THE NUN IN THE WORLD

THE NUN IN THE WORLD

Religious and the Apostolate

by

LEON JOSEPH CARDINAL SUENENS

Archbishop of Malines-Brussels

LONDON

BURNS & OATES

Translated from the French by GEOFFREY STEVENS

First published December 1962
2nd impression March 1963
3rd impression May 1963
New revised edition November 1963
2nd impression February 1964

MADE AND PRINTED IN GREAT BRITAIN BY
BILLING AND SONS LIMITED, GUILDFORD AND LONDON, FOR
BURNS AND OATES LIMITED, 25 ASHLEY PLACE, LONDON S.W.1

FOREWORD

THE Second Vatican Council is an invitation to an examination of conscience. It is a matter of getting clear what is essential in the Church and what is only incidental, what must remain and what is dependent on times and circumstances. This sorting out is necessary in many sections of the Church's pastoral work.

With this idea in mind we hope to examine in these pages the place and the mission of nuns in the Church in terms of the world as it is today. This study is of interest to the whole Church, for the nun is called to play a leading role. In putting the emphasis on the part she has to play, we shall at the same time bring to light the chief problems that concern the whole field of pastoral work.

The study should also give us a better understanding of the meaning of religious vocation by freeing it of the anachronisms which fetter it at present.

We shall be concerned only with nuns belonging to orders and congregations dedicated to apostolic work, and thus the contemplative life, which is on a different plane and has different immediate goals, will not be the object of our direct consideration.

When we talk of nuns we have also in mind all souls dedicated to God whose object is visible apostolic propagation and who, though their methods and forms are different, share the same basic vocation. We have also made free use of the word 'religious'—albeit with feminine pronouns—to indicate that, *mutatis mutandis*, what is said applies also to male religious who are not priests.

It is of all these chosen souls that we are thinking in this book. May the Council mark for them too the dawn of the spiritual spring-time of which Pope John XXIII has spoken. In the analysis of their present position—to which we bring as much love and respect as we do candour—our aim it to help them deploy on a global scale the inexhaustible treasure of their devotion and the wealth of their spirituality.

But we should first explain the title. We speak of "Religious and the Apostolate", and of the nun's progress in the apostolate of the Church today. But this should not give rise to a misunderstanding. The life of a religious is of its nature apostolic. Religious are already apostles in virtue of the consecration effected through their vows, as well as by the principal activities to which they dedicate themselves. And so when we speak of advancement in the apostolate we do not mean that nuns are now to pass from a non-apostolic role to one that is apostolic. If the phrase were thus to be interpreted, then the whole intention of this book would be misunderstood. Rather, what we mean by the term is a certain utilization of latent capacities, enlarging the nun's vocation by opening new dimensions. But again, it is not a question of adding to an already overcrowded timetable. What we are asking is that the horarium be streamlined according to norms dictated by the hierarchy of values. A proper balance must be achieved by concentrating first of all on the essential and indispensable factors of the religious life and on the primary tasks which God expects of us. Now one of these essential factors of religious life is most assuredly its apostolic dimension, and it is upon this that we wish to dwell. We intend to sketch, as it were, a modern theology of the nun's vocation. And we do this with the desire to keep our whole attention fixed on those things which God is requiring of us at present.

Malines,
  15th September, 1962
  Feast of the Seven Dolours

CONTENTS

Part I: THE POSITION TODAY

Part II: TOWARDS AN APOSTOLIC RENEWAL OF THE RELIGIOUS LIFE

LETTER FROM THE VATICAN
SECRETARY OF STATE

Secretario di Stato   Vatican
  di Sua Santità   29 November, 1962.

YOUR EMINENCE,

The Sovereign Pontiff has learnt that Your Eminence, having already shed light on various aspects of the Apostolate of the Church in a series of extremely pertinent works, has now been working on a study of the role of the nun in the world today.

Well aware of the pastoral zeal by which Your Eminence is inspired, His Holiness is greatly pleased to see Your Eminence devoting your time and talents to a problem which today forms the main concern of many pastors. There can, indeed, be no doubt that the present conditions of the Apostolate indicate the need for useful reforms in certain spheres, particularly a better utilization of all the apostolic forces at the Church's command.

Among these, nuns hold a place of honour and every encouragement should be given to any effort which will enable the spiritual treasures they possess to be placed more directly at the service of the Apostolate.

His Holiness takes pleasure in thinking that the study prepared by Your Eminence will shed new and valuable light on this question and as token of his fatherly goodwill He sends you with this letter his wholehearted and paternal apostolic blessing.

Please accept, Your Eminence, the expression of my highest esteem with which, venerating the sacred purple,

I have the honour to be once more,

Your Eminence's most humble, devoted and obedient servant in Jesus Christ,

✠ A. DELL' ACQUA,
Subst.

Part I

THE POSITION TODAY

1

THE WORLD WE LIVE IN

THE TEMPO OF THE WORLD

In order that the position of women in religion may be accurately assessed in the contemporary world, it is necessary to consider both them and the world in which they have to live. These two distinct things have their own separate internal evolutionary laws, their own vital rhythm. Religious in the world cannot occupy a real place without taking into account the evolution of modern society. Yeast is not placed beside the dough it is to leaven, but right in it. Somehow, then, the two vital elements must be brought into harmony.

Contemporary society, our society, the one in which we live and which it is our duty to save, which Christ has entrusted to us, is a society evolving with bewildering rapidity in all its aspects at once. It is characterized by a set of sociological phenomena which we must recognize if we are not to remain on the fringe of things and miss all dialogue with the world for lack of contact or even of a common language.

The world of today differs from that of yesterday in a number of ways. We shall consider at length only those differences which have a more direct effect on women in religion.

A CHANGING WORLD

Our world is a world in a continuous state of transition,

3

a state in which everything is questioned. We no longer live in an age when daily lives were solidly framed in tradition, and there were institutions to safeguard values that were never called in question. On all sides tradition is foundering and conformism falling in ruins. The world of today wants to re-think and revise everything, to take the universe apart to see what makes it tick. The emphasis is on personal values, on freedom, responsibility, inventiveness and creation.

The man of today has seen everything, read everything, heard everything; he is determined to explore everything, greedy of experience, anxious to set foot in unexplored fields.

THE WORLD AS A UNIT

Our planet has seen more revolutionary development in the last quarter of a century than in all the preceding nineteen. In the technical sphere, from the first atom-bomb to the interplanetary rockets of today, man has made giant strides and these are probably no more than a beginning, raising the curtain for what is to come.

In this world in which geographical distances have ceased to have any meaning, we are confronted with the spectacle of concepts and ideologies being brewed together on a scale previously unimaginable. We can hear a tele-vised broadcast of a U.N. session before those present in person, since radio waves travel quicker than sound waves. Anyone may see with his own eyes and hear with his own ears international conferences taking place in Tokyo or Melbourne. Every evening we can tour the world sitting in an armchair before our TV set. No aspect of human life remains alien to us. Through all the mass-communication media—press, radio, cinema—we are subjected to psycho-logical and moral influences attempting to mould the man of today to the image of this developing society. Matters are not treated on a provincial scale nowadays, nor even on a national or continental scale, but on an inter-continental scale—until such time as this is superseded by the interplanetary scale. To set a problem in other than global terms, said a certain statesman, is to put it on un-sound premisses.

And that, whether we like it or not, is how we stand today.

A WORLD ON THE MOVE

In this world our human ant-hill is astir in all directions. Flying from Europe to America is a matter of a few hours. One has only to spend a few moments at an air terminal to realize the extent to which the world has become a cross-roads of peoples. In addition, we are experiencing considerable internal migration and the rural world is more and more giving place to an urban civilization. Millions of uprooted country people swarm to the suburbs of our octopus cities. This move alone loosens their re-ligious roots, to say nothing of the moral repercussions of crowding masses of human beings into inadequate space with all the disastrous consequences to family life which this entails.

NEW VALUES

It is not only in the field of technical progress that our world has become a 'new' world in comparison with that of twenty, thirty or forty years ago; men in our times have acquired new standards. The old ideals have lost their full meaning and new ones have taken their place.

Men aspire to equality among themselves, to fraternity and solidarity. Feudalism is a thing of the past, and Queen Anne is really dead. Certain social distinctions are no longer accepted and privilege is denied. Everything which reminds people of the manners of an earlier age, the artificial etiquette of Courts, certain bourgeois customs and conventions, marks of respect in so far as they are pompous or obsequious—all these belong now to the past.

Men look for frankness, efficiency, directness, sincerity, brevity and sobriety. Art must be deprived of its flourishes and useless complexities. Human relationships are being rediscovered.

A PARADOXICAL WORLD

We must be able to understand this development and to distinguish what it holds of truth if we are to have any success in the task which we must undertake of analysing it and judging it objectively in the spirit of faith.

The atmosphere of the world could well permeate us if we are content to remain passive to its influence instead of trying to guide it. For the movements which course through it are as powerful as they are dangerous. Technical progress is one thing; the use to which mankind puts it is something else. The day after Hiroshima, Denis de Rougemont wrote, "The bomb is not dangerous; it is a thing . . . ; what is terrifyingly dangerous is man".

The astounding success of technical achievement intoxicates our contemporaries who barely fall short of idolatry in their respect for science. Gagarin, the man in the first sputnik, was told by his masters to declare that the heavens were empty, that he had not met God in orbit. Men today can hardly bring themselves to admit the existence of anything they cannot calculate or measure. They can no longer see God where He is, infinitely close to them, in the depths of their innermost being, giving them life, sense and purpose. They look for Him through a telescope, if indeed they seek Him at all, so closed are their minds to what they cannot see, to mysteries beyond their comprehension.

Mankind, thus deprived of its roots, is dragged helplessly by the fearful tides of materialism.

This materialism, whether it be admitted or remain under cover, does its best to rivet man to earth, to deprive him of his soul, and to block his spiritual horizon. These are evil times for the disinterested avocations where money is not the supreme criterion of success. Everything conspires to rob man of his sense of perspective and proportion. "What does it profit a man if he gain the whole world and suffer the loss of his own soul?" These words no longer have any meaning for the masses who never raise their eyes to heaven. Material well-being absorbs all their energies and becomes an end in itself.

Man suddenly sees his standard of living raised—in our countries, at least—and he begins to have more free time at his disposal. Work he accepts, but he expects also relaxation, week-ends, paid holidays and so forth; a continual increase in leisure is an integral part of existence. The nervous tension which is a feature of modern life demands holidays in the open air, sport and physical culture. Every evening people switch on the TV and allow entry to whatever the waves bring, be it healthy or unhealthy, as if they were a beach open to whatever the waves of the sea might wash up.

What is man going to do with this leisure, which he hails as human and social progress? What chance is there for keeping the Christian Sunday in the mass week-end exodus from the towns? Books, films and broadcasts which should be enriching our culture, what message have they? What answer do they propose to the fundamental questions man asks himself about his own nature, about the problems of suffering and death and the beyond? Are not these media of mass-communication all too often little more than muddy rivers, casting up wave upon wave of cheap literature extolling irreligion and indifferentism?

Our age is full of positive values, but also full of paradoxes. We must love it, yet defend ourselves against it;

B

collaborate with its enthusiasm, yet direct it; admire it, yet set limits to it; encourage it along every path that can lead to good, yet warn it of the pitfalls and precipices that flank the way. We must turn man from himself and make him aware of the Saviour who remains for him, too, in the heart of the twentieth century, 'the Way, the Truth and the Life'.

The Christian of today must possess a vital and clear-sighted Christianity which will demand of him certain alliances and certain reservations, certain adherences and certain denials, a generosity of views that will enable him to welcome all manifestations of brotherly goodwill, and a charity secure from compromise which will move him to share with others the treasures of life which he enjoys.

Every great speaker, it has been said, has two geniuses, his own and that of his times. The same is true of every Christian dedicated by the very fact of his baptism to the work of the apostolate. He must have his own genius—that is, he needs the Spirit of the Lord to enlighten him and inspire his enthusiasm—but he must also know the spirit of his time, its susceptibilites and reactions. Since he belongs to two worlds, that of God and that of mankind, he can only be the mediator between them if he is at the same time loyal to both.

The Christian life will always be a paradox. But in our times especially, being a Christian demands a greater maturity and clearsightedness, as well as a deep sense of responsibility if we are to bring Christ to the world in which we live.

It was necessary to do this rapid sketch to serve as background to the following chapters. In fact it is the context in which women in religion have to play their part and find their place. But before going on to a consideration of their present role in the world, we must describe what has happened to woman in the world of today, what her place is in the current process of change. A religious is a woman of her times, so the question of woman's status is a vital one for her. She cannot renounce her femininity, and it is in fact just this which should be placed at God's service. "The more holy a woman is", wrote Léon Bloy, "the more woman she is." Which we can translate, "The more a religious has the qualities of her times, the better will she realize her vocation".

2

WOMAN TODAY

WE shall be talking about women in the fully developed
countries: in Africa and Asia the situation is quite different. There, too, however, a change is taking place and
the trend seems likely to be irreversible. According to a
recent U.N. report, only nine countries continue to refuse
women the right to vote and to be elected.

CHRISTIANITY AND FEMINISM

Christianity started a new era for women. In revealing
to the world the divine adoption open to all the children of
God, Our Lord proclaimed at the same time the fundamental equality of the sexes and raised the dignity of
woman for all time.

Reacting against the laws and customs of the Greco-
Roman world, the Church in her turn proclaimed the
equality of man and woman before God and in the realm of
morality. The extent to which this equality was disregarded
in olden times when it came to judging questions of
adultery or divorce, and the extent to which custom
favoured man at the expense of woman, is well known.
The Church, however, has always fought for the emancipation of women so that they should be accorded equal rights
with men in the organization of their lives and the enjoyment of their freedom.

She also fought for the emancipation of unmarried

women, in providing for the vigorous growth of religious orders. By her respect for dedicated virginity she brought into relief the nobility of woman and her right to choose her own vocation.

In spite of the rough manners of that time, the chivalry of the Middle Ages also constituted a tribute to the dignity of woman and a sign of respect for her.

If we pass on from the Middle Ages to the Renaissance we note that as the de-christianization of society proceeds, so the civil authority interferes more and more in matrimonial matters and introduces the idea of the incompetence of the married woman.

Later on, the civil law was to place more and more emphasis on this legal incompetence and to approve measures tending to the disruption of family life. Christians all too often have gone along with their times, breathing without realizing it the air of paganism. Their conservatism led them to confuse authentic Christian tradition with human traditions which were no more than the product of their times and the anti-feminist prejudices thereof. At the end of a chapter on the feminist movement of the nineteenth century, Canon J. Leclercq wrote:

There is no doubt that the position of woman as established by the laws and customs of the nineteenth century was not entirely in conformity with her rights and her mission, but it is regrettable that in this feminist movement there were too few Catholics drawing their inspiration from the tradition of the Church. In general, Catholic intellectual circles adopted a defensive attitude consisting of defending, as if it were Catholic tradition, a civil code inspired by a man's world in the throes of becoming pagan. . . .

This explains why countries with a Catholic tradition . . . are those in which woman has advanced least, and why Catholic circles, which have great influence in the middle classes, often show so little understanding of the needs of women today.[1]

THE EMANCIPATION OF WOMEN

However that may be, the past is done with and we must now take into account what Lucien Romier called 'the Emancipation of Woman'. He himself set this advancement at the end of the nineteenth century because he was particularly aware of the economic liberation of women. The date is in any case unimportant: what is important is that this emancipation, which was achieved after a mighty struggle by women themselves, is an accepted fact and is continuing at great speed under our own eyes. To convince ourselves of this, let us take a glance back into the past, as one might do, for example, in the field of transport to show the amount of progress between Stephenson's *Rocket* and a Trans-Europe Express, or between Montgolfier's first balloon and an interplanetary rocket.

Then

A swift return to the past will permit us to assess progress in feminine emancipation. A comparison of the woman of today with her sister of 1700 or 1800 would be rewarding: certainly the picture would not be lacking in colour and picturesque detail. Nothing highlights the evolution of customs more than a family album where one can compare our ancestors with their counterparts of today: hats and dresses are just one sign of the different modes of life in different epochs.

Then—a woman's life was spent almost exclusively in the home. Her existence was bounded by the three K's: *Kirche, Küche, Kinder* (Church, Cooking and Children). A respectable unmarried woman never went out unchap-

[1] *Leçons de droit naturel*, Vol. III, La Famille, Ch. VI, p. 395.

eroned. No woman could exercise any public office. Welfare, administration, diplomacy, the universities, government, and a host of other fields, were all the exclusive domain of the male. Women did not so much as vote. It is not so very long ago that academic authorities were against women attending universities, while their admission to the faculty has only very recently been gained by a narrow victory in certain Catholic circles.

The idea of a lady ambassador, or senator, or air-pilot was just inconceivable. It went without saying that even for equal work there was no question of equal pay for women. A girl was not supposed to express an opinion in the choice of her husband, but to sit passively by while her parents arranged matters.

Woman lived imprisoned in a sort of immutable destiny, in the framework of an idealized pattern set up by men which remained invariable. She was supposed to be docile, faithful, resigned, hardworking—but all within well-defined limits and sheltered from the draughts and winds of the outside world.

Now

A new type has been born—modern woman. She does not passively accept her fate, she takes charge of it. Freed from her former shackles, she develops in an atmosphere that allows her to make use of her natural gifts. Greater life-expectation gives her, once her children are grown up, an extra life as it were. The culture available to her is wider and she has more leisure. All these new factors affect her position and her activities in the world and open to them almost unlimited opportunity for expansion.

A kind of feminine passivity, with life spent in retreat, has now given place to an ever more well-defined activity. Our industrial civilization has torn woman from her hearth and opened the doors of factories and offices to her.

Two world wars mobilized millions of women behind the front where they successfully replaced men.

The classical picture in which initiative lies with the man, and woman's part is submission, is no longer current. Penelope at her weaving, Marguerite at her spinning-wheel, Juliet on her balcony, Sister Anne shut up in her tower living on expectation . . . nowadays they all smack of folklore.

There is nothing in this advancement as such that militates in Christian eyes against the subordination to her husband in the home demanded by St. Paul, but this subordination can no longer be realistically carried over to the whole of life.

The advancement of woman is today a *fait accompli*, it has become a part of our customs and is accepted without question. Never before has woman's influence been so noticeable. Never has her psychological ascendancy been more pronounced. She plays her part sometimes even in the sphere of high policy. Thanks to the development of her personality and culture, she takes part in her own characteristic manner in the social, economic and literary life of the world. She no longer acts through man by her influence on him, but in her own right and under her own colours.

Women are to be found in Parliament, in the Cabinet, at the Ministry of Health, in scientific research centres, in the worlds of art and letters, and in the great social services. They have created for themselves an important place in the great technical field of communication media of press, cinema, television and radio. They write and speak and act, and their opinions and feelings are given their full weight in every sphere. We have seen new posts created, especially designed to suit them in the widest variety of circumstances. This shows that they are wanted, accepted and effective. They are expected to humanize the social services and make them less bureaucratic and theory-ridden, and better able to be adapted to individual cases and the complexities of special circumstances.

THEIR AMBIVALENT ROLE

Women's contribution to our present civilization is considerable, for good as also, alas! for evil. Who can say what damage is done to mankind's moral conscience by women who publicize in the most shameless manner their nervous crises, their divorces, the amorality of their spectacular lives, their unbridled luxury and their disgust with life? People do not realize clearly enough the extent to which certain campaigns led by women with a great deal of noisy publicity—in favour of divorce or abortion or birth prevention—strike at the roots of family life and shake the most sacred values of Christian civilization.

Woman has the awe-ful choice of being Eve or Mary: she is rarely neutral. Either she ennobles and raises man up by her presence, by creating a climate of beauty and human nobility, or she drags him down with her in her own fall.

We can apply the words of Joseph de Maistre to her, "Man may make the laws, but morals are made in the family." For the heart of a family is the wife and mother. Woman holds the moral destiny of the world in her hand today more than at any other time in history. She makes it in her own image and contributes in a positive way to the formation of public opinion in her articles, magazines and books. She takes part in the exchange of ideas and makes her influence felt in the drafting of laws as well as in social activity, whether it be in the field of education, medical care or leisure.

This unprecedented role of woman opens a new era in the history of mankind. A type of society which had imposed itself on mankind for thousands of years has disappeared never to return. A new type of society, already existing in the more civilized countries, will be adopted tomorrow by other continents where woman's evolution has been slower but is still inexorably continuing. The women of Africa and Asia will also look at the world with open eyes and play their part with their men in fashioning it. Such is the foreseeable course of history.

Lenin was able to write, "The experience of all movements of liberation proves that the success of a revolution depends upon the degree of participation by women".

This is a phrase not to be forgotten. Christianity is the greatest and most radical revolution for freedom in all history. The apostolate is simply that action of Christ by which, through us, He seeks to pervade all men and all society. And it is in this light that the apostolic role of women who are consecrated religious stands out in bold relief. Their very womanliness, with everything positive that the term implies, cannot be betrayed or stifled, but must on the contrary be strengthened and brought to full flower through their vocation.

The place of women in our modern world opens up new dimensions in the apostolic activity of modern religious. It is to these that we will now devote our attention.

3

THE RELIGIOUS IN THIS WORLD

How does the religious appear in the world of today in the present state of woman's development? That is the question we must now examine.

We are not concerned here with describing the religious through the eyes of an unbeliever. Without faith, how could he grasp the meaning of life which exists only through and for Christ, in which everything is done in reference to Him? Without the faith which would solve the mystery for him, the religious life must appear an enigma, a waste of time, an inexplicable abdication of freedom, a closed door for which he has no key. It is but a short step from this to the conclusion that the religious life is a dwarfed, less than human life, based on repression and the absence of love; and it is a step easily taken, to judge from a certain stream of contemporary writing as tendentious as it is ill-informed.

What we are concerned with here is to see the religious through the eyes of a believer who regards her with sympathy and gratitude.

One thing that strikes anyone who is at all observant is the immense place occupied by women religious in the vast field of human suffering. "Who suffers," said St. Paul, "and I do not suffer with him?" Women in religion *live* this phrase—at the bedside of the sick, with the handicapped and the bedridden, with old people, lepers, deafmutes, and prisoners. They live it, through each day and through each year, with a devotion and disregard of self which compel our admiration. They are standing witnesses to the Church's maternal love, concerned with all our miseries, mindful always of the parable of the Good Samaritan and Our Lord's words about anything done "for the least of these, my little ones". They are the vanguard of the missionary Church in jungle, desert or arctic ice. Wherever there are missionaries they are to be found, perfect partners and helpers beyond price.

Another striking feature is the considerable place they occupy at all levels in the world of education. It is not uncommon for non-practising Catholics to confide their children to them. People know that nuns have given up the possibility of a family of their own in order to be at the disposal of all families, and to devote to them their most loving care and solicitude. Millions of children and adolescents receive instruction and education in establishments run or inspired by them. People admire the nuns of these teaching orders for their watchful devotion and the unstinted trouble they take.

There are undoubtedly other ways in which religious are present to the world, for example in social assistance and parish work; but those we have mentioned are the most striking, and it is generally on them that the opinions and appreciation of the faithful are based.

It would, however, be neither objective nor complete to ignore a number of regrets that one finds expressed in innumerable articles, discussions and conversations. In general these remarks are not concerned with the essence of the religious vocation but with the ubiquitous customs and usages which make the religious seem in the eyes of the faithful to be living outside the world they are trying to save, to be lagging behind the general progress of women.

Among these comments some deal with the psychological attitude of nuns, individually or as a community, while others are aimed at their social and apostolic attitude in the worlds of education and good works. Let us consider some of the more important ones.

PSYCHOLOGICAL ATTITUDE

Religious too often seem to be living in a closed world, turned in on themselves and having but tenuous contact with the world outside.

A community of nuns often enough gives the impression of being a fortress whose drawbridge is only furtively and fearfully lowered. The ideal of separation from the world leads, people believe, to a kind of psychological isolationism, conducing to a failure of dialogue with those in immediate contact with them for lack of common interests and a common language. Even if a girl before her entry to the convent was thoroughly involved with the world on account of the circles in which she moved or even on account of her apostolic work, after a time she loses touch. She goes into an enclosure which, if it is not hermetically sealed, at least looks out on the world through openings more like arrow slits than bay windows.

Layfolk are familiar with the lost feeling experienced on coming back from a holiday away from home. Life has not stood still in their absence, changes have occurred which must be taken into account: in short, for a matter of days after their return they feel out of things and it takes some time to re-adapt. But religious do not resume contact: the break was made once and for all and the gulf can only grow wider.

Again, physical and psychological detachment from the world leads a religious to turn in on herself and her own community. Her world shrinks and if she is not careful will end up no more than a few square yards in size. From this comes a distorted vision, seeing everything from one angle, measuring things against a diminished scale. From this comes also the contrived and artificial nature of certain customs in religious houses—a sort of 'house etiquette', a stilted, stereotyped and unnatural behaviour. It has been said of certain congregations of nuns that they are "the last strongholds of the very studied manners of the middle-class woman of the nineteenth century". People would like to see more spontaneity, less inhibition, more natural and straightforward reactions. It is not the respect and conventions they wish to see the last of, but the outmoded expression of them.

To put it briefly, the dusty old wax flowers should be replaced by living blooms drawing nourishment direct from the earth.

Most religious habits, too, seem to the layman to be ill adapted to current conditions, to have outlived their purpose, to be archaic and inconvenient. They raise at best an ironical smile when a nun is seen on her way to tend a sick person, flapping through the streets on her scooter with her habit and veil streaming behind her to the imminent danger of herself and other traffic.

SOCIAL ATTITUDE

The foregoing remarks were mainly concerned with the individual and collective way of acting on the part of religious in our modern world. In addition to these observations, it is also noticed that even in their proper sphere of activity, be this medicine or teaching, women religious are in danger of becoming mere "officials". In the former of these two fields, State control of the health service and the growing demands of administration make it more and more difficult for a religious to carry out her proper religious mission as such.

The hospital has developed considerably since the days

when foundresses of religious communities chose it as the field in which to bring succour to the crying distress of their times. In those days the care of the sick was first and foremost a matter of charity, and religious congregations were pioneers in the field of the corporal works of mercy. Today Ministries of Health have taken over much of the nursing and impose their own rules and regulations on what remains in private hands. The congregations have had to undergo certain changes by sheer force of circumstances. The necessity to have diplomas, the imposition of administrative controls and social legislation have all changed the view taken of the nursing nun, not by God, but by our fellow-men.

She appears less and less as a religious bending over the beds of sick humanity, in close contact with her patients, having time to . . . have time. Hospitals, clinics, maternity homes all have large numbers of lay staff and the role of the religious is often no more than that of ward-sister or administrative superintendent; she is sometimes snowed under by purely administrative or supervisory tasks; she becomes more and more like a professional nurse overburdened with technical duties. She is in danger of becoming a mere official.

She bustles about and 'does' for her patients, but she cannot meet all their demands, for as the population increases so does the number of sick persons needing treatment. The poetry which enshrined the nursing nun of an earlier age when she cared for her patients in a directly personal relationship in some place like the Hôtel-Dieu of Beaune is sinking further and further into the past.

What is true in the field of hospital work, today so laicized, is equally true in the scholastic world. The Church has played a great part in the education and instruction of children, an historic part and one that was in part at least plugging a gap. The Church did not wait for the evolution of the modern State which would take charge of the formation of youth. She also undertook pioneer work in other fields not specifically within her competence. It is related that the Capuchins of Paris formed the city's first fire-brigade! But the past is past.

Today one cannot but notice the profound changes that have taken place in our educational establishments due to the growing demands of public authorities and the increase in the school-age population.

A network of laws governs private as well as public education. One finds that the teaching religious appears more and more in the eyes of the layman to be just another teacher. The overburdened programme of work leaves less and less time for directly religious and apostolic contacts. Her pupils see her as a teacher who instructs them competently and devotedly in algebra or history and prepares them for their exams. The schoolmistress takes the place of the nun in the eyes of the pupil and parent alike.

Here again, the danger of her sinking to the level of a mere official is by no means imaginary.

APOSTOLIC ATTITUDE

One cannot but be impressed by the sum total of devotion represented by the religious life.

But devotion and the apostolate are not the same thing. The question which everyone who has the care of souls should ask himself is this: great as their devotion undoubtedly is, what apostolic return do the Church and the world get from the activities of religious today? Is there not perhaps some apostolic capital that could be put to better use? Are there not perhaps some fields of apostolic endeavour lying fallow, awaiting their cultivation?

It seems to us that the answer to the questions must be,

Yes. It is necessary, however, to be clear about what we mean by the apostolate properly speaking, and to define in advance in what ways devotion and the apostolate are different. This should make apparent what gaps there are to be filled.

Let it be clearly understood once and for all that in speaking of gaps we are by no means levelling any criticism at the religious of our times. It is not their fault if they have not been trained for nor asked to undertake certain missions that are necessary today.

We shall try later on to unravel the causes of this situation.

MEANING OF THE APOSTOLATE

Having said that, we must also take into account the fact that though the apostolate is as old as the Church itself, it is a duty that has become rather shadowy in Christian consciousness, partly because people have thought they were living in a Christian society, that is in a society where the non-believer was the exception. The revival of the apostolic conscience, and in particular the awareness of the need to organize it, are recent happenings. The last few Popes have issued urgent appeals reminding the faithful of their apostolic duty inherent in their baptism and *a fortiori* in the taking of religious vows. But the idea has not yet really penetrated our everyday views or the constitutions of religious communities.

It is of the greatest importance to insist on the existence of this duty and to clarify its meaning, that is to say to make it quite clear in what the idea of apostolate consists.

'Apostolate' is a word which is used in different senses which have developed in the course of time and which do not always give the same meaning. We shall use it here in its 'missionary' sense to denote the activities of the Chris-

C

tian sent by virtue of his baptismal vows to bring Christ
to the world, either by revealing Him to those who do not
know Him or by increasing His empire in those who know
Him already and training them to preach Him in their
turn. In both cases it is a matter of a supernatural communication of life to bring Christ into souls and into the
world and to foster His increase. It means working for the
expansion of the Kindom of God here below. The apostolate is the work of evangelization, either of spreading the
Gospel or of making it penetrate deeper into all human and
social activity. This apostolate is something we have to do
ourselves and train others to do after us : doing and making
others do are integral parts of the same whole. In the
following pages special emphasis is laid on the duty incum-
bent upon women in religion to draw into the apostolate
those lay persons with whom they are in closest touch.

This does not mean that the life of religious devoted to
education, care of the sick, or social work is not already
apostolic: it is, by reason of their consecration to this
work. As we said in the Foreword, it is not a question of
the advancement of religious from a non-apostolic to an
apostolic sphere, but it does mean that certain apostolic
factors have to be introduced into the very heart of the
religious life.

The tendency nowadays is to minimize the religious side,
properly speaking, of the apostolate which tends to be
overlooked in a welter of things which prepare for the
apostolate, ensure favourable conditions for it, support and
extend apostolic action, but are by no means to be confused
with it. We are not concerned here with clearing the religious apostolate—in the sense of the Gospels and the Acts
of the Apostles—from all that which, seen from that angle,
is but pre- or para-apostolic. Suffice it to say that the apostolate is the extension of Christ's mission in and through
the Church, a mission which consists of giving God to the

world, of acting in such a manner that men come to know God, to love Him and serve Him, to take their nourishment from Him, and to live the whole of the Gospel in every aspect of their lives.

The apostolate, then, in its character of evangelization is not to be confused with works of dedication, however necessary these may be.

There is a tendency also to use the term 'apostolate' for activities which are apostolic only in intention. This does not mean that this intention is without value or significance. But to over-extend the application of words is to render them so vague that they lose all real meaning and fade into insignificance. Let us be quite clear that any action whose final aim is to glorify God has a supernatural and redemptive value, but this is not to say that it is intrinsically apostolic. The word 'apostolate' is as much abused as the word 'prayer'. One hears it said sometimes that work is prayer. It is and it isn't. One can work in a spirit of prayer, and a very good thing too, but one must not confuse two separate values. We should add that in order to make a 'prayer' of one's work one must have acquired elsewhere the meaning of prayer. In the same way, if one wants to acquire the apostolic mentality that can affect even a course in geography it is extremely desirable to have acquired, by practice of the apostolate properly speaking, the proper orientation and perspective of life.

Given these definitions, it is easy to show in what way works of dedication are distinct from the apostolate. One can dedicate a whole life to the care of the sick, but one does not begin to be apostolic until one confides in them the secret of one's devotion, until one leads them to know Christ and does one's best to make Him loved. Devotedness opens another's soul to sympathy, disposes him favourably, and renders him attentive to what you have to say.

Yet, there still remains the passing on of the message, and the imparting of life.

A French bishop, Mgr. Huyghe, speaking about a community of nuns nursing in people's own homes, which had been established for thirty years in one particular town, gave the following account of what one of the nuns told him:

"We are now in touch with the third generation. When we came we knew only the old and the sick; we nursed the next generation; today it is the grandchildren of our first contacts who come to us for help. We have become completely acclimatized in this working-class quarter and we are welcome in every home. We have, of course, been able to help bring the priest to the bedside of the dying in many cases, but we have never succeeded in converting one single adult in good health. To anyone with eyes to see, it is clear that our quarter continues to become more and more de-christianized."

To which the bishop added this remark which is worth remembering: "One can dedicate oneself and still not reveal the person of Christ."[1]

This quotation turns the spotlight on a state of affairs that we cannot accept as normal and against which we must react.

We shall have occasion later to examine the real apostolic return from religious in the spheres with which they are already familiar. For the moment, it seems important to draw attention in general terms to a field of vast extent which remains fallow.

THE ADULT WORLD

An observer analysing the part played by religious today cannot help being struck by their absence from the main

[1] Quoted in *Equilibre et Adaptation*, p. 233.

spheres of influence at adult level, spheres where they have a right to be and where their talents are called for and their presence is needed.

As a general rule the life of a religious is dedicated to children, to the sick or to the elderly. No doubt it is possible to reach the family to some extent through the children or the sick, but such an influence is necessarily indirect and often sporadic. The grown-ups as such are outside their influence. Nevertheless it is grown-ups who run the world, create the climate of opinion and the atmosphere we all breathe. It has too often been said that to form the young is to assure the future. This is true, but only to the extent that the formation continues until the young adult goes out into life and founds a home; it is true, but only to the extent that the influence on youth is complemented by action on the adults who in their turn will form, or deform, the coming generation. The self-perpetuation of schools is a myth that has sometimes cost us dear. One recalls the remarks of a notorious communist about our schools: "We leave you the children; we take care of the grown-ups." Or again: "Teach them to read and write; we'll teach them to think." This surely is invitation enough to carry our work through to its logical conclusion. It is seldom that one sees religious playing any part at adult level, a level at which other women, however, make their influence felt, baneful as that influence so often is.

One does not see them, either, playing any part among adult lay-women whom the Church calls to the apostolate but who often lack anyone to stimulate and sustain them. One meets religious at various Catholic Action congresses which take place in their houses during the school holidays, but it is only in the kitchen or the refectory or perhaps at the closing session that they meet the public and the guests. One rarely sees them play any real part among

young Catholic Actionists who, though they have just left
their schools, seem to expect nothing more from them.

In most of our university cities nuns run halls of
residence for the female undergraduates. With rare exceptions their work is restricted to being hotel-keepers, house-
keepers or cooks. It is the exception when they manage
to put some real life into these homes where tomorrow's
adults are being shaped, or to produce any effective
spiritual guidance for them at this decisive stage of their
career. All the girls expect from them is board and lodging
—and the greatest understanding about their freedom to
come and go at will.

It may be argued that the youth in question hides itself
away and is jealous of its freedom. True. But it is also true
that our instructresses have not had the training to enable
them to maintain contact with the young adult woman
and remain close to her at a time when she has to make
choices and decisions that will affect her whole life.

In many towns and pilgrimage centres religious devote
their lives to running homes or boarding-houses and are
exclusively concerned with the domestic affairs of running
an hotel. How can one fail to deplore the fact that they
have no apostolic outlet for their abundant spiritual energies? They have consecrated themselves to God and to
souls for this work no doubt, but principally for something
quite different. Such employment of nuns devalues the religious vocation in the eyes of the faithful. Priests, too,
are worried to see so many dedicated souls harnessed exclusively to material tasks when there is such a crying
need for all persons of goodwill in directly apostolic work.
They, too, cannot but deplore the fact that the apostolic
return of such religious is not even equal to that of many
lay people in the world.

It does sometimes happen that an individual religious,
however dedicated, is unable to devote herself to apostolic

work. Nevertheless, the community as such ought to undertake it. The religious who, for some special reason, cannot
play a direct part in the work can make her contribution
to the apostolic work of the community by carrying out
her secular tasks for the love of God and souls. She will
thus enter into the great apostolic current so much desired
by the Church. But her case should remain the exception.

Let there be no misunderstanding. We are not criticizing
the obscure tasks which lack glamour, but the fact that
apostolic activities of far greater importance are on this
account deprived of their help. Obviously a truly apostolic
soul does not prefer one job to another on account of its
external glamour but for what it does, or makes it possible
to do, for souls. The whole matter is summed up in the
question : where and how are the cause of God and the
visible extension of His Kingdom best served?

4

DISQUIET AND LOSS OF ESTEEM

HESITATION ON THE THRESHOLD

THE picture we have just painted includes highlights as well as shadows. The positive contribution which religious can make is so great that it ought by itself to supply the deficiencies. Yet it remains true that the deficiencies, and the element of truth in current criticism, are hampering recruitment. Everywhere one hears complaints that recruitment does not keep pace with needs, nor indeed with the growth of population; that religious houses are closing down one after another; that the average age of communities is increasing. This is the same as saying that the vitality of the Church is affected in her life forces, in this élite of womanhood that is at once her glory and her means of exercising in a special way her role of spiritual motherhood.

Vocations are decreasing everywhere. It is significant that the least affected are the missionary and purely contemplative congregations. The ideals of heroic missionary work and of a life devoted to God in silence still appeal to youth. On the other hand, vocations in hospital and teaching congregations are falling off to some extent everywhere.

A Belgian bishop has drawn attention to the fact that in his diocese 78 out of 522 religious houses of women had to close in the last thirty years for lack of new vocations.

In one French diocese the numbers of religious in education and nursing dropped 30 per cent. in ten years.

In addition to this there is the factor of ageing communities. The age pattern of many of them makes it clear that the rate of recruitment is falling off. The Bishop of Tournai has revealed the following figures in a pastoral letter: nearly 30 per cent. of nuns are over 65 while only 10 per cent. are under 30. This factor of ageing communities will have to be taken into account when it comes to considering modernization and the adaptations necessary.

The falling off in religious vocations is serious in itself, but it would be less so if it were purely numerical. What is much more serious for the future is a sort of spiritual devaluation of the vocation which is noticeable among good Christian families, the lay apostolate and even among the clergy.

Among the many causes of this devaluation must certainly be ranged the de-christianization of society and its customs, the increasingly materialistic atmosphere in the world and in ourselves, the internal disorder and egoism lying under the surface of so many families, and the decrease of the spirit of faith. . . . But rather than draw up a list of those factors which lie outside our control, it would seem more useful and more to the point to analyse the causes for which the religious orders themselves are responsible, as these are indicated by recent investigations.

The complaints—even if they are not always and everywhere applicable and even if they sometimes underestimate the positive contribution of the religious congregations— are too numerous and too similar not to warrant the most careful study.

Vocations, we said, are on the downgrade in the teaching and hospital congregations. It is important to understand the psychology of a young woman hesitating on the threshold of these vocations.

If she is thinking of a teaching congregation, it is obvious that what attracts her is not the idea of teaching geography or algebra or the domestic arts; what she wants is to become an apostle of Christ, to bring God to the world in and through such and such a congregation. The attraction of a congregation lies in its apostolic value. Even if the girl is not herself fully aware of it, what decides her is the picture of a religious vowed to God and able to win souls for Him.

It is the same if she is considering a nursing congregation. What attracts her is not the profession of nursing as such—the time is long past when one had to become a nun in order to tend the sick. She weighs the pros and cons of a lay nursing vocation and if she then decides to enter religion it is in order to be able to give the sick, and through them the world, not only nursing care but also an overflow of Christian life and of happiness. She wants to be quite clear about the difference between being a lay nurse and being a nurse in religion. And the greater apostolic value of the religious life must be evident if she is to choose it. All studies of the problem of vocations should be informed by this fundamental truth.

DISQUIET WITHIN

Nuns themselves experience in a different but none the less real degree the difficulty of reconciling scholastic or medical demands with the spiritual and apostolic aspirations which formed their vocation. All Christians live a paradoxical life, since Our Lord demands of us that we should be in this world but not of it. Religious live this paradox in community, bound by a very definite Rule. It is not surprising that from time to time a problem arises on how to maintain the delicate balance between the demands of their spiritual, apostolic and professional life.

It often happens that a community has difficulty in finding a suitable compromise between the Rule which separates it from the world and its apostolic work which demands certain contacts with the world.

We should not ignore this problem which can, thank God, be perfectly solved, and has been solved already in certain congregations. We should rather study how to reconcile things which in fact belong together.

The Church values both the interior life and the apostolic life, separation from the world and the action of leaven in the world. One has only to take literally the repeated appeals she addresses to her favourite children, her religious, to see all these difficulties give place to harmony.

Everybody realizes the difficulties involved in adapting the religious life to the world of today. The first to realize it are the religious themselves who have often experienced a conflict within their own communities.

Young religious who have been in touch with the contemporary world are aware of the values appropriate to our time. They feel that certain customs of the religious life no longer fit in. A more direct and less inhibited manner, a wider human culture, and above all experience of apostolic movements before their entry into the novitiate, have opened new horizons to them and given them a sense of responsibility. They come to the convent not to give less of themselves but to give more, and they are very sensitive to anything which puts the brake on or lessens the apostolic ardour with which they enter. They want a religious life which, albeit different in expression, is yet of a piece with their immediate past. Young religious desire a spirituality which is enriched and animated by the Scriptures and communal liturgy. They want to be less dependent on 'spiritual exercises' and vocal prayer which is nonliturgical. It is important to take this into account. This conflict between the generations can be softened by the understanding of Superiors in many cases, but it exists, even if latent, throughout.

This dissatisfaction among young members is often matched by that of older sisters who are conscious of the need for change. For the better ones among them this may constitute a case of conscience : on the one hand they realize the need for change, on the other a certain conception of obedience urges them to adhere to the established order of things, to abide by the *status quo* in which accepted uses and customs are not questioned. Seen in this light, any innovation seems doomed in advance. Authority easily becomes a sort of gentle and maternal authoritarianism, and obedience becomes no more than a passivity which solves problems by ignoring them.

Another difficulty is often added by differences in apostolic perspective between a mother-house in Europe and daughter-houses overseas. The latter have often been driven to make the necessary adaptations and this results in comparisons to the disadvantage of the European houses.

These factors combine to bring about a most unfortunate result—the devaluation of the religious vocation in the eyes of the world. Let us pause a moment before this saddening picture.

LACK OF ESTEEM IN THE OUTSIDE WORLD

It is an undeniable fact that the wind of defeatism is blowing through the older, traditional congregations. It is widely held that they are all condemned sooner or later to extinction, that history has already passed them by, as has happened to so many previously flourishing congregations. A whole mass of popular literature underlines the pessimistic view of their situation. M. Baldwin, K. Hulme, A. Hure, F. Werfel, G. Walschap and even, after their fashion, Bernanos and Montherlant, help to sustain the prejudice against their survival. It is not rare to hear it maintained, even in our own Christian circles, that this is the hour of the secular institutes or that the world needs entirely new forms of the religious life. The tendency is to discourage those who want to renew the religious life in its traditional form : they are reminded about putting new wine into old bottles, told that tradition has become top heavy and a check on action, that they must resign themselves to seeing congregations which are out of step with contemporary life plodding painfully along on the fringe of the world's development.

The religious of today appears to the faithful to be out of touch with the world as it is, an anachronism.

She seems also to be behindhand in relation to other women, who have achieved emancipation while she remains 'in the schoolroom'. To restore to the religious life its original value, we must put it in harmony with the progress which has been realized in the world, and in woman's relation to that world. We must retain from the past all that is of permanent value while at the same time adapting it to modern conditions. In particular, apostolic activity must be able to profit from all those positive gains which women have secured in our time.

In order that the religious life maintain its intrinsic value, it must, as it were, get in step with modern developments. The position of a religious in the world today ought to be defined in terms relating to that world. To the question "What is a religious?" one ought to be able to answer, "A modern woman—not one of the eighteenth or nineteenth century—who has dedicated her life to God for the salvation of the world through the congregation to which she belongs."

Every phrase in that answer has its importance.

She must be seen to be a modern woman.

It is therefore essential that she should have her proper place in the development of ideas and customs that distinguish the woman of today from her sisters of a century or even half a century ago. Anything in the life of the religious which is at odds with the present place of women in society, is a hindrance to her apostolic activity.

She should appear as a woman vowed to God in the Church and in the world of today.

Her vows bind her to God—this is true at all times and constitutes the unchangeable element of her vocation—but they also bind her to the salvation of the world in which we live. This second aspect of her vocation makes it immediately clear that the religious must strive to bring her apostolate to the world *as it is*, and that she must be continually adapting to the demands of the moment. With even greater reason then must she be immersed herself in those streams of life which course through the Church.

This dedication to God for the salvation of the world must be fulfilled by each religious through her own congregation. She is thus placed on her proper path, a path which is defined by her Rule, which must be faithfully adhered to. When we say '*through* her congregation' we are making the point that the congregation is a means to a more important end, an end which draws it, as the sea draws a river, into the common stream of the evangelization of the world.

It only remains for us to examine in detail what this fundamental definition requires if we are to retrieve the situation and hasten a renewal which the world and the Church so urgently need.

What we have said, it must be emphasized, is the very opposite of defeatism. It has been inspired by complete and absolute faith in the value of religious congregations of the classic types. Without undervaluing the providential part played by secular institutes or that played in the world by the different forms of religious dedication which the Holy Spirit never ceases to raise up, we believe that it would be a grave mistake not to do all in one's power to reinstate the classic religious vocation to its true value.

Before seeking remedies for the present situation, it is necessary to analyse it more in detail. What are the causes of the discord we have noted? What is their origin? It is to the examination of these various factors that we shall now proceed.

5

CAUSES OF THIS SITUATION

IT is essential, if we are to have a renewal, to resolve the uncertainties underlying this predicament and to establish the causes which led to it. It is due in great part to a lack of harmony between the practice of religious life and the demands of the apostolate. How can this dualism have arisen, since the religious life is no more than a fuller version of the life we are called to by baptism and the duty of the apostolate is inherent in baptism? To appreciate this situation, at once paradoxical and abnormal, we must consider a great many different factors working together to produce the disturbing situation. Once the main causes are known, the remedies will be obvious: diagnosis is already one step on the road to a cure, a cure which is within our powers if we so wish.

For reasons of clarity we shall divide the various factors behind the present situation into historical, spiritual, canonical, psychological and sociological. Let us examine each of them briefly in turn.

A. THE HISTORICAL FACTOR

'Religious' synonymous with 'enclosed'

Anyone who knows the history of the various orders and congregations is aware that at their inception, and for hundreds of years, the concept of 'religious' was applicable only to contemplative orders.

A religious was by origin and by definition an enclosed person taking solemn vows. The idea of unenclosed nuns seemed something unholy. Slowly the active congregations had to fight their way, not without struggles and misfortunes, to gain the right to be included in the term 'religious'. The history of the cloister down the ages has much instruction to offer on this point.

Evolutionary Stages

Whereas deaconesses had played an important part in the primitive Church, including giving Holy Communion to sick women, nothing like this was permitted later on. Once the deaconesses had disappeared during the fifth century, the Church knew only the enclosed monastic life for the next thousand years. The most intransigent manifesto in favour of enclosure was the celebrated decretal *Periculoso* of Pope Boniface VIII in 1298 :

> We command by this present constitution, whose validity is eternal and can never be questioned, that all nuns, collectively and individually, present and to come, of whatever order or congregation, in whatever part of the world they may be, shall henceforth remain in the monastries in perpetual enclosure.

We had to await, alas! till the beginning of the sixteenth century to see a relaxation of the rigidity of the *Clausura*. It came at the end of a long conflict of ideas, between jurists and pastoral clergy, and led eventually to a certain apostolic 'advancement' for female religious.

The revolution took place in the second quarter of the sixteenth century. The impetus came from those male religious who abandoned the classic type of cloistered life and made their immediate aim the apostolate. It was typified by the Barnabites and, above all, the Jesuits : and it was to have its repercussions among the women.

D

Until then one had hardly conceived the idea of religious not subject to enclosure and taking solemn vows. The 'apostolic' innovation was to be resisted and to experience various difficulties which are instructive for us today. In the front of this battle was Angela Merici. In 1544 the Ursulines founded by her received approval and were not subject to enclosure. Her first twelve sisters were dispersed and accommodated each in her own parish. They devoted themselves in various quarters to a multiplicity of works, but especially to the education of young girls and particularly those of the common people whom no one else worried about. Unfortunately their freedom of movement did not last. They were obliged to accept enclosure, and shortly afterwards, in 1566, the Holy See ordered the suppression of all female congregations not in enclosure and subject to solemn vows. The Ursulines, who up to then had dressed like anyone else, were required to adopt a religious habit. It was the triumph of legalism.

In the footsteps of St. Angela Merici, St. Peter Fourier and Bd. Alix Le Clercq tried in their turn to avoid enclosure. The founder of the Canonesses of St. Augustine was quite clear about what he wanted: he wanted to establish free schools for day pupils and boarders and he wished the needs of the education of children to take first place over the rules of enclosure. "I have always thought", he wrote, "that it was necessary to say that they were first and foremost schoolmistresses . . . for fear they should be thought to be religious first and foremost."[1]

Canon lawyers made it hard for him. To add to his misfortune, Urban VIII rejected the idea of teaching nuns on account of a passage in St. Paul: *docere autem mulieri non permitto*. In the end the work was approved, not without trouble and worry, but within the classic framework.

At the dawn of the seventeenth century St. Francis de

[1] E. Renard, *La Mère Alix Le Clercq*, p. 292. Paris, 1935.

Sales, with St. Jane Frances de Chantal, tried to promote the
apostolic activity of women in the world. He was thinking
in terms of an unenclosed congregation, not taking solemn
vows, at the service of the poor and the sick and visiting
them in their homes. The Order was formed under the title
of Our Lady of the Visitation : the title itself is significant.
But the Archbishop of Lyons came down on the side of the
legalists, and despite encouragement from St. Robert
Bellarmine, who was consulted and who advised him to
adhere to his ideals, St. Francis bowed sadly before such
deeply rooted tradition.

The battle lost by St. Francis de Sales was to be won
by the exercise of patience and 'holy cunning' by St. Vincent de Paul. In order that his Daughters of Charity should
be able to leave their convents to serve the poor, he used
all his gifts of diplomacy to evade the rigours of canon
law. To avoid enclosure, obligatory for all female religious,
the institute was called a company and the novitiate, a
seminary; the superior was designated Sister Servant, and
their residence was called not convent or monastery but
just 'house'. He did not talk about religious but about
'daughters of the parish'. Aspirants were not given the veil,
but kept the *toquois* for headdress and wore the grey serge
dress of the common people.

He left instructions, famous today but very daring at the
time. Read what he writes, and repeats, to his daughters :

Should the local bishop ask you if you are in religion,
you will say that by the grace of God you are not, not
because you have not a high opinion of religious but
because if you were you would have to be enclosed and
that would mean goodbye to the service of the poor. . . .
Should some muddle-headed person appear among you
and say, "We ought to be religious. It would be much
nicer," then, my dear sisters, the Company is ready for

Extreme Unction, for whoever says 'religious' says 'enclosed'—but the Daughters of Charity must go everywhere.

In the Rules he wrote:

> They shall consider that they are not in religion, since that state is unsuited to the tasks of their vocation. The Sisters have no convent but the houses of the sick and the house where the Superior lives, no cell but a hired room, no chapel but the parish church, no cloister but the streets of the town; for enclosure they have obedience . . . for grille, the fear of God; for veil, holy modesty.[1]

Such, in brief, is the history of a battle fought for the liberty of the Spirit. St. Vincent de Paul established a beach-head, but he did not conquer the whole terrain. In the centuries separating us from him evolution has been taking place, as it still is, and the Council may well take it a decisive step further.

This historical sketch helps us to realize how it happened that laws suitable for the contemplative life came to be imposed for so long on those who were trying to map out a path for active congregations.

The Spirit of the Times

To this must be added that religious constitutions did not escape the spirit of their times and were marked, as other Church institutions were, by the ideologies and deficiencies of their epoch.

Those dating from the seventeenth century were greatly influenced by the viewpoint of the Council of Trent, which was much concerned with laxity and internal abuses.

[1] St. Vincent de Paul, *Correspondances, Entretiens, Documents*, Vol. IX, p. 533; Vol. X, pp. 658, 667, 662. Librairie Lecoffre, Paris, 1923.

Churchmen were thinking in defensive terms, not of attacking; they were concentrating on what was going on within the household more than on the world outside whose dechristianization had not yet come out into the light.

The eighteenth century, overshadowed by the French Revolution which was to bring it to a close, was not a century of religious expansion. On the contrary, the very foundations of community life were being jeopardized in a struggle for existence. The Revolution did, however, contribute unintentionally to the development of the religious life by revealing the inadequacies of traditional legislation concerning the vows.

As regards the constitutions drawn up in the nineteenth century, one must not minimize the influence in our countries of certain remains of Jansenism which placed great emphasis on the withdrawal from and the hatred of the world, and on the intrinsically corrupt nature of man as the result of original sin, on the fear of God divorced from love, on the contagiousness of sin, on the repression of natural tendencies. One has only to glance through some of the writings of the time to see the traces of this tendency, which only gradually died away.

If one also takes into account the fact that for centuries woman played no part except in the home and behind the scenes, one can understand why it was impossible to stress the idea of a religious woman 'in the world', since all women were in the background. Feminine emancipation put an end to this, but the results of this emancipation of women have not yet been fully felt in the organization of religious life. To the great loss of the apostolate of religious, religious life has lagged behind in the vast field of action opened to the direct influence of women by their emancipation.

As far as more recent constitutions are concerned, one must remember that the idea of an organized lay apostolate only crystallized into Catholic Action under Pius XI. The idea that every baptized person should be an apostle is slow to take hold in the Church. With this in mind, one cannot be surprised that the concept of vows of religion being an extension and fulfilment of baptism has not been sufficiently stressed, and one understands why the role of religious as the moving spirits of the lay apostolate among women has not even been touched upon in these constitutions.

In the nature of things one breathes the air of one's times and lives within their limits. Once more, it is not the fault of the religious, who are quite properly concerned with obedience to their Rule as it is and are not called upon as individuals to make adaptations of it.

B. THE SPIRITUAL FACTOR

The contemplative origin of religious orders explains in part why apostolic spirituality has not had the full development it merits. A purely contemplative spirituality has had gradually imposed upon it a spirituality more nearly directed at action, but the balance between the life of prayer and the life of the apostolate has never been fully attained at the spiritual level itself. One slips very easily from one to the other—or rather, the 'contemplative' aspect retains a primacy which on some points fits in badly with the very real needs of the active vocation.

First of all one must distinguish between contemplation as such and the contemplative life. Contemplation, that is prayer in its purest form, is a part of every religious life and should have a very important place in it, but the contemplative life means something quite different—a life arranged on the basis of complete aloofness from the world. The vocation of which it is the fulfilment is of the very highest value, but it is not the vocation of congregations with directly apostolic aims.

The contemplative life has been described, quite properly, as seeking God principally in Himself and for Himself. It corresponds to the duty of direct adoration and is centred on the liturgical life—*Opus Dei*—and on the virtue of religion. The apostolic life, on the other hand, is oriented towards God in Himself and the service of God in serving one's neighbour and bringing him to love God. In a famous phrase, the apostle abandons God for God's sake. The phrase is, incidentally, inexact, for the apostle does not abandon God but remains in communion with Him while serving Him through his neighbour and adoring Him through His creatures in whom He abides.

Again, for those vowed to the contemplative life, as for those confined to a bed of sickness, the apostolate has a different meaning and is exercised in a different way. The contemplative life is eminently apostolic in the intention which inspires it, even though it plays no visible and active role in the extension of the Kingdom of God.

The silence and prayer of contemplatives bring down graces. But these graces need active helpers if they are to be fruitful. God needs man; He needs our active collaboration just as He needs wheat for the Holy Eucharist and water for baptism. Grace normally moves in human channels ever since God became man and intended the Incarnation in a certain sense to be continuous.

The religious who is vowed to the apostolic life must extend her prayer by action on every possible occasion. For her it is not enough to take refuge in prayer—to 'pray for poor sinners'—in order to be dispensed from the action which might perhaps help them to get free of sin. Neither the primary importance of prayer, nor the fact that God can work miracles of grace unaided, may serve as an excuse for our inaction. A religious vowed to the apostolic life has her own way of responding to the demands expressed in prayer. "The temptation of active religious," a Superior-

General wrote to us, "is to want to become enclosed nuns and to organize their religious life accordingly."[1]

What is proper and useful in one sort of life, then, is not necessarily suitable for another : words written for a Carthusian monk will not apply without some modification to a Sister of Charity. Let us take an example. Everyone knows the unparalleled position held by the *Imitation* in the spiritual life. This book, which has with good cause nourished many generations of nuns, contains a whole treasury of wisdom—but one must know how to read it; it was written by a contemplative for contemplatives. This accounts for the insistence with which it harps on the importance of solitude and aloofness from the world. "Every time I go back among men, I feel less a man myself." "It is praiseworthy for a religious to go out but rarely, to avoid seeing or being seen by men." But none of this is true if one goes out, not for personal satisfaction but to look for the lost sheep or to serve God through mankind. The fact that the *Imitation* has nothing to say about the apostolate is fair indication that its orientation is quite different. The book, which was written as a reaction to the danger of worldliness threatening religious who had chosen the contemplative life, is to be read quite differently by one whose life is dedicated to the visible salvation of the world and who, for that reason alone, must in some way be in touch with people. Underlying all appears the conclusion that it is more worth while to withdraw from one's fellow-men and devote one's whole time to prayer. This is in conformity with the overall idea of the vocation of a monk vowed to silence, but it is not true without modification for others.

[1] Cf. *L'Eglise en état de mission*, Ch. III, L'Excuse mystique.

C. THE CANONICAL FACTOR

To the historical and spiritual factors we must now add the canonical factor. Canon lawyers, like anyone else, are men of their age. In the course of the years they have codified the religious life on the basis of the cloistered type of nun, and in the spirit of an age which treated woman as a minor to be protected from herself. Canon law still bears the marks of this kind of masculine mentality which has not yet entirely died out. It is well known that what one can only call the anti-feminist tradition has had a long innings.

It can be traced all the way back to Tertullian whose influence in the matter was powerful. Mindful of paradise lost through Eve, he wanted to keep women in subjection and clothe them in garments of mourning and penitence. Addressing women of all times, Tertullian cried out, "Do you not know that you are Eve? You are the devil's doorway. It was you who profaned the Tree of Life, you who dragged down with you him whom the devil dared not attack directly. It was you who thus disfigured the image of God which is man."

Ancient canon law reflects this unfavourable prejudice.

In the decretal of Gratian there are the following unequivocal passages:

> Woman was not made in God's image . . . so one can understand the desire of the law that women be subject to men and wives almost the servants of their husbands.

> It is clear that woman is under man's dominion and has no authority, nor can she teach, give evidence, make a contract nor be a judge.

Some theologians, like some preachers, have fallen into line with this idea and tried to make woman into a sort of perpetual minor. Even St. Thomas followed his master, Aristotle, somewhat too unquestioningly in this matter.

"In her particular nature woman is something defective and accidental. . . . If a girl child is born, it is due to weakness of the generative principle, or imperfection in the pre-existing matter, or to a change produced by external causes, for example by the humid winds from the South, as Aristotle says."

The eminent Roman canonist Father van Biervliet, consultant to the Congregation for the Affairs of Religious, having emphasized the anti-feminine attitude of the ancient canonists, came to the following conclusion.

It is not surprising that canon law long reflected the common conviction of woman's weakness and her incapacity in many matters. From this came the dominant concern to protect her and supply her deficiencies by men. A typical case is that concerning the enclosure of nuns. For centuries the adage *aut maritus aut murus* (either a husband or an enclosure wall) was the accepted principle. To defend woman against the attacks of a brutal and not very well organized world there was no other solution conceivable: a wife was protected by her husband, if need be by cold steel; but an unmarried woman concerned for her virtue had to be shut away. True, a woman is still exposed to danger, but in our modern society immorality is less open and it is easier to avoid it behind the protection offered by the regular constabulary and an ever-alert police.[1]

It would be easy to find many traces left by an unconscious anti-feminist attitude in the summary judgments given by canon lawyers and spiritual writers on the subject of feminine psychology.

[1] *Regina Mundi*, No. 5, 1956.

On the subject of this hard-dying prejudice, a Superior-General once wrote to us:

> One feels that some measures were taken in previous centuries by men who mistrusted the uneducated woman. It is worth noting also that the rules were often the same for male religious [she added] but men are cleverer than we are at getting at the spirit of a text and do not allow themselves to become prisoners of the letter.

The contemplative orientation of conventional spirituality, as supplemented by a series of canonical prescriptions, tends to inhibit rather than to favour apostolic zeal. It is only in recent times, since the repeated appeals of Pope Pius XII urging on all religious, including contemplatives, certain forms of apostolate, that we have seen more supple adaptations appear. The process of broadening the canon law is under way, but it is far from complete.

D. THE PSYCHOLOGICAL FACTOR

Strange as it may seem we must stress, among the causes of the situation we have described, deviations which affect the practice of the vows themselves. These vows are of sublime greatness, as the Church has often had occasion to repeat through the ages in reply to those who, every now and then, attack them as implying an alienation incompatible with human dignity and freedom. But their very greatness demands that they be interpreted in action down to the last detail with the purity of intention and delicacy of touch belonging to all things divine. Sensitive handling is necessary for all that concerns the depths of the soul. A fall on level ground seldom causes broken bones, but if one stumbles at a great height the risk is much greater: the height itself demands greater precautions and clear vision.

And this is greatly to the honour of the religious vocation.

There is danger of distortion as soon as one adopts a too negative interpretation of the vows; that is to say, when the emphasis is on detachment and renunciation rather than on the positive aspect of cleaving to God. A one-sided emphasis tends to confuse the means with the end, and to present the vows as an end in themselves when they are in reality only the means to a full expression of the love of God.

Let us confine ourselves in this connection to one aspect of the practice of the vow of obedience.

It has been rightly said that the vow of obedience is the very essence of the religious life. By itself it can attain even the object of the other vows and it embraces the whole of the religious life, unifying it in a basic contract with God through the authority which represents Him. Every religious understands its meaning and its value. The more fervent she is, the more she wishes to anticipate the orders and even the wishes of her Superiors. She does not therefore allow herself to question anything; in any case, feminine psychology gives her a tendency to docility and passivity. It is natural for her to obey: she easily accepts general directives, but will want to discuss the details, whereas man more easily calls the principle in question and will not be bothered with details.

The religious quite properly regards the orders of her Superior as an expression of God's will, and she does her best to renounce her own will and forget her personal preferences. If she is not asked in the name of obedience to undertake apostolic works or to open her heart to the broader apostolate which we shall describe, she has a duty to refrain from them even though she may be conscious of their necessity and urgency.

The canon lawyers have restricted her life within clearly circumscribed limits, which she respects even if she feels she is being subjected to a kind of canonical tutelage. She accepts the fact that she can be made use of without her own wishes being consulted; she does not complain because, quite apart from the vow of obedience, she is encouraged to do so by a natural subordination which makes her content to lean on masculine support. Nothing in her make-up suggests that she demand the freedom which men in religion enjoy. The exigencies of the priesthood doubtless account for some of this freedom, but not for all of it, and the differences between nuns and priests remain very marked. As a nun she will not allow herself to claim even a few of the rights that woman has managed to obtain bit by bit from man in our modern society.

All this shows that if the Rules themselves are not opened to the new apostolic perspectives which we are going to describe, the vow of obedience will prevent in advance any change coming from within.

E. THE SOCIOLOGICAL FACTOR

Finally, let us look at the sociological factor which has made profound changes in the field of action of our congregations, that is in the scholastic and hospital fields. The increasing socialization of life and the growing State control in areas previously left largely to private enterprise, have transformed the daily life of our religious and threaten to overtax them. We should then take a fresh look at the religious life, and in particular the daily timetable, in order to re-assert the necessary hierarchy of values and safeguard the primacy of the religious and apostolic character of the nun's vocation.

Social progress, welcome it though we must, has its price. Our religious, enclosed in a network of legislation becoming more and more complex and making more and more demands upon them, facing the falling-off in the vocations which would bring them relief and reinforcement, see their professional duties becoming daily more institutionalized, thereby narrowing the margin of security indispensable to their personal religious development and their apostolic development.

Formerly when a foundress chose education she saw it as a fundamentally religious task; diplomas and technical demands appeared only later. The progress made, which is incontestable, is not without its dangers from the religious and apostolic viewpoints.

Such, in brief, are some of the major causes of a complex situation in which a variety of circumstances has played a decisive part. We have tried to list them and analyse them, without however being exhaustive, in order to allow us in the second part of this book (intended to outline the programme for reform) to indicate the ways and means towards the necessary solution which, thank God, is within the grasp of our joint efforts.

Part II

TOWARDS AN APOSTOLIC RENEWAL
OF THE RELIGIOUS LIFE

6

THE INNER MEANING OF THE RELIGIOUS VOCATION

WE have come now to the positive and constructive part of this book. We must place ourselves in an attitude of humble receptiveness before the Lord and ask just one question: What are the thoughts and wishes of the Master on the part to be played by religious in our times? What does He expect from these most precious collaborators? What help does He require from them for the salvation of the world? In reading the following pages we must say with St. Paul on the road to Damascus, "Lord, what wilt thou have me do?" Everything is in that question. How to make God better known, better loved and better served. As Pascal said, only God can tell us about God. Only God can speak about the salvation of souls, whose worth He alone knows, having ransomed them with His blood. He alone is the Master in command, giving the necessary graces in overflowing measure for us to answer His call courageously and to overcome all obstacles. *Da quod jubes et jube quod vis*, said St. Augustine—give what you order and order what you wish. What matters is the glory of God and the salvation of the world: everything else is relative to this absolute. Being open to the breath of the Spirit, to His views not to our own, this is the first thing required of those who, whether from within or from without, are responsible for the destiny of the religious life. For others the sure way is to respond with their whole heart to the demands made of them by their Superiors. The generous carrying out of allotted tasks is an infallible channel for the grace which not only renders their work fruitful but also advances the time of the hoped-for apostolic revival.

CONGREGATIONS AND SECULAR INSTITUTES

As we begin this second part, which is intended to be a contribution towards hastening that 'spiritual spring-time' desired by the late Pope as the fruit of the Council, it seems to us important to point out the present relevance of our traditional religious congregations and the necessity to preserve them.

As we have said, one frequently hears it repeated in different circles that the classic type of religious has outlived her *raison d'être* and that the future lies with secular institutes or with some new form altogether. The 'classic' religious, they say, are prisoners of the past and fettered by Canon Law; they can never become the salt of the earth as one would have wished. Their Rule itself hinders them, and is an effective obstacle to their penetrating the world. From this, people conclude that the answer is to let the past be past, that it is a waste of effort to attempt to move the mountains of tradition, and better to start from scratch and make something to measure which fits the needs of our time.

A curious thing is that this defeatist attitude finds involuntary support among certain religious who think that apostolic adaptation to the world is the job of secular institutes and that nuns of the traditional type should not be asked to do more than they do now.

What we want to explain here is why, in spite of the existence of these secular institutes, the active traditional congregations are still indispensable and why we firmly believe in the apostolic wealth which they hold for us today.

The religious state is defined in the Church today as "an established manner of living in community, by which the faithful, in addition to the precepts common to all, undertake to observe the evangelical counsels, through the practice of the vows of obedience, chastity and poverty" (Canon 487).

What typifies the regular type of religious life, then, is the life in the community in which the religious consecrates herself to God by the vows of religion. This communal life under obedience, lived within a framework and according to a Rule approved by the Church, constitutes a public affirmation of the transcendency of God and the reality of the supernatural. Religious are witnesses to God's right to be loved and served above all things. They set the world a problem: Whence comes the secret of such vocations? How is this devotion nourished? What is the source of their joy in the midst of the great human suffering to which they minister? Where can one find the key to such a life? What Bergson said of saints and heroes is particularly applicable to them—their existence is a challenge.

This in itself demands that they bear a sign, wear a distinctive habit, so that they are recognizable in ordinary circumstances. The habit must be simple and suitable—we shall come back to this—but it must also retain its function as a visible sign. The religious community as such is called upon to bear witness in a manner visible to all.

The secular institute has a different object. In the Constitution *Provida Mater Ecclesia* the Pope defines it as a society "whose members, in order to achieve Christian perfection and a full exercise of the apostolate, bind themselves to practise the evangelical counsels, while remaining in the world". This apostolate is exercised by them in their professional life, generally speaking on their own, wearing no distinctive habit, and living as far as possible the ordinary life of the world.

The comparison of the two kinds of life is alone enough to mark their differences and to show that the religious life answers a different purpose and retains in full its *raison d'être*.

THE PRIMITIVE CHURCH AS PROTOTYPE

The religious community as such constitutes a 'sign' by which the Master ought to be able to make Himself known; a convincing sign of brotherly love lived according to Jesus' words, "So they may perfectly be made one. So let the world know that it is thou who hast sent me." It is a fraternal community trying to continue in the world the prototype of the primitive Church described in the Acts of the Apostles :

> There was one heart and one soul in all the company of believers; none of them called any of his possessions his own, everything was shared in common. Great was the power with which the apostles testified to the resurrection of our Lord Jesus Christ, and great was the grace that rested on them all. None of them was destitute; all those who owned farms or houses used to sell them, and bring the price of what they had sold to lay it at the apostles' feet, so that each could have what share of it he needed. (Acts IV, 32–35.)

The religious community is linked by its very origin to the *vita apostolica*, to a life lived in the manner of the Apostles. It professes to be the incarnation of the Gospel in all its reality, and therefore particularly in the matter of its social repercussions. That fraternity of Christ's disciples went as far as a certain pooling of property which, although recognizing the right to private ownership, controlled its use for the common good. Religious life continues to express before the eyes of the world the social implications of evangelical brotherhood as a consequence of the voluntary association of members and the practice of the three vows.

As Fr. Carpentier writes:

> Limited to groups of volunteers, the *vita apostolica* organizes here below a social order and a way of life in which love solves all the problems of mutual understanding. . . . The religious life is seen as a public witness and has therefore a duty and acquires a mandate of public influence that is of interest to the Church as the supreme universal society. Its mandate is first of all to exist as a community and to bear witness among Christians and in human society. . . . It is also the accredited witness of the perfect evangelical life . . . the permanent charismatic witness to the Gospel's social message to humanity. . . . The religious life is no more than the baptismal life fully evolved along the lines of the social structure of the Gospel.[1]

At a time when Communism is trying to impose by force a new social order which destroys the spiritual personality of man, it is more than ever important that the Church should be able to offer the world the picture of living communities, where a voluntary communism reigns, based on divine worship and brotherly love, as a foretaste of what in many aspects a society open to social Christianity and faithful to the Gospel would be.

This apostolic life, it should be noted in passing, includes the supreme reason for its existence—the apostolate *par excellence* which consists of 'testifying with great power to the resurrection of Our Lord Jesus Christ'. This testifying must continue in the Church to the end of time, for the

[1] *L'Episcopat et l'Eglise Universelle*, pp. 427, 430, 433. Ed. de Cerf. Paris, 1962.

world can only survive on a living faith in the resurrection of Christ.

This, then, is the ultimate mission of our religious communities, and one can see why the Church shows special favour for them and desires to see them flourish.

All vocations have a reason for their existence, and the Church gives her blessing to them all. It is not our concern here to show the magnificent part which souls dedicated to God in the world can and do play; it is simply to make the point that the existence of secular institutes does not dispense the regular religious from their mission within the world.

THE IDEAL OF THE RELIGIOUS LIFE ALWAYS MODERN

The religious dedicates herself to God—but also to her brethren. To deprive her of the expression of the latter is to misunderstand the nature of her vocation.

St. Benedict used to ask those who sought admission to the novitiate, "What are you looking for?" If one put the same question to a young postulant to some apostolic order or congregation, she would answer, "I want to consecrate my life to God for the salvation of the world, nothing more and nothing less". She has in her, in the magnificent phrase of Gregory XV about St. Ignatius, 'a soul greater than the world'—*animam gerens mundo majorem*. In order the better to consecrate herself to God and souls, she is prepared to renounce the greatest joys of human love, of creating a home. She wishes God alone to be the breath of her soul and the inspiration of her heart.

This humanity which she wishes to serve embraces all souls whom she can reach, especially those who do not yet know Our Saviour and are wandering far from Him. In order to realize this ideal, she accepts the religious vows which are, with reason, represented to her as the great evangelical means of increasing in her the theological virtue of charity in relation to both God and man.

Joyfully she surrenders her heart and her body in order to belong to Christ alone and to have no other spouse.

Joyfully she surrenders her freedom for obedience; obedience which is not bondage, but a means of assuring the maximum return from her life and of strengthening and sustaining her apostolic impulse and co-ordinating it more effectively with the work of others.

Joyfully she renounces ownership of goods in order to intensify her absolute availability, in order to be quit of all cares but the service of God.

The vows, as she regards them, are not shackles on the apostolate but a liberation and a means to freedom. They are the price of a freedom which places itself at the disposal of the Spirit, which breathes where it will and which is always going forward : "Where the Spirit is, there is liberty."

Such is the ideal anticipated by the postulant : she must not be disappointed. In sanctioning a congregation the Church gives her guarantee that the way is sure and that faithful adherence to the Rule should lead to spiritual expansion and greater love for others.

Nowadays a postulant will already have had a glimpse of the dedication to the apostolate of which she dreams through her participation in various works and movements before entering the convent. She will already have experienced the joy of revealing Christ to others; will have come across ardent souls; known homes 'in a state of grace, and of mission'—her own perhaps. She will have seen with her own eyes what a Christian presence can achieve for good in the midst of the day's work; and also what a few hours a week devoted to directly apostolic work outside her professional activities can do. She will dream of giving to Our Lord and her fellow-men twenty-four hours out of the twenty-four. She wants her life to be even more unified. One love inspires her, a double love. She wants to go from God to God in prayer, and from God Himself to God in her fellow-creatures in the apostolate.

If her vocation is to overseas missions, the ideal of total dedication is perhaps more striking; but genuine apostolic zeal is a part of all religious vocations.

She renounces everything in order to dedicate herself to spiritual motherhood, to a supernatural fruitfulness incomparably superior to any other, however noble. She wishes to follow the Master wherever He may choose to go.

When a religious chooses an active order rather than a contemplative one (to which other laws apply), it is because she wants to exercise her apostolic zeal in a visible and tangible manner, to contribute not a marginal comment but a part of the very text of life.

SCHOOL OF SANCTITY

The religious life remains for the Church one of the treasures which give expression to her holiness—"I believe in the Holy Catholic Church," we say in the Creed. Religious offer themselves to the Church so that she may lead them to holiness and to nothing less. They enter into the mystery of sanctification of which Our Lord was speaking when He said, "I sanctify myself for them". What in Him was overflowing fullness is for them a progression and an increase. With Him and in Him they hope to sanctify themselves for the world. By renouncing human love they sanctify the conjugal love of others; by their renunciation of riches they are an invitation to detachment from the material possessions that so often plague mankind; by their renunciation of their own will they proclaim the fact that adherence to the will of God is the only liberty.

They sanctify themselves for the world.

They sanctify themselves also by sanctifying the world. If it is true that no one can give what he does not possess, it is equally true that the surest way to have anything is to give it away: spiritual treasure can only be possessed when one passes it on to others; one keeps only what one loses. In the words of Christ, "It is the man who loses his life for my sake that will save it".

Magnificent ebb and flow: sanctity increasing *in order* to give more of itself and increasing *because* it gives itself.

BELONGING TO GOD

The religious strives for sanctity with a view towards her apostolate, and by means of it. She is one of the Lord's chosen members, the portion He has reserved for Himself. In her own way, she is to God what Mary is. In the words of St. Louis de Montfort, "Mary is God's paradise, His ineffable world. The Son of God has entered there that He might work His wonders, that He might preserve this paradise, and take delight within it."

The spouse of Christ, the religious, is the result of the triumph of His grace: she is a victory-hymn of Jesus who in every age finds some souls who leave everything for Him. In answering His summons, the religious quits a world which she knew and in which the only thing she despised was sin. She renounces for a higher love treasures whose value she understands perfectly well; yet she joyfully offers Our Lord all that makes the world so attractive. It is a triumphant affirmation of God's supreme place.

BELONGING TO THE WORLD

Nevertheless, the religious brings with her the world she leaves behind and finds it in a supernatural way in the very heart of her vocation.

When God gives a soul that special grace which is what a vocation is, He is undoubtedly showing a special love, but this love embraces all mankind. Loved by God for her own sake, the religious is also seen by Him as the representative of her race.

When God loves, or chooses, or shows a preference, He does not do so as we do. When we prefer one thing to others, or choose one thing from among others, what we do not prefer or choose necessarily falls back to second place. But when God loves or favours it is in order that the whole world may thereby be enriched. She whom God loved above others, whom He chose from among all creatures, who was 'blessed among women', was loved and chosen and blessed in order to become the Mother of Christ and thereby the mother of all mankind. Our inclinations and our capabilities are made to match the particular form of apostolate that God asks of us. It is through us that God intends to love others; it follows, then, that each grace we have received must be converted into apostolic action for the benefit of the world.

The religious gives herself to God, but also brings with her in her striving towards God the whole of mankind for whom she makes herself responsible. For her more than for anybody should St. Augustine's words be true: "Do you want to know if God is there? When you turn to Him, have you the interest of humanity in your heart? When you try to approach God, do you bring with you human kind and all its cares? Do you bring with you those whom He gave you to love? If mankind is present in your tenderness and love, God is there."

The religious is not of the world, but she is in it; she takes it with her when she enters her convent; and the world expects the enrichment it has a right to as the result of her sacrifice. If the religious is not to fail God she must not fail mankind. She fulfils a function as mediatrix between God and man, and a mediatrix must join and bind together the two banks of the river; she must throw a bridge across and see that it is firmly anchored on both sides. If she belongs fully to her time and is rooted in the world as it is, the religious can only accept realistically and logically the conditions which will allow her to fulfil her proper mission in the Church today.

7

RETURN TO SOURCES

WE must keep this ideal of the religious life constantly
before our eyes if we wish to do our part, so far as it concerns us, in making reality coincide with the ideal. We
cannot disappoint this young girl who has seen the possibility of giving herself to God and mankind and wishes to
do so; the religious life she finds on entering must correspond to her highest aspirations.

In order to give the religious vocation its proper value in
the world today, it is essential to establish quite clearly the
balance between the religious life and the apostolic life. So
long as there is dualism there will be conflict. There can
be no question of opting for the religious life at the expense
of the apostolate, or for the apostolate to the detriment
of the religious life. The religious life and the apostolic life
are not opposites but are almost identical, each containing
or implying the other. So long as one thinks in terms of
defending the religious life against the encroachment of
the apostolate, or of encouraging it at the expense of
the apostolate one's approach is superficial and no solution
is possible. The demands of the apostolate grow out of
the demands of the religious life as a flower stems from its
parent plant. The only reason for consecrating one's life to
God for the salvation of the world is to achieve a greater
apostolic influence than one could in the world. We believe
that this fundamental unity and harmony will best be seen
if we go back to the origins of the religious vocation as

they are to be seen in the Gospels and the Acts of the Apostles, as they emerge in the course of history and are exemplified in the lives of the Foundresses. This return to tradition—and, if need be, beyond tradition—allows us to recapture Péguy's 'first morning' and to relive in their pristine freshness the intuitions that led to the birth of religious congregations.

This return to the well-springs leads us first of all, of course, to what is and always will be the model for all Christian life and all religious life—the Gospel. It is here that we must seek the thoughts and wishes of the Master.

THE GOSPEL

No constitutions or customs can override the Gospel. The value of any rule derives from its constant reference to the one valid basis, the word of God. Nothing in the religious life may conflict with a single verse of the Gospel, for it exists only to translate each line of it into the language of everyday life and to give it material existence. All that one should be able to read between the lines of any constitution is the Gospel which should be its very fabric.

Now the Gospel is not a book based on fear and timidity. On every page we are invited to go forward boldly in the name of the Lord into the world that is to be saved. It is not only by words and phrases that this invitation is conveyed, but also by the fundamental mystery the Gospel reveals to us—the Incarnation of the Son of God.

The Word, Scripture tells us, thought it no deprivation to leave the bosom of His Father to come into this world to redeem it by His Incarnation, by becoming one of us, so that we might partake of the divine. This prodigious fact, which is emblazoned across our horizon like a rainbow, constitutes the most astonishing appeal to us to 'approach', to make little of distances, to cross the abysses and to be all things to all men.

THE MASTER'S EXAMPLE

The example of the Master who, in one great surge of love, came from heaven to earth to "seek out and save that which was lost", will always be our model.

Our Lord came and He went; it is up to us, too, to go in search of that which was lost and must be saved. Jesus came and multiplied His contacts with men in order to reveal His Father to them. Christianity, let us not forget, is first and foremost the bringing of God to man, the communication of His truth and His life. The Church is Jesus Christ 'passed on and spread abroad'.

The Master came and He went to His brothers by adoption. These included His disciples, naturally, but also the Pharisees and the Sadducees, the Samaritans whom one 'simply doesn't know', and the sinners whom one avoids.

He came and He went as a doctor goes to the sick and not to the healthy. He said so Himself.

He came and He moved in circles which 'respectable' people despised and thought it unhealthy to frequent.

He came and He went into the house of Zaccheus and walked in the market place and on the roads and paths of His country, unceasingly, tirelessly.

He came and He went among men and spoke with them.

He spoke sometimes cryptically, sometimes clearly, according to the circumstances. Sometimes He spoke but one word, or a half-finished phrase, or He made a long speech, as on the Mount; sometimes it was a point-blank question, sometimes the answer to another's question, sometimes a meaningful silence. But He spoke to men, whether assembled in crowds or encountered individually at the village well or on the shores of the lake. He spoke as 'no other man has spoken' and His theme was always the same: He spoke about His Father so that men might discover that they were the sons of God and brothers of one another.

He spoke because He was the Ambassador of God, the prototype of all missionaries.

He spoke because He was, in every fibre of His being, the Living Word, the Word made flesh.

From this we can realize that a Christian is not a Christian if he does not participate in this same mission, if he does not echo this same Word, if he does not in his turn bring God to man with all his strength and energy.

THE MASTER'S COMMAND

To the example of His own life Jesus added the explicit command to go into the world in His name.

One command is written in words of fire in the Gospel: Go out to the whole world and proclaim the Good News to all creation.

It is an order that admits of no attenuating gloss, no exegetical restrictions, no plea of impossibility.[1]

It is the order that governs every life dedicated to God and our fellow-men: in that life we must keep it ever before our eyes.

It was the final charge given the Apostles at the end of three years of instruction during which He had never ceased to make it clear.

"As the Father sent me, so I also send you."

"I have appointed you to go and bear fruit, fruit that will be lasting."

"I send you as sheep among wolves."

"I send you to the lost sheep of Israel."

The Gospel is full of such exhortations in which the Master charges His disciples to be the heralds who will go out into the highways and byways to invite the many to God's banquet.

Everything in the Gospel breathes calm courage and the

---

[1] Cf. *L'Eglise en état de mission*, Ch. VIII, Le Commandement du Seigneur, where this theme is developed.

certainty of a divine assistance that will never be lacking. "You will do greater things than I."

St. Paul was the faithful echo of Our Lord when he wrote to Timothy words which should figure in the heading of all Rules of Life : "The Spirit he has bestowed on us is not one that shrinks from danger; it is a spirit of power, of love and of discipline."

THE ACTS OF THE APOSTLES

The whole Gospel is an invitation to the direct apostolate, to walk upon the waters.

And this is how the disciples understood it. The Acts of the Apostles are just an account of the courageous loyalty of Jesus' disciples at odds with the pagan world they were trying to penetrate. "We cannot not speak," they were to tell their judges. Among these disciples, moreover, women had a special place.

It was women who, disregarding the danger of compromising themselves, accompanied Jesus on the road to Calvary while the Apostles, with the exception of John, had fled.

They appear again, loyal and unbroken, at the foot of the Cross, at the empty tomb on Easter morning.

Women gave themselves fearlessly to the propagation of the faith and the service of the infant Church even though for some of them it meant martyrdom.

They are constantly met, either as deaconesses or as private persons, in every branch of the apostolate. It is worth reading again certain passages in the Acts, or in St. Paul's epistles, where he lists the intrepid women who worked with him. Nowhere in Scripture is there any trace of contempt or disdain for women. Jesus trusted them— and they did not disappoint His trust. If we really want to go back to sources, reading the Acts is an essential item on any programme of apostolic reform in any field.

THE FOUNDRESSES

The Acts of the Apostles are carried on throughout the history of the Church, in particular by those generous and saintly souls who were responsible for the founding of the various religious orders and congregations. Their lives are a faithful echo of the Gospel.

To bring out the missionary zeal that underlay the foundation of the active congregations, there is nothing better than to study the lives of the Foundresses.

Pope Pius XII emphasized this point very strongly in the repeated and moving appeals he made for an *aggiornamento*, that is a modern adaptation.

"Most of the time," he said during the Congress of Religious in Rome, "those who wrote the rules of religious institutes planned their new foundations in order to fulfil some urgent function or to answer a need that suddenly appeared in the Church and had to be dealt with then and there. If, therefore, you want to follow the example of your Foundresses, your attitude must conform to theirs."

Many of these Foundresses have been canonized, which means that the Church has formally set the seal of her approval on their life and purpose. What they all had in common—and some of them to an almost unbelievable degree—was the apostolic zeal which led them to minister to material and spiritual distress. They went further and further in their efforts to save souls and to make Christ known to all men everywhere.

Their history is glorious—and at the same time sad: glorious on account of the Foundresses who represent initiative, tenacity and Christian audacity; sad on account of the opposition they encountered from men who were slaves of the anti-feminist prejudices of their time and prisoners of routine or of too narrow a canonical definition of the term 'religious'.

F

The history of congregations is all too often the account of a series of obstacles to be surmounted in order to win the right to go where the distress to be relieved was most pressing, of the right to the freedom of action vital to their work.

In so many cases the story of the Foundresses recalls that of Veronica, braving the criticism and hostility of the mob to come to the Master to wipe the blood and dirt from His face. Their zeal was directed to Christ crucified in the souls of sinners, to Christ unknown or wrongly known. Like Veronica, they did not presume to think whether it was ladylike to mingle with a crowd of Pharisees and soldiers; they went to Christ with the courage born of love —and God blessed their action and their work.

Another striking thing is that the Foundresses never lost sight of the fact that their *raison d'être* and that of the young foundation was to bring Christ to those in material or spiritual distress. They faced sin and sought the sinner, the lost sheep. They took Our Lord at His word and went out to invite people to come and be nourished at the eucharistic banquet and take sustenance from the word of God. They went. . . . One might almost use that as a sort of refrain in their lives which were in no way enclosed or cloistered. They did not wait within walls until the police brought abandoned infants or delinquents to the door; they were penetrated with the mystery of the Visitation and hurried with Our Lady into the hill country to be of service to others.

The sick, delinquents and children were their special care and received from them both material help and religious sustenance.

The work of the first companions who rallied to them was, by human standards, on a very modest scale, but they never lost sight of the directly religious aim they had adopted.

After the death of the Foundress the work grew. Where to start with there had been a bare handful of sick or orphans, their numbers today are reckoned in hundreds or thousands. Socially this undoubtedly represents remarkable progress, but a progress which from the apostolic viewpoint has been dearly paid for. Technical progress, and mere weight of numbers on top of that, have obscured the original insight of the Foundresses whose first care was the work of spreading the Gospel. We must therefore constantly come back to first origins if we are to maintain a balance between the various elements of the religious life.

How this will work out, we shall have to see as we go along. Suffice it to mention here the extent to which the lives of the Foundresses show up the main points and prevent the wood from becoming obscured by the trees. To recapture the initial inspiration is to breathe the sweet air of the Gospel. Times have changed and methods have become outdated, but we must not betray the original spirit. All communities must guard jealously, or rediscover, the original 'marching orders' which made their Foundresses pioneers of the direct apostolate. On the subject of true loyalty to tradition, the following words of J. Chevalier are very true :

> Identity of life supposes a continuous change whose very continuity assures unity. In time there is always some element which is changing, but it only changes in order that some other element may remain constant.[1]

Let us, then, examine the main activities of religious today in the light of their origins, and try to see what available or latent apostolic possibilities we can find there and how they can best be enlarged.

[1] Quoted in *Equilibre et Adaptation*, p. 238.

8

A BROADER VISION

Organizing for the Apostolate

BEFORE going exactly into what constitutes for the main categories of religious the apostolic advancement which is the theme of this book, we should like to draw attention to some fields of action which have not been opened up or which lie fallow in part and which should be shared among these categories according to their particular gifts. One can, and indeed must, admire what is already being done, but preoccupation with the salvation of the world urges us to find out what still remains to be done and makes us anxious about the harvest abandoned for lack of labourers. To the man who said he had faithfully fulfilled the law, Jesus said, "In one thing thou art still wanting . . ." In the spirit of the Gospel we should try to find out what duties we have not yet fulfilled, rather than enumerate those which we have done our best to fulfil. It is not a question of abandoning the duties of one's state, but of seeing just how far these duties can be extended; it is not a question of embarking on new tasks instead of traditional ones, but of carrying the latter to completion, of following one's vocation to its ultimate conclusion, of 'becoming what we are'.

This extension which is indispensable for apostolic reasons is also essential to the balanced development of our nuns themselves and to the survival of our schools and institutions.

Growing State control in the fields of education and

medicine put the accent on the professional side of the life of religious. Officialism threatens them : both teachers and nurses sometimes feel themselves to be more teacher or nurse than nun. This is the cause of the disquiet of which we have already spoken.

"One thing is still wanting . . ." This one thing, though often not clearly seen or not seen at all, is the possibility of a more direct apostolate.

It is not a question of adding new tasks : the nun's day, like that of the rest of us, has only twenty-four hours. It is a matter of the practical revision of the scale of values and of reserving a special place for certain specified apostolic activities in the same way as a special place is held by the spiritual exercises prescribed by the Rule. Only if this is done can the real professional life of nuns be fruitful. Their spiritual and apostolic activities are the special portion that God reserves to Himself.

We do not intend to put forth a fixed and invariable definition of what 'God's portion' will consist of. It must be made to suit each case and should be introduced gradually in a manner still to be decided upon. In the next chapter we indicate some adaptations which may make the change-over easier. The essential is to realize that this integration is indispensable for the full vitality of a soul vowed to God, for, let us not forget, in choosing the religious life the postulant was not principally drawn by the prospect of becoming a teacher or a hospital worker : she wanted these activities to be the means whereby she played her part in the salvation of the world. It is in any case only to the extent that she is clearly fully apostolic that a nun will draw others to follow in her footsteps. A religious must be in a position to convey the best of herself.

It is essential to her spiritual joy that she be able to communicate to others the secret of her great love. It is hard to imagine a girl who could never talk to anyone about her fiancé: she needs to make him known and appreciated by others. "I believed, therefore I have spoken," said St. Paul. From the overflow of his faith words sprang up—they had to. Silence is agony for anyone who wishes to proclaim his discovery of the Messiah from the housetops. The religious, the bride of Christ, knows the same feeling and demands to be given the means of pursuing her apostolic vocation to the end. Her task is not done until she can give Christ to others by gathering round her other souls whom she can set on fire with love of God. She must bring Christ to life in them and make Him present in every facet of their lives as individuals, and as members of a family and society. She must teach these people, then, how to give Christ to others in whatever walk of life may be their own. A whole field of apostolic action among the laity opens up for the nun who knows how to discover such people, how to group them into appropriate Catholic Action movements already existing, or into some new movement to meet a present need, how to inspire their goodwill and keep it alive.

It is an immense field with boundless perspectives, this apostolate of bringing Christ to those who do not know Him, and introducing Christian standards into every aspect of the lives of so many who are Christian in name alone. The world is full of religious illiterates who cannot read God in the book of life, as it is full of Christians who have done no more than glance through a few pages, if that, of the Gospel. This is the world that claims the nun's attention.

Certainly not every religious is suited to every kind of apostolic action; the particular kind of activity must be chosen to suit each individual, including the Sister-cook, and an apostolic outlet must be found for each in keeping with her capabilities. We must be firmly convinced that, in comparison with the surrounding world which is spiritually undernourished to a scarcely credible degree, our nuns are overnourished and have a surplus they can distribute to those around them. Consider the time devoted to the nourishment of their souls: Mass and Holy Communion, meditation, spiritual reading, instruction, recollection, retreats—all these are storing up divine energy in them, making as it were high-tension power stations of them. Consider also how the Church surrounds them with loving care: the Superiors' orders, the Rule, the customs of the house, examination of conscience, spiritual direction, mutual support, canonical visitors, and so on all the way up to the Sacred Congregation for the Affairs of Religious— everything combines to ensure their spiritual welfare and to fit them ideally to be the inspiration of the lay apostolate among women. It would not be reasonable if all this care and trouble ended in their lives being concentrated on a restricted number of pupils or patients without there being also some outlet to the world in need of salvation. It would not be reasonable for the life of a religious to be turned back on itself and sheltered from the winds blowing in the world outside. Nuns do not dedicate themselves to God in order to live a petty, patterned life in a confined space cut off from the world.

It remains for us now to explain the extent and nature of the apostolic element to be incorporated in the religious life.

Today nuns are particularly active in education and the care of the sick, and it is in these two fields that they are most numerous. It is there, too, that we must go to study the question of apostolic yield. What we say of them can easily be applied to other categories by making the necessary minor adjustments.

EDUCATION

The Basic Apostolate

To avoid all possibility of misunderstanding, we must start by saying that the educational work carried out by our religious institutes is in itself an apostolate.

We must repeat here all that we said in our book *La Question scolaire* concerning the Christian atmosphere which should pervade all the instruction given to children who are baptized. The Christian outlook on life is not conveyed to the child by religious instruction alone: it is in all subjects, and particularly those which concern man more closely—history, literature, ethnology—that youth learns to see everything in the light of Christ and to acquire that integrity of judgment without which the Christian life is impossible.

The forming of youth is in itself an apostolic work so long as it respects the essential aim. Why, in the last analysis, do we develop the child's faculties by teaching him algebra or Latin or history if it is not to increase the value of this growing Christian, to make him better suited tomorrow to spread the thought and the life of Christ in the world which will be his? This *consecratio mundi*, this christianization of the world, can be achieved only by fully human and fully valid Christians. Only to the extent that Christianity has penetrated them will they be able to radiate it to other individuals and to society.

The natural order does not exist. There exists only a supernatural order, which alone is real and willed by God. It is in this supernatural order that all human potentialities are fully realized. Thus, in undertaking to make of a Christian, a man, the educator is endeavouring to form a Christian who is complete. But this can only be achieved by the continuity and harmony of an integrated education where all disciplines work together towards a common goal.

The whole atmosphere of a class or school should permeate every subject, even those most remote from sacred things.

Each subject taught can and must be integrated in an all-embracing Christian perspective. There can be no dualism between science and faith, since they are approaches to the same truth that comes from God. Teaching itself is only one element of the living synthesis of true Christian education. To be successful, Christian education demands that it is not only the mind that must be formed but also the will, the character and social and apostolic sense. All this supposes coherence and co-operation among educators; it supposes also an incontestable apostolic effort, which is the very soul of our institutions. The religious, whose whole being is vowed to God, is especially qualified to give the young such an integrated education which, being centred on God, embraces and unifies all the different facets of human culture.

SPECIFIC TASKS

What we have said so far applies to the basic apostolate inherent in our institutions in so far as they are true to their Christianity. They are the stock on to which specific apostolic tasks must be grafted if we wish Christian education to give its maximum yield and fulfil the Church's hopes.

Let us glance now at the various branches of the field entrusted to teaching nuns and see if we cannot find some occasions for apostolic action.

First of all, within the schools.

Apostolate in Schools

It is not enough that nuns themselves are fully conscious of the apostolic duty. They must communicate this conviction to the girls in their care.

Their young charges must be educated to a Christianity

that is complete—that is, apostolic. This means that each pupil must receive practical and progressive training. And this must be done in the ordinary way of school life. One must be able to offer the pupils a variety of works and movements capable of stirring their enthusiasms and generosity so that they can do an apprenticeship in social and apostolic work. A single standardized quasi-obligatory movement cannot take into account the diversity of talent and vocation among the girls. Such movements and organizations as can be made available would gain by being affiliated to diocesan, national or international societies, since they would profit from their know-how and experience. However, certain organizations of a purely local character are not excluded. Too often in our schools there are only a very few girls engaged in any such activity, a tiny minority. We cannot accept this anomalous situation. It must be understood that a fully Christian education must be given to all pupils; the means to achieve this must therefore be provided. Once the principle is agreed and the means at hand, some girls will choose a movement that is directly apostolic while others will go for something which is of a more social or charitable nature, but which indirectly leads to apostolic contacts. There are many mansions in the Father's house—but they should all be inhabited.

As in English schools, where the timetable allows a set number of periods for physical culture but leaves the choice of games or sport to the individual, our institutions must allow for a choice of apostolic or social work. Parents should know that this is part and parcel of Christian education, and it would be a good idea to explain to them what such an education entails.

The preservation of our faith is also at stake. We are no longer in the age of traditional Christianity handed on from one generation to the next. To remain alive, faith must propagate : like fire, it must set alight to its surroundings or it will burn out and die. A generation that has not learned to radiate its faith, to communicate it to others, is doomed to spiritual sterility. Catholic schools were not set up for the purpose of presenting diplomas to young ladies entrusted by their parents to our care, but in order to make of them apostles who have diplomas. A school does not earn the title of Catholic just by giving religious instruction and making it possible for the pupils to attend Mass. For a school to be Christian it must produce committed Christians needed by the Church and the world. This is a perfectly normal requirement of Christianity.

It must not happen, an American bishop once said to us, that our colleges produce nothing but "Old Girls". Our education is successful only if it turns out a dynamic, conquering, Christian faith. Anything else is failure.

It might sometimes happen that the very number of pupils makes it impossible to organize things so as to ensure this kind of fully Christian education. In that case we shall have to be bold and cut down the numbers, for if we do not, we shall be defeating our own ends, which are not to get as many diplomas or scholarships as possible but to turn out girls capable of playing the part that Our Lord expects of them in society.

After-school Apostolate

If education is to be an integral affair, teachers cannot just forget about their pupils when they leave school. The whole range of the pupils' lives should be the object of their active and fruitful solicitude.

Formerly the pupils confided to the nuns' care lived like them in a closed world: society was Christian or at least imbued with Christian morality. But this traditional Christianity is giving way to Christianity as a matter of personal preference. Today when a child leaves school it has often to go to a family profoundly unsettled on both human and

Christian planes, and in any case to a world becoming more and more pagan, in which everything is a matter for doubt and questioning.

Life after school threatens to undo what education has achieved *intra muros*. And nuns cannot afford to ignore this fact. But this negative reason is not the sole reason: education must be a co-operative effort by teachers and parents. Upon this depends the efficacy of an action that should be continuous and complementary. A child's education is at the mercy of the parents who can either further it or entirely disrupt it. The co-operation of the parents is essential, and it pertains to the religious to make them understand this. This means that she will be obliged to concern herself, in a certain degree, with the Christian education of the parents themselves. One cannot separate what life has bound together with the closest ties. Education is one: school and family are like the two halves of a Gothic arch. The education of children, as one philosopher expressed it, is the family reaching maturity. The religious has therefore a part to play in ensuring the continuity of this common work.

A teaching nun wrote to us very appropriately on the subject of this continuity:

Experience has shown that all is not done when one has spent oneself without counting the cost to provide our children with a Christian education. This education is the foundation of Christian society, but we must also help in the construction of the entire edifice in the persons of the young adults, and so continue our work as educators right to the end.

Thinking of the position of nuns, she added:

But what can we do? Our rules are framed in terms of the world as our Foundresses knew it; they did not envisage the world of their successors, a world necessarily very different from theirs. So we see our nuns vowed, if nothing is done to remedy the situation, to be the guardians of only those sheep that are within the fold and to allow those sheep to stray which, once outside the fold with no shepherd to follow them, leave the flock and get lost in such great numbers along the road. Yet how great is the price of a soul! Christ died as much for grown-ups as for the souls of children. We must therefore go out and find them wherever they may be.

Family Apostolate

School is more than just an assembly of pupils. Each child is an open door to a family, a door revealing endless vistas of family action. First there are the natural contacts: parents like to meet their daughters' teachers. These contacts must not be restricted to Reverend Mother or the Directress of Studies but should extend to all who are directly responsible for the girls. This will serve to multiply the occasions for dialogue, and allow for their continuance.

Parents' associations, which happily are being formed in various places all over the world, can be an increasing occasion for contacts: one must make the most of the latent apostolic opportunities they offer. What a wonderful thing it would be to have a hand in the steady, solid work of forming Christian families and organizing the best of them into various family movements or Catholic Action movements aimed at christianizing the others. But this supposes that one does not sit idly by and wait for the parents to come and ask for an interview. It means that educators must approach the families. Of these families those who do not come of their own accord are often the ones who most need attention. This supposes, too, that the 'family' part of apostolic work is recognized as an integral part of the duties of the educator's state.

It also supposes a freedom of movement which, in turn, demands some necessary adaptations. If the end is desired, the means to it must also be sought: and there can be no doubt about the desirability of an end demanded by the salvation of souls.

It is hard to overstress the importance of this 'missionary' action in the basic cell of the social body, the family. In visiting the parents at home one takes advantage of all the real, stable and human values which the family represents. At home the child is natural, genuine, her true self—and so are her parents. Outside the home they are subjected to a mass of influences which make them adopt artificial attitudes. This is an elementary observation. Social pressures exert their full force as soon as a man steps outside his own front door; if these pressures do penetrate unbeknown into the home, then at least he is in a better position to resist them there and to exercise his freedom. His true nature is stripped of its layers of social veneer and asserts itself at home. And here, too, a man may make what use he will of his freedom. To bring one's message into the home is to deliver it in an atmosphere of freedom where it stands a far better chance of lasting effect than otherwise.

Lay Staff

Nuns, however, do not act alone. More and more, they share their educational responsibilities with lay mistresses. This fact is of great importance in the matter we are considering. Nuns alone cannot ensure that each pupil is educated for the apostolate: lay mistresses and lay teachers must be brought in, and this means that they too must have training to fit them for this task: they must, as it were, take a degree in 'apostolics'. Who is to blame for the frequently heard complaint that the collaboration of the lay staff is restricted to their professional sphere? Have we prepared them for the apostolic role in the instruction we gave them in teacher training? Have we trained them, initiated them in instruction in the techniques of the apostolate as they were initiated in the techniques of teaching languages or the sciences? There is a vicious circle here and it is a matter of urgency that it be broken. Once this is done, instead of regarding the lay invasion as a necessary evil to be borne with, we can see it as a providential opportunity to relieve our nuns of a part of their non-religious duties and enable them to devote themselves more effectively to a wider apostolate which should include in particular the post-school work—that is, first and foremost, their former pupils.

Old Girls

Too often the organization which brings Old Girls of a school together once a year or so is rather academic and has no apostolic significance. Nevertheless, these souls remain in the charge of their mistresses whose mission is not completed until a Christian home has been established and everything has been done to make it a success worthy of the children of God. Their mistresses must keep in touch with them, devote some time to them, take an interest in their lives and try to get them interested in some apostolic or social work suitable to the circumstances in which God has placed them. Many factors will doubtless arise to weaken contact between mistresses and girls, not least among them the desire of the latter to be on their own and be 'allowed to grow up'. But it is the mistresses' job to find the right psychological approach that will enable them to maintain or create contacts. By means of existing movements, or new movements created for the purpose, somehow the work of education must be carried on among the young grown-ups. For some of them this contact will be, by the grace of God, a determining factor in awakening or sustaining the beginnings of a vocation; how else can one hope to preserve a vocation if all contact is lost at the very time when life's most important decisions are being made?

For others this contact will be a permanent source of grace, always at hand, according to circumstances. All that we said in *Love and Control* about the part to be played by educators in preparing their charges for betrothal and marriage should be recalled here.

But how can these needs be met if a nun cannot be near her old pupils; if she cannot reach them; if the Rule does not allow her the means to go to them; if her Constitutions forbid such contacts; if in fact this apostolic aspect of her task is not written into the Rule itself; if the Rule does not both fix the proper conditions and ensure the possibility?

Outsiders

Ought we not also to think about the other young people, who are not former pupils of our schools, but who must also be taken under our care?

Certainly our existing organizations and youth movements do their best to reach these young women, and we must do what we can to help them in this. But there will always be a number who will have nothing to do with any movement, yet must be evangelized. The field of young women is far too often left uncultivated. Who better than our nuns could take on the job?

It will not always be done directly by personal contact, but perhaps by organizing young Christian women in such a manner that they can penetrate the area. Who has not heard of moving examples of lay apostles radiating a warm and living Christianity in so-called impenetrable areas?

Unfortunately these lay apostles are a mere handful. It is up to religious to find more of them, to group them together, train them, and stimulate them.

This type of apostolic action, 'beyond the frontiers', must be well organized. It could be accomplished by the joint effort of several religious congregations working together according to some overall plan. Each congregation, while guarding its own characteristics and pursuing its particular mission, should, at the same time, collaborate with the clergy and apostolic groups to bring the Gospel to these young women who live outside the pale of more conventional, institutionalized influences.

The pedagogical techniques of such work will have to be studied more closely. All we wish to do here is draw attention to a world in distress, waiting to be christianized through the efforts of our educators.

The 'Poor' and the 'Abandoned'

Older adolescents are the abandoned children of our era. Formerly a Vincent de Paul or a Jean-Baptiste de La Salle collected from the streets the small children who had been materially, morally or intellectually abandoned. Today young adults—that is, between 16 and 25—are a class particularly in need of attention. They are the spiritual orphans of our time, up against the problems of life, alone, turned in on themselves, yet so anxious to be understood and to be tactfully and discreetly guided. The unpleasant exploits the papers report from everywhere in the world are the work of victims of this abandonment. No doubt the parents bear the primary responsibility for this state of affairs which is too often due to moral poverty in the home—however, we are not concerned here with analysing causes but with finding remedies.

The religious of today, drawing inspiration from the special love their Foundresses showed to young children, ought at the present time to show this same love to our abandoned adolescents. For these young girls have more need than ever of being loved and understood, and helped.

G

Given the choice of means, one would have liked to have opened special schools for them, since this would bring the girls into contact with a formative influence. The same pastoral concern would dictate the choice, whenever possible, of the sort of school which prepares girls of different social backgrounds for occupations that are rich in human contacts.

Formerly the Foundresses showed a particular love for the poor. Free schooling means that as far as education is concerned there are no longer any poor. But "the poor we have always with us". The evangelical preferences of the Foundresses would be best respected today by opening clubs or other places where young women deprived of normal Christian influence will be welcomed and can spend their free time. Modern society accords an ever-increasing place in life to leisure and amusement, and it would be hard to overestimate the importance that the environment of leisure has assumed. All mass communication media are propagating a concept of life which is invading our homes and capturing the adolescents; and it is a concept that is materialistic, pagan and as far removed from Christianity as it is possible to be.

The teaching nun is the obvious person to teach girls how to organize and occupy their spare time in a profitable manner—avoiding the dangers.

The environment of leisure extends beyond the home: travel, week-ends and holiday camps have assumed great importance in the lives of our young people. The presence of a nun during these times of naturalness and openness would be a great blessing for them.

We asked a group of Mothers General how they would answer the classic objection which tends to reject any new ideas and which is expressed something like this: "The duties of our state as teachers already constitute an active apostolate. Why look for anything else?" Their unanimous reply, which seems to us to be clear, courageous and conclusive, was:

"Teaching is sometimes the only way for the Church to get a foothold in, say, mission lands.

"But this teaching, even of non-religious subjects, must always quite definitely be done in the service of evangelization, religious education and the direct apostolate.

"Under pressure of circumstances, burdened with the preparation of new courses, the correction of exercises and a multitude of disciplinary and administrative chores, a nun no longer has time for the essential; she risks becoming a mere distributor of texts, a supervisor, with practically no real apostolic contact with her pupils.

"There is no question of denying the supernatural merit of these tasks carried out under obedience and often with love; but they no longer have any value as witness. Sometimes the only impression they convey is of being all too human—or not human enough—and are a source of scandal. This is obviously not what our Foundresses intended.

"This deviation from the original intention is resented by our young religious. Particularly if one has been active and had a certain amount of responsibility in apostolic movements, one wants to give one's life, not to become a supervisor or a teacher of grammar but to bring Christ to souls. Neither the pupils nor the lay staff have sufficient opportunities of seeing the nuns in their true role of persons dedicated to the love and service of Our Lord. And what might not be said of the spiritual crises and difficulties in the spiritual development of some of our religious! We should like to make our own the words of Mgr. Maury addressed to priests in charge of religious: 'Whatever position a nun holds in the Church, she must have the task of evangelization and the opportunity to carry it out.'"

CHARITY

Charitable Works

Another field in which our religious expend themselves
with such generosity is hospital and social work, mainly
for the benefit of the sick, the handicapped and the aged.
Nuns are to be found wherever suffering humanity calls
for help: to them is confided the ministry of the Church's
maternal pity. Their devotion moves people and wins their
hearts. This living day in, day out example of charity commands respect.

The sick expect to be cared for physically, no doubt, but
they expect something else from nuns—moral comfort,
support in their trials, attentiveness. Perhaps attention is
what the sick need most: they want someone to listen to
their life-history and their troubles, and it is by listening
patiently for hours that the religious wins the right to speak
and to utter the few words which count. She has the delicate task of gradually introducing to her patients the mystery of suffering, to show them how God can be met in the
midst of pain and how this encounter can put everything
in its proper perspective. In order to fulfil this mission,
which is inherent in her vocation as a nursing nun, she
must have the time, the secret of personal contact and the
ability to communicate.

We have seen that the increasing complications in the
organization of nursing tend to limit the nun to purely
technical tasks, perhaps as ward sister or supervising the
work of lay nurses and probationers. She is so overworked
that the most she can hope for is occasional fleeting contact with the sick.

Devotion and Evangelization

There is no doubt that the religious consecration of the
nun gives her work a supernatural value, but it still remains

to complete this work by the sort of directly apostolic work we envisage for teaching nuns. This apostolic complement to her technical work is vital not only to the development of the nun herself but also to foster vocations. The danger of officialism is perhaps even greater for nursing nuns, for medical care does not produce the same directly apostolic opportunities as teaching does.

Nuns know and feel that devotion and evangelization are not synonymous. Their unselfish devotion to the sick rouses everyone's admiration and often paves the way for more intimate contact, but devotion as such is not the apostolate. This does not mean that devotion must be reduced: only that some means must be found to complete it by direct apostolic action. Our Lord's share must be kept sacred, both for the sake of the sick and for that of the religious herself, who is thereby enabled to give the best of herself. Devotion, which is the giving of oneself, prepares her for the apostolate, which is the giving of Another through herself. If this is kept in mind we shall begin to see all sorts of valuable but previously hidden possibilities for radiating Christ. Many of these possibilities can become fact provided that a certain amount of time is made available to fit them into the routine of life.

Steps to be Taken

There are first of all certain steps to be taken with regard to the sick, as a group or as individuals. Individual contacts with them of a less fleeting and superficial nature will encourage their confidence. A great many moral troubles are confided to nuns who come to the sick with Christ in their hearts. There are wounds too deep to be probed by the X-ray that need to be tended by her care. There is suffering which longs albeit unconsciously to know its Saviour. Among collective approaches we have communication media like broadcasting where a 'Sick People's Hour' in appropriate circumstances could create a tonic atmosphere that would benefit both body and soul.

A sick person is normally not alone in the world. Contact with his family should supplement the contact established with him. In some cases this will reveal a need for social services; or in the intimacy of the home it may become apparent that there are religious deficiencies, situations that need to be set to rights, or sin at work. Briefly, a vast field for apostolic action can be opened up by anyone who has eyes to see and ears to hear and the gift of gaining people's confidence. Patients will then return to homes which, in the meantime, the religious has since come to know. This should make it possible for her to visit there, or to get someone do so, to assure oneself that they are keeping the good resolutions they have made. Suffering is like a retreat during which Our Lord speaks without words to the heart of the sick person in his weakness and dependence on others.

In the same line of thought, why should we not try to organize days of recollection or retreats for ex-patients— and their families? Or if it cannot be done on the spot, a little discreet propaganda for existing retreat houses would be a valuable contribution. The dialogue which physical suffering so often starts between God and a soul must be followed up and its fruits be brought into everyday family life. In addition to what one can do oneself, there is a vast field in which one can get things done by others if one knows how to organize and train them.

An effort must be made to enlist more and more collaborators from among those who, in one way or another, participate in the work of nursing. First of all this must be done in the nursing schools, which must be treated as 'mission territory' just as other schools, and later among probationers, lay staff and others within the orbit of our hospitals.

Although it is true that the hospital nun is in greater danger of becoming a mere technician than her teaching sister, it is also true that every nun is, as such, essentially a teacher. Her vocation gives her the right and the duty to make Christ known to those about her.

If the field of free-time occupations of young grown-ups is more accessible to teaching nuns, that of their attitude to life in general is open to nursing nuns. Their studies and qualifications fit them to organize and inspire Catholic Action groups, or family groups in which questions of family and marital morals can be dealt with : we are thinking of all the evils lurking behind the words abortion, divorce and birth control.

These tasks follow on perfectly naturally from their jobs in the hospitals. It is not so long since nuns were not allowed in maternity wards : their presence seemed inadvisable if not actually 'unsuitable'. Permission to change this was not achieved without a great struggle, though now everyone appreciates the value of the change.

Not content with simply opening maternity hospitals, the religious have frequently undertaken various programmes designed to give a Christian formation to the young mothers. These enterprises, which we welcome with joy as being at once both a symbol and a challenge, greatly help the young people to resolve in a truly Christian manner delicate matrimonial problems common in many homes today. This is a perfect example of that higher apostolic value of the religious life which one would like to see realized in many fields at present.

The help which nursing nuns specializing in educating young women for family life can give is of inestimable value. These young women have an urgent need to be familiar with Christian teaching on the moral and psychological problems which they constantly meet in best-sellers, films and in everyday conversation. Overhearing the conversation of some of our young people not long out of school, one often has difficulty in believing that they have had a Christian education, so much is their philosophy of life patterned on that of a world steeped in materialism, amorality and neo-paganism. More than ever before they need someone to discuss with them the vital problems the solutions of which will shape the world of tomorrow, and which can only be unlocked with the key of the Gospel.

In the face of the tidal-wave of immorality which is sweeping over those parts of the world which have remained Christian, we need rescue teams; and these teams must be readily available, properly trained, and prepared to speak frankly and directly. Light must be thrown on the turmoil, and counter-currents set up by the various organs of Catholic Action if souls are not to be swept away in the dark. Our nursing religious must take an active part in this healing work.

The misfortunes of the whole world are our concern, it has been said. This applies to religious too.

They must look beyond the four walls of their convents. It happens sometimes that an institution, say a home for sick children, is situated in the middle of a completely de-christianized area. A large number of nuns is there to care for the sick. Quite right and proper! But could they not set aside some time for the instruction of the laity to re-christianize their surroundings? A religious house is not a world of its own : it must take its place in the world and do its share of the work to be done, while still not losing sight of its main object.

To all women in religion we should like to repeat the motto of the Seigneurs de Gruuthuse, *Plus est en vous*. They have far greater apostolic riches than they imagine. The Church demands that they dare to have faith in all aspects of their vocation, that they dare to believe too in the resources available in the laity. To do something oneself is good; to get other people to do it and thus multiply the activity is better still. We must be imbued with the idea of a geometrical progression in our contribution to the apostolate. "I have done nothing", one great apostle of our time used to say, "unless I have trained ten others to do what I do and to do it better." If nuns can grasp this, a great step forward will have been made towards the salvation of the world.

9

THE PLACE OF THE NUN
IN PASTORAL WORK

PASTORAL work as a whole necessarily involves the integration of various elements into this whole. This whole is in the first place the universal Church, and then the local Church and its various offshoots.

Let us start, then, by situating the nun in the Church as such.

THE UNIVERSAL CHURCH
Bride of Christ, Bride of the Church

The nun is a dedicated person; she is called to live as a bride of Christ. This is her fundamental vocation and her inalienable glory. This 'marriage to Christ' which is at the heart of her religious profession, is at the same time a marriage to the Church, for the simple reason that one cannot separate the Head from the Body, Christ from His Mystical Body. "The Church and Christ", said Joan of Arc, "are one." Religious consecration in which the nun is vowed, body and soul, to Christ, dedicates her at the same time to the Church. They are one. "What God hath joined together, let no man put asunder." These words of Our Lord apply here too. Baptism, and consecration in religion, cannot be merely set side by side, since the former already implies those demands which are fully realized within the latter. The religious life is but the full flowering of the baptismal vows, the completion of the gift of herself to

Christ and the Church. The religious consecrates herself to Christ as He is now living in the Mystical Body of His Church.

By this fact alone, the nun's apostolate must be part of a Church-wide perspective. "The world is my parish" aptly expresses the normal Christian view. The nun, that 'high-powered Christian' (if I may use the term), ought to be able to say, "The world is my convent". She has no right to limit her horizon to the four walls of her school or hospital or clinic: it should extend as far as the interests of the Church. A nun has charge of souls, of all the souls she can reach in any way, directly or indirectly, personally or through others whom she trains.

This universality also comes from the fact that her apostolate will be tied in, as an integral part of a much greater whole, with the apostolate of the bishop on the diocesan plane and with that of the Pope, supreme head of the Church, on the universal plane. Under each of these headings it is the salvation of the world that is entrusted to her. Christ must continue by means of His nuns to love souls, all souls, since it was for them that He died and because redemption is for all.

It was to serve the Church that a religious entered this or that particular congregation. The specific aims of her life will vary according to the congregation she chose, but the general purpose is common to all—dedication of one's life to the salvation of the world. In a true Christian perspective, the whole is greater than its parts: it is not the putting together of a number of dioceses that makes the Church, it is the Church who creates the dioceses. It is the same with congregations of religious: they must serve the Church; only the means and methods differ. 'Parochialism' is a denial of the primacy of the whole.

The Church's Bride in Our Times

Loving Christ does not mean loving an abstraction. It means loving Him who is living within the Church of today. This is an important truth and the foe of all anachronism. It should make immediately obvious the urgent need to live in tune with the Church and the world of our own times. It is in and through the Church of today that the Holy Spirit operates. It is today that we must hear His voice and share His views. *Hodie si vocem Domini audieritis, nolite obdurare corda vestra.* "If you hear the voice of God today do not harden your hearts", the Liturgy tells us. Today is the day we have to meet God.

One does not achieve sanctity in the same way at every stage in history : the road to perfection is charted through the world that is, in the current of graces at present flowing to the Church. It follows that one's first duty to the spirit of a Foundress, who in her time moved within the Church's grace, is to do as she did and conform to the current needs and graces of the Church. The Foundress herself invites—nay insists—that her daughters express the love of Christ which inspired the foundation in a living, up-to-date, modern manner. Not, of course, for the sake of being modern, but in order to be able to correspond to the graces which God gives His Church today.

Attention must therefore be paid to the supernatural trends in the Church, the spiritual Gulf Streams as it were, which appear from time to time and enrich and vivify the Church.

Having seen their place in the Church as a whole, religious must now fix their position locally in matters apostolic.

THE DIOCESAN CHURCH

Our Lord confided His Church, and hence the apostolate,

to the Twelve, with Peter at their head, and to their successors. Bishops were placed by the Holy Spirit to guide the Church. Any apostolic action, whatever its nature, must tie in with and extend the apostolate of the bishop.

It is the bishops in their dioceses and in union with the Sovereign Pontiff who are the Apostles [writes Mgr. Renard]. As successors of the Apostles they are charged, as were the first envoys, the first Vicars of Christ, with the task of taking His place after His return to His Father, of founding and building up the Kingdom of God which is the Church. "As my Father has sent me, so I also send you. . . ." "Who listens to you, listens to me." Bishops are, then, by right and by commission, responsible for the apostolate in their own dioceses: the apostolate for the whole of the Church in the diocese, and therefore its organization, is the responsibility of the bishop beyond all shadow of question. Indisputable as the apostolic duty of every baptized and confirmed Christian is, it is the duty of but one cell in a whole organism. Now the head of the whole organism is Peter, and the head of the diocesan organism is the bishop. For the Church which has been confided to him, the apostolate and its organization in all of his territory depend directly on the bishop.[1]

The Bishop and his Priests

But the bishop chooses for himself helpers who take part in his apostolate and assist him in it. One does not simply become a priest just as such, in a vacuum, in one's own way: one is a priest of a certain diocese, attached to the Apostle of the place and in vital touch with him. This association in the priesthood and apostolate of the bishop is more im-

[1] *L'Evêque et son Eglise*, L'action catholique et l'évêque, pp. 152-3. Cahiers de la Pierre qui vire.

portant than individual priestly functions as such. For these very functions themselves are but the manifold extension of the episcopal apostolate. Just as a priest shares in the priesthood of his bishop, so also he shares in his apostolate. We could apply here those words in St. John which describe the entrance to the sheepfold. "He who enters by the door is the shepherd of the flock." To enter by any other way is to be guilty of unlawful entry. The bishop is the door, the passage-way through which must come any authentic apostolate within the Church of God.

> It is in the essence and nature of priesthood that priests are constituted into a college; the priestly body, if I may use the expression, is by its nature dependent upon the bishop, stemming from him, participating as a body in his plenary priesthood, making with him and in him only one 'priest'.[1]

Priests and the Laity

If, then, the bishop as head of the local Church must enlist the aid of collaborators, these in their turn must extend their effectiveness by means of the Church's members. This is the essential relationship between priest and people. The link has dogmatic as well as pragmatic value. The overall work of the pastorate is not in the first place demanded by public order but by the exigencies of the Faith.

Christ is only complete in His members: the Christian is not fully Christian unless he be bound together with other Christians. If this is true for everyone who has been baptized, how much more true must it be for those souls who are dedicated to God.

The idea of the priest as a complete entity in himself

[1] B. Bazatole, *L'Episcopat et L'Eglise Universelle*, L'Eglise au sein de l'Eglise locale, p. 344.

has been developed too far: too often has it been said that having recourse to lay assistance was due to shortage of priests and not, as it should be, part of the very nature of things.

The idea of a priesthood cut off and isolated from the laity is theological nonsense, apart from being a handicap to any effective apostolate. A priest must be associated with the laity or his apostolate is paralysed. From the very outset, his ministry loses its missionary character since, alone, he cannot possibly meet the demands inherent in such work.

A priest whose function is not extended by the co-operation of the laity is an anomaly, a contradiction.

Lack of co-operation not only brings a real danger of the priest being isolated and tempted to despair in the face of the size of his task, it also threatens to paralyse the laity by preventing them from giving of their best.

We must constantly come back to the underlying theme: Christ wants to attract members to Him for His work of evangelization. In our apostolate we must respect the purpose of this fundamental wish.

It follows from all this that a priest is only fully a priest when he is head of certain members united to him in a union which does not, however, stifle initiative or legitimate autonomy. In this extension of the priestly function the first to enrol are those who are already dedicated to God, so that with Him they can bring this vital concept to the laity.

Priests and Religious Communities

Much has been written about priest-laity relationships, but not enough has been done to integrate into this concept the proper place of the nun, who is the immediate extension of the priesthood without however raising a barrier between the priest and the laity. She must take her inspiration from our Blessed Lady, to whom God Himself gave her role of mediatrix.

Mary is the intermediary between Christ and us in that she helps us to unite ourselves with Him; she does not come between Him and us; she wants to unite us, bring us nearer to Him and introduce us into His presence. Mary is the means chosen by God to ensure that our approach to Him is more certain. Mary's mediation is not something supplementary, parallel to the mediation of Christ, it is at the very heart of His unique mediation. The Church invites her nuns to be responsible for the female laity; they have the task of spiritual motherhood. Leaving to the priest his specific functions at the altar and in the administration of the Sacraments, the nun should contrive to be the spiritual inspiration of lay-women. This is not the task of the priests of the parish, but of the nuns.

A parish is not well balanced pastorally unless nuns complement the work of the priest. Religious education, just like all education, needs their help. There should be a 'mother' in the parish family, and too often the post remains vacant. The lay-women of the parish should be able to fall back on nuns for support in the same way as the men rely on the priests, who are near to them. Particularly in the mission field there are many ways in which nuns can, within limits, replace the priest : for instance by organizing a Sunday service in places without priests.

A Superior General wrote to us on this matter :

> People complain bitterly about the shortage of priests . . . and in the mission field it is really terrible. One solution seems indicated : make the maximum apostolic use of the devotion of nuns.

In the same spirit, Cardinal Cicognani, Secretary of State to Pope John XXIII, wrote some months ago to the French teaching nuns on the occasion of their Sixth National Congress.

It is not a matter of indifference to the general good of the Church that women called by God to the religious life and more particularly dedicated to parish work should enter fully into the apostolic aims of the parishes where they are helping. Even from the merely human point of view experience shows that a group achieves its full effectiveness only if there is identity of views and action among its members. This is the case in a parish where the clergy, religious of both sexes, Catholic Action groups, and all the faithful, co-operate in pastoral work, each carrying out the task proper to his or her state.

Just as the priest has too often been pictured as separate from the laity, so it is often with nuns. Rarely do we think of the amount of help that nuns should be contributing to the apostolate if they would respond fully to what Christ expects of them. Each one of them should have a group of disciples about her. This, of course, supposes that they have grasped what the role of the laity in the Church is, and that they firmly believe in the royal priesthood of all the faithful of which St. Peter spoke.

It has rightly been said that redressing the pastoral balance must begin by 'converting the priest to the laity'. Congregations of religious need a similar conversion : they must believe in the priesthood of the faithful, in an apostolic laity. In this way they will better understand the capital importance of the part they have to play in inspiring the laity.

Nuns and Lay-women

The appearance of the lay apostolate in the organized form in which we know it today is something new in the

H

history of the Church. It is natural, then, that this should start a new chapter in the long history of the apostolic development of nuns. Where the apostolate expands, so does the role of the religious. The creation of Catholic Action in all its various forms immediately raises the question of where the place of the nun is in all this.

Here is what Mgr. Renard has to say on this:[1]

Our times have seen the birth and growth of Catholic Action and the increase in importance of the part played by the laity in the Church. For the last ten or fifteen years nuns have been receding into the background, eclipsed by the fortunate upsurge of a laity courageously accepting its responsibilities in the City of Man and the City of God. Even the clergy have sometimes been affected by this lay activity. Some priests have rallied to the defence of their rights and have tried to stem the rising tide of men and women who, as baptized Christians, wanted to have their say and play their part. . . . This same feeling of inferiority and envy in relation to a militant laity has, very humanly, appeared here and there among nuns; they remember their own ardent, enthusiastic and militant youth when they were at grips with the world, discovering nature and the world in a spirit of freedom and dedication; they admire and envy the girls of today and their freedom, their being able to carry on their work till all hours of the night, taking part in lively study groups, discussing and revising their approach with other fighters like themselves, living as part of a team— while they themselves, the nuns, are tied by their Rule, dependent on their Superior, hampered in their work by the habit and the Rule, prevented even (they think) from achieving their desire for poverty and abandonment to

[1] *Vie Spirituelle de la religieuse d'aujourd'hui*, pp. 12–13. Desclée de Brouwer, 1960.

God by having a comfortable convent and security for
the future. In short, the religious life seems like a cage:
they are protected, of course, as in a fortress, but they
cannot go out and fight the enemy where he is—outside.

These remarks are important. We must guard against this
sort of inferiority complex which threatens to cheapen the
religious vocation. To remove this, religious must realize
the magnificent part they have to play in the renewal of
the Christian laity, in this work of 'putting the Church on a
missionary footing'.

The emphasis has been put back on the apostolic duty of
each baptized Christian. The laity of today is better able to
understand Lacordaire's definition of a Christian as 'a man
to whom Jesus Christ has confided other men'. But baptized women will not fulfil their task nor awake to full
apostolic consciousness unless nuns grasp their role of providing inspiration and stimulus for them. Note that I do
not say 'direction'; the direction of the lay apostolate lies
in the hands of the laity, but their spiritual inspiration is
the responsibility of the priest, and so of those who function as direct extensions of his office, that is to say nuns, his
spiritual lieutenants. A nun is not a directress but a teacher,
training those responsible for carrying out the tasks. How
very desirable it is in any case that the instruction of young
women should be in the hands of a nun rather than in those
of a young curate, for to reach the necessary stage of instruction requires many prolonged contacts between teacher
and taught. It has not been sufficiently stressed that the
absence of religious is responsible for the delay in the
general mobilization of lay-women which recent Popes
have demanded.

The religious life cannot attain full usefulness unless it be
re-appraised in terms of this new dimension, the laity.

There can be no doubt that every congregation whose

object is the active apostolate is already expending its zeal on some task normal to its constitution, whether it be teaching or nursing. Within this duty of their state—this 'professional' duty, one might say—there is plenty of room for great devotion, but this duty also includes, as an integral part of the religious vocation, the further duty of inspiring the laity. In plain terms this means that it is the nun's task to take part in the triple task which Pius XII set before priests when he said they must discover, train and make use of lay apostles. There are tasks to be done of recruitment, of instruction, of training, of starting things going, of organizing things which are worth considering. Nuns must know how to train the laity for its tasks, how to start movements or put life into them, how to co-ordinate various activities to ensure the highest yield. The dominating thought must be to find people who will 'multiply'.

One must be imbued with the idea of making the 'apostolic most' of the time available in order to train others.

There is a subtle temptation to rest on one's laurels. We are easily satisfied with the good—the perfectly genuine good—we are doing, and forget about what remains undone, about all that we could and should have turned to apostolic profit. One must always come back to that phrase of Lavelle's, "The greatest good we can do to others is not to display our treasures to them but to show them their own".

A nun does not respond to the greatness of her task unless she is dominated by the idea of rousing up and training the great mass of lay-women.

In conjunction with the priest she must accept responsibility for the salvation of souls. A convent can never be an island among the waves but must be a promontory jutting out towards the high sea.

Addressing the nuns of his diocese, the Archbishop of Toulouse, Mgr. Garrone, wrote:

I wish you all an ever-increasing desire to co-operate in the general life and apostolate of this diocese where your mission has placed you. You must integrate yourselves fully and without confusion, contributing your personal value and your value as religious. You must be aware of the surroundings in which you find yourselves. You must be ever more and more united in your common effort, working together fraternally and effectively without overlapping or confusion. Should one congregation among you live its own little life apart from the rest, without reference to the general good or the present needs and activities of the Church, it will have no vocations: and that will be a good thing.

Complementary Truths

When a new idea makes its mark, it often happens that complementary truths take a back place. This is what happened when emphasis was, very happily of course, put on the advancement of the lay role in the apostolate. The time is now ripe to fill in the picture by including the advancement of the nun's role among the laity.

Some years ago it may have seemed that 'life in religion' and Catholic Action were mutually exclusive. In order to get the lay apostolate going, it was necessary to insist on their own responsibility for it, on the mandate they had received from the hierarchy. The part to be played by religious seemed to be outside all this. All that was asked of nuns was that they should find out what it was all about, give some encouragement from the side-lines, and pray. The idea of active co-operation did not come up even in important official documents. To quote one example, the proceedings of the Fifth Provincial Council of Malines in 1937 merely recorded:

At every opportunity educators will draw the attention of their young charges to the splendour and the necessity of lay participation in the apostolate of the hierarchy, and will exhort them to join now, and later, organizations appropriate to their age and condition. What we have just said in general terms about masters also applies in its entirety to men and women in religion who are engaged in the education of boys and girls. They must take care to inform themselves about all aspects of Catholic Action. Special courses arranged in various places with this end in mind are strongly recommended.

That was how we saw things at that time. A positive role for nuns had not been envisaged. We do not intend to analyse the causes of this state of affairs, but only to record a typical fact.

In practice the instruction of militant apostles, as for instance, those in Catholic Action, was rarely entrusted to nuns, from whom the only collaboration asked was material assistance in as discreet a manner as possible. From there it was but one step to believing that nuns had no place in the apostolate.

Papal Directives

Since that time, Pius XII himself gave nuns associated with Catholic Action in Italy a clear statement of what he expected of them, on 3rd January, 1958. He asked that nuns should collaborate with the clergy in the education of young women.

Though it is true that the priest at the altar, from the pulpit or in the confessional, must contribute to the spiritual education and wisdom and prudence of young women, since they are souls committed to his care, it is also true that he must find in you the indispensable collaborators who live in close contact with these girls and can help, support, comfort and console them. The

Church is therefore counting on you as direct interme-
diaries whom the priest can use for the education of
young women.[1]

He asked them to train apostles:

Are the pupils in your schools ready, each in the field
which Providence will assign to her, to collaborate in the
reconstruction of the world? . . . To train young people
to look at the world with Christian eyes, to see it as it is,
to know what it should be like, and to work towards its
conforming to God's plan, these are the practical aims of
every Catholic educational or instructional institute.[2]

He asked them to train leaders:

In this atmosphere of intense training we see the providential birth of the Catholic Action Association. What
needs to be done is to place in the souls of pupils a leaven
of overflowing life and courageous action; to place at the
head of the others a group of resolute pioneers who are
capable of swift action and of carrying with them any
who may be tempted to lag behind or to fall out. These
will be your collaborators in the difficult task of educating your pupils to be Christians. If your local Association can create this leaven, it will not only be good for
the health of your Institute but it will also constitute
an excellent school for those who will later become
leaders.[3]

Much has, quite properly, been made of the ideal of
the lay apostolate; just as much has been made of the
ideal of marriage. However, this should not lead us to
forget the ideal of the priesthood, nor the ideal, still to

[1] R. Carpentier, S.J., *La Vie Religieuse—Qu'en pense L'Eglise?*, p.
212. Paris, 1959.
[2] Ib., p. 215.   [3] Ib.

come to life, of the religious as the inspiration of the laity, the apostle of lay vocations for women, and the collaborator in the founding of truly Christian homes. There is too great a tendency, even in parishes, to relegate nuns to inferior tasks which could as well be done by others. Their place is not just in the sacristy, or looking after children and sick people. Ordinary healthy grown-up women in the world have a crying need for their help.

Two decrees of the Roman Synod promulgated by Pope John XXIII make clear the extent to which the Holy See is preoccupied by the integration of nuns into the total pastoral picture. The first emphasizes the breadth of their role.

> Since all religious strive for the highest and most perfect virtue, let them remember that their vocation is wholly and fully apostolic, is no way bounded by the limits of place, of things, or of time, but extends everywhere and at all times to anything that touches the honour of their Spouse or the salvation of souls.

The second deals in particular with their part in the organization of lay-women.

> As regards women's associations (of Catholic Action) and particularly those of young women, it will be useful to call upon nuns to complete and perfect the task of the chaplain upon whose task prudence places certain limits. Let Superiors see to it that their nuns are suitably trained for this form of apostolate; let them freely accord permission to attend congresses and courses with this object; all these means of training being, of course, subject to approval by their ecclesiastical authorities. (Art. 649.)

"Come to Us"

The world of women ought to appear to a nun's eyes as a mission field entrusted to her. The *Acts* describe how St.

Paul, hearing a voice which said to him, "Come to us in Macedonia", set out at once so as not to disappoint their expectation. This same invitation comes today from the depths of the unconscious of a spiritually undernourished world, and it is addressed to nuns. We cannot remain deaf to its appeal. "What others expect of us," says Bernanos, "God expects of us."

One example of a large-scale pastoral operation in which nuns played a noble part has recently come to us from a large Latin-American country. One district had become infamous in the last dozen years or so for the number of crimes committed there. Two years ago, taking advantage of a period of comparative freedom from *la violencia*, a general mission was organized in all parishes of the diocese. Drawing on every part of the country, teams were set up of a priest, a brother or seminarist, a layman and two nuns. These teams, with a perseverance equalled only by their courage, visited every single household. Two years later, commenting on the success of this unique form of apostolic mission, the bishop said, "These criminals—these *bandoleros*—confessed first of all to the nuns then they went and asked the priest for absolution".

This example, exceptional though it admittedly is, shows how wrong it would be not to have the courage to believe in the apostolic fruitfulness of nuns. Everyone must be convinced of this, and follow it to its logical conclusion.

The Duty to Increase

If we really want to produce an answer commensurate with the needs of souls, then it is of the greatest importance that the clergy co-ordinate their apostolate with that of nuns and lay people, and that all be constantly thinking of ways to multiply the number of their collaborators.

For a nun to teach the catechism to twenty children is a very good thing. but it is more important that she should train other adults to teach catechism in their turn. She should be preoccupied, not so much with doing things, as with seeing to it that things are done. She should exercise a role of supervision and control with the purpose of increasing the extent of apostolic activity. I have no right to spend my time producing a 10 per cent. return if I can make it earn 100 per cent. We only have to imagine for a moment what the power and range of the Church's activities would be if every nun in the world were aware of the necessity for her to inspire a group of lay people; if each could imitate our Saviour in sending disciples out in pairs to the missions. I am thinking, for example, of how the effectiveness of a nun is literally multiplied tenfold if she but knows how to inspire a group, say a Praesidium of the Legion of Mary. I use this as an example, since the Legion exists in all five continents, because it is very easily handled, and because its supernatural harvest is exceptional and manifestly blessed by God. But whether it is the Legion of Mary or any other Catholic Action movement, the principle remains and should be accepted by all nuns.

In writing the Life of *Edel Quinn*, that heroic young woman who at the cost of her own health went and founded the Legion of Mary in British Central Africa, I often thought of the paradox presented by the example of a young lay-woman arousing some thousands of apostles in her passing. What a harvest there might have been if each missionary nun had known before embarking for the missions just how to promote and organize a lay apostolate.

To clarify this idea of multiplication of one's personal contribution, I would like to tell the story of a conversation between two Mothers General about helping the clergy. One related how the parish priest of her parish had asked her one Christmas Eve if the nuns could help by singing the Nativity Mass in the parish church. She agreed, but the next day she asked the priest not to make the request another year on account of the inconvenience caused to the community. "That's what you would have done, isn't it?" she ended. The other one, however, who had grasped this principle of "seeing to it that things are done", answered her, "I should have accepted, as you did. And then, as you did, I should have asked the parish priest not to repeat his request next year. But then I should have added, 'But, Father, if you would like us to go round the parish and find you some volunteers to start and train a choir, we shall willingly do so'."

The answer lies there. And the example is applicable to a thousand different situations. It is a matter of getting the right viewpoint—a viewpoint that is much rarer than one imagines. People think only of what they can do themselves, only rarely of what they can achieve with others. Yet the salvation of the world depends on seeing things like this. If we are not to be completely overwhelmed by the magnitude of the masses needing christianization or re-christianization, we must be able to apply this basic principle in practice.

The Place of Nuns in the Pastoral Structure

Once nuns are conscious of the scope of their mission and have assumed their rightful position within the overall pastoral apostolate, it is obvious that they have a place at all levels of the pastoral structure: parish councils, diocesan unions, national councils and, one day no doubt, international councils.

In the letter we have already quoted, written by Cardinal Cicognani to nuns in the name of Pope John XXIII, express mention is made of the presence of nuns at parish councils.

The temptation sometimes experienced to treat nuns as no more than useful assistants for the less important tasks, must be opposed by the conviction that they are first-class propagators of the Gospel and very often constitute a necessary link between the pastor and his flock. This being so, why should their voices not be heard in councils where pastoral work is planned, as is the case already in many parishes? Associated thus with the apostolic decisions of the clergy, they cannot fail to put them into better effect in the exercise of their duties, be they liturgical, catechetical, educational or medical. The clergy and the parish will gain by it, and in the same way the nuns themselves will be in a better position to develop their vocations among a laity whom they know.

This by no means implies that a congregation of religious should renounce anything of its own specific objectives, nor that the community as such has to be integrated into the parish context; it implies, however, that one or other of the members must act as a link between the convent and the parish or diocese and serve as a coupling in the co-ordination of the whole. Without this the community would not be participating in the duty common to all, in the unity of action which is the concrete, visible, dynamic expression of the mystery of Christ living in His mystical body.

The mere acceptance by nuns of this broader view of which we have been speaking will mean that their action will reach the parents of their pupils, the relations of their patients, their former pupils, the laity—in short, a number of people living in their parish who can be reached in this manner. We are well aware that their efforts are often addressed to a floating population, difficult to identify with any particular locality. This difficulty, which is due to the conditions of modern life, indicates that to the apostolate carried out on a parish level there must be added pastoral work within the various sociological strata, on a plane which includes larger areas. This sort of apostolate is much easier in the country than in towns and cities. In any case, there is no avoiding the issue; each community must somehow make its contribution to the general work of the pastorate.

In 1949 the cardinals and archbishops of France declared, "It is important that the clergy should be able to get nuns to enter into the stream of parish life and do not deprive them of their apostolic responsibilities".

The bishops of France, in plenary session in 1960, speaking of the necessary change-over from a conservative attitude to pastoral work, added, "This demands bold revisions of habits of thought and action : the Spirit of God is there to inspire everyone—priests, religious and laity—with the necessary clarity of vision and courage".

Nuns, then, have their place not only at parish level but also at diocesan or national level, everywhere in fact where women are engaged in the lay apostolate. They have an active part to play in contributing to meetings and congresses the particular treasure which is theirs.

One cannot but greet with joy the notion of such an integration of religious into the work, for it will be of the greatest advantage to the entire Christian community. This mutual aid in the apostolic field brings to its full life and reality the union of all Christians who share in brotherly love the same Eucharistic Supper. To communicate together at the same altar leads naturally to communion together in the same apostolic work—a work which is one whole, yet diversified by the gifts of each worker. What a magnificent opportunity of offering the world the shining example of full Christian brotherly love, for surely the *cor unum et anima una* are still the sign whereby the world shall recognize the disciples of Jesus.

It is clear that in order to be able to respond to these needs, nuns are going to have to adapt themselves, if only because their work with the laity will have to be mostly in the evenings or at week-ends. And at a deeper level, the whole question of formation must be reconsidered. We must investigate the requirements of a training which will enable the religious to respond to the full demands of their mission. It is to this consideration that we will devote the following chapters.

10

NECESSARY ADAPTATIONS

THE nun's task in the world of today cannot be accomplished without certain modifications in the customs of the classical type of religious life.

It is not surprising that as the Church became aware of the growth of the field of its apostolate she issued many appeals through her Popes and bishops for modification of the religious life to suit the new needs.

Such modification, needless to say, does not touch the essence of the religious life nor the unalterable core which characterizes a life dedicated to God. It concerns only bringing it into line with the current needs of the apostolate. And it goes without saying, too, that these modifications are not the responsibility of individual nuns, but must be made by competent authority if we are not to have disorder and anarchy, or warp the religious spirit, or just scratch the surface of the problem.

THE POPES' APPEALS

With these reservations in mind, one should get the right attitude by re-reading the urgent exhortations of the Popes, particularly Pius XII. It is worth recalling two passages from an address by Pius XII to religious teachers on 13th September, 1951.

It is possible that certain elements of the daily schedule, certain regulations which are not just interpretations of the Rule, certain customs perhaps more in keeping with another age but which nowadays only complicate the task of education, should be adapted to the new circumstances. . . Your aim is to serve the cause of Jesus Christ and His Church according to the needs of the world of today. It would therefore not be reasonable to persist in customs or ways of doing things which hinder this service or even perhaps make it impossible.

This invitation to do some pruning is completed by another exhortation to be of their time.

With the help of the Holy Spirit, minds and hearts must be revived and renewed so as to be able as far as possible to cope with the way of life of our epoch and with its spiritual distress.

(12th November, 1950)

Echoing the repeated appeals of the Holy See, many bishops all over the world asked that the necessary changes be made to meet the apostolic needs of the age.

These appeals to our various congregations to place themselves more widely and more squarely on a missionary basis came up against a number of difficulties. But one must repeat with Newman that a thousand difficulties do not constitute a doubt. Obstacles are not insurmountable. All that is needed to get over them is in the first place the spirit of faith to reveal clearly the imperative necessity of the end in view, courageous perseverance, and finally a sense of humour to enable one to keep one's sense of proportion and keep smiling in spite of the difficulties. If it is possible to say *Sacramenta propter homines*—Sacraments exist for men and not the other way about—one should also be able to say, with even greater force, *Regulae propter salutem mundi*—rules are made for the salvation of men.

In this chapter we shall run through the main points which may be thought to constitute handicaps to missionary zeal.

The necessary changes affect a number of aspects of religious life, among them:

the balance between prayer and the apostolate;
the allocation of time;
the balance between the requirements of enclosure and those of the apostolate.

1. THE BALANCE BETWEEN PRAYER AND THE APOSTOLATE

Praying by Action

A proper balance between prayer and apostolic action is essential to a life vowed to the apostolate. This balance is easily obtained if prayer is gauged in terms of depth and if activity is truly apostolic. Prayer is not an island in time unconnected with the rest of life, and its value is not measured by the clock nor by the multiplicity of exercises. Our Lord did not say we must pray for an hour, or two hours, or three: He said we must pray always. This supposes a life of prayer, a permanent state of communion with God. Seen in that light, as a state of union, prayer is uninterrupted: this is the essence of the matter. The true apostolate is prayer in action. Note that it is not the action as such that constitutes prayer, but supernatural apostolic action. One is right to be on one's guard against 'the heresy of activity' which is a mere display of human energy, bordering often on a state of agitation, and restricted to the level of purely human techniques. The supernatural action which is the apostolate we are talking about consists in communicating life and grace, in giving Christ to others. This giving is spiritually vivifying in itself

I

and also in its returns. There is no break between prayer and the worship of God on the one hand, and on the other, the work of evangelization in the strict sense where one shares the theological virtues of faith, hope and charity with others. The apostolate is a supernatural reality continuing the work of the Redemption. Quite naturally it will be steeped in prayer before, during and after the activities which it requires. Incongruity only exists between superficial prayer and action which is purely human.

In the practice of our Christian life we must not only turn our prayers into action but also turn our actions into prayer.

Turning our prayers into action means embodying in the apostolate, and by means thereof, all that we ask for in prayer; it is what transforms prayer into action and is the essential complement to the *Thy Kingdom come* of the Our Father. The apostolate is the outcome of true prayer, and its guarantee and touchstone.

And inversely, we must 'pray' our actions right from the start, for 'without God we can do nothing', without Him we are totally incapable of achieving good.

Spiritual Exercises

In practice a very large part of the life of prayer is devoted to 'spiritual exercises'. These exercises have a very important place in the organization of the religious life.

There is, each day, one meeting between God and man which unites them in a unique manner and which is beyond compare. We are speaking, of course, of the holy sacrifice of the Mass and of the Communion which is its culmination. For this is the summit of the spiritual life of all religious. That is why all that has been done to stress the value of the Mass in the eyes of the laity is eminently applicable to nuns as well. Their piety must nourish itself at this primal source. The liturgical revival is as much a boon to religious houses as it has been for the laity : they cannot remain outside it, for their own sakes as well as for that of their pupils. They must profit, and see that others do too, from the instructions issued by the bishops commending dialogue-Masses in community, and also solemn Masses. The pupils should be encouraged to take an active part in these liturgical functions, so that later on they will be able to enter fully into the community life of their parish.

Spiritual exercises serve as a frame for the Mass, thus lived and brought to life, and prolong its action through the day. These exercises cannot be left to individual initiative, but they should be restricted to what is essential, and should really constitute communal prayer. There is a need to amend and simplify them, and to give their piety a more biblical, liturgical, ecclesiastical and apostolic bias. At the start of one's spiritual life it is reasonable that much time is devoted to vocal prayer and communal exercises designed to instil the habit of prayer.

Spiritual progress will make more time available for personal prayer. It will be as well to allow for some freedom in these exercises and to reconsider their distribution which tends at present to divide the day into too many short periods. Certain out-of-date and redundant devotions—and there are enough of them in all conscience—must be mercilessly eliminated. Spiritual exercises, if they are too numerous and ill-suited to the needs of those who use them, tend to make the life of prayer mechanical and stilted. They become an end in themselves instead of keeping their place as means. If, however, they are properly understood, they can lead gradually to a permanent state of prayer and communion with God. This sort of result will come particularly from short periods of interior concentration which will punctuate the day like resting places where one can breathe deeply of the air of the supernatural and unite oneself more consciously with God.

It is difficult to understand why active religious should be bound to recite the whole of the canonical office in choir. St. Ignatius marked out the way for active religious when, for sound apostolic reasons, he omitted certain practices more suitable to the contemplative Orders. And would it not be as well to have a look at the musical side of offices sung in a manner irritating to modern ears? It is hard to imagine a modern girl being attracted by the high-pitched quavering of certain tones. It would be better to adopt a more relaxed and natural manner of singing. The singing of Lauds and Vespers, the liturgical prayers *par excellence*, in choir could well suffice for active nuns and would ensure their participation in the great prayer of the Church: the rest of the office could be voluntary and left to the discretion of the individual.

Spiritual reading for professed nuns could be spread out through the week (not through the day) so that the same number of hours could be devoted to it without cutting both the day and the reading mechanically into sections. No doubt the nuns would thereby derive greater benefit from the reading. The examination of conscience and the chapter of faults should be reviewed in the spirit of the times and perhaps benefit from current practice in certain movements where they have a 'review of life'. One should aim at more candour and openness between nuns, more mutual sincerity, more real sharing, at constructive self-criticism in common, with a view towards closer co-operation in the accomplishment of their great mission. This means that religious usages as well must move in the missionary dimension, that one should question oneself before God, together and singly, about the response that has been made to His invitation to each individual to share in the salvation of the world.

All these observations tend to the creation of a more supple and open conception of the religious life, allowing freedom to the Holy Spirit and to the action of grace in souls, and helping souls to embody in their lives the essential one-ness of prayer and the apostolate.

2. ALLOCATION OF TIME

How, one might ask, are the supplementary or increased tasks put forward in these pages going to be fitted into an already overloaded timetable? Look how much there is to be done in one day, count the numbers of demands for their services . . . and have pity on the nuns!

Scale of Values

This is a major difficulty and must be examined with the eye of faith. There is a theology of time, just as there is a theology of work. Time must be used and filled in accordance with the scale of values which a sincere and generous faith reveals. Which brings us back to the fundamental question: Why were we created? We are created to know God and to make Him known, to love God and to make Him loved, to serve God and make others serve Him. This is the overriding consideration for every baptized person; all the more so, then, for a religious solemnly vowed to God. She must be imbued with a sense of the importance of time. We have not a minute to lose when the glory of God and the salvation of the world are at stake. This means we must review, and review again, the use we make of time. *Caritas Christi urget nos.* We have no spare soul, no spare life, and it is to this generation that we have to convey God's message. This does not rule out relaxation —which is essential for good work—but is just a reminder of the precious value of time. Time is money, the saying goes. It is true. One could say with Newman, "Time is eternity", which is the same as saying that time is souls. The way our day is filled must be rigorously examined in relation to this scale of values.

> Everything is grace, undoubtedly; everything can contribute to redemption [wrote Fr. Courtois]. But at a time when there is such a shortage of men and women to work in the Father's field, faced as we are with the immense tasks of the apostolate requiring, as the Sovereign Pontiff has himself made clear, the maximum effort from everybody, it is vital that a considerable part of the time at the disposal of nuns should be spent, under obedience of course, in direct evangelization.[1]

This call to the duty of evangelization, echoing St. Paul's "Woe to me if I do not preach the Gospel!" is also in a certain way addressed by the Church to contemplative nuns. We know that the Sacred Congregation for the Affairs of Religious on 19th March, 1952, basing itself on the Constitution *Sponsa Christi*, required of women in religion, including those in enclosed Orders, that they take on certain works of evangelization. "It seems", wrote the Congregation, "that the time has come to harmonize the monastic life, including in a general way that of nuns dedicated to a contemplative life, with an appropriate degree of participation in the apostolate."

Our scale of values demands that God be served first, and that priority be given to serving Him as directly as possible, through one's neighbour. Supernatural things are in a class of their own. We must give our time to God, and give God to men, in as personal a way as possible. Once these principles are granted, we must proceed to make the consequent adjustments in the timetables followed in religious communities. Fundamentally, it is in relation to God that we must view these adaptations. The earth re-

[1] *L'Heure de Jésus*, Ed. Fleurus, pp. 133–4.

volves round the sun, not the sun round the earth : we must accept Copernicus' teaching—and apply it to God, the sun of our existence as individuals or as communities.

The problem is one of balance, of proportion. Professional duties will continue to take up the greater part of the day : in this, nuns are applying in practice the principles of Christianity and are working (and very effectively) for the salvation of the world. They must make the most of all opportunities for evangelization occurring within the framework of their professional duties. But they must also set aside some periods for the organization, inspiration and guidance of lay-women who, having had this training, will in turn be able to introduce the practical requirements of the Gospel among those with whom they work or spend their leisure hours. Without the assistance of nuns, the female laity will never play the essential part desired by the Church. Without the religious, lay-women will never be as fully organized as is desired, nor will they receive the inspiration which could enable them to undertake the apostolate on a vast scale.

Nuns must regard the time set aside for this spiritual inspiration of the laity as sacrosanct. This time, which will have to be squeezed in somewhere in the week, or perhaps only every other week, will necessarily be short—but it must at all costs be found. The order of exercises must be altered and allocation of duties rearranged until this is managed. This means that the daily schedule of the community may have to be adjusted to suit the times convenient for the laity : the shepherd has to suit his pace to the sheep, not the other way about.

The Temptation of 'Urgency'

We must beware of the temptation to believe such adaptations impossible. No one doubts the necessity of eating—and one manages to find the time for it. The same applies to what God asks of us: we must find time to feed the multitudes who hunger and thirst for God and who, directly or indirectly, expect to receive the bread of life from us.

The balance we must find will entail a better distribution of work. Some tasks will be dropped or passed to others. The risk that they will be less well done must be accepted, for the balance between spiritual exercises, the apostolate and professional duties must be achieved at any price.

When arranging the allocation of time one must never fail to distinguish between urgency and importance. Unless one is constantly on one's guard, one is perpetually tempted to confuse them, and one can end by spending one's time rushing from one urgent task to another, in a permanent state of tension and always having to deal with some new emergency.

One must know how to stand back a bit and give priority where the proper scale of values places it. It is not enough for us to lead 'full' lives regardless of what they are full of: their first charge must be the work Christ demands of us, in the order dictated by Faith. The temptation to deal with the most urgent things first is a subtle one; to do so enables one to see immediate results and enjoy a quiet conscience and a sense of achievement in spite of the major omissions one is unknowingly responsible for.

As the Very Rev. Fr. De Gryze, Superior General of the Scheut Fathers, wrote to his missionaries:

Hard work can also be a danger: one can do a great deal of work and not give enough thought to one's method of work. Not planning one's work and not co-ordinating it can mean a lot of wasted effort or only half-effectual work. A passion for activity can make one a slave to immediacy and detail. This leads to a short-sighted inability to view the scene as a whole and to take the future into account. Too much realism can be fatal, or at least very weakening. We may suffer from lack of imagination, inability to see things in perspective, and be wanting in original and creative ideas. We may forget that preaching the Gospel is a process of growth and therefore demands a constant return to its source and continual adaptation.

3. THE WORLD AND CLOISTER

Double Demand

The chief obstacle to the apostolic advancement of nuns seems to be the conception of enclosure and what it entails. There is an apparent contradiction. How can one apply both parts of Our Lord's words to His disciples when He said they were not of the world yet must not flee the world.

To be separated from the world and yet to be present in it to inspire it and save it is a situation paradoxical enough for all Christians but particularly so for nuns. The apparent contradiction is resolved when one realizes that for active congregations the separation is an attitude of mind rather than a matter of walls and grilles. In her heart the nun has renounced the privilege of founding a home, has left her family and chosen renunciation as her path. However, this break with the world is not made in order to isolate herself from the world but to give expression to her greater zeal in its regard. It is the price of a spiritual motherhood opening its arms to all the world's distress. The nun withdraws only that she may be the more present, just as yeast begins by working against the tendency of the dough and ends finally by permeating it and raising it. To isolate the yeast from the dough for fear of contagion is to miss the whole point. By its very nature the apostolate implies a risk, just as the yeast runs the risk of being overwhelmed by the dough. But it is a good Christian risk which makes Christianity an adventure worth living. Without risk even human activities come up against a blank wall. If you exclude all risks of contagion, you exclude care of the sick; if you insist on avoiding all risks from wind and wave, you prohibit travel by air and sea. The Christian apostolate would just be two meaningless words if all risks were barred.

That in no way means that one does not have to take the necessary precautions. Every time an aircraft lands, everything is inspected and checked for the next flight. Incidentally, to maintain its serviceability an aircraft must fly regularly: a regular flight routine is a guarantee that the mechanism remains in a good state.

In the same sort of way, nuns are asked to go to the world to save it.

So much emphasis has been put on this notion of danger that it is important to redress the balance by emphasizing the 'necessary presence' idea. The religious life has quite properly been hedged about with safeguards, sometimes down to the smallest detail. Nobody disputes that the world is full of pitfalls, is pagan and getting more so. One must advance circumspectly, not rush in recklessly. But when a vehicle is fitted with powerful brakes, one does not hesitate to take it on the road for fear of spoiling the brakes; brakes are fitted to provide safety at high speeds, not to keep one down to a snail's pace. By all means let us make sure that our brakes are in good trim, but then let us fix our sights on the horizon and start moving, however hard the road ahead may be.

This dual attitude towards the world—loving it and yet fleeing it—comes from the fact that Our Lord uses the word in two senses. At one moment the world represents the assembly of forces arrayed against God, something to be resisted and fought; at another it is the assembly of men who have to be saved; men in their insignificance but also in their grandeur, in their zeal for good, in the uneasiness of their unconscious search for God.

The argument *Prudence* v. *Audacity* might as well be between deaf people so long as prudence and audacity are assumed to be incompatible opposites. Agreement can only be reached when it is understood that prudence is meant to be in the service of boldness. Precautions are necessary so that the flight may be secure.

Realism in the Apostolate

The separation of religious from the world cannot be such that a nun can no longer play the part of mediatrix between God and the world. One must avoid giving the impression that nuns live in a sort of ghetto, or a hot-house, and that their knowledge of the world is limited to what they pick up from their pupils or patients.

Lay people complain of a certain childishness, naïveté, an old-fashioned air, a too narrow outlook among nuns so that they never see the whole picture and can never really know the world. Cut off from the world, the nun is in danger of not getting a realistic picture of the spiritual ills that afflict mankind.

Without going into details about rules of enclosure, which everyone wants to see simplified in the revision of the Code of Canon Law which will follow the Council, it seems appropriate to indicate the basic principle which will probably guide its provisions. This principle is that woman can no longer be treated as a minor. The practical corollaries of the principle must also be accepted. We do not in any way deny the differences between the sexes, but in the service of God and man there is a substantial degree of equality in all dedicated souls. In principle, therefore—and leaving aside the priesthood and certain special cases—women in religion should have the same treatment as men in religion, due regard being paid to feminine psychology. Women are no longer minors and one no longer has the right to consider nuns as unable to undertake enterprises that their sisters in the world undertake in many different spheres of modern life.

Enclosure and the Apostolate

Everything we said in Chapter 8, 'A Broader Vision', would be nullified by a rigid conception of enclosure. How would it be possible to meet all the needs, to make the necessary contacts with families in their own homes, to ensure the spiritual stimulation of the laity, to achieve the realism essential for any 'made-to-measure' apostolate, if teaching and nursing nuns remained confined *intra muros*? It would be equivalent to nullifying the Church's claim to missionary zeal. It would be basically to misunderstand the full scope of the duties of their state intrinsic to the vocation of active religious today. One example will suffice to show how a rigid conception of enclosure threatens today to paralyse teaching nuns in the carrying out of their primary mission.

When a congregation, whatever its original nature may have been, undertakes the work of educating young Christians, it binds itself *ipso facto*, in justice to the children, to the parents, to society and to the Church, to do the job fully and properly and to adopt all necessary means to do so. Now, education today requires the presence of nuns in various spheres which did not exist yesterday. But the congregation has undertaken total education. This means that the mistress cannot be separated from her pupils by some enclosure rule which forbids her presence where it is necessary to fulfil the mission entrusted her by the parents and the Church. We know the influence that their spare-time activities have on children, how these out-of-school activities can affect them for life, and the risk there is of undoing in the course of one week-end or one holiday all that has been achieved at school. This emphasizes the necessity for extra-mural contacts with young adolescents who need training in the various apostolic movements, guidance for their study-trips, and social, family and cultural formation.

Besides this out-of-school world, there are the day-to-day events which need the presence of the nuns with the children or with their parents in the case of bereavement, or accident, ill-health or suffering, to give only a few examples. To hand the pupils over to the lay staff in such circumstances, because the rules of enclosure forbid nuns to leave the convent, is to cut off the human and Christian contact at the very moment when nuns could best fill the important role expected of them.

And unless enclosure rules are made more flexible, how can nuns fulfil their mission to the laity alongside whom they live—parents, lay staff, former pupils, etc. They can only do so if they are able to approach those who do not come of their own accord to them. If they have no contacts, how can they manage to train even the best candidates for the apostolate in their respective circles? Apostolic vocations have to be sought out and fostered: they do not normally appear in a flash of lightning, but as the result of repeated contacts and persuasive insistence. They have to be gained one by one. A fervent religious house is like an electric power station, capable of the greatest distribution of power—but someone has to go out and wire up the circuits connecting the outside with the source of power.

There is nothing insoluble about the problem, only one must have the will to solve it. The Decree of 31st May, 1957, allows Superiors much latitude in permitting visits outside which would serve the apostolic work of the house. The only trips expressly excluded are those for personal interest or satisfaction—which is only wise. There can never be question of visits to people's homes being transformed into a search for personal satisfaction : the intention must always be to do a service. Instead of making use of the latitude permitted in the matter of trips outside the convent only to acquire new diplomas or arrange matters of finance or health, all one needs to do is to add to the list of accepted grounds that of apostolic activity.

One Mother General, who shares these views, wrote to us :

> Our Constitution says, "No one will leave the convent except on important business of the Institute." Up to now the interpretation given to these words has been to apply them only to trips made necessary for professional reasons or for the material maintenance of our houses. Having now understood that 'important business of the Institute' should include anything that helps to achieve our aim of 'making God known and loved', we have not hesitated to include in the phrase all visits demanded by the apostolic needs of our time.

Enclosure and Family

Another question which must be re-thought is that of periodic visits by religious to their families. The religious has chosen a new family; her house is her convent and her fellow-nuns her sisters. Being at home means in the first instance being in her convent, and that is how she sees it. Visits to families must not be regarded in the same light as a boarder's holidays, but rather as a reconciliation of two duties : that of maintaining a certain distance from the world, as properly desired by every religious, and that of *pietas*, family charity—and sometimes even justice—towards one's own people, without mentioning the matter of apostolic presence. For always and everywhere, among her family as much as anywhere else, the religious must be the bearer of Christ; her visible interior joy will be a striking apostolic witness. Her presence in the family home should be a grace for everyone, including herself, for contact with the realities of life will give her more understanding of others and a better appreciation of her own vocation.

Our modern world is more sensitive to a thoughtful and refined expression of filial piety. No doubt the younger generation of nuns will appreciate this more than the older ones who might in some cases be confused by what might seem to be laxity. But these latter need only be shown the extent to which these family visits tie in with the general policy of the Church today, and they will accept them whole-heartedly.

When a parish has a Vocation Day, the nuns who come from that parish should return there for the occasion. Their very presence will be a stimulus to vocations. This is as it should be, and the religious ought not to view these visits as laxity or accommodation to the world, but rather as an obligation deriving from the virtue of piety.

The arrangements for, and frequency of, family visits are things which have to be settled. The customs in force for male religious may serve as a useful guide, but the important thing is to find a balanced and sensible solution, free of petty provisions, which takes local conditions into account and which is open to suitable interpretation by the appropriate ecclesiastical authority if necessary. It is impossible to legislate for every eventuality since situations vary so greatly. Superiors, however, should avoid the temptation of applying automatically the norm of 'one day a year', instead of assuming their full responsibility in this regard. They should remember what Aristotle said—that true equality consists in treating unequal things unequally —and train their communities to understand the good sense of it.

The Religious Habit

Another, somewhat more obvious, problem arises when there is question of nuns mingling with the world—that of the religious habit.

On account of their aims, secular institutes generally do not wear a distinctive habit, but in our view it remains necessary for religious congregations. We have already shown the necessity for a visible and understandable collective witness: some sort of habit which is a distinctive sign is therefore necessary. It has its own nobility, it reminds us of the nun's exclusive dedication to God, and witnesses to Christ in a world which has forgotten Him. Often, the habit facilitates apostolic activity. It inspires confidence, makes it easier to keep conversation on a spiritual plane, renders people more open to discuss personal matters, and is always a joy and a help to those who wear it.

But the habit must be in keeping with the needs of our time. The world today has no patience with mere ornamentation, useless complications, gofferings and other oddities, whether starched or floating in the wind, which belong to another age: anything contrived or lacking in simplicity is rejected, as is anything unpractical or unhygienic, or anything that gives the impression that the nun is not only apart from the world but also a complete stranger to its evolution. The habit must be fully adapted to the nun's apostolate: as it is today, it often inhibits her social contacts. In de-christianized circles it acts as counter-propaganda, giving the impression that Christianity is out of date, archaic.

It is astonishing to note the timidity, the inertia, with which those responsible have answered—or rather, have failed to answer—the repeated appeals of Pius XII and other qualified authorities; appeals, incidentally, which are well known and commented upon among the laity.

What modifications have been made have generally been minimal; what is wanted is a radical modernization to twentieth-century standards, not to those of some past age. A serious factor in this anachronism is that the visible exterior leads one to fear the existence of an interior inability to adapt to current needs. Some habits exist which prevent nuns from taking part, as they should, in certain educational and apostolic activities, or which embarrass lukewarm lay people and which in many cases are an obstacle to the discretion sometimes needed for house visits.

Some lay people may have a sentimental, historical or traditional attachment to certain habits, but this should be no excuse for giving way to the temptation to keep things unchanged. We must love the Church of today and progress in step with her, according to her wishes and recommendations. This is true even if the origin of the habit lies in some dream or apparition, for it is to Christ living and speaking in the Church today that we owe our loyalty. Saints, and Foundresses of congregations, were models of faithfulness to the Church. One knows how even such favoured souls as St. Teresa of Avila and St. Margaret Mary inculcated in those around them that it was the Church alone, speaking through her human hierarchy, who had in the last resort the authority to decide upon the ways and means of the supernatural order. Loyalty to the Church on the part of nuns is but respect for the loyalty displayed by their Foundresses.

A Direct Manner

Those, then, are the main aspects of revision which interest us to start with. No doubt there are others, less important from the apostolic point of view but which would help from a psychological standpoint to create a better harmony between the religious life and the legitimate aspirations of the contemporary world. There must be,

K

wherever possible, dialogue on the same wavelength: there are secondary aspects of the religious life which would gain by being modernized. Why should there not be a periodical spring-cleaning to get rid of encumbrances and things which are an unnecessary stumbling-block to the modern mentality? The young woman of today likes a clear, direct, simple and frank manner; she should not be put off by an archaic vocabulary or a sort of ritual which is not of our times. These things, small in themselves and of only relative value, have a symbolic importance for our contemporaries: it should never happen that some out-of-date custom should stop a hesitant vocation at the threshold. One cannot hesitate before such minor sacrifices, for it is a question of vocations, which are worth the elimination of a few incidentals.

Let us read again the words of Pius XII which our pages have sought only to comment upon and paraphrase:

> The art of education is in many ways the art of adapting oneself to the age, temperament, character, capacity, needs and reasonable aspirations of the youth of today . . . adapting oneself to the rhythm of the general progress of humanity. (May, 1951.)

In September, 1952, the Pope returned to the charge in connection with the vocations crisis. He called upon Superiors General to see that "customs, the kind of life or asceticism of religious families did not constitute a barrier or a source of failure". He was speaking, he continued, of "certain customs which, though they formerly had some meaning in a different cultural context, no longer have any and in which a young, fervent and courageous girl would find nothing but fetters inhibiting her vocation and her apostolate".

Adaptation is not Relaxation

To end this chapter on the changes demanded by the needs of the apostolate, one last clarification seems useful.

There must be no mistake: the adaptations we have spoken of do not imply any relaxation or any compromise with the spirit of the world. Nuns who would like to modernize their life and their institutions on those lines have entirely misunderstood our thinking. To adapt apostolically is not to introduce luxury or excessive comfort, nor to follow every craze in order to be right up to the minute, and thus exude an atmosphere of worldliness and superficiality. No, it means quite a different sort of adaptation and one that has as its fruit: a religious life more religious because more apostolic, a more intense life of prayer, a more exacting spirit of renunciation, and a more authentic supernatural spirit. The liberty of action called for is always under discipline and obedience and will be exercised under the control of Superiors aware of the current needs. Far from being an excuse for following one's natural inclinations, apostolic work will be a harsh school of mortification, penance and renunciation. When one knows the self-denial required to start the smallest Catholic Action group, when one knows from experience what it costs to bring just one soul back to God, one knows that 'nature' does not get one very far and one must plunge into the supernatural in order to persevere.

We hope these remarks will prevent any misunderstanding, and will help readers to understand the deeper meaning of these pages.

11

THE REQUIREMENTS FOR ADEQUATE TRAINING

THROUGHOUT these pages the reader may have been tempted to compare the ideal put forward with certain things as they actually are, and our proposals will perhaps have appeared a trifle utopian. We are perfectly well aware that the actual realization of an ideal is achieved only by a transition which takes time, and that one must take into account the human 'material' and individual and collective psychology.

That is why we must now approach the problem which is the key to final success: the problem of providing for our nuns an adequate training which will enable them to meet all the current demands of their vocation.

This training must take place in several fields, all of them necessary and mutually complementary. It must be spiritual, apostolic, professional and social. Let us study these in turn.

SPIRITUAL TRAINING

The Novitiate

At present, spiritual formation is given within the framework of the canonical year of novitiate to which the Church, with good reason, attaches a great importance and which ought to be observed quite rigidly. The reasons for this are not difficult to understand. The girl who has just left the world to consecrate herself to God must start by getting away from the world she is leaving. She must discover for herself that which she has so far only perceived fleetingly—intimacy with God. In calling her, as He once called Andrew and John, the Master has repeated the invitation, "Come and see". He is inviting her to open out, little by little, the horizons of her spiritual life. She must learn to know herself, to correct her faults, to discover the meaning and value of her vows and of life in community. The novitiate ought to establish peace in her soul, strengthen her vocation and be a sort of prolonged retreat like Jesus' forty days in the desert before He started His public life. The Church wants her future religious to be Mary before being Martha so that later she can the better be Mary and Martha together in one vocation.

A new world opens before the novice: she has to discover the meaning of prayer, continuous communication with God, life in the presence of God. She must learn to see with the eyes of faith, to hope in the invisible realities, and to love not with her own heart but with that of God. She must enter into the mystery of Christ, grasp the vital significance of the doctrine of the Mystical Body and the Redemption. The future religious must understand the spiritual motherhood which it will be her role one day to exercise. She must become familiar with the lives of the Saints, that 'Gospel in pictures'. Now all this cannot be done in a day, and takes time to mature. This mere enumeration of the more fundamental requirements is sufficient to show that it is not easy to accomplish all that is demanded. There is, in the first place, a lack of time. But there is also, particularly in small congregations, a lack of personnel available for this work of education. Small congregations would profit by setting up, with the necessary guarantees, a common novitiate. But that would not be the whole answer; everyone is aware of the need for greater consistency in the present training and for some supplementary training.

In the nature of things the indispensable initial training cannot provide a complete initiation in one year—nor even in two.

And thus was born the idea of the juniorate.

The Juniorate

The Holy See is in favour of this idea of the *Grand Juvénat* which would prolong the training period in a different context, and it would like to see the progressive introduction of some years of juniorate.

Fr. Gambari of the Sacred Congregation for the Affairs of Religious explained the object as follows:

> The object of the juniorate is to continue, consolidate and perfect religious instruction both general and particular and also to give the professional instruction necessary for a suitable apostolic activity. The whole should be informed and guided by personal religious growth which is the individual response to religious and professional training.

On the duration, he adds:

> A minimum of two years and a maximum of five should be devoted to the juniorate. Between these limits the period would be settled by each religious family according to its own needs and capabilities.[1]

No one can fail to see that this innovation, which is still in its earliest stages, bids fair to make a solid contribution towards enabling religious to profit fully from the treasures of their vocation.

Some Aspects of Spiritual Education

Throughout the period of the novitiate and juniorate there must be a deepening of that spiritual life which is

[1] *Le Grand Juvénat selon l'esprit et les directives du Saint-Siège.* Article in *Supplément de la Vie Spirituelle*, No. 54, 1960.

common to all Christians. Yet, there must also be an ever more profound experience of what is specifically the religious life as this is expressed in the spirit of each congregation. The practice of the vows will be decisive in this apostolic education. If the vows appear as means of detachment in order to make one more available, then their practice will, far from being a hindrance, enhance apostolic zeal. Initiation into the practice of obedience will have a considerable influence on the orientation of a religious life. That is why we shall spend some time on it.

Education to Real Obedience

The three vows of religion are very closely related and this relationship is embodied in obedience, the pivot of the religious life.

> What is the religious state if it is not the subjection of the individual, and therefore of his whole life, to the service of God? . . . When he abandons his will to his Superior, the religious gives up to him, and through him to God, all acts that would arise from his will . . . in other words, the matter of the vows of chastity and poverty. Thus one can truthfully say that the vow of obedience achieves the object of the other two vows and so embraces the whole of the religious life.[1]

The central place of obedience in the religious life demands particularly careful training in it. Obedience must be lived as a positive virtue, a stimulus rather than an invitation to passivity. If it is not properly understood, it will tend to inhibit missionary zeal; properly understood, it will, on the contrary, guarantee its full freedom. Obedience does not mean lack of personality, initiative or responsibility. It is rather a giving of our deepest will to God so

[1] Dom O. Lottin, *Etudes de Morale, Histoire et Doctrine*, p. 255. Duculot, Gembloux, 1961.

that we may serve Him all the better in the way indicated to us by authority, His interpreter. Obedience cannot be productive unless there is openness, reciprocity and dialogue. Submission must not be confused with passivity. Real submission carries out loyally the orders given, after having raised, if necessary, the points which seem to favour another course. The nun who is most passive is not necessarily the most submissive, nor the most obedient.

Although it comprises it, obedience is not in the first instance an exercise in mortification. The prime consideration is not the abdication of one's own will nor the submission to a person, it is loyalty to the common good as an expression of God's will. Everyone must do the job of his station, the Superior as well as the subordinate. And one must never forget that both Superiors and inferiors must be trained in this sense of co-responsibility which is essential to the success of their common efforts. The Superior has the final decision, the last word—but not the second-last word. It is normal and sensible that subordinates be asked for and give their views before a decision is made. The common good demands that this be done with respect and loyalty, and in some cases privately; but thereafter the common good demands loyal adherence to the decisions made.

The proper motive is essential if obedience is not to defeat its purpose entirely. To think that one obeys in the first instance in order to renounce one's own will, is to start on a path that leads nowhere; the primary reason for obedience is not to mortify oneself but to serve God and one's neighbour. One does not obey in order to please someone, but to respond to God's will. Passive conformity is not obedience : obedience has nothing in common with 'complacent paralysis'.

Passivity, when indulged in as a policy, tends to favour the *status quo* and gives rise to immaturity. An adult cannot renounce the right to obey as an adult. This does not mean that one obeys any less perfectly: quite the contrary. A genuine obedience, based on forgetfulness of self and inspired by the theological virtue of faith, sees Christ in all legitimate authority. Education in this sort of obedience is something requiring skill and tact which should be carried out by both parties under the constant guidance of the Holy Spirit. It is probably more difficult for a woman to carry it out than for a man. Pius XII himself once remarked to the Mothers General, "What psychology teaches is doubtless true, that a woman in authority does not manage as easily as a man to strike the exact balance between severity and kindness". (15th September, 1952.) To exercise command without stifling the personality of one's subordinates but making on the contrary the most of their initiative and intelligence is the mark of true authority.

Respect for Natural Qualities

Complete religious education does not end with initiation in the supernatural virtues and the vows—it ought also to build up the natural feelings of rectitude, loyalty, justice and social sense.

We must develop in the nun of tomorrow the sense of respect, tact, discretion; she must know the cost of time and the value of silence. She must learn to talk and express herself clearly. She must know how to open out, to share her treasure, and to listen, to be 'pure attention to the existence of another'.

She must develop, suitably balanced, the gifts of the heart; lack of feeling is not a good quality. As Fr. Voillaume wrote:

The love of perfect charity must give rise to a delicacy of feeling which is not only purified but also enlarged and refined, and will permit it to express itself towards

God and man with all the treasures of tenderness, friendship, sweetness and strength of a human heart. The perfection of man, who has become the son of God, cannot be achieved by the suppression of what is most beautiful in him. The heart must therefore not be confined or brutally repressed; it must be directed; its sensitiveness must not be destroyed, but purified and brought under control. To purify and control is entirely different from stifling and lessening: it is to make the heart larger and the sensibility more delicate so that both may be placed at the service of supernaturalized love.[1]

The natural virtues must be developed, both in order to provide grace with good soil for its labours, and also so that those human qualities essential to any genuine dialogue may be manifested to our lay people who are particularly sensitive to their presence in religious. Anything that dehumanizes or defeminizes the nun lowers her apostolic value. One must beware of any trace of Jansenism, a one-sided insistence on the supernatural virtues must not be the cause of neglecting the natural virtues.

APOSTOLIC EDUCATION

Spiritual education would be dangerously incomplete if it did not go hand in hand with a progressive theoretical and practical education for the apostolate. The latter must take into account the new conditions of our time. The greatest single new factor is that the laity has become conscious of its apostolic mission in the Church. From which it follows that the apostolic education of nuns would be incomplete if it did not include instruction in the role they have to play as inspiration for the lay-women alongside whom they will constantly find themselves.

[1] *Au coeur des masses*, pp. 376–7.

The object of apostolic education will be to teach the religious how to give Christ to the world, how to put the Gospel into practice in all its aspects, and how to train others to be in their turn agents of christianization.

The religious has to have a double apostolic training. On the one hand she must be prepared for her task as teacher or nurse with its direct apostolic extensions, and on the other she must learn how to train the laity and thus multiply apostolic action in the world.

The Holy See, in speaking of the means of developing the apostolic sense, gives the following directive in Art. 47 of the General Statutes of *Sedes Sapientiae*.

> During the entire period of formation and probation Superiors and Masters will not fail to impart a taste for the apostolate to their pupils; more, they will make it their duty to give them moderate exercise in it in accordance with the mind of the Church and the nature and purpose of the institute.

By the same token, let us not forget the wish expressed by the World Congress of Major Superiors in Rome as reported in the *Osservatore Romano* of 16th December, 1957.

> With regard to non-priest members, whether male or female, of religious institutes, this Congress expresses the wish that special attention be paid to the indispensable part these persons have to play in the creation, training, organization and apostolic inspiration of the adult laity. It is their task, under the direction of and in close harmony with the clergy, to collaborate in the work of setting the entire Church on a missionary footing, associating themselves in the threefold task commended to priests by Pius XII of discovering lay collaborators, training them, and making use of them in order to increase

the apostolic yield. [Letter to Lenten Preachers, 1954.] This role may be compared with that of N.C.O.s in an army, where they are an indispensable element of liaison and co-ordination. So that they may more effectively fulfil this very important aspect of their religious vocation, a practical introduction to the apostolate seems highly desirable with a view to the instruction and training of the laity.

This progressive introduction to the apostolate has not yet acquired its own science of teaching, though the importance of it is clear. The apostolic gift is seldom innate. Few people have a natural or supernatural genius for the apostolate. However, there is much that can be learned, and faith in the Holy Spirit does not dispense us from a humble apprenticeship spent in acquiring those techniques needed in dealing with people, either individually or in groups. While admitting the sovereignty of grace we must also realize that it demands of us that we love God not only with our whole heart but also with our whole mind, with method, imagination and a sense of organization.

There must be, one day, centres in which the apostolate is studied and its methodology constantly improved and made more effective. But even now, the attempts which have been made in this direction allow us to discern the main lines which will be followed in its future development.

Some Necessary Conditions for Initiation to the Apostolate

To be adequate, the initiation must be practical. Theoretical courses are not enough. There is what is called a 'learning by doing' for which there is no substitute. All the theories one may propound about the art of swimming are not as valuable as one swimming bath. The slow, continuous apprenticeship in constant contact with life remains an indispensable means of training.

Since it is to be practical, the training must be by stages spread out over a number of years.

It will produce results only if it is well adapted, proportioned to individual needs and capacities, and carefully supervised. It must be integrated, as an equal partner, with other aspects of education: it cannot be relegated to the side-lines as something merely supplementary.

In the light of what has already been said, one can see that preparation for the apostolate must be widened to correspond to the complexity of the duties which it involves.

Not only teaching nuns, but also nursing nuns will tomorrow be in contact through pupils and patients with a background of parents, relations, ex-pupils and ex-patients, all members of the laity. This means that they will be confronted, one way or another, with the problems of the adult laity. Therefore, they must be prepared not only to fulfil their specific role as teacher or nurse, but also to carry out their mission to inspire and educate the laity. The scope of the training will depend on the various conditions of time and place. Depending upon whether the religious houses in question exercise their function in a Christian area or in one which has become de-christianized, there will be different problems for which they must be prepared. No stereotyped scheme can be outlined here, only a general orientation.

Apart from a real acquaintance with the problems involved, training for the apostolate involves knowing about the various organizations and movements in which today's efforts at christianization are channelled. The religious must become familiar with the various spiritual programmes available to the laity, and they must have a knowledge of the work being done in such areas as aid to the poor, social action, family rehabilitation, etc. Most especially, they must be informed, both in general and in particular, with regard to the various youth organizations and Catholic Action in all its multiple modern facets. If one cannot know in detail or have practical experience of everything, at least one must have some experience of those areas in which one will have a part to play or which the bishops wish to be given special support. It is not necessary to be able to organize every type of movement, but some must be known thoroughly and there must be a working knowledge of others which is sufficient to interest and direct the young people and others whom one may be able to reach.

PROFESSIONAL TRAINING

In addition to spiritual and apostolic training, there must also be the indispensable professional training. Anyone who undertakes the role of teacher or nurse must perfectly fulfil the technical requirements. Nuns must be distinguished for their capability in this matter: it is an elementary duty in justice to those who will be confided to their care and at the same time it will indirectly increase the value of their religious influence.

On the eve of the Council, Pope John XXIII wrote to the nuns of the whole world:

Let all those who dedicate themselves to the active life remember that it is not only by prayer but also by works, that we will ensure that the new direction being taken by society will draw its nourishment from the Gospel. . . . And since the scholastic, charitable, and welfare fields cannot use people who are unprepared to meet the increased demands imposed by present-day regulations, devote your efforts, in accordance with obedience, to completing your studies and gaining the diplomas that will put you in a position to overcome all obstacles. And thus, in addition to your required and proven competence, your spirit of dedication, patience, and sacrifice will be better appreciated. (2nd July, 1962.)

One must start from the idea that every religious, even though, humanly speaking, she may not be gifted, can and must be developed professionally to her full capacity. It is a duty we owe to God not to leave one single talent buried. In our more advanced countries means are not lacking to increase the professional training of all religious.

On the subject of teachers, Pius XII said on 13th September, 1951 :

> See that you provide them with a good preparation and training corresponding to the requirements of the State. Give them generously all they need, especially books, so they can follow, later on, the progress made in their subject and be able thus to offer the young a rich and stable harvest of knowledge. This is in conformity with the Catholic concept which accepts with gratitude all that is naturally true, beautiful and good since it is the image of the divine truth, goodness and beauty.

The more capable nuns should be trained to make their voices heard in all human matters where questions are raised about the life of grace in souls and obedience to the laws of God. Abortion, divorce, birth prevention, public morals, juvenile delinquency, neglect of children, social legislation, status of women . . . nothing of all this should be unfamiliar to them. Priests of great ability have given themselves to the study of these things, but there is a dearth of nuns qualified and specializing in these fields.

The Pope excludes nothing : each nun must have the chance to put her talents to use, whether it be in teaching, care of the sick or social work. It is to be hoped that nuns have access to libraries that are kept up to date, and periodicals and current books; that they are able to attend congresses and study-groups and that these in turn are open to attendance by nuns. Study-trips in search of information should be authorized so that they can benefit from experiments outside their own neighbourhood. They should follow closely all that is being done in the various fields by government or by private enterprise.

One must not be afraid of being too ambitious. If woman today has such a place in social life, then the nun with the qualification of her professional training has a reserved seat in the same row. Wherever public opinion is formed, wherever educational laws are drafted or laws concerning the home or health, the nun has a part to play.

SOCIAL TRAINING

In order to meet what is demanded of them today, nuns must be aware of the social realities which condition the world they live in. They have to know not only the various kinds of common misery but also what causes them. They must be initiated into the great social problems which affect a man's life today. If a room is flooded, it is no good just mopping the floor: one must find out where the water is coming from and do something about it. Charity is not just an individual thing between individual persons, it is a social thing. What does loving one's neighbour as oneself mean then? It is not just a question of giving alms or being kind to individuals, it means caring about society itself and trying to even out its inequalities and let the light of justice shine.

We must not forget that one measure may abolish or alleviate the material and moral misery of millions of human beings in a moment. Our nuns, therefore, must be able to situate their work in the social context of our own times, taking due notice of the psychological components of the present-day world. All this requires, on their part, presence, openness, and readiness.

As teachers they will have to introduce their charges to the great problems of the working classes and all that is implied in the sombre words 'social justice' and 'poverty'. Older girls should have close knowledge of the anguish of a family at grips with sickness, uncertainty and inadequate wages; they should have seen a slum and its promiscuity; they should know something of marginal cases which the law covers inadequately if at all; they should understand the reason for things like strikes and demonstrations. Our young people should be trained to choose their career in the light of the social service which it implies. The governing class will be powerfully influenced by the moral judgment given on the social phenomena by young adults who have to behave as Christians not only in their private lives but also in their social lives. They have their contribution to make towards the necessary redress.

Everything mentioned in the Encyclical *Mater et Magistra* should be broken down into concrete realities for our pupils. We must be able to set up social and mutual assistance teams which can teach young women of the leisured classes to seek out moral and physical distress, not with excessive maternalism but with a deep sense of service and a clear knowledge of the requirements of social justice.

All this presupposes some training of the teachers. It is difficult to imagine a teacher of today who is not familiar with the great trends of our age or who cannot trace the source of the profound stirrings which shake our society. Communism covers one third of the world: one cannot ignore it, and it is no good just condemning it. One must know its origin and the partial truth responsible for its birth before being in a position to condemn its atheism.

L

We must have the courage to face up to certain situations. As Fr. Van den Hout once wrote:

> Our western civilization has failed in its primary mission. A Christian civilization, it could and should have christianized the universe. Deeply apostate, it sought only to exploit the universe for purely worldly, even basely materialistic ends. But if the white races have been able to enrich themselves to an unbelievable degree, it has been at the price of enormous and terrible social injustices. Its cornering of wealth, its creation of an immense proletariat, its culpable lack of concern in the face of the appalling misery of millions and hundreds of millions of human beings undernourished and dying of starvation, have aroused and built up an enormous rancour that falls easy prey to the apostles of human pseudo-liberty.

The social education which is necessary for teaching nuns is also necessary in other forms for other kinds of religious who are in contact with the world. They have to deal with, one by one, the souls which Providence places in their path and give them the best they have—the living Christ. But they must know that these souls are influenced by the world around them and do not easily resist the undertow and the many currents to which they are prey. Religious must know about these currents in order to guide their own actions and also in order to help christianize the circles where souls are fashioned and so often de-christianized.

Mgr. Bonet, Chaplain-General of the Workers' Catholic Action in France, has not hesitated to declare:

> It is through women that working-class society will return to being a Christian society, and it is through the nun that the working-class woman will become an enlightened and effective factor in the christianization of the working-class world.

This declaration, which is valid for all social classes, is worth remembering. A social education adapted to the nature and needs of each religious congregation will give each nun an incomparable power of penetration and will be nothing but gain for the realism of her approach and the efficacy of her apostolate.

CONTINUING THE FORMATION

Continuous Education

This varied education begun during the juniorate cannot be considered as completed when the juniorate ends. Our age has started on the road of continuous education on account of the incessant development of new techniques. If he is not to become very quickly out of date, an engineer or a doctor must keep abreast of developments in his field. For the doctor it is an obligation in justice to his patient who has a right to the best treatment. The acquisition of a degree or diploma is less and less the end of study : rather, it is the beginning. A French scientist made the sally that France was "a country where one learns a great deal at school and where one acquires a number of very difficult diplomas all of which allows one to learn nothing else for the rest of one's life". That will serve as an opportune warning against the fetishism of diplomas and against all kinds of stagnation.

Continuation studies are today equally necessary for our nuns, and Superiors must take care to see that they are carried out. If industrial concerns organize refresher courses for their technicians in order to ensure productivity, it is only right and proper that we should do the same to ensure a better apostolic yield. This is one sphere, at least, in which the children of light can learn something from the children of this world.

On the spiritual and apostolic plane this refresher education must be carried out if we are not to risk a lack of balance. Professional necessity makes a number of our religious acquire the necessary diplomas and benefit by the valuable training they afford, but if religious and spiritual education does not keep pace there is a risk that in the course of years there will be such a differential that the humanitarian aspect of their work would overwhelm the Christian aspect. What the world needs far more than Christian humanism is a thoroughly human Christianity. This means a continuous and suitable religious education. We have agreed to raise the intellectual and professional level of our nuns at the instance of the State. It is necessary now that our own requirements of life lead us to concentrate on the imparting of an integral religious formation which will then be developed until it reaches the full flowering of maturity.

Second Novitiate

A certain number of congregations provide for a sort of third year or second novitiate. This idea should be expanded and deepened. Straightway one comes upon the necessity of grouping together the smaller congregations so that they can have the benefit of these refresher courses which require a directing staff difficult to obtain with the talent available to a small group. Such courses would be taken regularly at intervals still to be determined and should cover every aspect of the life of our nuns, that is to say not only their spiritual life but also their apostolic, professional and social life. Each aspect has its own requirements. Deepening the spiritual life can be done in a special house, in silence and recollection—in retreat, in fact. But other forms of refresher training could not be carried out in those conditions. In fact it will be necessary to learn new apostolic techniques and bring old methods up to date, in the same way as nuns will have to review and bring up to date their theoretical and practical knowledge of their professional and social work. All this involves contacts, movement—in fact courses. What will be needed will have to be worked out for each type of refresher course. The four aspects —spiritual, apostolic, professional and social—must all be dealt with, but not necessarily all within one year. The incidence and programming will have to be studied.

This will need sacrifices, adaptations and an imaginative effort in order to make available nuns who are not easy to replace; but the results will be worth the trouble involved.

Nuns have dedicated their lives to God in their communities; it is right and proper that the communities do what they can to foster a renewal which will increase the yield both natural and supernatural of these dedicated souls. Steps will have to be taken to ensure that all nuns are included. The Superior and her assistants must love each member of the community individually and develop all her energies and all her natural and supernatural gifts. All this is part of the permanent education towards which we must strive. There is nothing like it to dispel the danger of spiritual sclerosis and to ensure that God is served with joy. "A soul which raises itself raises the whole world." A religious, brought to the full realization of her potentialities with regard to all these four aspects of her vocation, will draw an ever-increasing multitude of souls after her as she makes her way to God. Superiors have a duty to be ambitious for their daughters. They were chosen by God and God has in reserve a superabundance of grace to allow them to respond adequately to their vocation.

12

HOW TO HASTEN THE RENEWAL FROM WITHIN

THE renewal proposed in these pages depends on the co-
ordination of the efforts made within and without, that is
to say the efforts made *by* the congregations and *for* the
congregations.

In this chapter we should like to analyse what can be
done from within to speed and promote advancement of
the religious and, as a consequence, allow her to benefit
from the pastoral revival which the Church hopes to introduce at all levels.

This improvement will depend on the attitude to be
adopted on the questions of enclosure and allocation of
time. Unwillingness to move in these two matters would
ensure in advance the failure of any attempt at renewal.
On the positive side, integration of the apostolic meetings
we shall describe into the life of a community will be a firm
guarantee of the will to adapt.

As we said before, the necessary revisions must not be
the work of individual nuns—their vow of obedience requires them to obey a Rule, not to change it; but it is
legitimate for them to collaborate in bringing about changes
once competent authority has agreed in principle. The competent authority is alone responsible for directing the revision process. To do so, it is necessary to enter into all the
aspects of renewal. What is, in fact, the best way to set

about revision? We believe that the initiative lies in the first place with the General Chapters.

GENERAL CHAPTERS

The General Chapter of each congregation provides for the periodical revision of the constitutions. The instrument is available, therefore; let us see how it works.

A congregation is governed in ordinary affairs by one of its members, the Superior General, assisted by a Council and in extraordinary affairs by the General Chapter. Necessary revisions are first of all the concern of the General Chapter—the highest authority of the congregation. Part of its normal function is to see that revisions necessitated by new needs or new circumstances are carried out.

I was told by the Superior General of a very important congregation that formerly this used to be almost exclusively a question of maintaining tradition. It was only just recently under Pius XII and principally since the first Congress of Religious (1950) and that of Superiors General (1952) that anything has seriously been attempted in the way of adaptation. I asked him to tell me what were in his eyes the most important reefs to be avoided at a General Chapter, and he gave me the following points:

Chapters are convened in a hurry and are almost always insufficiently prepared for. Improvisation occurs when the Chapter is called only on the death of a Superior General. Lack of information is due both to the absence of any continual source of information between the Chapters and to the insufficient information available in the preparatory stages of the Chapter. Adequate consultation between members is needed, as well as preliminary studies and enquiries. Also, too long intervals between Chapters are undesirable in our times when everything evolves so rapidly. Moreover, the Chapter should be really representative. Representation is often one-sided. This arises from the preponderance of *ex officio* members over elected members, of Superiors over ordinary members. A certain concept of religious obedience and of what is 'suitable' leads a number of religious to send Superiors as delegates to the Chapter rather than choose men principally for their competence. There is also a tendency to choose older rather than younger men, and in the case of congregations working in several fields, to overstress one or other of them.

Another danger to be avoided is the tendency to attach no importance to anything except the elections and to treat other business, i.e. problems of adaptation, etc., as subsidiary; or again to put all the emphasis on religious problems at the expense of apostolic questions, or to be concerned only with maintaining tradition, not with adapting it.

Once the Chapter is in session there are other dangers to be avoided. The Superior General and Council must be careful to remember that, in Chapter, they have no power of decision. The delegates to the Chapter are there precisely to exercise some control over the administration and to ensure that what they deem to be the best interests of the Community are truly realized. There is danger that the Chapter will fail in its object due to a mistaken sense of deference among its members who dare not bring deficiencies to light or make suggestions for fear of upsetting some Superior, or of seeming to be too revolutionary. Members must not lose sight of the fact that they are there not to listen to the Superior General dictating but to deliberate and legislate in common. The temptation to be passive or easygoing must be resisted. In order to prevent the Chapter lasting too long, one is inclined to refer problems 'to the wisdom of the Superior

General and Council' or else to rush through them at high speed.

The above comments seem to us of the greatest importance. To emphasize one of the points brought out—insufficient preparation—one might use as one's inspiration the preparatory work for the Council. The pre-preparatory committees followed by the preparatory committees cleared the ground and analysed some 9,000 suggestions received. Similar preparatory work for a General Chapter would have to be carried out with the greatest freedom, discretion and frankness. To get at people's real reactions is not always easy, for people do not like to say, to their faces, at least, things which they think may offend their Superiors. Preliminary studies will have to be made up of very precise questions, and conducted with eyes and ears wide open. It may be advisable to question certain reliable lay witnesses. The sort of question to be put might be, 'What is it in the religious life as seen by a young woman of today which stops her from entering and turns away vocations?'

The question does not cover everything, of course, and is not intended to evoke all the multiple causes which, from the outside, militate against vocations, but it is direct and precise and is part of the main question of how to hasten renewal from within.

It is easy to see how much more realistic and effective a General Chapter would be if it were preceded by a thorough enquiry addressed to all members of the congregation.

REPLACEMENT OF SUPERIORS

If we are to hasten the renewal from within, a point of primary importance is that of the duration of the term of office of Superiors. The Central Council of another great congregation whom I consulted on this point, sent me a note which summarizes considerable experience in the matter and which seems pretty well in harmony with what we have already cited about General Chapters.

It is noted that with few exceptions most female congregations have a Central Council composed of a majority and sometimes a totality of older members. Commonly enough elections for renewal of terms of office have their own particular psychology: a nun very easily feels that she must not be ungrateful to a retiring Superior even if there is an obviously competent candidate to take over her office, and so she votes for the present holder. Another point is that although freedom to vote as one wishes is theoretically guaranteed there is often a fear, founded or unfounded, that in the end the votes do not remain secret, and this obviously inhibits freedom. Finally, most of the time a serious renewal is almost impossible, owing to the fact that the Superior General, once in office, nominates at her discretion all the general staff of local Superiors who are therefore devoted to her and who are *ex-officio* members of the next General Chapter. Thus it follows that the tendency to maintain the *status quo* can easily prevail.

Present legislation is in itself and quite apart from personalities which are not under consideration here, a source of inaction and a major obstacle to renewal from within.

It is to be hoped that any revision of the Code will take this situation into account and that remedies for it will be studied. It will be enough to revise a few things on this point.

Election procedure should be improved so as to guarantee freedom and secrecy.

Capitulantes, i.e. members of the Chapter called upon to elect the new Superior General, should comprise at least as many elected delegates as *ex-officio* members.

There should be an increase in the percentage of votes required to re-elect an office holder and there should be, in accordance with the wishes of the Sacred Congregation for the Affairs of Religious, no recourse to the process of postulation which allows terms of office to be prolonged by special permission beyond what the rules provide.

Legal expression should be given to the Church's expressed preference for periodic changes of government; an age limit should be fixed, and the wish should be expressed that as a matter of principle the retiring Superior should not, as is the present tradition, be a member of the new Central Council.

Legislation forbidding direct or indirect influence on elections should be strengthened. It should also be more severe in allowing a retiring Superior to be nominated as Superior to another house, since this can result in a lifetime tenure of office being exercised in a succession of houses. Nuns find difficulty in accepting that a one-time Superior is no longer such and must take her place in the ranks.

All this has been on the juridical plane. It goes without saying, however, that any renewal must be supported on the psychological plane by the creation of a mentality which will welcome these new ideas. Renewal will only be obtained at this price. One may hope that nuns, being clearly aware of the Church's wishes today, would be happy to adhere to directives which they know to be inspired by the greatest good of their communities.

Cardinal Larraona, at that time Secretary of the Sacred Congregation for the Affairs of Religious, expressed himself with all necessary clarity on this subject in 1952, addressing the Congress of Mothers General in Rome :

The Sacred Congregation is not in favour of re-elections beyond the term stipulated in the Constitutions; indeed it is opposed to them in principle. Superiors and *Capitulantes* are obliged to observe the law of the Church just as their subjects are. The prolonged retention of one person in an office tends to prevent the training of other Superiors and restricts the choice too narrowly. . . . In the case of a possible 'postulation' . . . the judgment of the Sacred Congregation will henceforth be strict, since the confirmation of a re-election beyond the fixed term will constitute an exception which should be rare.[1]

Superiors ought to take pleasure in preparing their successors, in distributing responsibility, in regularly introducing the younger element into the government in order to be more attuned to the times—God knows, we are evolving rapidly enough in these days of space flights!

The Mothers General during their Congress in Rome in 1952 expressed the following wish:

For the continuous training and perfecting of Superiors . . . one must not exclude the younger nuns from office, nor insist on conditions not demanded by Canon Law. They should not persist in re-electing the same persons, for the Church's mind is that the law and constitutions of the congregation should be obeyed and they find it good that there should be alternation in the office of Superior so that Superiors shall not be deprived of the benefits of obedience. Let it be remembered that where other conditions are equal or nearly equal between a Superior in office and a new candidate, it is preferable to elect the latter. Regrettable crises will thus be avoided and one will have a greater number of religious trained in governing.[2]

[1] Sacra Congregatio de Religiosis, *Acta et Documenta Congressus Internationalis Superiorissarum Generalium*, 1952, p. 271.
[2] Ibid., p. 299.

What a good example, incidentally, can be shown by a retiring Superior who receives an ordinary appointment and shows by her joyful humility the truth of what she has been teaching. If she is appointed again to office later on, she will be all the better qualified for having once more seen things from the other side and will be nearer to her subjects and better able to serve them.

PERIODICAL REVISION

Periodical revision is normal and healthy; a rule must be adapted to reality—which means that it must be brought up to date to keep pace with the developments of reality.

Actually it will not be the Constitutions so much as the Directories and Customaries that will be subject to revision. These are the *vade-mecum* of everyday life: the spirit of the Rule is brought to life in a thousand concrete details. It is these things which often either inhibit or encourage liberty of apostolic action. They must be carefully checked, for their provisions control the whole life of a congregation. It often happens that with the passage of time they become an obstacle and a hindrance to enterprise instead of a stimulus and support.

Once Customs have been in use for ten years, one may be sure that danger level has been reached and that some paragraphs at least have no longer any connection with reality.

In the course of the necessary revision a negative work is first necessary—the elimination of everything that hinders the apostolic developments previously described. After that comes the task of making positive provision for the four-dimensional training we have spoken of.

APOSTOLIC MEETINGS

Among those measures which can serve to promote and sustain the apostolic renewal of the religious life, we would like to draw particular attention to the value of apostolic meetings held in community. The sole aim of these meetings should be the stimulation of individual effort with a view to responding more perfectly to the demands of the Church's modern apostolate. The Constitutions should provide for these meetings in principle, while the Directories could legislate more in detail for their practical management.

What we are saying, in effect, is that the integration of apostolic activities ought to have an official place in the life of the community. They ought not to be left to chance nor treated as poor relations. Such activities as these should not be abandoned to amateur efforts or, worse still, be withdrawn from the control of obedience. Rather, it is necessary that this sort of activity be incorporated in the normal life of the community and not just be a fringe activity. The hours set aside for it must be part of the normal routine and take their place among other duties as spiritual exercises, differing in form, but animated by the same spirit. Since the whole community is involved, it is to be expected that place will be found regularly for well organized apostolic meetings which will follow a determined pattern. These meetings, for which provision will be made in the timetable, will consist of a 'sharing' of apostolic activities with mutual exchange of information and criticism and co-ordination in the distribution of tasks. It is easy to see why the community should meet at regular intervals to consider as a body the way in which each individual effort should be directed and to follow up and co-ordinate results. Without something like this there would be the tendency for the work to get no further than the expression of personal inclinations and unrelated impulses. A community will never really get going in this new dimension of the apostolate unless each of its members is assigned a definite task which will cause her to discover new possibilities of religious activity and of which she will be called upon to give account. The meetings are essential for cohesion of the work and for the spirit underlying it. They could be compared to spiritual exercises, a time for prayer which is fixed but in no way excludes prayer at other times: on the contrary, one prays at fixed times in order to accustom oneself to the climate of prayer. Similarly, the apostolic meetings we are talking about are a powerful means of placing the soul in a state of constant apostolic awareness.

In the case of a large community it would be better to divide it up into groups or 'apostolic teams' of ten to twelve nuns. This would avoid over-long meetings, would increase the yield of each member and give her the maximum of personal responsibility. To avoid dispersal of effort, there could be periodical meetings of all the teams or their representatives. All this, of course, must come under obedience: it will be the Superior's responsibility to nominate the members and officers of each group and to exercise overall control of their activities.

The teams will give the community all the advantages on the human plane of group psychology. The necessary discretion will allow individual nuns to put the best of themselves at the disposal of the common good. The meetings will be a stimulus to community life. Once they have been successfully tried out, it will be up to a General Chapter to give them official status.

It would be interesting to hear about enterprises of this nature so that others can benefit from the experience.[1]

---

[1] Information and details about the integration of apostolic meetings into community life will gladly be furnished by the Conseil Pastoral Diocésain des Religieuses, l'Archevêché, Malines.

APOSTOLIC GUIDANCE

So far we have dealt with getting the renewal under way. Once the principle is accepted, it may be useful to have qualified guides or advisers who can both start enterprises and assist in integrating the apostolic meetings into the community life. This sort of task could be given to 'apostolic' visitors, that is to specially trained nuns who would be able to place their experience at the disposal of communities. They could be found within the communities or 'borrowed' from communities which have the necessary experience. Their assistance would greatly facilitate the setting up of new enterprises and the avoidance of mistakes. A great many problems are much more easily dealt with by someone on the spot and a 'visitor' would be a great encouragement to face up to all the 'impossibilities', which usually disappear if one has the courage to believe that they will.

13

HOW TO HASTEN THE RENEWAL FROM WITHOUT

IN order to make the most of her own apostolic possibilities, the religious of today needs help from outside and she should seek all possible co-operation in the same way as she appeals to the authorities on whom she is dependent.

An exceptional opportunity of making a decisive turning point in the development of the apostolic aspect of the religious life is available. It is none other than the Second Vatican Council now being held in Rome with the object of encouraging a spiritual renewal throughout the Church.

THE COUNCIL

The bishops have expressed or passed on several thousands of proposals. It is to be feared that the Superiors of our congregations have not made their voices heard enough nor made known their wishes on the subject of the things that hinder or inhibit their vitality and power to radiate Christ. But it is not too late: what was not done before the Council can be done afterwards. It would be reasonable to suppose that a place will be found for them on some post-conciliar consultative committee and that the thousand complex questions to be solved about the religious life of women will not be left in exclusively male hands. In any case a possibility of dialogue is desirable.

But that is for the future.

But at this moment the Council could cause a decisive step forward to be taken in the matter of apostolic advancement of nuns by deciding to appoint a committee to study the problem. The Council could determine some basic guiding principles and instruct the Committee for the revision of the Code of Canon Law (which will sit immediately after the Council) accordingly. It is usual for the Code to be amended from time to time, for the law should be patterned on reality and not the other way about. There is normally some time-lag between the need for revision and its being made. A Roman canon lawyer used to say by way of encouraging the promoters of useful changes, "You must be the torrent: we canonists will provide the river-bed for you". Put in another way, the canon lawyers cannot do anything useful unless they know what is wanted and are encouraged to do the necessary work. In the hope of achieving this, it could be respectfully but insistently demanded of the Conciliar Fathers that they:

Affirm the principle of the new role of the nun as the one to inspire and direct the feminine laity both young and grown up.

Express the wish that adequate theoretical and practical training for this role be given to young nuns.

Express the wish that nothing in the Constitutions should be a hindrance to the needs of the apostolate in the world of today and that Constitutions be revised in this sense.

Express the wish to see the religious life so organized that this new function becomes an integral part of community life and has by right its recognized place therein through the organization of special meetings to control and foster specific activities.

The Council's agreement to this would be of incalculable importance and would furnish a decisive impetus.

NATIONAL AND DIOCESAN FEDERATIONS

Associations of Major Superiors

Adaptations within communities could also be greatly helped from outside by the use of those means of collaboration which exist already. Thus diocesan and national federations of religious are obvious instruments of renewal. So also are the Associations of Major Superiors, which, at the instigation of the Holy See, have come into being in many places. Their task is to overcome inertia, routine and the spiritual or intellectual laziness which everywhere favour a policy of no change. They permit religious to compare problems, exchange views and to work out concrete proposals to be submitted to higher authority. These periodical meetings and exchanges provide a remarkable opportunity for progress. They were in fact started by the Holy See with an eye on the changes that will be necessary. No doubt a part of the problems to be studied will deal with the internal arrangements of the religious life, but most of these problems affect the apostolate. They must be studied with the constant idea of being always one step ahead of apostolic needs while still respecting the principal object of each institute.

One cannot fail to welcome a flourishing set of associations grouping together religious engaging in school and hospital work and parish schooling. A movement has been started which arouses a justifiable hope. Books and periodicals, congresses and study-sessions are attacking the problems of the religious life with courage and objectivity.

The Holy See is generous in its encouragement. The question of the nun's position has been brought out into full daylight. One must hope for active participation on the part of qualified religious in the search for concrete ways and means of solution. Listening to lectures is not enough. Investigations must be carried out and practical proposals put forward; it may be a long business but it is a work that should command the devotion of all.

Particularly welcome is the institution of training sessions for Superiors.

Training Sessions for Superiors

Behind every serious reform lies the problem of training Superiors. Until recent years, election to office was regarded as all that was needed. People are beginning to realize that there is something missing and arrangements for training Superiors are becoming more numerous. This is a step in the right direction, particularly since the training is not only for Superiors as such, but also for assistants, mistresses of novices, all those who in one way or another have the fate of the community in their hands. The Superior must be able to make a team out of her Council and must show by example what it means to take over collective charge of a community. Several heads are better than one—not only for intelligence but also for wisdom, and above all to harmonize the various complementary aspects of community life and to avoid the stifling effect of maternalism centred in one person. Authority grows in stature by giving due importance to its subordinates. In any case the Church in her laws has always emphasized the part to be played by Councils in the government of religious houses. Any training which will help Superiors to work as a team with their Councils will be of the greatest benefit.

Training Centres

The renewal can also be greatly helped by the establishment of training centres for nuns. Some centres have already been established to provide suitably prepared nuns with the opportunity of acquiring a solid philosophical and theological training. Why should it not be possible for nuns who have taken this instruction to run retreats or days of recollection, or direct spiritual and apostolic sessions of lay-women or girls? *Regina Mundi*, the Pontifical Institute for nuns in Rome, where teaching is in four languages, indicates by the very fact of its existence what the mind of the Holy See is in this matter. The time will come no doubt when a complementary practical introduction to apostolic work will complete the object of this Institute.

It is desirable that centres of training in methods of apostolic work should also be opened for the teaching in theory and in practice of anything that can increase the power of penetration of the apostolate.

One must in fact learn how to carry out the apostolate and how to teach others to do so; which means knowing how to find apostles, how to convince them, and how to train them. This in turn means knowing how to organize and co-ordinate an apostolate on many fronts. This can only be done by attending courses in order to learn, from the inside, all about the main apostolic movements which the hierarchy considers to be necessary in any given area.

A great deal of energy has been given to studying theoretical problems: the same sort of effort is now needed in the practical sphere to find concrete ways and means. It is not enough to know a message and understand it and formulate it to oneself, one must learn by practice—for it is something to be learned—how to transmit the message naturally and supernaturally to others. Schools of this sort, either independent or attached to some existing institutions, would be of great help in the training of nuns. They should be for the apostolate what the *Lumen Vitae* centres are for catechesis. But, let us say it again, they must be based on *practical* training; the temptation to be content with lectures and theoretical instruction must be resisted.

Naturally enough one thinks about the part that could be played by teacher training colleges (*Ecoles Normales*) where tomorrow's teachers are trained. If it were possible to prepare a course of apostolic methodology there and grant a certificate, one would have established something resembling a training academy which would be an important step towards increasing the apostolic yield in our schools.

One would like to see programmes started to establish these centres of methodology and to study their syllabus and its application. Experience would show the best methods for this new sort of instruction rendered necessary today by the vast apostolic problems facing us and, in the case of religious, by the part they have to play in inspiring the laity with whom they come in contact.

Regrouping

The regrouping of dispersed forces is a potent means of increasing their efficacy. Unorganized and dissipated use of the personnel available is one of the main reasons for the loss of so much energy. The need for regrouping communities that are too small on their own is admitted: the Holy See is favourable to it as a matter of principle and makes provision for many different forms of it. One of these is federation, which has been introduced for enclosed nuns and which allows complete autonomy but makes provision for certain common services. Besides federations there are unions, which unite congregations of the same type. There is a whole range of possibilities combining autonomy and unity in various proportions.

There is also room for complete fusion either by two small congregations uniting to form one larger one, or by the absorption of a small congregation into a large one. There is no doubt that this sort of regrouping can appreciably speed up the desired reforms and permit adequate training. Each case is a special case and there is no question of studying all aspects of the matters here: all we wish to do is to note the place of regrouping in the general perspective of renewal: it is by no means a negligible place and the idea merits favourable consideration and careful study by all congregations with reduced numbers.

It is easy to see the benefits to be expected from such fusion; greater choice of personnel to fill important posts, much less need to 'double up' on duties, a freer positioning of forces, and the greater availability of property, real and otherwise, which can be useful in extending the field of activity.

A real love of souls combined with genuine detachment from self will lead the Superior General and her Council to forget themselves and their natural and understandable predilections and base their decisions on the needs of the Faith and the interests of God.

One must not wait passively until higher authority takes the initiative nor till things have gone so far that fusion is no longer possible. Let all Superiors General to whom this applies have the courage to take the first step, to map the course, and to plan for a union which would be for the good of all. Once they have created the right atmosphere and made the first approaches, the work of the ecclesiastical authorities is greatly simplified—they have only to sanction a union which has already taken place in spirit.

In cases where the grouping together of small communities is found to be impossible, it is desirable, as we have said, that they join forces to establish a novitiate common to several congregations (which will themselves remain independent) and to arrange for the second novitiate about which we have spoken; our congregations have everything to gain by getting away from isolationism and particularism. The habit is happily becoming commoner of arranging retreats and recollections for members of several congregations together. Experience shows that exchanges between congregations are a great stimulus and source of fruitfulness.

Regrouping is the practical way of allowing nuns to get the maximum benefit from good lecturers and preachers who are too few in relation to the number of religious communities to be able to meet all the demands on them as things are at present.

14

PROSPECTS FOR
THE FUTURE

IT remains for us at the end of these pages to look to the
future and to see what hope for re-christianization the
apostolic advancement of nuns holds out.

We can say that tomorrow's society will be what our
Christian families are. These Christian families themselves
will be the reflection of the nun who trained the wife and
mother of tomorrow to be a Christian woman, conscious
of her duties as an apostle.

An immense responsibility but also a vocation all the
more magnificent because its place is in the very heart of
natural and supernatural life.

In the Family

"Society will be reformed by woman, or it will not be
reformed at all," wrote Fr. Rijckmans.[1] A phrase of wide
significance.

It can be applied literally to Christian society, which will
be what the Christian woman of tomorrow makes it, for it
is she who builds, stone by stone, both the earthly city and
the city of God.

Archetype of the social cell, the family is also the first
cell of the Church. It is the first sanctuary, built of living
stones, where God establishes a dwelling.

[1] *L'aide des Laïcs au soin des âmes*, p. 90.

To build a family is to build the Church, to work, basically, for the salvation of the world.

The nun who has understood these pages will always see the family as the final objective of her activities. She will instinctively place the pupils she teaches or the sick confided to her care in their family context. Every nun being essentially an educator—whether she belongs to a teaching or nursing order—she will carry her teaching to its end, that is up to and including the family, whether it is a question of creating a Christian home, consolidating it or bringing it back to health. As an educator, she will carry out this function to its full extent in relation to lay-women whose full capacity for radiating Christianity she will bring out.

Usually a nun comes from a thoroughly Christian home. She should keep the picture of this home constantly before her eyes as an incentive to make Christ live in other homes. She must not regard the picture as a relic of the past but as something to be projected into the future in the service of others.

What a wonderful thing before God and man is a family which fully accepts the Kingship of Christ.

They pray together and their common prayer links souls together by ties stronger than blood.

They kneel side by side at Communion and allow Our Lord to transform each one of them into His own image as they nourish themselves on Him.

They work together in the same spirit of duty. The children, seeing Christianity lived by their parents in every aspect of life, acquire without realizing it the spirit of the apostolate and of devoton which is at the root of all generous vocations.

The Source of Vocations

This picture, albeit incomplete, of a Christian family is

kept by the religious in her heart so that she may give it to the world. Through the children she teaches or the sick she cares for she is working within the framework of the family, even though indirectly. Children, the sick, the aged, all open a door for her to their families: she can never forget it and she must exploit it to the full.

By her contribution to the christianization of families the religious is preparing the ground in which great vocations can germinate and mature, the good ground of the parable which receives the seed and yields a hundredfold harvest.

These will be vocations to the lay apostolate, to entering the religious life, and to the priesthood.

Lay Vocations

Lay vocations on the one hand prepare for, support and extend the action of the priest, and on the other christianize their own circles by the natural and supernatural power of radiating Christ.

Who can be blind to the immense field of action open to nuns trained for this work and called upon to arouse, organize and sustain lay-women who (let us say it again) without them would never be mobilized on a scale to meet the requirements.

Religious Vocations

Our Lord will not be outdone in generosity. He will respond to the generosity of active congregations by assuring them of the new life the need for which is now so urgently felt. They will be the first to benefit from the increase in vocations. The sight of their apostolic courage will be an inspiration and a great attraction for the young.

This is also valid for contemplative vocations which are vital to the Church to supply the high tension current feeding all apostolic efforts. Contemplatives have chosen silence and real separation from the world for love of God and for the salvation of the world. Active religious have chosen speech and the direct transmission of God, but the impulse of love is the same. The silence of one gives power to the words of the other; those on their knees give strength to those who must march. There are reckoned to be some 60,000 contemplatives in the world. In relation to the total of 1,000,000 or so women in religion altogether they can be regarded, as one writer said, as the 6 per cent. return on capital which God reserves to Himself.

Priestly Vocations

Finally, it is true for priestly vocations, the most exalted manifestation of God's predilection. Without the priesthood Christ's visible mediation would disappear from among us, vocations, both apostolic and contemplative, would fail for want of inspiration and support, sacramental life would wither. Without the priesthood there would be no Eucharist. Without the priesthood humanity would die of spiritual starvation.

All these graces come from God of course, but also through the co-operation of man. It is the home that gives man's first response to God.

When she consecrates her life to the young and the sick and through them to the salvation of the family, the religious places herself at the very heart of the religious and moral future of a country.

She holds the key of the Kingdom. The Church can say to her in the words of Scripture, "My fate is in your hands".

The Keynote is Joy

In furthering that advancement in the apostolate of which we have been speaking in these pages, the religious will not only render an invaluable service to the world, she will also discover the secret of a deep and integral religious maturity.

In agreeing to carry out her teaching role to its proper conclusion she will have to exercise to a greater extent the theological virtues of faith, hope and charity. Nothing will help her spiritual development more. The heart can only expand when the horizon widens and one can breathe deeply of invigorating air. A great joy will follow her acceptance, and a great hope will arise in the Church. Let her not be afraid!

When St. Peter was told to walk to Jesus on the waters, all went well so long as his eyes were fixed on those of the Master. It was only when he turned his eyes away to judge the changes of the wind that he became afraid and began to sink. And Our Lord said, "Why didst thou hesitate, man of little faith?"

This passage of the Gospel has a special meaning for the religious authorities called upon to promote the apostolic zeal of our active congregations. The Master speaks to them again today through those who speak in His name, "Sail across the water, pay no attention to contrary winds or the movements of the waves".

Our Lord will be at hand to steady their steps and to overcome the 'impossibilities' of mere human wisdom. He will be there to encourage them with His smile, with His fortifying grace, with His power which laughs at the world and Satan. He will put into their hands, insofar as their faith is alive and creative, the power of the Resurrection itself.

The holy women who approached the Saviour's tomb on Easter morning asked themselves how they were going to roll away the stone. But they started out without having found an answer to the problem, and the Lord solved it magnificently for them.

We have the right and the duty to count upon God's

grace since He does not ask the impossible and gives what He asks for. The essential is to start out, with faith.

It is said of Louis Blériot that on his first flight he placed in the cock-pit of his plane, directly in front of him, a small statue of Our Lady upon which there were inscribed these words: *"Regarde et prends ton vol"* : "Fix your gaze on me, and fly".

And it is with this message that we wish to close.

Let our nuns, too, fix their gaze on the Blessed Virgin. Let them accept courageously the necessary changes and sacrifices. Let them offer themselves to continue in the contemporary world the spiritual motherhood of our Lady under whose aegis the Vatican Council has so auspiciously begun its work of pastoral renewal in the Church of God.

The Voice
from
the Whirlwind

The Voice
from
the Whirlwind

The Problem of Evil and the Modern World

Stephen J. Vicchio

Christian Classics, Inc.
Post Office Box 30
Westminster, MD 21157
1989

First published 1989

Library of Congress Catalog Card Number: 89-61356
ISBN: 0-87061-162-3

Printed in the USA

Contents

The Voice
from
the Whirlwind

Introduction

> However much concerned I was with the problem of
> the misery of the world, I never let myself get lost in
> broodings over it; I always held firmly to the thought
> that each one of us can do a little to bring some
> portion of it to an end. Thus I came gradually to rest
> content in the knowledge that there is only one thing
> we can understand about the problem, and that is that
> each one of us has to go his own way, but as one who
> means to help to bring about deliverance.
>
> Albert Schweitzer,
> *Out of My Life and Thought*

This book is concerned with why the world is not such
an easy place in which to live. Human beings, as its
apparently most sentient creatures, live daily in a morally
ambiguous environment. Most of us experience
contentment, happiness, and even profound joy. But these
experiences are all too often interspersed or punctuated
with unwarranted suffering, excruciating pain, and sometimes irrational violence. Although human life may at times
seem like heaven on earth, it can also be more like scenes
from a Kafka novel or a scarred canvas of Edvard Munch.
This book is primarily concerned with the problem of
reconciling these two kinds of experiences with belief in a

God who is said to be all good, all knowing, and all powerful.

For readers looking for a simple answer to this question, you need read no further: none will be found here. In fact, much of this book is done in the spirit of what the Medieval churchmen called the *via negativa*. A good portion of this book is taken up with showing what I think is wrong with most of the traditional answers to the problem of evil. In the fourth and fifth chapters I try to make some sense out of what we can know about the problem.

Throughout the book, I continually refer back to three criteria for what I think would count as a good answer to the problem. It would probably be good to state them here, early on, so that you can begin to decide whether you agree with me. First, any serious philosophical or theological response to the problem of evil must be true to the tradition from which the problem originates. The problem of evil is a peculiarly Judeo-Christian problem because of the attributes of God in that tradition. Any answer that tries to dismantle the problem by changing the attributes of God is either engaging in a kind of theological shell game or has unwittingly absconded from the very tradition it is trying to save. Second, any answer to the problem of evil should be one that is logically consistent. It should be clear, concise, and internally coherent, looking more like Ockham's razor than a Rube Goldberg device. Third, a good answer to the problem of evil must take the individual sufferer seriously. In the history of western philosophy, it is rare to find a response to the problem of evil that meets this third condition. What seems vaguely plausible from the pulpit or philosophy lectern rarely passes the test of the everyday suffering of the reflective individual. When placed in the pressure cooker of real suffering, most answers to the problem of evil melt and stick to the bottom of the pot. Above all, what I try to do in this book is place any ostensible theological response to the problem within the context of these three criteria. I leave it to you to judge whether I have been fair in my assessments.

The principal dilemma in acknowledging the various kinds of help I have received in the writing of this book is that there is a real danger of leaving someone out. It would simply be within the bounds of common courtesy, however, to thank the following: John Titchener, Thomas Benson, Paul Holmer, Randolph Miller, William Jones, Dean McBride — all teachers from whom I have borrowed or stolen many things.

I must also acknowledge the friendship and advice from Sr. Virgina Geiger, Margaret Steinhagen, Maureen Robinson, Sr. Robin Stratton, Fr. Joseph Gallagher, J.J.C. Smart, Peter Coxon, D.W.D. Shaw, Kathleen Cahill, Julia Thorpe, Leon Wurmser, Albert Dreyfus, and Marguerite and Umberto Villa Santa, who all contributed in material and other ways to the completion of this manuscript.

I must also give a special acknowledgement to my supervisor at St. Andrews University, George Hall, who read this work when it was still a Ph.D. dissertation. Finally, I must reserve a special kind of gratitude to my parents. Through their individual and collective lives, I have learned many profound lessons about taking the sufferer seriously. It is to them this work is dedicated.

Stephen J. Vicchio
Baltimore, MD
Winter 1989

I.
The Varieties of Theodicy

I stand near Sorberanes Creek, on the knoll over the sea, west of the road. I remember this is the place where Arthur Barclay, a priest in revolt, proposed three questions to himself: First, is there a God, and of what nature? Second, whether there is anything after we die but worm's meat? Third, how should men live? Large time-worn questions no doubt; yet he touched his answers, they are not unattainable; But presently lost them again to the glimmer of insanity.

Robinson Jeffers

I want to be there when everyone suddenly knows what it has all been for. All the religions of the world are built on this longing.

Fyodor Dostoyevski

In *Escape from Evil* Ernest Becker observes that "what man really fears is not so much extinction, but extinction with insignificance."[1] This holds true, I think, not only for the fear of death, but also for human responses to suffering. Death, disease, and natural calamity are brutal reminders of how little control human beings have over the world. Although we often imagine ourselves immortal and impregnable, the cruel facts suggest that our physical existence is limited more or less to the Biblical seventy years. The presence of evil in the world is a terrible burden that demands a response. Thus, when we are confronted with it, "our lives become meditations on evil and a planned venture for controlling and forestalling it"[2] and when that is not possible, for making meaning out of it.

People in all cultures face problems that cannot be resolved with the use of either common sense or scientific expertise. To be human is to suffer and die, and to have one's aspirations and desires subject to failure and frustration. The transitoriness of life and the uncertainty that plagues human ventures confront all people with situations in which, as sociologist Thomas O'Dea has remarked, "Human knowledge and social forms display a total-insufficiency for providing either means of solution or mechanisms for adjustment and acceptance."[3]

It is clear that religious systems provide, or attempt to provide, the context in which the existence of evil, both moral and natural, is integrated into the larger picture of reality. Religious systems, if they are to be lasting, must have something to say in what Paul Tillich has called the "boundary situations," when our capacity to say yes to life is most threatened. And that "something to say," I think, must consist of at least two important elements. First, religious responses to suffering must have an existential element. Indeed, the experience of suffering is first an existential one, an experience to be lived through. It is usually only later that it becomes an intellectual one to be explained. Clifford Geertz has come very close to making this same point when he writes: "The problem of suffering is, paradoxically, not how to avoid suffering, but how to make physical pain, personal loss, worldly defeat, or the helpless contemplation of others' agony something bearable, supportable, something, as we say, sufferable."[4]

Religious responses to suffering must also exhibit another important dimension: they must deal with evil in a coherent and intellectually honest way. Religious forms of life must not only help the suffering, they must also help the sufferer give meaning to the experience.

The various ways in which the religions of the world have attempted to give meaning to suffering might be called the study of comparative theodicy, from the Greek *theos* and *dike*.[5]

Peter Berger, in his book *The Sacred Canopy*, has suggested a typology that may be helpful in differentiating among various styles of theodicy making.[6] The general vocabulary and system of categorization employed by Berger provide a rather neat hermeneutical tool for interpreting the various responses to the problem of suffering.

Berger begins by defining a theodicy as "the part of a belief system that serves to maintain religious meaning in spite of evil and suffering."[7] He very carefully points out that theodicies are by no means employed to make people happy or even necessarily to show them that they may be redeemed. "Indeed," he suggests, "some theodicies carry no promise of redemption at all except for the redeeming assurance of meaning itself."[8] Nevertheless, Berger maintains

> It is possible to analyze historical types of theodicy on a continuum of rationality-irrationality. Each type represents a particular posture, in theory and practice, vis a vis the anomic phenomena to be legitimized or nomized. [9]

According to Berger's scheme, theodicies can vary in type, from an irrational identification of the self with society, as in primitive societies or the covenantal relationship of the ancient Hebrews, to the most rational type of theodicy found in Indian religious forms of life — the "karma-samsara complex." Berger suggests that Vendantic Hinduism and Hinayana Buddhism should be considered the most rational form of religious responses to suffering because these traditions are governed by a series of rewards and punishments in successive incarnations according to the degree to which one has been faithful to the tasks imposed by former lives.

Somewhere between these poles of the rational and the irrational, Berger finds several intermediate forms that include "this worldly" messianic-millenarianism (Jewish Sabbatianism and cargo cults), "other worldly" compensations (exemplified by the elaborate mortuary customs of the ancient Egyptians and Chinese), and dualism, in which all evil is ascribed to some ultimate reality other than God. Berger cites Manicheanism, Mithraism, and Zoroastrianism as examples of this third type, though the view taken by John Stuart Mill in his *Three Essays on Religion* can also be seen to fall quite naturally in this category.[10]

Into this intermediary cluster of theodicies Berger also places types more common in the West, such as those found in the Book of Job, as well as those stressing the redemptive power of the suffering of an incarnate deity, as in most forms of Christianity.

There is much to recommend Berger's work. Though he has clearly based his study on the pioneering work of Max Weber, Berger considerably broadens the discussion by including an analysis of a number of traditions to which Weber has paid little or no attention.

The Sacred Canopy is an ingenious and comprehensive piece of scholarship,[11] but it is not without its conceptual problems. The major flaw in Berger's method of categorization seems to rest on his rather dubious assumption that one can clearly assess the comparative degree of rationality in each of the various theodicies. One would be hard pressed, I think, to come up with clear, sufficient, or even necessary conditions for calling something "rational." Alvin Plantinga points to this very sticky problem:

> Now an apparently straightforward and promising way to approach this question would be to take a definition of rationality and see whether belief in God conforms to it. The chief difficulty with this appealing approach, however, is that no such definition of rationality seems to be available. If there were such a definition, it would set out some conditions for a belief's being rationally acceptable, conditions that are severally necessary and jointly sufficient. That is each of the conditions would have to be met by a belief that is rationally acceptable; and if a belief met all these conditions, then it would follow that it is rationally acceptable. But it is monumentally difficult to find any non-trivial necessary condition at all.[12]

Nowhere in Berger's chapter on theodicy does he entertain the question of what the proper definition of the "rational" might be. Indeed, it may well be the case that by examining various religious forms of life from the outside and measuring them by use of a rather murky and implicit notion of rationality, Berger has missed the particular coherence of each, in the same way that Americans sit bored and confused at a cricket match until suddenly they understand the rules of the game.

In some ways Berger succumbs to the same intellectual elitism that was present among anthropologists and sociologists of religion at the end of the last century and the beginning of this one. Individuals like E.B. Taylor, Max Muller, and Sir James Frazer all began with certain assumptions about the level of "rationality" among "primitive" peoples and then developed elaborate theories about the origin of religion based on the study of the "pre-logical" frames of mind of these people.[13]

In some of the literature from this period, "primitives" were not labelled "irrational" or "pre-logical" but rather "unscientific." Perhaps one of the clearest examples is to be found in E.E. Evans-Pritchard's *Witchcraft, Oracles and Magic Among the Azandes.*[14] Evans-Pritchard suggests that the African Azandes believe that some of the members of their tribe are witches capable of various occult influences on the tribe and its individual members. Given this belief, the sorts of activities the Azandes engage in with reference to these particular members of society are quite understandable; indeed, quite logical. But Evans-Pritchard indicates that although the Azandes are logical, they reason unscientifically, for they don't check their truth claim in a scientific way.

Peter Winch, in an influential article, "Understanding a Primitive Society,"[15] objects to Evans-Pritchard's point of view. Winch suggests that hidden in Evans-Pritchard's perspective is the assumption that the Azandes' view of witches must be seen as a possible scientific claim. Winch also objects to the notion that "being in accord with objective reality" can only be understood within the context of scientific reasoning. Indeed, he suggests that Evans-Pritchard's notion of "reality" and "being in accord with reality" are really shorthand ways of saying "that which is verified by science," and it is only within this context that Evans-Pritchard's comments are intelligible. Winch remarks:

> Evans-Pritchard is trying to work with a conception of reality which is not determined by its actual use in language. He wants something against which that use itself can be appraised. But this is not possible; and no more possible in the case of scientific discourse than it is in any other. We may ask whether a particular scientific hypothesis agrees with reality and test this observation and experiment. Given the experimental methods, and the established use of the theoretical terms entering into the hypothesis, then the question whether it holds or not is settled by reference to something independent of what I, or anybody else, care to think. But the general nature of the data revealed by the experiment can only be specified in terms of criteria built into the methods of the experiment employed and these, in turn, make sense only to someone who is conversant with the kind of scientific activity within which they are employed.[16]

Winch continues by arguing that there are other contexts where "reality" and "being in accordance with reality" are also meaningful, and these may have little or nothing to do with scientific views of the world. Winch is not proposing a new kind of relativism here.[17] What he is doing, I think, is sketching out in a more definitive way some remarks made by Ludwig Wittgenstein regarding the realization that we cannot determine the meaning of a concept disconnected from the use that particular concept is given in a certain

language game.[18] Whether and how language is meaningful
can only be determined from inside that particular language
game. Berger attempts to stand outside the traditions he has
analyzed, as if he could be an ideal observer in these
matters, and has tried to discern which theodicies are the
most rational and which the least. But in taking this kind of
approach, he fails to take into account the contexts in which
each of these particular answers to the problem of evil is
placed. Winch sums all this up quite well:

> The check of the independently real is not peculiar to
> science. The trouble is that the fascination science has
> had on us makes it easy for us to adopt its scientific
> form as a paradigm against which to measure the
> intellectual respectability of other modes of discourse.
> Consider what God says to Job out of the whirlwind:
> "Who is it that darkens counsel by words without
> knowledge? ...Where wast thou when I laid the
> foundations of the earth? Declare if thou hast
> understanding. Who hath laid the measures thereof?
> Tell me, if thou knowest? Or who hath stretched the
> line upon it? ...Shall he that contendeth with the
> Almighty instruct him? He that reproveth God, let him
> answer it." Job is taken to task for having gone astray
> by having lost sight that Job has made any sort of
> theoretical mistake, which could be put right, perhaps
> by means of experiment. God's reality is certainly
> independent of what any man may care to think, but
> what reality amounts to can be seen from the religious
> tradition in which the concept of God is used, and this
> use is very unlike the use of scientific concepts, say
> of theoretical entities. The point is that it is within the
> religions of language that the conception of God's
> reality has its place, though, I repeat, this does not
> mean that it is at the mercy of what anyone cares, to

say; if this were so, God would have no reality.[19]

Wittgenstein makes several remarks about Sir James Frazer's *The Golden Bough,* which amount to the same thing. One of Wittgenstein's major objections to Frazer's work is that the latter makes the beliefs of the peoples he studied look like mistakes or false hypotheses. Wittgenstein puts the matter this way:

> Frazer says it is very difficult to discover the error in magic and this is why it persists for so long — because, for example, a ceremony which is supposed to bring rain is sure to appear effective sooner or later. But then it is queer that people do not notice sooner that it does not rain sooner or later.[20]

Berger, in judging these various theodicies according to their degree of rationality, seems to commit the same kind of error. He has some notion of what it would mean to think or act rationally, and he applies this notion quite unreflectively to the traditions in question.

Another important problem with Berger's typology is that it ignores several of the most important responses to the problem of evil to be found in the Western tradition. Little or no mention is made, for example, of retributive justice, the idea that evil is God's tool for punishing the guilty and warning those who are tempted to sin. He also makes little reference to the contrast theodicy, the notion of evil as privation, the free will defense, or various teleological theodicies that have been offered in the Judeo-Christian tradition.[21]

A third and perhaps most important flaw in the method of categorization found in *The Sacred Canopy* is that Berger gives very little attention to the various presupposed ontological underpinnings of each of the traditions' answers. If more time had been spent in looking for what Wittgenstein called "the hidden grammar" of each of these faiths, a very different typology might have resulted.[22]

I would suggest that we might place in one group Brahmanic Hinduism and Theravadan Buddhism. Although Berger is correct to point out that these two religions share the important notions of karmic rebirth and transmigration, he says nothing about an even more crucial metaphysical presupposition that they have in common: the individual personality or soul is obliterated when one reaches nirvana or moksha. For both the Vedantic Hindus, as well as the small raft Buddhists, it is that instant when it will become clear that the phenomenal world, as well as the individual personalities in that world, were fundamentally illusory. Reality for both of these religious traditions collapses into a kind of ultimate monism. As John Bowker suggests:

> The individual who has an adequate grasp of Brahman
> will find that suffering falls away in insignificance.
> Since everything that happens is a manifestation of
> Brahman, it follows that true understanding only
> arises when the accidents of time and space are
> penetrated and seen to reveal Brahman. Brahman
> pervades all things without being exhausted in any
> one of them; which means that suffering and sorrow
> cannot be the final truth of existence.[23]

The *Katha Upanishad* makes the same point about the fundamental monistic character of ultimate reality:

> As fire, which is one, entering this world becomes
> varied in shape according to the object it burns, so
> also the one Self within all beings becomes varied
> according to whatever it enters and also exists outside

them all. As air which is one, entering this world becomes varied in shape according to whatever it enters and also exists outside them all. Just as the sun, the eye of the whole world, is not defiled by the external faults seen by the eye, even so the one within all beings is not tainted by the sorrow of the world, as he is outside the world. [24]

Bowker expresses the relationship between this ultimate monism and the problem of evil quite well:

Suffering occurs as a problem for Hinduism only when duality in the universe, the contrast between pain and pleasure, is seen as an abiding truth about existence. Then, inevitably, the individual self spends itself in trying to find a solid and secure home in objects that prove ephemeral and transitory. Suffering ceases to be a problem when it is realized that the individual self can transcend occurrences of suffering by finding its identity in Brahman. [25]

If the phenomenal world and all that it contains is an illusion, [26] then there can be no individual personalities. Of course, where there are no individual personalities, there can be no individual suffering. Where there is no individual suffering, there can be no problem of evil. The problem of evil is not solved in these monistic faiths, it is dissolved. [27] Thus we might call this first type of response to the problem of evil the "religions of dissolution."

A second cluster of theodical responses might be labelled "religions of solution," for rather than dissolving the problem of evil, they attempt to solve it. Religions of solution are most dramatically exemplified in the ancient Persian faith, Zoroastrianism. Religions of solution can be easily identified by two necessary conditions that taken together become sufficient. First, they are committed to an ethical dualism. In these faiths human beings are thought to be endowed with freedom of choice and thus have the power to choose between two real alternatives, good and evil. The other necessary condition is that there is at least one other eternal principle in the universe besides God.[28]

Geddes MacGregor points quite clearly to the gist of these two necessary conditions when he writes:

> God, though indeed as benevolent as the devout say, eternally faces conditions not of his own making. As in the *Timaeus*, God is the divine artist ever working on a recalcitrant and eternal stuff. Upon this inchoate stuff, he is imposing order. The stuff is 'evil' in the sense that it can be an obstacle that the divine goodness has to overcome and subdue. All the chance and arbitrariness commonly associated with the naturalist view of the universe are in it. It is physic (nature). To say that nature is cruel is to read into it human interpretation. Nature is simply indifferent; but that seems as cruel as when sailors talk of the 'cruel seas,' which of course are cruel only in the sense in which a brick wall seems cruel when I run into it. In this view even God finds nature like that, and in our struggle with nature we find ourselves co-workers with God. The scope of this struggle is presumably far greater than ours and his power and skill far beyond ours in coping with nature, but the task is essentially the same.[29]

An example of the religions of solution where this competing force takes on the character of a personified deity can be seen in Zoroastrianism, where there is a belief in two eternally opposed deities. One, Ahura Mazda, is totally good, while his counterpart, Angra Mainya, is thought to be absolutely evil. The radical conflict between these two gods is evident throughout the nature of the universe and human life. In the Zoroastrian view the conflict between good and evil on earth is an indication of the fundamental cleavage at the very root of being. The daily conflicts between good and evil in our characters and lives is only a manifestation of the universal war between these two eternal powers.

Zoroaster, the prophet, puts it this way:

> I will speak out concerning the two spirits of whom, at the beginning of existence, the holier spoke to him who is evil: "Neither our thoughts, nor our teachings, nor our wills, nor our choices, nor our words, nor our deeds, nor our convictions, nor yet our souls agree."[30]

And again, Zoroaster points to this fundamental split in reality:

> In the beginning the two spirits who are well endowed twins were known as the one good and the other evil in thought, word and deed. Between them, the wise chose the good, not so the fools. And when these spirits met they established in the beginning life and death that in the end the evil should meet with the worst existence, but the just with the best mind. Of these two spirits, he who was of the lie chose to do the worst things; but the most holy spirit, clothed in heaven chose righteousness (or truth)...as did all those who sought with zeal to do the pleasure of the wise lord by doing good works.[31]

In these two passages Zoroaster implies the metaphysical dualism that underlies his faith by suggesting that Ahura Mazda and Angra Mainya are twins, identical, eternal, and presumably equal in power and strength. This ontological dualism is the key to understanding the duality of human life, and thus brings us to the Zoroastrian answer to the problem of evil. Evil has its source in the bad god, Angra Mainya. Human beings, through their volitions, can choose to ally themselves with "he who was the lie" or with the good god, Ahura Mazda. The problem of evil is solved, not dissolved, by turning toward the good god. This position is logically sound, indeed perhaps irrefutable, because the Zoroastrian ethical dualism corresponds rather neatly to their basic metaphysical presuppositions about ultimate reality.

A somewhat milder form of the religions of solution, and one that is much closer to the quotation by MacGregor, can be found in sections 30a to 48 of Plato's *Timaeus*, as well as Book X of the *Laws* and Book II of *The Republic*, where Plato devises the following dialogue:

> Goodness, then, is not responsible for everything, but only for what is as it should be. It is not responsible for evil.
>
> I agree.
>
> It follows, then, that the divine being, being good, is not, as most people say, responsible for everything that happens to mankind, but only for a small part; for the good things in human life are fewer than the evil, and, whereas the good must be ascribed to heaven only, we must look elsewhere for the causes of evil.[32]

In Book X of the *Laws* and section 29 of the *Timaeus*, Plato makes similar references to the notion that god is not the cause of evil.[33] If we look carefully at these texts, it becomes clear that Plato has made this assertion for two reasons. First, the souls, although created by the demiurge, once made, have autonomy and thus the power to initiate evil.[34] And second, unlike the god of the Old Testament, Plato's god does not create *ex nihilo*. Instead, he brings order to a pre-existent chaos.[35] And some of that chaotic stuff remains eternally resistant to change.

Plato answers the question of the origin of evil by suggesting that it ostensibly could have two sources: the souls or the unordered chaos. His position can be seen as a religion of solution, for it meets our two necessary conditions cited above. First, like Zoroastrianism, Plato's position includes a commitment to ethical dualism. And second, his position presupposes a metaphysical notion that there are two eternal substances, the demiurge and at least some elements of the preexistent chaos that predate the existence of the souls.

Various forms of the finite deity doctrine popular among modern Western thinkers might also serve as good illustrations of the religions of solution. The first appearance of the finite deity doctrine in modern philosophy can probably be attributed to David Hume.[36] Since the late eighteenth century, this position has not suffered from a lack of supporters. John Stuart Mill, E.S. Brightman, H.G. Wells, John McTaggert, Albert Einstein, F.H. Ross, and Peter Bertocci have all at one time or another identified themselves as believers in a finite god doctrine.[37]

John Hick rightly points out, however, that there are really two different but related finite deity doctrines.[38] He refers to the first as "external dualism" and suggests that his position is best characterized by John Stuart Mill. The other position he calls "internal dualism." It can most clearly be seen in the work of E.S. Brightman. The difference between the two would seem to reside in the fact that in the external variety the limitations on God's power come from the outside (as in Plato), while in the internal version the limitations can be seen as coming from a given to be found in the nature of the deity itself.

Brightman refers to this limitation in God's nature when he says:

> The Given consists of the eternal uncreated laws of reason and also equally eternal and uncreated processes of nonrational consciousness which exhibit all the ultimate qualities of sense objects (qualia), disorderly impulses and desires, and experiences of pain and suffering, the forms of space and time, and whatever in God is the source of sure evil.[39]

Although this passage suffers from a crusty opaqueness, the point to be made, I think, is that evil, whatever it may be, is not something willed by God but rather an eternal part of his nature. Hick seems to take the same view of the passage in question when he comments:

> He (Brightman) unites under one label of deity two diametrically opposed realities, namely the perfect and holy will of God and the evil nature that opposes that will.[40]

If Hick is correct about Brightman, and I believe that he is, it should be clear that Brightman's internal dualism meets our conditions for a religion of solution. Whether it possesses the same internal consistency as Zoroastrianism or the metaphysics of Plato is, of course, another question.[41]

John Stuart Mill's external dualism, on the other hand,

seems quite logically consistent. In discussing the source of natural evil, Mill suggests the following possibilities:

> There is no ground in Natural Theology for attributing intelligence or personality to the obstacles which partially thwart what seems the purpose of the Creator. The limitations of His power more probably result either from the quality of the material — the substance and forces of which the universe is composed not admitting of any arrangements by which His purposes could be more completely fulfilled; or else the purpose might have been more fully attained, but the Creator did not know how to do it; creative skill, wondrous as it is, was not sufficiently perfect to accomplish his purpose more thoroughly.[42]

Either scenario painted by Mill in the passage above would be sufficient to produce a solution to the problem of evil. If God is not all powerful, there is nothing he can do about certain aspects of the make-up of the universe. If he is not all knowing, he might be quite capable of doing something about natural evil, but not at all sure how to go about it.[43] Another possibility that Mill does not entertain is that God is omniscient in all matters except with respect to the existence of evil.

Mill does not explicitly state his position on the origin of moral evil, but Hick suggests the following reading of Mill:

> Presumably, he (Mill) would have to hold that matter and energy together with the laws of their operation, as to the circumstances that God had not created and with which he had to contend, somehow necessitates man's moral frailty and failure. He would presumably argue that such a psycho-physical creature as man,

organic to his material environment and subjected by
it to a multitude of strains and stresses, must
inevitably become self-centered, and that from this
circumstance have developed the moral ills of human
life.[44]

Hick makes an additional observation about Mill's
position:

Nor does this seem to be an unreasonable speculation.
This form of dualism is capable of being expanded
into a comprehensive and consistent position, and one
that has the great merit that it solves the problem of
evil.[45]

McTaggert seems to follow the same basic line of
thought on this issue:

It seems to me that when believers in God save his
goodness by saying that he is really not omnipotent,
they are taking the best course open to them, since
both the personality and goodness of God present
much fewer difficulties if he is not conceived as
omnipotent.[46]

A little further on, McTaggert concludes:

It is not a very cheerful creed, unless it can be
supplemented by some other dogmas which can assure
us of God's eventual victory. But it is less depressing
and less revolting than the belief that the destinies of
the universe are at the mercy of a being who, with the
resource of omnipotence at his disposal, decided to
make a universe no better than this.[47]

Another modern version of the limited God theory, and therefore a religion of solution as well, can be found in the doctrine known as panentheism, or what is more often called the process view of God. This position has its historical roots in Plato's *Timaeus*, and they extend up through Socinus in the sixteenth century to modern thinkers such as Alfred North Whitehead and Charles Hartshorne.[48]

Although Whitehead's contributions to process thought are immense, in many ways his thought is much more difficult and inaccessible than Hartshorne's.[49] Like the rest of Whitehead's philosophy, his thoughts on God are frequently expressed in highly technical language. Often, they are not fully worked out. For these reasons, it seems best to comment on Hartshorne's version of process theology rather than on that of Whitehead.

For Charles Hartshorne, God is as good as it is now possible for him to be. God is, in effect, developing, improving, and has not yet managed to eliminate evil, if such an elimination can ever occur. As human beings struggle against both natural and moral evils, we can assist God in his own development.[50] In Hartshorne's version of the finite deity theory, God cannot know the future, hence he can never be absolutely certain about how the details of history will work out. According to Hartshorne, this fact is due both to the randomness of nature and because he has endowed human beings with freedom of choice. Because God is situated in time and was not the creator of the universe, he suffers and rejoices with human beings, but he cannot control them. God and humans may enter into a partnership, aligned in a project to reduce or eradicate evil, but God cannot force them to assist him. Any conforming to God's will comes about through persuasion, not coercion.

Hartshorne believed that his model will solve the

problem of evil for the theist. If God is subject to the limitations of the basic structure of a universe he did not create, then the laws of that universe are eternal necessities, not matters that could be altered by divine decision. Thus, Hartshorne has a ready-made answer to the problem of evil. The process answer to the problem of moral evil can best be understood by looking at the following quotation from David Ray Griffen, a member of the youngest generation of process thinkers:

> God does not refrain from controlling creatures simply because it is better for God to use persuasion, but because it is necessarily the case God cannot completely control his creatures.[51]

Since omnipotence, for the process thinkers, does not involve omnicausality, there is no logical commitment to God being the active cause of all moral evil existing in the world. When moral evil is introduced into the world it is through human, not divine, initiative. In the process view, mankind is responsible for the ubiquitous moral evil in the world, not God. And since God suffers as the world suffers, the pain we inflict on our fellow humans is ultimately inflicted on God as well.

But the problem of theodicy is not completely solved by making room for human freedom and responsibility. God suffers with us not only in our sinfulness but also in our finitude. Much of the pain and suffering in the world is not the result of human volitions. It comes as the result of the structure of the universe being the way it is. Nothing immoral is involved when man A and man B are both interested in the same beautiful, intelligent woman. But at least one of those suitors is doomed to failure and its accompanying pain. In process thought, God did not make the universe the way it is, a universe that appears to be necessary[52] and in which fulfillment of competing interests is incompossible, that is, possible separately, but not possible at the same time.

Thus, we see that Hartshorne's position on the problem of evil is quite similar to the external forms of the limited God theory.[53] There is something about the universe as a whole that makes it impossible for God to be all powerful. Also, in Hartshorne's view God is not omniscient with respect to the future. Jim Garrison, much influenced by the process perspectives of Hartshorne and J.A.T. Robinson, shows clearly that the degree of human freedom suggested in the process point of view makes the traditional conception of God's omniscience inappropriate. He makes a similar remark about God's omnipotence:

> Thirdly, while God does commit what we define as intrinsic evil as well as what we define as intrinsic good, God as infinitely free and powerful (though not omnipotent), can use those intrinsically evil and good acts committed by God and humanity alike and good acts committed by God and humanity alike instrumentally for a higher purpose.[54]

The process perspective qualifies as a religion of solution in regard to the problem of evil for two reasons. First, human beings possess freedom of choice, and the universe is such that they have both the possibility of good and evil moral choices. Second, the process thinkers of the Griffen-Hartshorne persuasion are committed to an ontological presupposition about the preexistence of the universe that makes God less than omnipotent with respect to the given structure of the universe.

Once again, as we have seen in the other forms of the

religions of solution, the process answer to the problem of evil can be said to be both logically sound and providing a clear and cogent way out of the dilemma.[55]

If we now return to Berger's *The Sacred Canopy*, and even grant him the use of his rather fuzzy notion of what "rationality" amounts to, it is clear that his claim that Plato's view (and we might add the other limited God theories as well) belongs somewhere in the middle of his continuum of theodicies is mistaken. These dualistic answers to the problem of evil are quite logically sound by any ordinary usage of that term. Moreover, Hinduism and Buddhism, the religions of dissolution, are also highly rational responses to the problem of evil, but not for the reasons Berger would have us believe. Berger believes the Indian traditions should be counted as the most rational by virtue of their rather neat balance of debits and credits with respect to the law of karmic rebirth.[56] But if that were the real reason for making this judgment, then certainly the retributive justice of the Deuteronomic code should be counted as just as reasonable. The same notion of "reaping what one sows" is at the heart of the biblical idea of *lex talionis*.[57]

It seems to me that a better reason for considering the religions of dissolution to be rationally cogent responses to the problem of evil is that by suggesting that individual life[58] ultimately ends in a reabsorption back into the One, they have developed a metaphysical monism that matches quite well with their ultimate ethical monism. (If we have no individual personalities, we can have no individual evil, either moral or natural.)

But although both the religions of dissolution and the religions of solution are logically consistent, they are still not without their difficulties. The monistic religions of dissolution are unsatisfactory for at least three important reasons. First, there seems to be no real connection between the karmic law and their ultimate end point, nirvana. If it is the case that at bottom level all of reality is of the same substance, why is so much emphasis placed on this series of rebirths that seems to "pretend" that individual personalities and the phenomenal world are real? Second, this position quite simply seems to offend common sense. The phenomenal world may ultimately be an illusion, but it certainly appears to be real.[59]

One might raise an important objection at this point and suggest that I have failed to understand the particular religious forms of life of the Brahmanic Hindus and Theravadan Buddhists. But I could reply by pointing out that the adherents of these traditions also seem to take the phenomenal world, as well as the individual personalities in it, a good deal more seriously than they might if they were really to hold fast to the basic metaphysical assumption on which these faiths are based.

Another way of looking at this second objection is to see that in a real way ultimate monism tends to offend what Wittgenstein would call the "certainties" of life, the foundational principles we hold to be true, without evidence, but on which all our other judgments about the world are based. Many of the comments Wittgenstein makes in *On Certainty* in regard to skepticism could also be made with reference to any view that the phenomenal world is an illusion.[60]

A third problem with regard to the monistic responses to the problem of evil is that they seem to leave a very important question unanswered. We may at once admit that the phenomenal world, and thus evil, is an illusion, but we still seem to be left with the inexplicable problem of viewing it as if it were real, and that seems to present the monistic faiths with another kind of problem of evil to replace the old one.

The religions of solution, it seems to me, also suffer from some intractable flaws, though I have no real quarrel with the logical cogency of these views. The real problem I have with dualistic answers to the problem of evil is that they seem to know so much more about what God is like and what he is doing than I do. Although they each represent a logically possible state of affairs, I see no clear reason for picking any one view over the other, for example, that God is omnipotent, omnibenevolent, but terribly absent-minded.[61]

Another more fundamental problem I have with the religions of solution is that none of the limited God theories seems to be describing a God that is even remotely similar to the God of Abraham, Isaac, and Jacob, or even the God of the philosophers for that matter.[62] The process theodicy is tempting, but their God hardly seems like the one to whom I might be interested in praying. Indeed, what does prayer amount to for Hartshorne's God? It strikes me as more like a committee meeting where God takes suggestions for how the universe might be straightened out.

I am also not at all sure precisely what it means in the process view to say that God is "in time." At the very least it can be said that Hartshorne's view of time suffers from a lack of development. I am reminded of Unamuno's remark, "Time is the most terrible of mysteries, the father of them all."[63]

It should be kept in mind, however, that the criticisms of both the religions of solution and the religions of dissolution that I have outlined do not lie on purely rational grounds. In the case of the latter, they lodge more in the realization that absolute monism seems counter-intuitive, even, it seems to me, to those engaged in that particular form of life. I have criticized the religions of solution not so much for logical shortcomings, but rather as failing to present a picture of God that is sufficiently enough like the orthodox Christian conception that he is worthy of worship.

John Hick seems to raise a similar point about John Stuart Mill, in particular, and the religions of solution in general, when he writes:

> From the point of view of Christian theology, however, a dualism of this kind is unacceptable for the simple but sufficient reason that it contradicts the Christian conception of God. Mill's type of dualism does not face, and therefore does not solve, the problem of evil as it arises for a religion that understands and worships God as that than which nothing more perfect can be conceived. Dualism avoids the problem— but only at the cost of rejecting one of the most fundamental items of the Christian faith, belief in the reality of the infinite and eternal God, who is the sole creator of heaven and earth and of all things visible and invisible. The belief is so deeply rooted in the Bible, in Christian worship, and in Christian theology of all schools that it cannot be abandoned without vitally affecting the nature of Christianity itself. The absolute monotheism of the Judeo-Christian faith is not, so to say, negotiable; it can be accepted or rejected, but it cannot be amended into something radically different. This then is the basic and insuperable Christian objection to dualism; not that it is intrinscially impossible or unattractive, but simply that it is excluded by the Christian understanding of God and can have no place in Christian theodicy.[64]

The rejection of the religions of solution as orthodox responses leads us to the realization of a third cluster of religious perspectives on the problem of evil. This group might most aptly be labelled the "religions of paradox" and includes Judaism, Christianity, and Islam, though, as will soon become apparent, I will confine my comments almost exclusively to the first two of these traditions. This third type is called religions of paradox because each embodies a distinctive combination of monism and dualism, or of an ethical dualism set within the framework of an ultimate ontological monism.[65]

These faiths seem committed on the one hand to the metaphysical presuppositions that God is all good, all knowing, and all powerful, as well as being creator of the universe in some *ex nihilo* way, while at the same time holding that both moral and natural evils exist. Another way then to state the necessary conditions of the religions of paradox is to say that they are simultaneously committed to the truth of two propositions: first, belief in a God who possesses the omni-attributes,[66] and second, belief in an ethical dualism that sharply distinguishes good from evil.

Unlike the limited God theories of the religions of solution, in this third type we have a conception that most closely resembles the classical conception of God in the Judeo-Christian tradition. In being faithful to that conception of God, however, we seem to leave no room for the existence of evil. At first blush this seems to be an insoluble problem, and thus we see the appropriateness of the name, the religions of paradox.

Brand Blanshard seems to put the conundrum quite succinctly:

> The question at issue is a straightforward one: how
> are the actual amount and distribution of evil to be

> reconciled with the government of the world by a God
> who is in our sense good?[67]

After raising this question, Blanshard goes on to answer
it:

> So straightforward a question deserves a straight-
> forward answer, and it seems to me that only one such
> answer makes sense, namely that the two cannot be
> reconciled.[68]

But before we too quickly concede victory to Blanshard,
we must recognize he makes no mention of God's power
and intelligence. This immediately allows us an escape
hatch through which the problem raised by Blanshard might
be solved — the limited God theories of the religions of
solution. One could readily end the argument with
Blanshard by simply suggesting, with John Stuart Mill or
David Hume, that God is either not omnipotent, not
omniscient, or perhaps both.

David Hume puts the dilemma for the religions of
paradox in perhaps sharper detail:

> Is He (God) willing to prevent evil, but not able?
> Then He is impotent. Is He able but not willing? Then
> He is malevolent. Is He both able and willing?
> Whence then is evil?[69]

Augustine raises the problem in almost identical terms:

> Whence, then, is evil, since God who is good made all
> things good? It was the greater and supreme good who
> made these lesser goods, but Creator and created are
> alike good. Whence then comes evil? Could he who

was omnipotent be unable to change matter wholly so
that no evil might remain in it? Indeed, why did he
choose to make anything of it and not by the same
omnipotence cause it wholly not to be?[70]

The problem seems no less acute for Thomas Aquinas:

It seems that God does not exist; because if one of
two contraries be infinite, the other would be
altogether destroyed. But the name God means that He
is infinite goodness. If therefore, God existed, there
would be no evil discoverable; but there is evil in the
world, therefore, God does not exist.[71]

Among contemporary philosophers, the problem of evil
for the religions of paradox is given almost identical
formulation. Consider this comment from J.L. Mackie:

The problem of evil...is a logical problem, the
problem of clarifying and reconciling a number of
beliefs. ... In its simplest form the problem is this:
God is omnipotent, God is wholly good; and yet evil
exists.[72]

These words of H.J. McCloskey seem quite familiar:

The problem of evil is a very simple problem to state.
There is evil in the world; yet the world is said to be
the creation of a good and omnipotent God. How is
this possible? Surely a good omnipotent God would
have made a world which is free of evil of any kind.[73]

All of these comments seem to agree on three points
that produce the horns of the dilemma for the religions of
paradox. All five thinkers, in their own particular language,
express the belief that evil exists, while at the same time

ascribing to a cluster of metaphysical presuppositions that include God's omnipotence and omnibenevolence.

But if we look carefully, we can see that in each of the five examples something crucial is missing. In order to see more clearly what has been left out, consider the example of Crunch, the greatest rugby player in the world. In fact, he plays with such power and grace that Crunch is seen by most experts to be invincible. In addition to Crunch's skill and love for the game, he is also known as the most sportsmanlike and gentlemanly character on the pitch. The only problem with poor Crunch is that no one has sent him a copy of this season's venue, and since he lives far outside of town, he has no idea when the games are being played.

The purpose of this example is to show that it is logically possible for a god to exist who has essentially the same problem as poor Crunch. This deity could be all good and all powerful, but completely unaware that evil exists. Evil could be a peculiar blindspot or lacuna in this god's knowledge. He would be perfectly happy to do something about evil; indeed, because of his goodness he would be compelled to do something about it, but he just doesn't know that it is there. This position calls for no limitation in God's power. He would not only be quite willing, he would also be quite able to fix the evil, if only he knew about it.

What we have in this answer, of course, is another version of the limited God theories. And, indeed, if this is a logically possible state of affairs, and I think it is, it is a quite simple solution to the problem as stated by the five representatives above. It might be added that this solution suffers from the same flaw Hick has pointed out in regard to the other limited God theories. But it does, nevertheless, meet the formulations of all five inquisitors head on. As the problem is stated by all five, however, it does not involve the religions of paradox.

It should be clear that what is needed to create the dilemma as it exists for the religions of paradox is the notion that God is also omniscient.[74] Thus, the proper formulation of the problem of evil for the religions of paradox would look something like the following: God is by definition omnipotent, omniscient, and omnibenevolent, yet evil exists in the world in both moral and natural forms.[75]

In the next chapter we will examine these terms very carefully. A careful analysis will be made of omnipotence, omniscience, omnibenevolence, moral evil, and natural evil in an attempt at getting clear on what these terms mean and how they are related. Additionally, we will discuss whether the problem of theodicy, as formulated by the religions of paradox, really involves one in a formal, logical contradiction.

Notes

1. Ernest Becker, *Escape From Evil* (New York: Free Press, 1975) p. 2.

2. Ibid., p. 3.

3. Thomas O'Dea, *Introduction to the Sociology of Religion* (Englewood Cliffs, N.J.: Prentice Hall, 1966) p. 63.

4. Clifford Geertz, *The Interpretation of Culture* (New York: Basic Books, 1973) p. 171.

5. Leibniz appears to have been the first to use the word
    theodicy in its distinctive modern sense. In a letter
    written in 1697 he spoke of employing the term as the
    title of an impending work, and in 1710 the work duly
    appeared. The complete title was *Essais de Theodicees
    sur la Bonte de Dieu, la liberté de l'homme et l'origine
    du Mal.* Since that time the word theodicy has been in
    common use in French, German, and English.

6. Peter Berger, *The Sacred Canopy* (New York: Anchor
    Books, 1969).

7. Ibid., pp. 53-54.

8. Ibid., p. 60.

9. Ibid. Berger's analysis leans very heavily on an earlier
    model offered by Max Weber in "Das Problem der
    Theodizee," in *Wirtschaft und Gesellschaft* (Tubingen,
    1947).

10. Important distinctions among these thinkers will be
    discussed later in the chapter.

11. Other classifications of types of theodicies can be
    found in Brian Hebblethwaite's *Evil, Suffering and
    Religion* (London: Sheldon Press, 1979) pp. 14-39;
    Charles Barrett's *Understanding the Christian Faith*
    (Englewood Cliffs, N.J.: Prentice Hall, 1980) pp. 230-
    260; and John Hick's *Evil and the God of Love* (London:
    Macmillan, 1977) parts II and III.

12. Alvin Plantinga, "Rationality and Religious Belief,"
    Nous, vol. 15 (1981) pp. 41-42.

13. Cf. E.B. Tylor, *Primitive Cultures* (London: Longmans,
    1891); Max Muller, *Lectures on the Origin and Growth
    of Religion* (London: Longmans, 1878); and Sir James

Frazer, *The Golden Bough* (London: Longmans, 1914).

14. E.E. Evans-Pritchard, *Witchcraft, Oracles and Magic Among the Azandes* (Oxford: Clarendon Press, third edition, 1976).

15. Peter Winch, "Understanding a Primitive Society," *American Philosophical Quarterly*, vol. 1 (1964) pp. 307-324.

16. Ibid., p. 309.

17. A more detailed discussion as to why I think Winch and Wittgenstein are not epistemological relativists is carried out in chapter 5.

18. Ludwig Wittgenstein, *Remarks on Frazer's The Golden Bough*, edited by Rush Rhees (London: Cambridge University Press, 1979).

19. Ibid., pp. 308-309.

20. Ibid., p. 2.

21. This same point might be made regarding the other traditions Berger mentions as well. In the Hebraic tradition, for example, one can identify at least the following traditions: the *yetzer ha ra* or evil imagination tradition, the richly mythological response of the Kabbalists, the fall narrative in Genesis 3, and the resurrection response in Daniel 12. I suspect the same kind of variety is to be found in other traditions.

22. Ludwig Wittgenstein, *The Philosophical Investigations* (Oxford: Basil Blackwell, 1953) section 373.

23. John Bowker, *The Problems of Suffering in the Religions*

of the World (London: Cambridge University Press, 1970) p. 212.

24. "Katha Upanishad", in *The Principle Upanishads*, trans. Sri Purchit Swami and W.B. Yeats (London: Faber and Faber, 1937).

25. John Bowker, *Problems of Suffering*, p. 215. Both Hinduism and Buddhism also have a number of alternative explanations for suffering. Theravadan Buddhism, for example, postulates the four noble truths as the *sine qua non* of the problem of evil. The various sects of Mahayana Buddhism and sectarian Hinduism have also developed highly mythologized responses to the problem of suffering, sometimes quite different from the traditional monistic answers offered by the religions of solution.

26. A rather beautiful Hindu account of the illusory character of the world of the senses can be seen in the Indian tale of Vishnu and Narda. Lord Vishnu grants the wish of Narda that he be shown the secret of maya (the illusory nature of the phenomenal world.) But before revealing the secret Vishnu requests that Narda bring him a drink of water. The disciple goes to a nearby village, seeking to fulfill the Lord's request. While in the village, however, he quickly falls in love, eventually marries, raises children. Several more years pass. Finally, one day a severe flood carries away his wife and children. Grief stricken, Narda collapses into the darkest despair. He lapses into unconsciousness, but when he awakens he hears the comforting voice of Vishnu. "Where is the water you have gone to fetch me? I have been waiting here for more than a half an hour." Heinrich Zimmer, *Myths and Symbols in Indian Art and Civilization* (New York: Harper Torchbooks, 1961) pp. 32-34.

27. A curious echoing of this monistic position can be found in Mary Baker Eddy's *Christian Science*, where the reality of the phenomenal world is upheld, while the reality of natural evil is not. More sophisticated versions of western monism can be found in the writings of Spinoza and Nicholas Berdyaev.

28. I have used the phrase "at least one other eternal principle" here for it is logically possible that there could be more than two gods who were exactly equal in power and intelligence. The most important aspect of this second necessary condition is that at least two of these eternal principles cannot overcome each other.

29. Geddes MacGregor, *Philosophical Issues in Religious Thought* (Boston: Houghton Mifflin, 1973) p. 149.

30. R.C. Zaehner, *The Teachings of the Magi: A Compendium of Zoroastrian Beliefs* (London, 1956) Yasna xiv. 2.

31. Ibid., Yasna xxx. 3-6.

32. Plato, *The Republic*, F.M. Cornford, translator, Book II, 379 (London: Oxford University Press, 1970) p. 71.

33. Plato, *The Timaeus and Critias*, A.E. Taylor, translator, (London: Methuen and Co., 1929) pp. 26-27; *Laws*, T.J. Saunders, translator (London: Penguin Books, 1970) pp. 437ff.

34. Plato, *Timaeus*, 39e to 42, pp. 36-40.

35. Ibid., 47-48, pp. 45-47.

36. David Hume, *Dialogues Concerning Natural Religion* (New York: Hafner Publishing Co., 1959), particularly

sections xi and xii.

37. J.S. Mill, *Three Essays on Religion* (London: Longmans Green, 1885); E.S. Brightman, *A Philosophy of Religion* (Englewood Cliffs, N.J.: Prentice Hall, 1940); H.G. Wells, *God, the Invisible King* (London, 1936); John McTaggert, *Some Dogmas of Religion* (London: Edward Arnold, 1906); Albert Einstein, *Out of My Later Years* (New York, 1950); F.H. Ross, *Personalism and the Problem of Evil* (New Haven: Yale University Press, 1940); Peter Bertocci, *Introduction to the Philosophy of Religion* (New York: Prentice Hall, 1951).

38 Hick, *Evil and the God of Love*, pp 31-39.

39. Brightman, *Philosophy of Religion*, p. 337.

40. Hick, *Evil and the God of Love*, p. 39.

41. Peter Coxon, Lecturer in Hebrew and Old Testament at the University of St. Andrews, has suggested that this view of God may be quite like that expressed in some of the earliest portions of the Old Testament. Carl Jung expresses a similar point of view in his *Answer to Job*, translated by R.F. Hull (Princeton: Princeton University Press, 1973).

42. Mill, *Three Essays on Religion*, pp. 176-177.

43. Some of the lesser known versions of external dualism include Christian Ehrenfels' *Cosmology*, translated by Mildred Focht (New York: Comet Press, 1948); Edwin Lewis, *The Creation and the Adversary* (New York: Abingdon and Cokesbury, 1948). Also, a new version of the external limited God theory has appeared recently in a very popular book in both Great Britain and America entitled *When Bad Things Happen to*

Good People, by Harold Kushner (London: Pan Books, 1982). Kushner's position very much resembles Mill's.

44. Hick, *Evil and the God of Love*, pp. 34-35.

45. Ibid., p. 34.

46. McTaggert, *Some Dogmas of Religion*, p. 243.

47. Ibid., p. 244.

48. Geddes MacGregor suggests some affinities between Whitehead and Brightman, *Philosophical Issues in Religious Thought*, p.149. Hick makes a similar judgment in *Evil and the God of Love*, p. 36.

49. There are some important differences between Whitehead and Hartshorne that should not go unmentioned. Whitehead employs an empirical method. His metaphysical point of view is arrived at through seeking to identify, by empirical means, those elements that are necessary to all experience as human bodies. Hartshorne seems much more committed to using *a priori* reasoning to reach his conclusions.

50. Charles Hartshorne, *The Divine Relativity* (New Haven: Yale University Press, 1948) pp. 134ff.

51. David Ray Griffen, *God, Power and Evil* (Philadelphia: Westminster Press, 1976) p. 276.

52. This is another important place where Whitehead and Hartshorne disagree. Whitehead argues that the ultimate metaphysical principles on which the universe operates were initially established by divine fiat. Hartshorne and Griffen suggest that these laws of the universe are necessities.

53. In the preface to *God, Power and Evil* Griffen writes, "In John Hick's *Evil and the God of Love* the

Whiteheadean position is not even mentioned except for the false suggestion that it is essentially the same position as E.S. Brightman's." Ironically, in the remainder of the book Griffen never returns to the task of showing why we should not view the two positions as versions of the same point of view.

54. Jim Garrison, *The Darkness of God: Theology After Hiroshima* (London: SCM, 1982) p. 52.

55. For more on process thought, as well as on process theodicies, see the following: Delwin Brown, *Process Philosophy and Christian Thought* (New York, 1971); John Cobb, *A Christian Natural Theology* (Philadelphia: Westminster Press, 1965); Charles Hartshorne, *The Divine Relativity* (New Haven: Yale University Press, 1948); and *A Natural Theology for Our Time* (Lasalle: Open Court Press, 1973).

56. In a real way Berger confuses two separate theodicies with a single one. Monism and karmic rebirth are logically independent notions that need not be found together.

57. For good examples of the notion of retributive justice among the ancient Hebrews, see Deut. 11: 13-21; chap. 28; Lev. chaps. 26-28 and Num. 12: 1-15.

58. I have used the expression "individual life" here rather than soul because there is a fundamental difference in the Indian traditions on this point. The Buddhist notion of skandas is more like David Hume's idea of the self as a bundle of perceptions than it is like the Christian or even Hindu notion of the soul.

59. This discussion is quite like the Buddhist story where the young student asks his teacher what the holy man would do, given the world is an illusion, if he were

about to be attacked by an illusory tiger. The monk
responded, "I would climb an illusory tree."

60. Ludwig Wittgenstein, *On Certainty* (Oxford: Basil
    Blackwell, 1977).

61. This view, or something quite like it, is suggested in
    James Branch Cabell's novel, *Jurgen* (London, 1919),
    particularly chapter 49.

62. Geddes MacGregor suggests in *Philosophical Issues
    in Religious Thought* that because "Brightman and
    other exponents of the view have wished to exhibit it
    as compatible with traditional Christian theism, they
    have tried to minimize its dualistic aspects." p. 149.

63. For more on puzzlements about time, see Book XI of
    Augustine's *Confessions* and Ronald Suter's
    "Augustine on Time With Some Criticisms From
    Wittgenstein," *Revue Internationale de Philosophiae*,
    vol. 16 (1962) pp. 319-322.

64. Hick, *Evil and the God of Love*, p. 35.

65. John Hick, in his article "The Problem of Evil" in *The
    Encyclopedia of Philosophy*, edited by Paul Edwards
    (New York: Macmillan, 1967) suggests that this
    combination of monism and dualism exemplified in
    Judaism and Christianity represents "the main
    contribution of western thought to the subject."
    vol. III, p. 136.

66. It is not clear when these omni-attributes first began
    to be used in reference to God.

67. Brand Blanshard, *Reason and Belief* (New Haven:
    Yale University Press, 1975) p. 546.

68. Ibid., p. 538.

69. David Hume, *Dialogues Concerning Natural Religion,* p. 178.

70. Augustine, *The Confessions and Enchiridion,* translated and edited by A.C. Autler (Philadelphia: Westminster Press, 1955) chapter V. A very similar phrasing of the problem can also be found in Book XI of *The City of God.*

71. Thomas Aquinas, *Summa Theologica,* I ques., 2 ans. in A.C. Pegis, *The Basic Writings of Thomas Aquinas* (New York: Macmillan, 1945)

72. J.L. Mackie, "Evil and Omnipotence," *Mind* (April 1955) p. 209.

73. H.J. McCloskey, "God and Evil," *The Philosophical Quarterly,* vol. 10, no. 39 (April 1960) p. 97.

74. In J.L. Mackie's recent book, *The Miracle of Theism* (Oxford: Oxford University Press, 1982) he came to realize the importance of including the attribute omniscience in any discussion of the problem of evil. He amends his version of the problem to read: "According to traditional theism, there is a god who is both omnipotent (and omniscient) and wholly good, and yet there is evil in the world. How can this be?" p. 150.

75. For the most entertaining formulation of the problem of evil, see Tertullian's *Adversus Marcionem,* ii, 5-6.

II.
A Clarification of Terms

I know that one has no right to say things like that. I know. Man is too small, too humble and inconsiderable to seek to understand the mysterious ways of God. But what can I do? I'm not a sage, one of the elect, nor a saint. I'm just an ordinary creature of flesh and blood. I've got eyes too, and I can see what they are doing here (in a concentration camp). Where is the divine mercy? Where is God? How can I believe, how can anyone believe, in this merciful God?

Elie Wiesel

Apparently with no surprise
To any happy flower
The frost beheads it at its play—
In accidental power—
The blonde assassin passes on—
The sun proceeds unmoved
To measure off another day
For an approving God.

Emily Dickinson

In the first chapter it was suggested that the dilemma of the problem of evil for the adherents to the religions of paradox can be expressed in the following group of propositions, all of which are held to be true:

God is
    omnipotent
    omniscient
    omnibenevolent
    and evil exists (in both moral and natural forms).

Judaism, Christianity, and Islam are called religions of paradox with respect to the problem of evil because they seem to involve one in an apparent contradiction or paradox about the origin and existence of evil. Another way to put this idea of apparent paradox, as I suggested in the first chapter, is to say that Judaism, Christianity, and Islam seem committed to an ethical dualism set within the framework of an ultimate metaphysical monism.

In this present chapter, we have two distinct but related aims: First, to get clear, as best we can, on the meaning of various terms used in formulating the apparent paradox (omnipotence, omniscience, omnibenevolence, moral evil, and natural evil). And second, to discuss briefly whether the use of these terms in formulating the problem of evil as framed by the religions of paradox involves one in a logical contradiction. The first of these tasks shall take some time, so we must keep the second task in the back of our minds.

In the religions of paradox, God is endowed with characteristics that radically distinguish him from all other forms of being. He is thought to be wholly limitless throughout the whole range of His existence. Unlike the God of Hegel, or that of the process theologians, the God of traditional theism does not need the world as a sphere for His self-development. God's essence is identical with His existence, as Thomas Aquinas held when he suggested that the most appropriate name for God is that disclosed to Moses, according to the Vulgate text of Exodus: qui est, He who is.[1]

If the God of classical theism is thus infinite, he must possess all properties in a mode that is free of limitation. The properties we shall now be concerned with are omnipotence, omniscience, and omnibenevolence. In this discussion we will make no attempt to prove the existence of the God of classical theism. Rather, we shall show that given the existence of God as He is traditionally conceived, the following definitions of His attributes would seem to be the most logically compelling and consistent.

OMNIPOTENCE

Let us begin this discussion by considering for a moment this note from Frederick Ferre's *Basic Modern Philosophy of Religion:*

> Different theistic traditions interpret this term differently. Some insist that "omnipotence" must involve the possibility of God's doing literally anything — whether it be "making a stone so heavy that He cannot move it", or "killing Himself", or other standard conundrums and dilemmas — while others interpret "omnipotence" as the possibility of doing anything logically possible or anything worthwhile.[2]

Ferre rightly suggests that when we say that God is omnipotent, philosophers, as well as the common man, may mean by that term one of two things.[3] Either (a) an omnipotent being is one who can do absolutely anything, or (b) an omnipotent being is one who can[4] do anything that is logically possible. For reasons that will become apparent later, we must also offer a third formulation of God's omnipotence: (c) an omnipotent being is one who can do anything that is logically possible and is consistent with his other attributes.[5] Let us proceed by first examining formulation (a).

The notion that an omnipotent being is one who can do absolutely anything is at least as old as the philosophy of René Descartes. His belief in this interpretation of omnipotence is actually connected to and dependent upon another Cartesian notion that the truths of logic and mathematics are made true by virtue of the will of God. In a letter to his friend, Father Mersenne, on April 15, 1630, Descartes makes this point very clearly:

> The mathematical truths which you call eternal have been laid down by God and depend on Him entirely no less than the rest of His creatures. Indeed, to say that these truths are independent of God is to talk of Him as if He were Jupiter or Saturn and to subject Him to the Styx and the Fates. Please do not hesitate and to assert and proclaim everywhere that God who has laid down these laws in nature just as a king lays down laws in his kingdom.... If God established these truths He could change them as a king changes his laws.[6]

A short time later, Descartes sent Mersenne a second letter on this same point:

> As for the eternal truths, I say once more that they are true or possible only because He knows them as true or possible. They are not known as true by God in any way which would imply that they are true independently of Him.... In God willing and knowing are the same thing, in such a way that by the very fact of willing something He knows it, and it is only for this reason that such a thing is true.[7]

It should be clear that Descartes thought the laws of

logic and simple mathematics were necessary truths, and so he counted them among his small bag of simple and distinct ideas. But although he thought they were necessary truths, he did not think that they were what Geach has suggested Descartes would call "necessarily necessary truths."[8]

Descartes makes a reference that amounts to this same point in a third correspondence with Mersenne:

> It would seem rightly so if the question was about something that exists or if I was setting up something immutable whose immutability did not depend on God.... I do not think that the essence of things and the mathematical truths which can be known of them are independent of God, but I think they are immutable and eternal because God so willed and so disposed.[9]

And again in a fourth letter:

> It was free and indifferent for God to make it not be true that the three angles of a triangle were equal to two right angles, or in general that contradictories could not be true together. Even if God had willed that some truths should be necessary, this does not mean that He willed them necessarily or to be necessitated to will them.[10]

In Descartes' point of view, God freely establishes the laws of logic in much the same way He has established the laws of nature. Although once he establishes the laws of logic, they are then necessary, it does not mean that he willed them necessarily.

Still, Geach has his problems with Descartes' interpretation of the concept of omnipotence:

Descartes' motive for believing in absolute omnipotence was not contemptible; it seems to him that otherwise God would be subject to the inexorable laws of logic as Jove was to the decrees of the fates. The nature of logical truth is a very difficult problem, which I cannot discuss here. The easy conventionalist line, that our arbitrary way of using words is what makes logical truths, seems to me untenable, for reasons that Quine among others has clearly spelled out. If I could follow Quine further in regarding logical laws as natural laws of very great generality; laws revisable in principle, though most unlikely to be revised in major theoretical reconstruction, then perhaps after all some rehabilitation of Descartes on this topic might be possible. But in the end I have to say that as we cannot say how a supralogical God would act or how He could communicate anything to us by way of revelation, so I end as I began: a Christian need not and cannot believe in absolute omnipotence.[11]

The problems with absolute omnipotence to which Geach gives hints are difficulties noticed by Thomas Aquinas as well. This is precisely what led him to conclude, in the *Summa Theologica*, "Nothing which implies contradiction falls under the omnipotence of God."[12] In a following passage he gives a more detailed account of his reasons for holding this point of view:

Whatever implies being and nonbeing simultaneously is incompatible with the absolute possibility which falls under divine omnipotence. Such a contradiction is not subject to it, not from any impotence in God, but because it simply does not have the nature of being feasible or possible. Whatever, then, does not involve a contradiction is in the realm of the possible

with respect to which God is omnipotent. Whatever
involves a contradiction is not within the scope of
omnipotence because it cannot qualify for possibility.
Better, however, to say that it cannot be done, rather
than God cannot do it.[13]

The central flaw with the notion of absolute omnipotence, as Thomas and others have pointed out, is that it
inevitably commits one to a host of rather bizarre contradictions. For example, if God can do absolutely anything
could He make His left hand so heavy that His right hand
could not pick it up? Notice that if we give an affirmative
answer then after God made His hand sufficiently heavy
there would be something He could not do, namely, pick it
up. Hence, He would not be omnipotent. On the other hand
(no pun intended) if we answer no, God could not make His
left hand so heavy that His right hand could not pick it up;
then immediately there would be something that He could
not do, and consequently He would not be omnipotent. We
could ask similar questions about whether God could create
a thing that was simultaneously itself and not itself, but I
think the point about the inherent weakness in the concept
of absolute omnipotence has already been made.[14]

Let us now examine the second formulation: (b) an
omnipotent being is one who can do anything that is logically possible.[15] Our first task is to get clear on what we
mean by the "logically possible" and the "logically impossible." Aristotle suggests a very simple and cogent pair of
definitions: the logically possible is found when it is not
necessary that its contrary is false. The logically impossible, he suggests, is to be found when its contrary is necessarily true.[16]

To cite an example from the realm of simple mathemat-
ics, it is impossible that 2 plus 2 $\approx$ 4, because its contrary 2

plus 2 = 4 is necessarily true. If I define a triangle as "a three-sided figure whose angles are equal to 180 degrees," it makes no sense to say that God could create a four-sided triangle. This is no limit on God's power. It is a limit in our ability to find meaning in a meaningless sentence. This, of course, applies to the physical world, as well as the world of mathematics and geometry. To ask if God could slide two beads up the rod of an abacus, then two more beads up the same rod, and without creating another bead, produce five beads at the top of the rod, is to ask God to do something that is logically impossible. This is not a limitation on God's power. It is a limitation on our ability to make sense of what it means to say that two beads and two beads equal five beads. To expect God to do the logically impossible is to expect God to do what cannot be done by any being. Indeed as Thomas Aquinas suggests, if the sentence is logically contradictory, there is nothing to be done.

The importance of the above examples should be clear. If the elements of a concept are contradictory (for example, a round-square), then the concept can never be substantiated. It is, in effect, a pseudo-concept that refers to nothing at all. When we become critical of God because He cannot make a round square or a married bachelor, we are chiding Him for not doing something when there is nothing there to be done. When there are things to be done, an omnipotent being can do them, provided they are not contrary to His nature. Thus, the proper definition of an omnipotent being is one who can do anything that is logically possible.

C.S. Lewis points unambiguously to this same notion of omnipotence and suggests that the first alternative, formulation (a), involves meaningless combinations of words that do not suddenly acquire meaning simply by virtue of the fact that we preface them with the words "God can."[17] Thus

Lewis concludes:

> His omnipotence means the power to do all that is
> intrinsically possible, not to do the intrinsically
> impossible. You may attribute miracle to Him, but not
> nonsense. There is no limit to His power. If you
> choose to say "God can give a creature free will and at
> the same time withhold free will from it," you have
> not succeeded in saying anything about God.... It
> remains true that all things are possible with God: the
> intrinsic impossibilities are not things but nonentities.
> It is no more possible for God than for His weakest
> creatures to carry out both of two mutually exclusive
> alternatives; not because His power meets the obsta-
> cle, but because nonsense remains nonsense even
> when we talk it about God.[18]

Still, with all this said in its favor, (b) is, nevertheless,
an inadequate definition of the concept of God's omnipotence, though it might now do quite satisfactorily as a formulation for any being *x* who is said to be omnipotent. In
order to see why this is the case consider whether an
omnipotent being could commit suicide or sin. Surely, there
is nothing amiss in saying that both of these actions are
logically possible. There is nothing logically incoherent or
contradictory in saying that an omnipotent being could, for
example, tell lies or take his own life.

But if we make the stipulations that this omnipotent
being is also eternal and omnibenevolent, then it follows
that it would be logically impossible for him to tell lies or
think himself out of existence. God cannot sin because it
contradicts his omnibenevolence. He cannot commit suicide
because he is eternal. Thus, the proper formulation of God's
omnipotence is (c) an omnipotent being is one who can do

anything that is logically possible and is consistent with his other attributes.

OMNISCIENCE

Once again, perhaps it is best to begin with a helpful note from Ferre's *Basic Modern Philosophy of Religion*:

> As in the case of omnipotence, different theistic traditions interpret omniscience differently. Some allege that the term involves God's knowledge of even future events, in which case the traditional problem arises in explaining how future human actions can be considered genuinely free and undetermined (if they are so considered) and at the same time known with perfect assurance by God. Others maintain that "omniscience" will be satisfied as long as God knows all there is to know; and if future indeterminate actions are not yet, it is no imperfection of knowledge not to know what is not yet knowable. Omniscience on this view would be complete knowledge on all actualities and all possibilities and the distinction between them.[19]

In this passage, Ferre makes an important distinction between two different views of omniscience: (c) for every proposition p, if p is true, an omniscient being knows that p, but only in so far as p is determined now by what is already the case. And (d) for every p, if p is true, an omniscient being knows that p. We will also examine the less convincing formulations of God's omniscience: (a) for every p, an omniscient being knows that p, and (b) for every p, if p, an omniscient being timelessly knows that p.

Version (a) can be seen to be an inadequate definition of omniscience, for if we were to take a proposition like

"Vicchio is a member of the Royal family." and substitute it for *p*, we would have the following: "Vicchio is a member of the Royal family, and an omniscient being knows that Vicchio is a member of the Royal family." But clearly this will not do. Any satisfactory formulation of omniscience must take into account the distinction between knowing something false and knowing that something is false. An omniscient being does not know false propositions but he should know when propositions are false. We must there- fore amend our definition to take this into account. Formulation (b) corrects the simple error of (a).

Formulation (b) of omniscience can be easily under- stood by looking at the following remark from Boethius:

> Since God lives in the eternal present, His knowledge transcends all movement of time and abides in the simplicity of its immediate present. It encompasses the infinite sweep of past and future, and regards all things in its simple comprehension as if they were now taking place. Thus, if you think of the foreknowl- edge by which God distinguishes all things, you will rightly consider it to be not a foreknowledge of future events, but knowledge of a never changing present.[20]

Thomas Aquinas was also a staunch proponent of this view. In the *Summa Theologica*, he writes:

> Things reduced to acts in time, are known to us, suc- cessively in time but by God are known in eternity, which is above time.[21]

St. Anselm, addressing God in the *Proslogion*, develops a similar perspective:

> You were not, then, yesterday, nor will you be tomor-
> row, but yesterday and today and tomorrow you are,
> or rather, neither yesterday nor today nor tomorrow
> you are, but simply, you are, outside of time.[22]

What these three figures have in common is that they all
view the concept of omniscience as the ability to know the
past, the present, and the future, simultaneously, as if happening all at once. From this it follows, all three would
argue, that it is terribly misleading to talk about God knowing the future. For in reality, his knowledge of the future is
a knowledge of an eternal present, for He is outside or
above time.

The major difficulty with this view of omniscience can
be found in the last sentence of the above paragraph. It is
very difficult, if not impossible, to figure out what it
means. It is not at all obvious what it means to say that any
being is "above" or "outside" time. But whatever those
expressions may mean, if they mean anything at all, they
are surely not intended to suggest that God does not know
every action that is performed by all His creatures. But it is
also clear that His creatures perform actions that by their
very nature could not be performed simultaneously. For
example, I may open the window in my study in the morning to allow some air in the room, and later, after the sun
has set, I may close it because I then have a chill. But I
cannot perform both of these actions at the same time. I
must perform the first action before I can perform the second. It makes no sense to talk about closing an already
closed window. In order for God to be omniscient, he must
know the sequence. It makes no sense to say that God
"sees" me opening and closing the window simultaneously.

A similar kind of difficulty with formulation (b) of
God's omniscience is pointed to by Anthony Kenny:

> The whole concept of a timeless eternity, the whole of
> which is simultaneous with every part of time, seems
> to be radically incoherent. For simultaneity as ordi-
> narily understood is a transitive relation. If A happens
> at the same time as B, and B happens at the same time
> as C, then A happens at the same time as C. If the
> BBC programme and the ITV programme both start
> when Big Ben strikes ten, then they both start at the
> same time. But on St. Thomas' view, my typing of this
> paper is simultaneous with the whole of eternity.
> Therefore, while I type these few words, Nero fiddles
> heartlessly on.[23]

Elsewhere, Kenny suggests that this same kind of difficulty with formulation (b) has been expressed by Suarez in
De Scientia Dei Futurorum Contingentium. Suarez analyzes
the passages mentioned above from Anselm, Thomas
Aquinas, and Boethius, and adds a fourth by Augustine. He
goes on to suggest that although all four thinkers believe
that presence or coexistence is both a necessary and sufficient condition for explaining God's knowledge of future
events, they are mistaken. Kenny explains:

> Suarez insists that though temporal things coexist
> with the whole of eternity, because eternity coexists
> with all times, past, present and future, yet these dif-
> ferent times do not coexist with each other. God coex-
> ists now with one thing and now with another thing,
> without changing in Himself: like a tree standing
> motionless in a river which is successively present or
> adjacent to different masses of flowing water. The
> only sense in which things are eternally present to
> God is as objects of His knowledge. The statement of
> their presence, therefore, is a restatement of God's
> knowledge of the future, and not an explanation of it.[24]

In contemporary philosophical circles, two other major objections to formulation (b) of God's omniscience have been raised. The first of these might be called the argument from indexicals. It can be found in the work of A.N. Prior and is also followed by Norman Kretzmann and Nicholas Wolterstorff.[25] In short, Prior suggests that if one is committed to the view that God's knowledge is timeless, then an undesired by-product of this position is that God's knowledge would be restricted to those truths that do not change over time. Prior puts the problem this way:

> I want to argue against this view [formulation (b)] on the ground that its final effect is to restrict what God knows to those truths, if any, which are themselves timeless. For example, God could not, on the view I am considering, know that the 1960 final examinations at Manchester are now over. For this is not something that he or anyone else could know timelessly. It's true now but it wasn't true a year ago (I write this on 29 August 1960) and so far as I can see all that can be said on this subject timelessly is that the finishing date of the 1960 final examination is an earlier one than the 29th August, and this is not the thing we know when we know that those examinations are over. I cannot think of any better way of showing this than one I've used before, namely the argument that what we know when we know that the 1960 final examinations are over can't be just a timeless relation between dates, because this isn't the thing we are pleased about when we're pleased the examinations are over.[26]

Nelson Pike successfully challenges Prior's position by arguing that he has not identified a range of facts a timeless being could not know. Rather, he has merely pointed out certain linguistic forms a timeless being could not use when talking about his knowledge.[27] Indeed, Pike points out that the fact reported in an expression like "It is raining in St. Andrews on 17 April 1984" could be expressed by God in sentences that do not employ temporal indexicals. H.N. Castenada and Richard Swinburne[28] employ similar strategies in answering Kretzmann's version of the indexical argument against formulation (b) of God's omniscience. Swinburne writes:

> A knows on 2 October the proposition "It is now 2 October." Surely B on 3 October can know that A knew what he did on 2 October. How can B report his knowledge: By words such as "I know that A knew yesterday that it was then 2 October." How can we report B's knowledge: As follows: B knew on 3 October that on the previous day A knew that it was then 2 October. Hence...B knows on 3 October what A knew on 2 October, although B will use different words to express the same knowledge.[29]

Castenada points to a similar resolution:

> If a sentence of the form "x knows that y knows that _____" formulates a true statement, the person x knows the statement formulated by the clause filling in the blank.[30]

What Pike, Swinburne, and Castenada all point to is the realization that if you know that Washington, D.C. is in the United States, and I know that you know that Washington, D.C. is in the United States, then it is clear that I know the same fact that you know. Castenada and Swinburne suggest that Kretzmann's dilemma is really a pseudo-problem, the result of Kretzmann not noticing how words like "now" and "current" function in certain types of discourse. Once one gets clear about the logic of these quasi-indicators, the problem suggested by Kretzmann and Prior disappears.

A more telling criticism of formulation (b) of God's omniscience has been suggested by William Kneale in his "Time and Eternity in Theology."[31] In that article Kneale attacks the notion of God's knowledge being timeless because he (Kneale)

> can attach no meaning to the word "life" unless I am allowed to suppose that what has life acts...life must at least involve some incidents in time and if, like Boethius, we suppose the life in question to be intelligent then it must involve also awareness of the passage of time.[32]

This same argument is ratified and embellished by J.R. Lucas in his *A Treatise on Time and Space* and by Richard Swinburne in *The Coherence of Theism*.[33]

The thrust of this final criticism of God's timeless omniscience is that if one believes that God is outside time, as Boethius and Thomas Aquinas have suggested, then one must deny in effect that God is a person. Lucas' suggestion for resolving this dilemma is to argue that since minds are necessarily in time but only contingently in space, it is reasonable to suppose that everything that exists is present to God spacelessly, but not timelessly.[34] I think Lucas' suggestion is a sound one, but enough has been said already, I think, to cast serious doubts on formulation (b) of God's omniscience. We shall now turn to formulation (c). For every p, if p is true, an omniscient being knows that p, but only insofar as p is determined now by what is already the case.

Friedrich Schleiermacher is a good example of this third account of omniscience. In his book, *The Christian Faith*, Schleiermacher describes God's foreknowledge in the following way:

> In the same way we estimate the intimacy of relationships between two persons by the foreknowledge one has of the actions of the other, without supposing that in either case the one or the other's freedom has thereby been endangered, so even divine knowledge cannot endanger freedom.[35]

What Schleiermacher seems to be suggesting is that God's foreknowledge, and therefore His omniscience with respect to the future, is based on God knowing His creatures so well that He has a very good idea of what each of them is to do in the future. The analogy often used in connection with this view of omniscience is that God sits in a high tower and, because of his knowledge of the predilections and characters of each of His creatures, He can establish what they will do next.

In order to better understand formulation (c) of God's omniscience, consider the following example. Two brothers exit from two different pubs at closing time on a particular evening. Both are quite intoxicated. Both have had drinking problems for a number of years. Both stumble out of their respective pubs and enter their automobiles, one headed north, the other south. Proponents of formulation (c) of divine omniscience suggest that God's knowledge of future contingent events would be analogous to a third brother who sits high in a flat in the middle of the same street on which the two brothers travel. Because he knows his brothers so well, the third can glance in both directions, spot both cars, and "know" that the brothers will come to an abrupt crash in the middle of the street. He does not cause the crash to occur, but he knows his siblings so well he realizes that the accident is inevitable. The believers in formulation (c) of God's omniscience might then go on to add that God not only knows about the future actions of the two brothers, but he also possesses this kind of knowledge about all the creatures he has made.

The problem with this view of omniscience is that the analogy does not quite work. For one thing, in traditional theism God not only knows that there will be a crash, he also knows the name of the ambulance driver, the hospital to which they will be taken, how much blood each brother will lose, and the number of cobblestones that will be covered by both vehicles before the collision. Indeed, the God of classical theism knows all these things before either of the dead brothers was born.

Formulation (c) of God's omniscience will not do as a proper interpretation. The reason is quite simple. If it were the proper definition we would be beset with the major difficulty that most human beings of normal intelligence would be logically possible possessors of the kind of knowledge attributed to (c). All (c) implies is that if one were able to make the proper kinds of inferences he could tell future events by virtue of the availability of those inferences now. But surely when we refer to the omniscience of God we mean to say a good deal more than that.

This leads us quite naturally to an analysis of (d) For every p, if p is true, an omniscient being knows that p. If it is true that it rained on this date last year in St. Andrews, then an omniscient being knows that it rained on this date in St. Andrews last year. If it is true that it is presently raining in St. Andrews and if it is true that on this date next year it will be raining in St. Andrews, then an omniscient being knows it is now raining in St. Andrews and that it will be raining in St. Andrews on this date next year.

The principal objection raised in connection with this formulation is that in using this approach God's omniscience seems to be incompatible with human freedom. There are various ways in which this problem might be phrased. For our purposes, we will take the following argument as being fairly representative:

i. If God is omniscient, he knows the future.

ii. If someone knows that *p*, it follows that *p*.

iii. If God knows some future event will occur, it could not be otherwise.

iv. If some future event could not be otherwise, then the event is necessary.

v. Human actions can either be free or necessary.

vi. If God knows future human actions, then they could not be otherwise.

vii. Therefore, if God is omniscient, there can be no free human actions.

This formulation of God's omniscience does not deny God's omniscience, but it does suggest that the absence of free human actions is the price paid for its truth.

The question this argument against omniscience addresses is one that is as old as the history of Christian theology. In a curious way the argument continues to reemerge in the history of the tradition.[36] But what is not seen by the proponents of the deterministic objection, of which our sample argument is an example, is that there is a fatal ambiguity concerning what is meant by the term "necessary" in premises iv and v. When speaking of the concept of necessity it is important to distinguish between necessity *de dicto* and necessity *de re*. Necessity *de dicto* is used to describe a class of propositions that are necessarily true, e.g., "If Socrates is sitting, then Socrates is sitting." Necessity *de re* is used in connection with statements that take the form " *x* is *y* necessarily," e.g., "Socrates is sitting necessarily." The latter use is a kind of shorthand for saying that nothing could prevent Socrates from sitting, while the former is related to tautological expressions.

Thomas Aquinas seems to make this same distinction between these two different uses of "necessity" when he speaks of omniscience:

> 'All that God knows must necessarily be' is usually distinguished: it can either apply to the thing or the statement. Understood of the thing, the proposition is taken independently of the fact of God's knowing, and false, giving the sense 'everything that God knows is a necessary thing.' Or it can be understood of the statement, and thus it is taken in conjunction with the fact of God's knowing and true, giving the sense 'the statement,' a thing known by God is, is necessary.'[37]

What Thomas is suggesting here is that someone who believes that "God is omniscient" and "There are some future free actions" are incompatible would be led to the conclusion "Future free actions are necessary." But two different interpretations of "Future free actions are necessary" can be given, for we have two distinct uses for the word "necessity." Thus "Future free actions are necessary" could mean:

(1) If God knows that 'Socrates will sit tomorrow,' then 'Socrates will sit tomorrow' is necessarily true.

(2) 'God knows that Socrates will sit tomorrow' entails that Socrates will necessarily sit tomorrow.

Although (1) is certainly true, (2) is not. There is nothing contradictory in saying that Socrates will not always be sitting as a matter of necessity. If Socrates is sitting, his sitting is necessary. But this does not show that Socrates always sits necessarily.

If we use this distinction between necessity *de dicto* and necessity *de re* to examine premises iii and iv of our sample argument against formulation (d) of God's omniscience, it should be plain that there is nothing contradictory in saying that God could know free human actions in advance. If premise iii and iv become suspect, the conclusion in vii does not follow.

Thus, our analysis of the concept of omniscience is complete. We have examined four competing notions of what it means to say that a being is omniscient, eventually settling on the most logically satisfactory formulation: (d) For every *p*, if *p* is true, an omniscient being knows that *p*.

OMNIBENEVOLENCE

Omnibenevolence is a synonym for perfect goodness. But moral goodness is not the same as perfect goodness. We can and often do attribute moral goodness to people who are morally imperfect. Most if not all people fail morally at some time or other (they are dishonest, unkind, selfish, etc.), but if generally they attempt to avoid these pitfalls, and are most often successful in these attempts, we call them morally good. A morally perfect being, however, acts well always, though failure to act in an evil way is not sufficient for calling a being morally perfect or omnibenevolent. On the other hand, one single act of evil is sufficient for saying a particular being is not morally perfect or omnibenevolent. An omnibenevolent being must not only avoid evil, he must also do the good. These two necessary conditions taken together become sufficient for calling a being morally perfect or omnibenevolent.

Of course, one initial problem with this definition of moral perfection or omnibenevolence is that we have said nothing about what it means to say an action is morally good. We often contrast morally good acts with good acts of other kinds. George might be a very bad harmonica player, for example, but his playing may be morally good because he does it for the enjoyment of people in an old age home. What is it, then, to judge that some actions are morally good?

I would suggest that to say an action is morally good is to say that that particular action is a better action, on balance, than any other actions that might be done in its stead. A morally good action is one we have an overriding obligation to perform. It is an action where the overriding reasons for doing it outweigh any reasons for not doing it. Conversely, a morally bad or evil action is one a moral agent should refrain from doing. When we say that God never does actions that are morally wrong we mean that in choosing between alternatives God never selects an action that is on balance worse than any alternative action He might have chosen instead. When we say that God is morally perfect we mean that God always chooses the action that on balance is better than any other action He could have performed.

But an important problem arises for our view of moral

perfection. The problem is sometimes referred to as the Euthyphro dilemma, for it is first found in the Platonic dialogues. Briefly stated, the problem is this: Does belief that God is morally perfect imply a moral standard external to God by which we measure God to see whether He is, in fact, morally good? Or is it the case that when we say that God is omnibenevolent it means that God is, by definition, morally perfect? In this second view God's nature, whatever it might be, is the standard by which we decide goodness. Both of these positions, as Plato has shown, involve their proponents in difficulties. If God is good in relation to some external source, then God could not be said to be the only ultimate reality. If this position is correct, the universe is one wherein its moral character was not ordained by God.

On the other hand, if God is good by definition, then whatever God commands is morally permissible, indeed, morally obligatory. Thus, if God were to decide that the ten commandments should be rearranged such that those that contain a "not" should have it removed, while those which contain no "not" should have one inserted, that would be morally acceptable since what is ethically "good" is solely determined by the will of God.

But as Mackie has skillfully pointed out, the horns of this dilemma need not impale us. They only do so if we make the mistaken assumption that moral qualities are atomistic, that is, they only come in unanalyzable atomic units that either are wholly dependent or independent of the will of God. Mackie suggests that we can, in fact, take them apart:

> It might be that there is one kind of life which is, in a purely descriptive sense, most appropriate for human beings as they are — that is, that it alone will fully develop rather than stunt their natural capacities and

that in it, and only in it, can they find the fullest and
deepest satisfaction. It might then follow that certain
rules of conduct and certain dispositions were appropriate (still purely descriptive) in that they were needed to maintain this way of life. All these would then
be facts as hard as any in arithmetic or chemistry, and
so logically independent of any command or prescriptive will of God, though they might be products of the
creative will of God which, in making men as they
are, will have made them such that this life, these
rules, and these dispositions are appropriate for
them.[38]

Mackie continues his analysis by suggesting that God
might require human beings to conform to this appropriate
life by enjoining them to obey certain rules. This would add
a certain objective and prescriptive element to these
descriptive truths. Mackie then adds that it might also be
the case that this appropriate life as well as these connected
rules are what human beings ought to strive to conform to,
though they may not be completely accessible to people in a
direct way, through some kind of experimental or empirical
method. Still, God knows what this appropriate life
amounts to and desires that people should live it. So,
Mackie concludes, it is perfectly coherent to hold that God
somehow reveals the sense of these corresponding rules.[39]

The importance of Mackie's response to the Euthyphro
problem lies in the fact that it allows us to say that the
descriptive component of moral distinctions is logically
independent of what God may wish, while at the same time
it suggests a prescriptive component that is intimately related to God's will. The picture of God as a divine ogre is
replaced by the belief that He demands of His creatures that
they should live in the best way possible.[40]

NATURAL AND MORAL EVIL

We have already spent some time in discussing what constitutes a moral evil. It is clear, however, that the willful causing of human suffering is different in kind from hurricanes that may take human lives or cancers that may cause suffering and death. The latter should be considered evil because anyone who desired them for their own sake would clearly be acting irrationally.[41] Another reason for viewing certain kinds of natural occurrences as evil is that an omnipotent, omniscient, omnibenevolent being who causes these things to happen, when he alternatively could have created a world without them, with no loss of overall balance of good over evil, would be thought to be an evil or malevolent being. If this were not the case, it would be difficult to figure out just what the problem of evil is about.

But this distinction between natural evil and moral evil is not always so clear cut. In order to understand this point, consider the following example:

Fred comes from a family with a long history of lung cancer and various respiratory ailments. Fred persists, nevertheless, despite warnings like shortness of breath and tightness in the chest, to smoke four packs of cigarettes a day. Before he opens each pack, he carefully notes the warning on the side. Eventually, after many years of chain smoking he contracts lung cancer, but when his friends inquire as to when he might think about giving up his cigarettes, he tells them, "Whatever happens will happen anyway. When your number is up, that's when you go, and not a day before or after that."

Now it should be clear that the disease Fred has contracted is a natural evil. At the very least, one could say that Fred has done nothing to prevent or forestall its occurrence. But because of this, it might also be said that if Fred is a competent moral agent, he is indeed experiencing a moral evil done to himself as well. Through his gross neglect, Fred is a victim of his own moral evil.

The above example shows that the distinction between moral evil and natural evil appears to be more a heuristic device than a neat logical distinction. Much of what we consider to be natural evil appears to have indirect human causes. We could eliminate much of the starvation in the world, for example, if the world's resources were allocated differently. Many people still suffer from diseases for which there are now known cures. Sometimes steps can be taken to avoid or forestall natural disasters, but they are not taken. In these instances it is quite difficult to say whether it is only a natural evil that has occurred.

This rather fuzzy distinction between moral and natural evil has led thinkers on the problem of evil to concentrate mainly on the problem of moral evil, since it seems to constitute the larger part of the problem. But we must keep in mind that if God possesses both omnipotence and omniscience, in addition to His omnibenevolence, then He is in some way connected to the existence of natural evils and may, therefore, be morally culpable.

J.S. Mill seems to be pointing to God's moral culpability for natural evils when he says the following:

> In sober truth, nearly all the things men have been hanged or imprisoned for doing to one another are nature's everyday performances. Killing, the most criminal act recognized by human laws, nature does once to every being that lives, and in a large proportion of cases after protracted tortures such as only the greatest monsters whom we read of ever purposively inflicted on their fellow living creatures. If by an arbi-

trary reservation we refuse to account anything murder but what abridges a certain term supposed to be allotted to human life, nature does this to all but a small percentage of lives, and does it in all modes, violent or insidious, in which the worst human beings take the lives of one another. Nature impales men, breaks them as if on a wheel, casts them to be devoured by wild beasts, burns them to death, crushes them with stones like the first Christian martyrs, starves them with hunger, freezes them with cold, poisons them by quick or slow venom of her exhalations, and has hundreds of hideous deaths in reserve such as the ingenious cruelty of a Nabis or a Domitian never surpassed. All of this nature does with the most supercilious disregard both of mercy and of justice....[42]

We must keep in mind in our discussion of the problem of evil from the perspective of the religions of paradox that if Mill is correct, then it seems that all examples of natural evil are also substantiations of moral evil as well. If God is a moral agent and He is responsible for the existence of natural evils, then in a real sense they may be seen as moral evils as well.[43]

One consistent way out of this dilemma is to make a distinction among what David Griffin calls "genuine evils," "apparent evils," and "*prima facie* evils."[44] By genuine evils we mean pain, death, disability, loss of freedom, loss of opportunity, etc., which, all things considered, the universe would have been better without. Another way to state the definition of a genuine evil is to say that it is an evil for which we cannot give a sufficient reason for its existence. An event or state of affairs is a genuine evil if its occurrence prevents the existence of some other event or state of affairs that would make the universe better than it is.

Prima facie evils are anything that may be labelled evil at first glance. Some *prima facie* evils, upon closer reflection, might turn out to be genuine evils. Other *prima facie* evils, however, may ultimately be seen as only apparently evil.

Apparent evils are those that, when considered from a larger context, are seen as merely apparent since their "evilness" may be viewed as compensated for by the goodness to which they contribute. In the final chapter of this thesis, we will once again take up the challenge posed by Mill. It is enough now, however, to simply mention the distinction among genuine evil, apparent evil, and *prima facie* evil.

I must confess that despite the important distinctions we have made in the last several pages in regard to the definitional problems involved in the problem of evil, much of what I have said here, nevertheless, seems too antiseptic, too clean. These distinctions seem not to capture the sense of the wanton cruelty and destruction that are the everyday fare of radio, television, and newspaper reports.

Examples of extraordinary cruelty are no less ubiquitous in the history of human culture. Almost three millenia ago, Ashurnasirpal II, King of Assyria, ordered that the hands and feet of the inhabitants of captured villages should be severed. The bleeding bodies were piled up in the town squares so that those who were still alive might suffocate or bleed to death.[45] As I write this, Syrian soldiers three thousand years later sit across from American marines in Lebanon. The weapons both sides carry make the cutting off of hands and feet seem like a more merciful practice.

The perception of evil is a direct and immediate experience of something that befalls individuals. We experience, each of us, evil done to us, and by empathy, evil to those we love, our friends and neighbors, and even to people we will never meet. It is not difficult to understand the pain suffered by the victims of Lt. Calley's massacres in Mai Lai or the mental anguish depicted so skillfully in William Styron's *Sophie's Choice.*[46] Voices like these cry over immense distances. That one person, anyone, should suffer unjustly is intolerable. If there were but one example of innocent suffering in the entire world, we would still have the obligation of asking why.

But Solzhenitsyn raises an interesting point about hidden suffering, about the impossibility of ever having just one example of innocent suffering. He tells the story of the eight-year-old daughter of one of the victims of Stalin's purges. After the father's death the girl lived only another year. During that time, Solzhenitsyn remarks, "She did not once smile." He adds, "When we count up the millions of those who died in the camps, we forget to multiply them by two or three."[47]

One is reminded of Edward Wallant's stirring and disconcerting novel, *The Pawnbroker*, in which the central character, Sol Nazerman, has lost his wife and two children in the Nazi death camps. Before the war, he was a university professor, specializing in Western intellectual history. After the war, he operates a pawnshop in East Harlem. His religious world view, which includes his definition of the meaning of suffering, has been totally shattered. Yet, when we count up the dead of the Holocaust, Sol Nazerman's name does not appear. The practical reality of suffering seems to be hidden no less in philosophically sophisticated discussions of the definition of evil than it is in the statistics concerning dead in Nazi Germany or the Soviet death camps.

The realization of the practical reality of suffering was brought home to me in a painful way when the memorial for the Vietnam veterans was recently erected in Washington, D.C. The monument is a series of interlocking pieces of black marble on which are placed the names of the 56,000 men and women who died in Vietnam. But rather than placing the names in alphabetical order, the designer of the stones chose to put the names in the order in which they died. This makes it extremely difficult to find any particular person in the dozens of panels. One summer day I traveled to Washington to find on the stones the name of a high school friend who had been killed early in the war. After several hours of looking for the name, I finally found it. After paying my respects, I began to look about me at the family members and friends of those who had fallen in southeast Asia. Often groups of three and four could be seen stroking the indentation in the stone that signified a particular lost friend or father, husband or son. It is in moments such as this that one realizes the truth of Solzhenitsyn's remark. Each of these names tells us the story of one tragedy, but there are also the three or four hidden stories we do not learn.

Let us now examine carefully what we have garnered from this second chapter. First, after a lengthy discussion we were led to the notion that God's omnipotence involves the ability to do anything that is logically possible and is also consistent with His other attributes. Second, in our analysis of omniscience we ascertained that the best definition of that term is to say if some proposition is true, God knows that proposition is true. Additionally, we have suggested that the proper formulation of God's omnibenevolence is to say that God always avoids the evil and does the good. We also demonstrated that the distinction between natural and moral evils, though not a strict logical distinction, is a good heuristic device for understanding the concept of evil. Finally, we made some very brief comments, which will be taken up again in chapters three and five, about the untheoretical character of suffering experienced first hand.

One remaining problem we are faced with in this chapter is whether belief in God's omnipotence, omniscience, and omnibenevolence, as well as belief in the existence of real evil in the world, commits one to a formal logical contradiction. Another way to phrase this question is to ask whether one may consistently ascribe to the truth of the following four propositions simultaneously:

    i. God is omnipotent.
    ii. God is omniscient.
    iii. God is omnibenevolent.
    iv. There is evil in the world in both moral and natural forms.

There can be no doubt that the religions of paradox are committed to the truth of all four propositions. If a formal contradiction can be derived from i through iv, then we would be forced to conclude that the paradox is not just apparent, it is genuine. And if this were to turn out to be the case, the best we could hope for would be a god who resembles that proposed by J.S. Mill or found in Plato's *Timaeus*.

But it should be clear to any student of elementary logic that belief in the truth of propositions i through iv does not involve one in a formal contradiction. This would still be the case even if we were to add

    v. God created the world *ex nihilo*.

J.L. Mackie seems to come to the same conclusion about

the logical compatibility of these propositions when he writes:

> However, the contradiction does not arise immediately; to show it we need some additional premises, or perhaps some quasi-logical rules connecting the terms 'good,' 'evil' and 'omnipotent.'[48]

Mackie then goes on to offer these additional premises or quasi-logical rules:

> vi. Good is opposed to evil in such a way that a good thing always eliminates evil as far as it can.
>
> vii. There are no limits (other than logical ones) to what an omnipotent, omniscient being can do.

From these two additional premises, as well as i through v, he derives something like the following:

> viii. A good, omnipotent, omniscient being would eliminate evil completely.
>
> ix. "A good, omnipotent, omniscient being exists" and "evil exists" are logically incompatible.[49]

Thus, if Mackie's analysis is correct, we may see the aptness of the name "religions of paradox." In response to the logical problem Mackie has outlined above, theologians and philosophers of religion have attempted to construct various theodicies. Some attempt to relax the paradox by suggesting alternative definitions of "good," "evil," "omnipotence," etc. But from a logical standpoint, most of these attempts end up as religions of solution or dissolution, depending on whether they attempt to change any of the first three propositions (solution) or concentrate their attention on the fourth (dissolution). Any theodicy that attempts to resolve the problem by denying any of the four propositions, however, inevitably strays from either the orthodox doctrine of God or the classical view of evil.[50]

In the remainder of this work we shall not be concerned with theodicies that attempt to abandon or modify the theistic attributes so as to avoid the logical problem outlined above. Instead, I shall assume the existence of what Hick has called the traditional belief in God as unique, infinite, uncreated, eternal, personal spirit of absolute goodness and power.[51]

In the next chapter, I shall discuss those theodicies in the Christian tradition that, in various ways, attempt to restate the alleged evil pole of the logical contradiction. Rather than modifying the theistic attributes, these theodicies attempt to restate the concept of evil without turning their position into a religion of dissolution. In these reformulations of evil the attempt is made to show that evil, as reformulated, is compatible with the existence of a God who is conceived as possessing the relevant attributes of omnipotence, omniscience, and omnibenevolence.

Notes

1. Thomas Aquinas, *Summa Contra Gentiles*, translated by Anton Pegis (New York: Doubleday, 1955) Book I, chap. 22, p. 121.

2. Frederick Ferre, *Basic Modern Philosophy of Religion*
    (London: George Allen and Unwin, 1967) p. 123.

3. In chapter 5 it is argued that the Christian form of life
    actually provides a fourth alternative to these three
    traditional notions of omnipotence.

4. "Can" is used here as the can of ability.

5. There are some less convincing definitions of
    omnipotence that, for the sake of brevity and clarity,
    I have not mentioned here. One other possibility is
    that an omnipotent being can do "anything he wants."
    This view is sometimes attributed to Augustine.
    Anthony Kenny in *The God of the Philosophers*
    (London: Clarendon, 1977), chap. 7, suggests that
    this formulation of God's omnipotence is defective,
    for any person on earth who realizes his limitations
    and then desires only those things he is capable of
    would be a possessor of omnipotence.

6. René Descartes, *Descartes' Letters*, edited by
    C. Adams and P. Tannery (Paris, 1964) I, 35.
    A modern formulation of this same notion can be
    found in H.G. Frankfurt's "The Logic of
    Omnipotence," in *Philosophical Review*, vol. 73
    (1964). There he argues that God "invents" the laws
    of logic in much the same way he makes the laws of
    nature.

7. Ibid., I, 147.

8. P. T. Geach, *Providence and Evil* (Cambridge:
    Cambridge University Press, 1977) pp. 9-10.

9. *Descartes' Letters*, VII, 380.

10. Ibid., IV, 110.

11. Geach, *Providence and Evil*, p. 11.

12. Thomas Aquinas, *Summa Theologica* (New York: McGraw Hill, 1963) I. ques. 25 ans. 4, p. 164.

13. Ibid., I. ques. 25 ans. 3, pp. 163-64.

14. For an interesting early Medieval discussion of omnipotence paradoxes, see the dinner conversations between Desiderio of Cassino and Saint Peter Damiani, recorded in the latter's *De Divina Omnipotentia*, reprinted in J. Migne's *Patrologia Latina* (Paris: n.d.) vol. 145.

15. "Logically possible" includes only those actions that are not contrary to his nature, when predicated of God.

16. Aristotle, *The Prior and Posterior Analytics*, edited by W.D. Ross (Oxford: Oxford University Press, 1949) 12, 32a., pp. 6-14.

17. Anthony Flew quotes this section of Lewis with approval in his "Divine Omnipotence and Human Freedom," *New Essays in Philosophical Theology* (London: SCM, 1955). This may be the only time Flew and Lewis agreed on anything having to do with the philosophy of religion.

18. C.S. Lewis, *The Problem of Pain* (New York: Macmillan, 1978) p. 28.

19. Frederick Ferre, *Basic Modern Philosophy of Religion*, p. 24.

20. Boethius, *The Consolation of Philosophy*, translated by Richard Green (New York: Random House, 1962) Book V, p. 116.

21. Thomas Aquinas, *Summa Theologica*, I, ques. 14 ans. 13.

22. Anselm, *The Proslogion in St. Anselm*, translated by Sidney Norton Dean (Lasalle: Open Court Press, 1962) p. 25.

23. Anthony Kenny, *Aquinas: A Collection of Critical Essays* (London: Macmillan, 1969) p. 264.

24. Anthony Kenny, *The God of the Philosophers*, p. 39.

25. A.N. Prior, "The Formalities of Omniscience," *Philosophy* (1962); Norman Kretzmann, "Omniscience and Immutability," *The Journal of Philosophy*, vol. 63 (1966); Nicholas Wolterstorff, "God Everlasting" in *God and the Gods: Essays in Honor of Henry Stob*, edited by C.J. Orlebeke and L.B. Shedes (Grand Rapids: Eerdmans, 1975).

26. A.N. Prior, "The Formalities of Omniscience," p. 116.

27. Nelson Pike, *God and Timelessness* (New York: Macmillan, 1970).

28. H.N. Castenada, "Omniscience and Indexical Reference," *Journal of Philosophy* vol. 64 (1967); Richard Swinburne, *The Coherence of Theism* (Oxford: Clarendon Press, 1977).

29. Ibid., p. 165.

30. H.N. Castenada, "Omniscience and Indexical Reference," p. 116.

31. William Kneale, "Time and Eternity in Theology," *Proceedings of the Aristotelean Society* vol. 61 (1960-61).

32. Ibid., p. 99.

33. J.R. Lucas, *A Treatise on Time and Space* (London: Methuen, 1973), pp. 300-308.; Richard Swinburne, *The Coherence of Theism*, p. 162ff.

34. Ibid.; one of the first modern versions of this theory that God is everlasting, but existing in time, can be found in Oscar Cullmann's *Christ and Time* (Philadelphia: Westminster Press, 1950).

35. Friedrich Schleiermacher, *The Christian Faith*, H.R. MacKintosh and J.S. Steward, eds. and trans. (Edinburgh: T. and T. Clark, 1957) p. 57.; James Ward, *Naturalism and Agnosticism* (London: A. and C. Block, 1915); F.R. Tennant, *Philosophical Theology*, vol. 2 (Cambridge: Cambridge University Press, 1930); both hold it is contrary to say that free choices can be known until they are made.

36. Cf., for example, Jonathan Edwards, *Freedom of the Will* (1754), section 12, quoted in Baruch Brody, *Readings in the Philosophy of Religion* (Englewood Cliffs, N.J.: Prentice Hall, 1974); and Martin Luther's position in *Luther Oder Erasmus* (Basil: Friedrich Rheinhart, 1972).

37. Thomas Aquinas, *Summa Theologica* Ia ques. 14 ans. 13.

38. J.L. Mackie, *Ethics: Inventing Right and Wrong* (London: Penguin Books, 1977) pp. 230-231.

39. Ibid., p. 231.

40. Ibid., pp. 231-232. For more on the Euthyphro dilemma, see the following: Kai Nielson, "An Examination of the Alleged Theological Basis of

Morality," *Iliff Review* (1964); Brian Hebblethwaite, *The Adequacy of Christian Ethics* (London: Marshall, Morgan and Scott, 1981) pp. 13-14; and H. Meynell's "The Euthyphro Dilemma," in *Aristotelean Society Supplementary*, vol. 46 (1972).

41. Bernard Gert, *The Moral Rules* (New York: Harper and Row, 1970).

42. J.S. Mill, "Nature," *Three Essays on Religion* (London: Oxford University Press, third edition, 1975) pp. 1-2.

43. Brian Davies in his *Introduction to the Philosophy of Religion* (London: Oxford University Press, 1982), as well as Michael Durrant in his *The Logical Status of God* (London: Macmillan, 1973) suggest that this problem can be overcome by arguing that God is not a moral agent. Neither writer, however, makes it clear how this view can be consistent with the claims that God is also personal and acts in history.

44. David Ray Griffen, *God, Power and Evil*, pp. 21-27.

45. L. W. Doob, *Panorama of Evil* (London: Greenwood Press, 1978).

46. William Styron, *Sophie's Choice* (New York: Random House, 1979).

47. Aleksander Solzhenitsyn, *The Gulag Archipelago* (New York: Harper and Row, 1974) p. 431.

48. J.L. Mackie, *The Miracle of Theism*, p. 150.

49. Ibid., pp. 150-151.

50. By the "classical view of evil" I mean here a biblical view as opposed to Augustine's view of privation.

51. John Hick, *Evil and the God of Love*, p. 35.

III.
An Analysis of
Traditional Theodicies

A bird sings now;
Merrily sings he

Of his mate on the bough,
Of his eggs in the tree:

But yonder a hawk
swings out of the blue,

And the sweet song is finished
— Is this story true?

And now have mercy,
on me and on you.

James Stephens

I have been ill and keep ill. I am president of the
Diabetic Society and diabetes keeps me in and out, in
and out of bed every two hours or so. This exhausts
and this vast return to chaos which is called peace, the
infinite meanness of great masses of my fellow creatures, the wickedness of organized religion give me a
longing for sleep that will have no awakening. There
is a long history of heart failure on my parental side

but modern palliatives are very effective holding back
that moment of release. Sodium bicarbonate keeps me
in a grunting state of protesting endurance. But while
I live I have to live and I owe a lot to a decaying civilization which has anyhow kept me alive enough in
the spirit of scientific devotion to stimulate my
curiosity and make me its debtor.

Forgive this desolation.
                                   H.G. Wells, shortly before his death,
                                       in a letter to Bertrand Russell.

In this chapter I shall offer a critical analysis of traditional Western theodicies that, in various ways, attempt a
restatement of the alleged "evil" pole of the logical contradiction sketched out in chapter two. Rather than modifying
the theistic attributes in order to resolve the problem of
evil, these theodicies attempt to restate the concept of evil.
In taking this approach, the proponents of these views can
thereby argue that the existence of evil, as reformulated, is
compatible with the existence of a God who is omnipotent,
omniscient, and omnibenevolent. A fair sampling of these
responses can be arranged conveniently into four groups:
(1) punishment and warning theodicies; (2) unreality of evil
theodicies; (3) evil is logically necessary theodicies; and
(4) teleological theodicies.

In each of these four categories we shall explore a number of variations. It will be the burden of this chapter to
show, however, that all of the restatements mentioned are
inadequate Christian responses for one reason or another.
Many of the theodicies about to be mentioned fail on logical grounds, but I will also suggest that some of these
attempts at theodicy fail either because they fall outside the
general bounds of the Christian tradition or because they
largely ignore the perspective of the victim of suffering. We

shall see that most if not all of the answers about to be mentioned fail to take the sufferer very seriously. We will recall from our discussion in the first chapter that this is one of the chief conditions necessary for a theologically viable response to suffering. Without this existential element, we have argued, answers to the problem of evil ring hollow or seem arbitrary and forced.

It is, of course, quite difficult to approach the problem with a true understanding of the practical reality of suffering. But without that understanding the task of theodicy cannot properly be undertaken.

Perhaps the best way to begin an analysis of traditional theodicies is to approach the concept of evil through a sympathetic observation of human suffering. In a real way, this is the only direct link we have with evil. Although we have been clear about what evil is in the previous chapter, it is, nevertheless, best understood, at least for the individual doing the suffering, in an ostensive way. Surely it is easier for a person to communicate the existential pain and reality of his suffering by having you suffer as well, than it is to have him verbally relate his feelings to you. Perhaps there is a bias in what I am suggesting: The practical reality of suffering can only truly be seen from the perspective of the victims, or at the very least from the perspective of those who are totally and profoundly sympathetic with those victims.

In an often quoted text, Gabriel Marcel has stated the importance of assuming this kind of perspective:

> In reflecting upon evil, I tend, almost inevitably, to regard it as a disorder which I view from the outside and of which I seek to discover the causes or secret aims. Why is it that the mechanism functions so defectively? Or is the defect merely apparent and due

to a real defect in my vision? In this case the defect is
in myself, yet it remains objective in relation to my
thought, which discovers it and observes it. But evil
which is stated or observed is no longer evil which is
suffered: in fact it ceases to be evil. In reality, I can
only grasp it as evil in the measure in which it touches
me — that is to say, in the measure in which I am
involved, as one is involved in a law suit. Being
"involved" is the fundamental fact; I cannot leave it
out of account except by an unjustifiable fiction, for
in doing so, I proceed as though I were God, and a
God who is an onlooker at that.[1]

I think Marcel is suggesting something central to the
study of theodicies. When the theodicist objectifies the evil
he views, or reflects upon it in a dispassionate way, he
deprives the evil of its "evil-ness" in relation to the very
real suffering of the victim, for whom the evil is experienced as intrinsic and ultimate in the present moment.

In viewing evil from a distance one is bound to form a
distorted conception of it. Indeed, if Marcel is correct, one
no longer observes evil but an objectification of it. In
removing oneself from the evil the theodicist becomes
something akin to the pilot of a small plane who wants to
understand a certain African tribe by flying over them at
10,000 feet.

In order to make this personal perspective of Marcel's a
bit clearer, consider the two following statements:

(a) On October 5, 1942 at Dulmo (in the Ukraine)
eight German Jews were exterminated along with
1,500 local Jews. They were led to an open air shooting range, where burial pits had been dug. The condemned handed in their clothing and other possessions, were directed to stand in the pits, and were
shot.

(b) The people undressed. The mothers undressed the little children without screaming or weeping.... They had reached the point of human suffering where tears no longer flow and all hope has been abandoned.... I heard no complaints, no appeal for mercy. I watched a family of eight persons, a man and a woman both about fifty.... looking at each other with tears in their eyes. The father was holding the hand of a boy about ten years old and speaking to him; the boy was fighting his tears.... The pit was already nearly full; it contained about a thousand bodies. The SS man who did the shooting was sitting on the edge of the pit, smoking a cigarette, with a tommy gun on his knee. The new batch of twenty people, the family of eight, and the baby carried in the arms of the woman with the snow white hair, all completely naked, were directed down steps cut in the clay wall of the pit, and clambered over the heads of the dead and dying. They lay down among them. Some caressed those who were still alive and spoke to them in a low voice. Then came the shots from the SS man who had thrown away his cigarette.[2]

It is clear that in the first statement above we have a concise, rather objective account of the facts of a given incident that occurred over forty years ago. This account describes the particulars of the case, but in so doing it contains nothing of the practical reality of the experience. One can read statement (a) with little or no emotion; no real sympathy is required.

In contrast, statement (b) is much more lengthy and detailed. But it is not just this fact that makes us more sympathetic to the second account. More facts could be added to the first account, but it is doubtful that this alone would make that description more sympathetic. In the second

account we are asked not only to recognize the particulars
of the case, but we are also asked to attempt to understand
what these human beings are going through in the final
moments of their tragic lives. We are asked to enter the
scene not as mere spectators but as participants in their suffering.

It is rare in present times to hear sympathetic accounts
of suffering. In contemporary Western culture we are beset
with news accounts often wedged between situation come-
dies and advertisements for mouthwash and underarm
deodorant. It is little wonder that contemporary theodicists
have fallen into the trap of objectifying evil.

John Hick, along with a number of other contemporary
philosophers of religion and theologians, would surely
object to my line of argument. In fact, Hick explicitly
asserts that theodicy is the task of the detached observer
rather than the victim:

> As has often been observed, in the case of human suf-
> fering the intellectual problem of evil usually arises in
> the mind of the spectator rather than that of the suffer-
> er. The sufferer's immediate and absorbing task is to
> face and cope with evil that is pressing upon him and
> to maintain his spiritual existence against the threat of
> final despair. He does not want or need a theoretical
> theodicy, but practical grace and courage and hope.
> We can therefore say, in Marcel's terminology that for
> him evil is not a problem to be solved, but a mystery
> to be encountered and lived through.[3]

Hick does not totally exclude the victim's perspective
from consideration, but surely he underestimates the ability
of the sufferer to formulate crucial questions in the midst of
his encounter with evil. "Practical grace and courage and

hope" are never completely divorced from some theoretical context. In fact, despite the disorientation and chaos that often occur in these situations, it is often in the very context of the agony and suffering that the problem of evil is most forcefully raised and seriously considered. Indeed, this is precisely one of the reasons why the Book of Job remains so poignant. Job not only has a practical concern about suffering, he also has a theoretical concern. The comforters, on the other hand, see it as a theological conundrum to debate. Here I would probably part company with Marcel insofar as Hick's interpretation of Marcel is correct. I think it is clearly wrong that the mystery of evil cannot be reflected upon at all within the experience of that evil. This is an anti-intellectual claim that seems to dismiss *a priori* any possibility of theodicy. If this *a priori* view were the correct one, we certainly would not need Job's friends coming along on three different occasions to discuss the intellectual alternatives.

On the contrary, I'd like to suggest that the search for a Christian theodicy is not, by definition, impossible, but that theodicists must be careful first to be logically cogent and second to be consistent, at least in a broad way, with the major tenets of Christianity, and finally, they must develop a method that captures the reality of evil as it is experienced by the sufferer. Theodicy, I think, cannot be done by using dim objectifications as one's focus of study. Evil remains a part of the sufferers, and this often keeps their theodicies honest. We should expect at least that much from the sympathetic theologian or philosopher of religion.

Perhaps one of the best examples in Western literature of a sufferer reflecting on the problem of evil in the midst of his encounter with that evil can be found in Leo Tolstoy's "The Death of Ivan Illych." It is a harrowing tale that describes, with compelling and grim realism, the decline and death of a legal official, Ivan Illych, who had reached the top of his profession as a public prosecutor. But at a deeper level, Tolstoy gives us the picture of Ivan as an ordinary, mediocre man — a typical member of a professional bourgeoisie. Before his illness, Ivan had spent his legal career objectively viewing other people's problems. He had always approached evil and suffering in the lives of others in a cold and legalistic fashion. But now it was his turn. He, Ivan Illych, was the victim. During his slow and painful dying, he saw, to his great horror, that his family, friends, and physicians had objectified his suffering.

> Ivan Illych went out slowly, seated himself dejectedly in his sledge and drove home. All the way home he kept going over what the doctor had said, trying to translate all those involved, obscure scientific phrases into plain language and find in them an answer to the question, 'Am I in a bad way — a very bad way — or is it nothing at all?' And it seemed to him that the upshot of all that the doctor had said was that he was in a very bad way...[4]

Those around him did not truly sympathize with his situation. In the midst of his suffering Ivan realizes the absurdity of viewing disease, loss of opportunity, and death from the point of view of an outsider.

> In the depths of his heart he knew he was dying but, so far from getting used to the idea, he simply did not or could not grasp it.
>
> The example is a syllogism which he had learned in Kiezewetter's *Logic*: 'Casius is a man, men are mortal,

therefore Casius is mortal,' had seemed to him all his life to be true as applied to Casius but certainly not as regards himself. That Casius — man in the abstract — was mortal, was perfectly correct; but he was not Casius, nor man in the abstract: he had always been a creature quite, quite different from all others. He had been little Vanya with a mamma and papa, and Mitya and Volodya, with playthings and the coachman and nurse; and afterwards with Katya and with all the joys and griefs and ecstasies of childhood, boyhood and youth. What did Casius know of the smell of that striped leather ball Vanya had been so fond of? Was it Casius who had kissed his mother's hand like that, and had Casius heard the rustle of her silken skirts? Was it Casius who had rioted like that over the cakes and pastries at the Law School? Had Casius been in love like that? Could Casius preside at sessions like he did?[5]

Finally, from out of the depths of his own suffering he formulates the crucial question of theodicy:

... he no longer controlled himself, but wept like a child. He wept over his helplessness, over his terrible loneliness, over the cruelty of men, over the cruelty of God, over the absence of God.

Why has thou done this? Why didst thou place me here? Why, why dost thou torture me so horribly?[6]

It is this spirit of Ivan Illych that is so often lacking in contemporary discussion of theodicy. Barth once said of Leibniz that "at bottom level he hardly had any serious interest (and from a practical standpoint none at all) in the problem of evil." It could be argued, I think, that Albert

Camus is essentially making the same claim against his character, Father Paneloux, in *The Plague*. Dr. Rieux, the atheist physician who is revealed as the narrator in the final chapter of the book, and the young priest are used as paired opposites in the novel. Rieux sees the problem of the plague as a purely medical one. Paneloux in the beginning of the book sees the existence of the disease as an intellectualized theological conundrum. Each of their views becomes tempered by the other's when they are thrown together in witnessing the death of an innocent child. Rieux is, for the first time, confronted by the larger questions, questions that require answers that go beyond his simple technical skill. Paneloux is forced to respond in an existential way to the reality of undeserved suffering.

It is this dual concern for existential understanding and intellectual rigor that is difficult to find in so many contemporary and historical theodicies. In reading much of the literature on the problem of evil, one gets the distinct impression that intellectual defenses are carried out with little or no reference to the real world, that solutions proffered would be quite useless in any practical situation where a sufferer was asking "Why?" Would anyone dare, for example, to suggest to a mother whose child had been recently killed in a senseless accident that evil was merely an illusion, a deprivation of good, or some prelude to a future eschatological harmony? Talk that is distantly plausible in the lecture hall often becomes strangely absurd when brought to the bar of concrete experience. Even from the pulpit we all too often forget that not only must we be intellectually honest, but we must also keep in mind that one of the other important tests of the worth of a theodicy is that it help the sufferer in his encounter with evil. If a theodicy fails this test, it is useless; it has ignored the practical reality of suffering.

Having made these comments about the central importance of the victim in discussions of theodicy, we might do well to look carefully and critically at a variety of restatements of the evil pole of the apparent logical paradox presented in chapter two. In our discussion we will attempt to show that the first three types (punishment and warning theodicies, the unreality of evil theodicies, and the evil is necessary theodicies) all suffer from some incurable logical ills, but the fourth type, teleological theodicies, will require a more extensive analysis in terms of how well it conforms to our second and third criteria: Whether they fit in a broad way into the Christian form of life, as well as how seriously they take the individual sufferer.

PUNISHMENT AND WARNING THEODICIES

Under this heading we can discuss two distinct but related points of view that find their origins, at least in the Judeo-Christian tradition, in the Torah. These positions might properly be labelled "punishment and warning theodicies," and "the free will defense."

In the earliest portions of the Old Testament, where the Hebraic understanding of man's relationship to God is both communal and covenantal, the existence of pain and suffering is most often seen as retribution for sins.[7] This view is most clearly expressed in the Pentateuch but can also be seen in early prophetic literature as well:

> Tell them, 'Happy is the virtuous man, for he will feed
> on the fruit of his deeds; woe to the wicked, evil is on
> him, he will be treated as his actions deserve.'[8]

This simple cause-and-effect explanation of suffering is written very deeply into scripture. It is explicit in the idea of the covenantal relationship in which the contract is inevitably followed by blessings and curses. It reached its height of formulation and theological importance in the Deuteronomic history, which even gave a retributive explanation for the fall of the city of Jerusalem to the Babylonians a century later:

> He built altars to the whole array of heaven in the two courts of the Temple of Yahweh. He caused his son to pass through the fire. He practiced soothsaying and magic and introduced necromancers and wizards. He did very much more things displeasing to Yahweh, thus provoking his anger....
>
> Then Yahweh spoke through his servants, the prophets, "Since Manesseh King of Judah has done these shameful deeds..., and has led Judah itself into sin with its idols, Yahweh, the God of Israel, says this, 'Look, I will bring such disaster as to make the ears of all who hear it tingle.... I will scour Jerusalem as a man scours a dish and, having scoured it, turns it upside down.'"[9]

This quotation contains both elements of retributive justice and, quite clearly, an element of warning to be heeded by any reader who might have apostasy planned in the near future.

But even as early as the seventh and eighth century prophets there had been questions raised about the distribution of this supposed deserved punishment. Indeed, it would seem that Jeremiah raises this question about the distribution of suffering in an anguished way rather than as an intellectual exercise.

You have right on your side, Yahweh,
When I complain to you.
But I would like to debate a point of justice with you.
Why is it that the wicked live prosperously?
Why do scoundrels enjoy peace?[10]

By the time of the writing of the Book of Job, we find a sustained attack on this theodicy of deserved punishment. This attack, of course, is placed in the mouth of the victim of suffering, Job.

In his article, "Will You Lie for God?", F.M. Cross describes the developed orthodox theodicy that Job and his comforters debate:

In the national development of Israel's religion, the confessions of this historical faith were elaborated. The Lord of Israel, it was said, will deliver an obedient nation; he will also bring down by plague or defeat a rebellious and proud people. In the circles of Israel's pious and wise, the older doctrines were further simplified and refined. The ancient Lord of Israel's community became rather the God of the pious individual, who prospered the godly in his lifetime and struck down the unrighteous in the midst of his folly. This weal and woe were the unambiguous signs of God's pleasure or wrath, direct evidence of man's integrity or sin.[11]

The orthodox line, Cross continues, is elaborated by Eliphaz, one of Job's friends:

Think now, who that was innocent ever perished, or where were the righteous destroyed?
As I have observed, those who plow falsehood and sow trouble reap the same,
By the breath of God they perish, and by the blast of

his wrath they are consumed.[12]
God sets on high the lowly, and the despondent are
lifted in victory.
He frustrates the designs of the crafty, so that their
hands achieve no success....
He delivers the orphan from violence; the poor from
the hands of the strong.
So the pauper has hope, and injustice shuts her
mouth.[13]

Job, however, counters this punishment and warning
theodicy with the perspective of the sufferer:

Look at me and be appalled, and put your hand on
(your) mouth.
When I call it to mind, I shudder, and chills seize my
flesh.
Why do the wicked live, reach old age, yea, and wax
great in power?
Their houses are free from anxiety, and God's rod
(falls) not on them....
They spend their days in prosperity, and in peace go
down to Sheol....
When you say 'Where is the house of the prince?'
'Where is the camp of the wicked?'
Have you not asked those who travel the roads, and do
you not accept their evidence:
That the wicked man is spared in the day of calamity,
that he is rescued in the day of wrath?[14]

The glib answer set forth by Job's friends does not
budge the protagonist. We have been told in 1:1 that Job is
"blameless and upright," and nothing the comforters have
said will change that.
Professor Cross strongly argues against the popular con-

ception that Job is a patient, orthodox, and long-suffering individual (an interpretation that is fostered by the fact that the author of the dialogues has utilized the setting of the folk tale before and after the main debates). To see Job in his true light, Cross argues, we must recognize him as a heretic in his own time and place. Job confronts his orthodox comforters, having endured restlessly their pastoral tones, their pious pomposity, their offense at his doubts and their refusal to admit questions, their endless stock of brilliant aphorisms, and observes that they are liars:

> Will you tell lies on God's behalf, and speak falsely for him?
> Will you show him partiality; will you prejudge the case in his favor?
> Will it go well when he examines you? Can you delude him as you delude a man?
> Nay, he will surely punish you if you secretly show him partiality.[15]

Albert Camus is also very highly critical of the punishment and warning theodicy in his novel, *The Plague*. A few weeks after the plague had deeply established itself in the town of Oran, the Jesuit priest, Father Paneloux, preaches a sermon that emphasizes the punishment and warning theodicy as the proper answer to why the town had been inundated by the dreaded disease. Paneloux traces the history of the plague in the Old Testament, noting that it served as an instrument used by God to strike down his enemies:

> In strict logic what came next did not seem to follow from the dramatic opening. Only as the sermon proceeded did it become apparent to the congregation that, by a skillful oratorical device, Father Paneloux

had launched at them, like a giant fisticuff, the gist of
the whole discourse. After launching it he went on at
once to quote a text from Exodus relating to the
plague of Egypt, and said: "The first time this scourge
appears in history, it was wielded to strike down the
enemies of God. Pharoah set himself up against the
divine will, and the plague beat him to his knees.
Thus from the dawn of recorded history the scourge of
God has humbled the proud of heart and laid low
those who hardened themselves against him. Ponder
this well, my friends, and fall on your knees.[16]

The plague eliminates the chaff, while at the same time
it winnows out the chosen:

If today the plague is in your midst, that is because
the hour has struck for taking thought. The just man
need have no fear, but the evil doer has good cause to
tremble. For plague is the flail of God and the world
his threshing floor, and implacably he will thresh out
his harvest until the wheat is separated from the
chaff....[17]

Paneloux concedes that to verify that deserved punishment is the cause of the plague demands that the wicked
only be afflicted. This would affirm, as Job's comforters
attempted to do, that the fact of suffering is *prima facie*
evidence of the sufferer's wrongdoing. But Paneloux also
seems to want to affirm that the judgment and punishment
of the wicked aids the salvation of those unaffected by the
plague, for it works as a constant warning to them. The
plague motivates the righteous to continue to conform to
God's will. It illuminates and underscores man's impotence
and exposes his arrogance and specious self-sufficiency.
Consequently, one may be humbly prepared for the necessi-

ty and acceptance of God's saving grace.[18]

But shortly after this first sermon an event occurs which radically changes Father Paneloux's view of the appropriateness of the punishment and warning theodicy. He and the physician, Dr. Rieux, are present for the death of an innocent child:

> They had already seen children die — for many months now death had shown no favoritism — but they had never yet watched a child's agony minute by minute, as they had now been doing since daybreak. Needless to say, the pain inflicted on these innocent victims had always seemed to be what in fact it was: an abominable thing. But hitherto they had felt its abomination in, so to speak, an abstract way; they never had to witness over a long time the death throes of an innocent child.[19]

The death of this innocent child forces the priest to view evil in a way where he is more than a spectator. He comes to see that the boy's death flagrantly contradicts the logic of the first sermon. In the face of this tragedy, suffering can no longer be seen as the result of deserved punishment. The plague has struck down the guiltless, and any error in discriminating between wheat and chaff must call into question the validity and applicability of the deserved punishment theodicy.[20]

Later in the novel, during the height of the plague, the priest gives a second sermon. In this second attempt at theodicy, Camus has Paneloux change his preaching style, as well as the content of his sermon. The pronoun "you" dominates the first sermon, clearly because the priest regards himself as a member of the class "wheat." In the second sermon, however, after he has witnessed the death of the innocent child, he speaks of "we," for the neat distinction between wheat and chaff has collapsed. The theodicy Paneloux ultimately employs in the second sermon will be discussed at some length when we discuss teleological theodicies later in this chapter.

In his film *The Virgin Spring* Ingmar Bergman includes a discussion that is very similar to Paneloux's dilemma in seeing the suffering of the innocent child. In the Bergman film a man discovers the body of his murdered daughter and shouts furiously at the heavens:

> You saw it, God. You saw it. The death of an innocent
> child, and my vengeance. You permitted it and I don't
> understand you.[21]

It should be clear that the punishment and warning theodicy is an inappropriate and illogical answer to the problem of evil in the religions of paradox, for the innocent suffer right along with the sinners.[22]

THE FREE WILL DEFENSE

A second more philosophically sophisticated form of the punishment and warning theodicy can be found in the writings of St. Augustine. In short, Augustine argues that far from being the victims of suffering human beings are actually the perpetrators. Theodicy (the justification of God's ways to man) is not Augustine's concern; rather his attention is focused on anthropodicy (the justification of man's ways to God):

> The will which turns from the unchangeable and com-
> mon good and turns to its own private good or to any-
> thing exterior or inferior sins: it turns to its private

> good when it wills to be governed by its own authority; to what is exterior, when it is eager to know what belongs to others and not itself; inferior things, when it likes bodily pleasures. In these ways a man becomes proud, inquisitive, licentious, and is taken captive by another kind of life which, when compared to the righteous life we have just described, is really death.[23]

In his book, *Emile*, the great French romantic Jean Jacques Rousseau develops the free will answer to the problem of evil with a simple certitude:

> Enquire no longer, then, who is the author of evil. Behold him in yourself. There exists no evil in nature than what you either do or suffer, and you are equally the author of both.... Take away everything that is the work of man, and all that remains is good.[24]

Although Rousseau's view of evil is tied to a still somewhat optimistic view of human nature, or at least its possibilities,[25] for Augustine, man has his capacity to sin because of the Fall. Adam and Eve were created by God in a state of innocence with the blessing of free will. But the gift was gravely misused. They rebelled against the rule of God and in so doing took upon themselves the responsibility for the origin of evil, both moral and natural. Thus, as Augustine puts it, there are two kinds of evil — "sin and the consequences of sin." The sorrows and sufferings that befall the human race are seen as the punishment merited by sin. Man brought natural evil upon himself, and as a sinner under judgment, he cannot rightly call God into question for not intervening to stop the evils that are the consequence of man's sin. Man simply gets what he deserves in his experience of sin.

This "free will defense" is a mainstay in the history of Christian theodicy. It was popularized and endorsed by Augustine in the fifth century, and in many ways remains the predominant view in Christian theodicy today. Its influence can easily be traced through the work of Thomas Aquinas, John Calvin, Martin Luther, Charles Journet, Karl Barth, and many others. In our own day, contemporary writers have done much to rehabilitate the free will defense to suit modern sensibilities.[26]

As historically important and pervasive as this Augustinian point of view appears to be, it suffers, nevertheless, from a number of important defects. The most obvious problem with Augustine's answer to the problem of evil is that it accepts as a literal truth the notion that the rest of the human race, countless numbers of people, are justly punishable for all eternity through the sinful deeds of two people. There may be acceptable ways of updating Augustine's view of the Fall so that modern people might be able to reconcile that view of human nature with the realities of contemporary anthropology. But whether Augustine would have been willing to allow this revision is doubtful.

Beyond this historical point, there is a second practical concern that raises doubts about the Augustinian free will defense. Augustine, and those who follow him, allow the focus of theodicy to shift too quickly away from the victims of suffering; the practical reality of suffering is simply ignored when the Augustinians move from theodicy to anthropodicy. A third problem is connected to the first. Augustine seems committed to a notion of an historical, temporal Fall, but it is clear that prior to the existence of *homo sapiens* on this planet the conditions necessary for the experiencing of profound natural evils were already present. In this context, there is no way we can see all evil as proceeding from the temporal Fall. Fourth, and perhaps most importantly, there is, I think, a basic and fatal incoherence that lies at the center of this theodicy. It is self-contradictory to say that a creator, at least in the religions of paradox, is not responsible in some sense for the origin of evil. In orthodox thought after the time of Augustine, God was seen to be an omniresponsible deity who foreordained evil, though God's omniresponsibility does not relieve man of his own responsibility on a different level for moral evils. The real point is this: the Augustinian approach seems to suggest a kind of self-generating evil. If Adam and Eve were *about* to eat from the tree of the knowledge of good and evil, how did they already seem to know what disobedience was?

A fifth question to be entertained concerning all versions of the punishment and warning theodicy, as well as the free will defense, is whether God could have made a world such that people had freedom of choice, but always chose the good.

Charles Peirce would have answered this question with a resounding no. He often refers admiringly to a book, *Substance and Shadow*, by Henry James, Sr., the father of Henry and William. The text contains several comments about this notion of creating a world where everyone chooses the good. Unfortunately, the book is also heavily laden with the rather murky theology of Emmanuel Swedenborg. Consequently, a better idea of the elder James's view of this "good" world can be found in the following excerpt from one of his letters:

> Think of a spiritual existence so wan, so colorless, so miserably dreary and lifeless as this; an existence presided over by a sentimental deity, a deity so narrow-hearted, so brittle-brained, and pretty fingered as

to be unable to make god-like men with hands and
feet to do their own work and go their own errands,
and contents himself therefore, with making spiritual
animals with no functions than those of deglutition,
digestion, assimilation.... These creatures could have
no life. At the most they would barely exist. Life
means individuality or character; and individuality
and character can never be conferred, can never be
communicated by one to another, but must be inward-
ly wrought out of the diligent and painful subjugation
of evil to good in the sphere of one's proper activity.
If God made spiritual sacks, merely, which he might
fill out with his own breath to all eternity, why then of
course evil might have been left out of the creature's
experiences. But he abhors sacks, and loves only men
made in his own image of heart, head and hand.[27]

Ninian Smart takes a very similar kind of approach to
the question of whether God could have made human beings
who always freely choose the good:

None of the usual reasons for calling men good would
apply in such a utopia. Consider one of those harmless
beings. He is wholly good, you say? Really? Has he
been courageous? No, you reply, not exactly, for such
creatures do not feel fear. Then he is generous to his
friends perhaps? Not precisely you respond, for there
is no question of his being ungenerous. Has he resisted temptations? No, not really, for there are no temptations (nothing you could really call temptations...).[28]

From all of this, Smart goes on to conclude:

... that the concept of goodness is applied to beings of
a certain sort, beings who are liable to temptations,

have fears, possess inclinations, tend to assert themselves and so forth; and that if they were immunized
from evil they would have to be built in a different
way. But it soon becomes apparent that to rebuild
them would mean that the ascription of goodness
would become unintelligible, for the reasons why men
are called good and bad have a connection with human
nature as it is empirically discovered to be. Moral
utterances are embedded in the cosmic *status quo.*[29]

Both the criticisms of James as well as those of Smart,
seem to miss the point. The question at hand is whether it
was logically possible to create a race of human beings who
freely chose to always do the good. James and Smart have
set about answering the question concerning what the consequences would be once God made such a race of people.
But concerning the question at hand, I see nothing logically
impossible in the suggestion that God could make a race of
people who always freely choose the good. In order to
understand why I am taking this position, consider the following example: Since the beginning of the human race
there have been a finite number of people who have existed
on earth. And in the finite amount of time *homo sapiens* has
been on this planet, they have made a finite number of
moral choices. Now let the two sides of a coin represent the
two choices for moral good and moral evil. And let each
flip of the coin represent one moral choice freely made. It
is, of course, logically possible that as long as we have a
finite number of flips, the coin could land on the same side
every time. It is highly unlikely, but it is still logically possible. If our analogy is a good one, then it is logically possible that there could exist a finite number of moral agents
who made a finite number of moral choices, but those
choices were always made for the good. There is nothing

logically contradictory or inconsistent in this. In both the James and Smart objections to this position it is implied that "God making beings who always freely choose the good" is incoherent. And this would certainly be true if we were suggesting that God *forces* men to freely choose the good. But that is not what this position is about. If God *forced* men to choose one way or the other, they certainly would not be choosing freely. But God could make creatures who had such good characters that although they had the ability to choose evil, they always preferred not to. Kant seems to be discussing this as a perfectly logical possibility when he refers to what he calls the "holy will."

J.L. Mackie arrives at the same conclusion by using the following formulation:

> If there is no logical impossibility in a man's freely choosing the good on one, or on several occasions, there cannot be a logical impossibility in his freely choosing the good on every occasion. God was not, then, faced with a choice between making innocent automata and making beings who, in acting freely, would sometimes go wrong: There was open to him the obviously better possibility of making beings who would act freely but always do right.

> Clearly his failure to avail himself of this particular possibility is consistent with his being both omnipotent and wholly good.[30]

Anthony Flew also concurs:

> Not only is there no necessary conflict between acting freely and behaving predictably and/or as the result of

caused causes; but also Omnipotence might have created only people who would always as a matter of fact
freely have chosen to do the right thing.[31]

In orthodox Christianity the character of Jesus has been
thought to be both fully human and fully divine. And in the
course of his earthly life, it is believed that Jesus never
sinned. Now clearly this notion of Jesus' sinlessness is
trumpeted among orthodox Christians because it was Jesus
the man who did not sin, though he was subject to all the
same temptations as the rest of us. If it were true that it was
Jesus the God who did not sin, this would be no more interesting than saying that a square did not become a circle. By
his very nature, Jesus the God cannot sin. Indeed, what
makes the story of Jesus's temptation in the desert so
poignant is that as a man Jesus was strong enough in character to stand up to such a giant temptation.

Now if God the father could make one human being who
was of such good character that he always freely chose to
do good, he could certainly make two. Indeed, in traditional
Catholic theology there is the belief that Mary, the mother
of Jesus, was also without sin. Now if God could make two
people of such good character that they freely choose not to
sin, he could make ten. If he could make ten, he could make
millions. If he could make millions, he could make everyone that way. God could have made any finite number of
people who have existed or will exist on earth of such good
character that they always freely choose the good.

Anthony Flew sums up our conclusion on this free will
defense quite well:

> If there is no contradiction here then Omnipotence
> might have made a world inhabited by wholly virtuous
> people; the free will defense is broken-backed ; and

we are back again to the original antinomy.[32]

It must be added here that it matters very little to our argument if Jesus or Mary actually did or did not always freely choose the good. All that need be the case is that it is logically possible that throughout either of their earthly lives, they did not sin.[33]

Another way of raising this objection to both the punishment and warning theodicy, as well as the free will defense, is to ask why God did not make Adam with the character of Jesus, the man, or someone as morally good, and Eve with the character of Mary, or someone with a similar moral character. Their descendants could be very different in most of the myriad ways humans differ, but they would have one thing in common: They would all be of such good moral character that they would always freely choose the good.

Another staunch defense of the free will theodicy can be found in the recent work of Alvin Plantinga,[34] an American philosopher who uses a clever combination of modal arguments and notions of individual "essence" to help circumvent problems for the free will defense.

Plantinga takes as his point of departure Leibniz's *Theodicée.* In that work Leibniz suggests that evil in the world is due to the imperfection characteristic of all finite existence. God in His omniscience recognizes that any created world would suffer from some imperfection. In His infinite goodness and knowledge he has chosen the least imperfect of these possible worlds, and by His omnipotence, He has brought it into existence. Thus, Leibniz concludes, this is the best of all possible worlds. His point of view had its severe critics, even in the late eighteenth century, when, for example, Voltaire in typical ironic spirit asked, "If this is the best of all possible worlds, what must the others be like?"

Plantinga begins his defense of the free will theodicy by suggesting that Leibniz has made what he calls a "lapse."[35] Plantinga argues that Leibniz might have followed a more successful route by proposing the notion that there are possible worlds that even an omnipotent, omniscient, omnibenevolent being is not able to bring about.

Plantinga develops this idea through a number of amusing examples about Maurice choosing oatmeal for breakfast, Paul selling his aardvark, and Curley Smith, the fictitious mayor of Boston who must decide whether to take a bribe in exchange for his dropping opposition to the proposed construction of a new highway.

Suppose that if Mr. Smith were to be offered the bribe, he would reject it. Then it is the case, Plantinga argues, that God could not bring about a possible world in which Mr. Smith existed, was offered the bribe, and accepted it. But suppose that if Mr. Smith were offered the bribe, he would take it. Then it follows just as in the contrary example, that God could not actualize a possible world in which Smith was offered the bribe and refused it. In either situation there is at least one possible world that cannot be actualized, even by an omnipotent, omniscient, omnibenevolent God. If we think for a moment of the number of possible free choices, it is clear, Plantinga suggests, that there are many possible worlds that God could not bring about.

In the second step to Plantinga's argument, he adds to this notion that there are possible worlds that even God could not bring about, a certain view of human essences that suggests people may be so corrupt that in the case of Curley Smith, for example, there is no possible world such that Mr. Smith exists and would refuse the bribe were he to be offered it. According to Plantinga, Curley Smith suffers from "transworld depravity."

Now suppose, Plantinga suggests, that transworld depravity is not only true of Curley Smith, it is true of the rest of us as well, indeed, true of any beings God could have created. The conclusion would follow that "it is possible that God could not have created a world containing moral good but no moral evil."[36]

Although this view would ostensibly account for the existence of moral evil, it says little about why the world contains natural evil. If Plantinga takes the Augustinian line that the natural disasters and hardships of life in the world are the consequence of human sin, we are still left with the thorny problem of why there were natural evils in existence before the advent of human life on this planet. Plantinga responds to this query with the rather *ad hoc* notion that natural evils exist as a by-product of the sins of the fallen angels.

J.L. Mackie, in his recent book *The Miracle of Theism*, poses some further difficulties for Plantinga's view:

> But how is it possible that every creaturely essence suffers from trans-world depravity? This possibility would be realized only if God were faced with a limited range of creaturely essences, a limited number of possible people from which he had to make a selection, if he was to create free agents at all. What can be supposed to have presented him with that limited range? As I have argued, it is not logically impossible that even created persons should always act rightly; the supposed limitation on the range of possible persons is therefore logically contingent. But how can there be logically contingent states of affairs, prior to the creation and existence of any created beings with

free will, which an omnipotent being would have to accept and put up with? This suggestion is simply incoherent.[37]

I think that Mackie is entirely correct. Plantinga does not show that it is possible that all free beings must suffer from transworld depravity. Indeed, it is odd that considering the fact that Plantinga believes in the existence of angels (which solved for him the problem of natural evil) he did not conceive of the possibility of the sinlessness of Jesus, the man, or Mary, his mother. Both of these logical possibilities seem like excellent counter examples to the notion that any created human who also had free choice would suffer from transworld depravity.

THE UNREALITY OF EVIL THEODICIES

There are at least three variations of theodicy that may be included under this heading: (a) that the amount of evil is insufficient to create a problem; (b) that evil is an illusion; and (c) that evil is a deprivation, a distortion of something intrinsically good. We shall discuss these in order.

The amount of evil is insufficient to create a problem.

This point of view has been openly advocated by very few serious thinkers; C.S. Lewis adopts a fairly sophisticated presentation of this theodicy, but he is quite the exception.[38] In its more simple forms this answer may lie behind the prevalent eternal optimism that characterizes the spirits of what William James would call the "healthy minded." On another level, I would suspect that this theodical formulation is widespread among many sincere and pious believers who have never carefully considered the problem of evil from the perspective of the victim, or perhaps among actual victims of suffering who refuse to ask the theoretical questions about the "meaning" of their suffering.

The central claim to this theodicy seems to be that the amount of evil in the world, including human suffering, is insufficient to disturb one's belief about God's omnipotence, omniscience and omnibenevolence. There is not enough evil to warrant the presumptuous act of calling God into account.[39] From a logical point of view, this idea is patently false. All that is needed for the problem of evil to arise is *one* example of moral or natural evil. Given the supposed attributes of God, a single example of evil is sufficient to create a problem. Even if a single example were not enough to create the problem, David Hume lists in his *Dialogues Concerning Natural Religion* a catalogue of woes that should be sufficient to convince any serious thinker that we are beset with more than enough evil to create a problem:

> But though these external insults, said Demea, from animals, from men, from all the elements, which assault us from a frightful catalogue of woes, they are nothing in comparison of those which arise within ourselves, from the distempered condition of our mind and body. How many lie under the lingering torment of disease? Hear the pathetic enumeration of the great poet (John Milton).
>
> Intestine stone and ulcer, colic pangs,
> Demoniac frenzy, moping melancholy,
> And moon struck madness, pining athrophy,
> Marasmus, and wide wasting pestilence.
> Dire was the tossing, deep the groans:

> Despair tended the sick, busiest from couch to couch.
> And over them triumphant Death's dart
> Shook but delayed to strike, though oft invoked
> With vows, as their chief good and final hope.
>
> The disorders of the mind, continued Demea, though more secret, are not perhaps less dismal and vexatious. Remorse, shame, anguish, rage, disappointment, anxiety, fear, dejection, despair — tormentors? How many have scarcely ever felt any better sensations? Labor and poverty, so abhorred by everyone, are the certain lot of the far greater number; and those few privileged persons who enjoy ease and opulence never reach contentment or true felicity. All the goods of life united would not make a very happy man, but all the ills united would make a wretch indeed; and any one of them almost (and who can be free of everyone), nay, often the absence of one good (and who can possess them all) is sufficient to render life ineligible.[40]

It may be that Hume is overstating his case for the ubiquity of evil. Nevertheless, his point is still well taken. There is indeed more than enough evil to create a problem for the theist. The human condition, as Thomas Hobbes suggests in the *Leviathan*, is one that is often "solitary, wolfish, brutish and nasty."

Hume's awareness of the potentially overwhelming magnitude of evil has been shared by many who have endured the unparalleled atrocities of the twentieth century. The realization of the omnipresence of evil has been brought home to our age, perhaps much more clearly than any other. Evil is a positive, real, and sometimes dominating force that often threatens us with senseless destruction. It frequently thwarts even the best of human purposes, and thereby calls into question beliefs about an all loving, all knowing, all powerful creator. Most notably, the World War II experiences of the Jews provide us with a constant reminder of the sometimes devastating reality of evil. Man's capacity for inhuman acts can be seen very clearly in the Holocaust; it was there that relations between human beings seemingly reached their all-time nadir on the scale of depravity and wanton cruelty. It may well be that people have always exhibited this pernicious hatred that seems to go beyond reason, but in the twentieth century we have had the technological skill and resources to demonstrate that hatred far more effectively. It would seem that in the Holocaust we came face to face with evil beyond which nothing greater could be conceived, evil that led some Jewish thinkers to believe that God had lost his morals.[41] There can be no doubt about this matter from the perspective of the victim: the amount of evil does indeed create a problem.

The alleged evil is an illusion. When seen from a larger, or divine perspective, it has a different character.

This statement admits at least two separate interpretations. The first is quite like the answer given to the problem of evil in the religions of dissolution. You will recall that in those traditions the problem is dissolved by suggesting that the whole world of temporal changing things is an illusion, and what we call evil belongs only to this phenomenal realm. Therefore, at bottom level, evil is unreal. A variation of this first approach is to say, with the Christian Scientists, that although temporal things are much as we see them, those we call "evil" are not real.

The other variety of this theodicy has been called the "aesthetic defense." It can be found in the works of Plato, Augustine, and chiefly among eighteenth century optimists.

Its adherents maintain that although individual instances may be seen as evil, when viewed in a larger context, these evils are apprehended as part of a greater good. Sometimes the example of painting is used to stress this point. Often when artworks are viewed close up or in segments they appear quite ugly. But when seen from a distance, or as a whole, the parts that formerly appeared ugly are seen to fit together in a grand pattern. Each of the individual parts, though some may be ugly, in its own way contributes to the beauty of the painting as a whole.[42]

Alexander Pope seems to hold this position in Epistle I of his *Essay on Man*:

> Cease, then, nor order imperfection name,
> Our proper bliss depends on what we blame.
> Know thy own point: this kind, this due degree
> Of blindness, weakness, Heav'n bestow on thee.
> Submit. In this, or any other sphere,
> Secure to be as blest as thou canst bear:
> Safe in the hand of one disposing Pow'r,
> or in the natal or the mortal hour
> All nature is but art, unknown to thee;
> All chance Direction which thou canst not see;
> All discord, Harmony not understood;
> All partial evil, universal Good:
> And spite of pride, inerring Reason's spite
> One truth is clear, whatever is, is right.[43]

One might begin to criticize the first version of the "evil is an illusion" theodicy by suggesting that it goes against the Biblical view, which clearly posits the existence of real, substantial instances of evil. Beyond this Biblical criticism, however, one may suggest that this theodicy falls short on at least two other counts: in terms of plain common sense and on the level of more restrained philosophical discussion.

On the common-sense level Dostoyevski has captured in a painfully detailed way the positive and sometimes crushing reality of evil:

> 'A Bulgarian I met lately,' Ivan went on, seeming not to hear his brother's words, "told me about the crimes committed by the Turks and Circassians in all parts of Bulgaria through fear of general rising of the Slavs. They burn villages, murder, outrage women and children, they nail their prisoners by their ears to the fences, leave them so till morning, and in the morning they hang them — all sorts of things you can't imagine. People talk sometimes of bestial cruelty, but that's a great injustice and insult to the beasts, a beast can never be so cruel as man, so artistically cruel. The tiger only tears and gnaws, that's all he can do. He would never think of nailing people by the ears, even if he were able to do it. These Turks took pleasure in torturing children too; cutting the unborn child from the mother's womb, and tossing babies up in the air and catching them on the points of their bayonets before their mother's eyes. Doing it before the mother's eyes is what gave zest to the amusement. Here is another scene that I thought very interesting. Imagine a trembling mother with her baby in her arms, a circle of invading Turks around her. They've planned a diversion; they pet the baby, laugh to make it laugh. They succeed. The baby laughs. At that moment a Turk points a pistol four inches from the baby's face. The baby laughs with glee, holds out his little hands to the pistol, and he pulls the trigger in the baby's face and blows out its brains. Artistic, wasn't it? By the way, Turks are particularly fond of sweet things, they say.[44]

It would be very difficult to read this passage and suggest that the evil depicted there is somehow illusory. Certainly for the victims, it is seen as very real. F.R. Tennant in his *Philosophical Theology* raises a philosophical objection to this "evil as an illusion" point of view:

> The empirical theist finds no comfort in the supposition that evil is an illusion of finite temporal experience, an inadequate idea, or an appearance which would dissolve away if we only saw *sub specie aeternitatis*. For if evil is an illusion, the illusion is evil.... The problem of evil is raised by the world as we find it, and it is not to be found by diverting attention to other-worldly cognition of a world order other than the phenomenal and the temporal.[45]

John Hick echoes this same kind of criticism when he suggests that the "evil as an illusion" theodicy merely "redescribes the problem." Evil may be an illusion, but we must ask why this illusion seems to cause so much suffering. Evil may be *maya*, but why is there so much *maya*? The problem remains just as thorny as it was before the terminology was altered.

H.D. Lewis comes to the same conclusion about the inadequacy of the "evil is an illusion" theodicy in his *Philosophy of Religion:*

> ...These views seem to me to be nonetheless vastly mistaken; Evil is genuine and positive, and I have indicated already some of the main defects in systems which question its reality. The practical effects of treating evil as mere illusion have already been noted. But it must be added in fairness to the religions and

cultures which tend to give evil, in the last event, no
proper place in the universe, that much in the initial
stages of the attitudes they represent involves a profound, almost obsessive, preoccupation with evil. It is
the unendurable spectacle of evil in its most distress-
ful and insidious forms that prompts the desperate
search for release or oblivion by which mind and heart
are alike averted from the reality of evil. This kind of
escapism cannot, in my view, be good for either the
individual or his society.[46]

Lewis's conclusion, however, seems to have fallen victim to the genetic fallacy. Since he has done a bit of amateur psychologizing to show the "origins" of this belief
about evil as an illusion, he concludes that the belief is
false. But the real problem with this position cannot be
found on psychological or anthropological grounds. It is to
be found in its logical incoherence.

John Wisdom gives a very good summary of the force of
these logical objections:

I will only say briefly that the theory of the unreality
of evil now seems to me untenable. Supposing that it
could be proved that all that we think evil was in reality good, the fact would still remain that we think it
evil. This may be called a delusion of mistake. But a
delusion or mistake is a real thing, as real as anything
else... .But then, to me at least, it seems certain that a
delusion or an error which hid from us the goodness
of the universe would itself be evil.[47]

It is true that the "evil is illusion" theorist could
respond to Wisdom by saying that seeing evil as though it
were real is just another illusion. But this new illusion
could then be pronounced a real evil, since it is now this

illusion that actually deceives us about the true nature of reality and hides the goodness of the universe from us. This could, of course, go on *ad infinitum*, for no matter how many times we call the last evil an illusion, we always leave what is real behind, which eventually in its turn is to be pronounced as evil because it hides from us the way things really are.

The aesthetic version of the "evil is unreal" theodicy can be dismantled on similar logical grounds. If Pope's line about "disorder" being merely harmony not understood is to be taken literally, the "partial evil" of the following line must, if he is to remain consistent, mean something like "that which in isolation really is evil." Line 12 of Pope's poem is, in fact, quite equivocal. It hesitates between two logically incompatible views, that partial evil isn't really evil, since only the "bigger picture" is real, and that partial evil really is evil, albeit a lesser evil.[48]

The alleged evil is a privation, a distortion of something intrinsically good.

The most detailed exposition of this theodicy is to be found in Books XI, XII and XIV of Augustine's *The City of God*, as well as in chapters three and four of the *Enchiridion*. In chapter three of the latter work Augustine explains the nature of evil in the following way:

> What, after all, is anything we call evil except the privation of good? In animal bodies, for instance, sickness and wounds are nothing but the privation of health. When a cure is effected, the evils which are present (i.e. the sickness and the wounds) do not retreat and go elsewhere. Rather, they simply do not exist any more. For such evil is not a substance; the

> wound or the disease is a defect of the bodily sub-
> stance which, as a substance, is good.[49]

A modern version of the "evil is privation" theodicy, which relies heavily on some Augustinian principles, can be found in Errol Harris's *The Problem of Evil*. In that work Professor Harris suggests that evil

> is not, therefore, anything substantial, but is merely
> the negative aspect of what in its positive being is
> good. To revert to our examples, disease is the posi-
> tive reaction of the organism to the effect of another
> positive influence (on the part of the viruses or bacte-
> ria, or the like) which tend to disrupt the organic self-
> maintenance of its system. Each positive trend is con-
> structive and self-maintaining but they come into con-
> flict. The evil involved is simply the degree to which
> the superior and more inclusive system fails to pre-
> serve its integrity. Evil is no positive entity or pro-
> cess. Similarly, stupidity is failure of insight and con-
> fusion of constructive thinking. So far as it is an effort
> to think and understand it is positive and good; and if
> it were not these at all it could not become confused
> nor would there be any attempt to comprehend which
> could fail. Lastly, if we did not constantly strive to
> satisfy our desires, did not seek contentment and per-
> sonal fulfillment, the material of moral action would
> be altogether lacking and so equally the means and
> occasion of moral failure. Wickedness is neither more
> or less than the persistent effort to fulfill oneself in
> ways which negate the very conditions of fulfillment
> both of ourselves and of others.[50]

A third example of "evil as privation" can be seen in the work of the Catholic scholar, Germain Grisez:

Evil thus has a negative character, it is in itself not a positive thing, but a lack of something. Yet not all lack is evil. The person who could murder another is not evil for remaining unfulfilled in this respect. Doughnuts are not evil merely because they really do have holes in them. But a person who attacks the foundation of the other goods in another person by killing him does something wrong, because the choice to act in this manner narrows the scope of one's freedom to an arbitrarily selected subset of all the possibilities a human person can wish to further. A hole in one's gas tank, which allows the gasoline to leak out, also is something missing; the lack of integrity of the metal is a privation in this case, since there ought to be metal where the hole is.[51]

What these examples have in common is this: given the basic belief that the created order is good, and that God is the source of creation, a theodicy follows from these two points that holds that evil has no independent, substantial reality. Augustine in the *City of God* rejects any theodicy that claims that evil is due to the material aspects of the world. Matter is good, God created it as good; therefore, everything created is good in its own way. Evil arises when that which is good is perverted or corrupted in some way. Augustine's chief concern in his privation theory is to show that evil is not something positive; rather, it is a lack of something.[52]

We have already suggested in some detail that any theodicy that does not view evil as something positive and real runs the danger of not taking the experience of sufferers very seriously. On an existential level, the level of experience, this theodicy is open to serious question. F.R. Tennant has rightly noted that the theodicist cannot easily argue that evil is a privation, unreal or nonexistent in the sense of being mere deficiency or negation. The privation theory owes its plausibility to the ease with which abstractions can be verbally manipulated. Tennant rejects this theodicy because he thinks it is reductionistic. He concludes:

> The fact that evil exists in the world is a primary datum for the empiricist theist, knowable with much more certainty than is the being of God.[53]

H.J. McCloskey arrives at the same conclusion about the *privatio boni* defense by taking a much more philosophically rigorous route. He is inclined to admit that certain evils such as blindness and deafness are privations of proper goods. But the question for him becomes one of whether we can easily explain all evils that way. He argues rather forcefully that we cannot.[54] W.I. Wallace, in his *Existence of God*, expresses a similar point of view on this matter:

> It may console the paralytic to be told that paralysis is mere lack of mobility, nothing positive, and that insofar as he is, he is perfect. It is not clear, however, that this kind of comfort is available to the sufferer of malaria. He will reply that his trouble is not that he lacks anything, but rather that he has too much of something, namely, protozoans of the genus Plasmodium. If the theist retorts that evil is nonbeing in the metaphysical not crudely material sense, it would seem appropriate for the victim to inquire why God saw fit that the finitude of his creatures should take just this form rather than some other. Really the "evil is nonbeing" ploy is a play on words, an unfunny joke. It is a sign of progress both in the philosophical acumen and essential humanness, that little is heard along these lines nowadays.[55]

The belief that evil and pain are mere privations of something good seems hardly a satisfactory theodicy. Admittedly, seen in its best light, however, the privation answer may be saying something fairly profound about evil never being an end in itself — that it often leads to, or is overcome by, the good. But this somewhat more sophisticated notion will be discussed under the teleological theodicies.

EVIL IS LOGICALLY NECESSARY

There are at least three versions of theodicy that could be included under the general heading "evil is necessary." We have already had occasion to discuss one of these, (a) Alvin Plantinga's free will defense, and we have made passing references to a second, (b) Leibniz's notion that this is the best of all possible worlds. Both of these positions suggest that we could not have had a world with no evil. For Plantinga, this is because any possible world that God could have made actual would be filled with creatures suffering from transworld depravity. For Leibniz, the sense in which God could not have avoided evil is not simply that it was logically impossible. Rather, it was logically impossible given the fact that this is the best of all possible worlds. Since God is morally responsible for seeking the best, there can be no element in this world that should have been avoided. But this argument is actually based on a not-too-subtle confusion. The proponents of this view are fond of using the analogy of color. If everything were blue, they suggest, we would not have blue as a concept. By analogy, if we did not have something to contrast with good, then the concept "good" would not exist. But it should be clear that this is false. If all the items in the world were the same shade of blue, it is quite true that we would not be able to distinguish the blue, but it would not follow that the blue did not exist. We might not be able to recognize the blue, but it would, nevertheless, still be there. The more coherent formulation of the contrast theodicy is that of Brody who suggests that in order to recognize or appreciate the good, we must have its opposite, evil. If all the objects in the world were blue, it is true that we would be hard pressed to recognize and appreciate the blue.

There are two main avenues of criticism we might explore with respect to Brody's version of the argument. The first assumes that what the contrast theodicy asserts is true. It then criticizes the argument on the grounds that there appears to be an immense amount of gratuitous evil in the world. The other avenue of criticism suggests that the premises on which the contrast theodicy is based are false, and thus it is an invalid argument. Let us begin examining the first criticism by entertaining an example.

Alvin, a free-lance painter, has been recently hired by the Parsimonious Paint Company to demonstrate their new line of indoor house paints. When applying for the job, Alvin was told by his interviewer that the company prides itself on its cost efficiency, and although he would be required to make demonstrations in homes all over Britain, he must, under no circumstances, waste any paint.

During his very first demonstration, Alvin is immediately beset with a serious problem. Mrs. Higgins, his first customer, has suggested that Alvin paint some of her white living room wall with their new "Lagoon Blue," so that she might see the contrast between the new color and what she formerly had. As Alvin begins to paint the wall, the voice of the interviewer reverberates in his ears.

How much of the wall should Alvin paint? Clearly, he

should paint enough so that Mrs. Higgins, a woman of normal intelligence and vision, can appreciate the contrast between her white wall and the new Lagoon Blue, but not a drop more than is needed to accomplish that task, for Alvin is not to waste any paint.

It is very unlikely that Alvin would have to paint half the wall, or even a quarter or an eighth. Indeed, all that would be required would be something like the following:

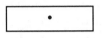

The first condition of his employment has been met, for Alvin, Mrs. Higgins, and any other observer of normal intelligence and vision can easily see the difference between the formerly all white wall and the small experimental dab of Lagoon Blue. The second condition has also been met — Alvin has wasted very little, if any, paint.

Now let the Lagoon Blue stand for evil, while the white represents good. God, in our analogy, plays the part of the Parsimonious Paint company as well as the painter, for He is responsible for the existence of the world and, if the analogy holds, He certainly would not allow any evil to exist that did not serve the important purpose of helping us distinguish evil from good. The question of course is quite simple: How much evil do we need to understand or appreciate the good? How much do we have? Certainly Dostoyevski and Hume would argue a good deal more than we need.

In the other criticism of the "contrast theodicy," the thesis that "in order to apprehend and appreciate the existence of something, you have to have its opposite" is denied. In order to understand why this premise is not acceptable, we must look for a moment at the orthodox Christian conception of heaven.[56] If the principle that underlies the contrast theodicy is true, how do the souls residing in heaven realize they are experiencing heavenly bliss? Surely it is not because they are having experiences of evil in heaven. One might respond by saying that they remember evil from when they were on earth. But clearly this will not do, for babies who died shortly after birth would have no such experiences.[57] Still, it could be argued, they would know they are in heaven because they could see people on earth suffering. But once again this will not do. If the souls were to watch for example, the senseless murder of an innocent person, by the very fact that the souls were of the kind of moral character that merited heavenly bliss, they should feel for the victim with appropriate sadness and distress. This would also serve the useful purpose of allowing a contrast between the evil done to the poor victim and the heavenly residents' condition of heavenly bliss. But it would seem that by definition souls in heaven should not feel sorrow, and so we are left with a curious paradox: The souls in paradise cannot know they are experiencing heavenly bliss because they can't experience or apprehend evil in heaven. If they could apprehend or experience evil in heaven, they would not, by definition, be in heaven.

One way out of this paradox is to suggest that the principle on which the contrast theodicy is based is false. Indeed, it seems perfectly plausible to say that the reason souls in heaven know what heavenly bliss amounts to is that they can contrast their condition, not with its opposite, but rather against the vision of God. They could know they are experiencing heavenly bliss by understanding that they are not God. The contrast need not be between opposites, it may be a contrast in degree rather than kind.

Plato seems to be suggesting the same notion in Book

Nine of the *Republic*, when he talks about the pleasures of taste and smell. These two sensations, Plato notes, seem not to depend for their existence on any prior experience of pain. Thus, the central notion of the contrast theodicy "in order to understand or apprehend the existence of something you must have its opposite" can be denied, and the argument can be seen as unsound.[58]

TELEOLOGICAL THEODICIES

There are at least two versions of the teleological theodicy: (a) the moral quality theodicy, and (b) the theodicy of future harmony. What these points of view have in common is that they both assert that evil in some way brings about good. They are different from the "evil is necessary" theodicies because the teleological approaches do not suggest that it is necessary that God brings about things the way he has.[59] The "moral quality" approach is so named because it emphasizes the moral qualities that often result from the human encounter with evil. The "future harmony" theodicy gets its name from its controlling belief that in some future harmony to come, a kingdom of God realized, all evils will be seen as actually resulting in good.

Baruch Brody briefly describes a version of the moral quality theodicy:

> One of the greatest goods we possess are our moral qualities of courage, mercy and compassion. But these qualities arise and develop out of the confrontation with evil and wrongs. So in order to allow us these prized moral qualities, God had to create a world in which evil exists.[60]

Richard Swinburne seems to have a similar perspective in his *Existence of God*, where he argues that natural evils provide, among other things, an opportunity for people to grow in knowledge and understanding:

> If men were to have knowledge of the evil which will result from their actions or negligence, laws of nature must act regularly; and that means that there will be what I call victims of the system...if men are to have the opportunity to bring about serious evils for themselves or others by actions of negligence, or to prevent their occurrence, and if all knowledge of the future is obtained through normal induction, that is from induction from patterns of similar events in the past then there will be serious natural evils occurring to animals and man.[61]

Swinburne entertains the possibility that God could have given people this knowledge by just informing them of it, rather than having them experience it. But if this were the case, he argues, no one would fail to believe in God, and thus everyone would be compelled to accept the divine word. Additionally, no one would be in a position to acquire knowledge of the way the world works on his or her own. Thus, Swinburne concludes:

> that a world in which God gave men verbal knowledge of the consequences of their actions would not be a world in which men had a significant choice of destiny, of what to make of ourselves, and of the world. God would be far too close for them to be able to work things out for themselves. If God is to give man knowledge while at the same time allowing him a genuine choice of destiny, it must be normal inductive knowledge.[62]

John Hick takes up this same point in the third edition of his *Philosophy of Religion*. He seems to agree about the necessity of God creating human beings at an epistemic distance from himself:

> The other consideration is that if men and women had been initially created in the direct presence of God, who is infinite in life and power, goodness and knowledge, they would have had no genuine freedom in relation to their maker. In order to be fully personal and therefore morally free beings, they have accordingly (it is suggested) been created at a distance — not a spatial but an epistemic distance, a distance in the dimension of knowledge...[63]

Hick also concurs with Swinburne on the preferability of having evil in the world so that human beings may perfect certain moral qualities:

> ...A world without problems and difficulties, perils and hardships would be morally static. For moral and spiritual growth comes through response to challenges. Accordingly, a person-making environment cannot be plastic to human wishes but must have its own structure in terms of which men have to learn to live and which they ignore at their peril.[64]

It is clear that Hick is in substantial agreement with Swinburne on the importance of the moral quality theodicy, but he also goes a good deal beyond it. Indeed, he seems to attach to the moral quality answer another point of view, which he feels is intimately related to it and makes it more plausible. He calls this second approach "eschatological verification." It is at the heart of what we have labelled the "future harmony" theodicy. He conveys the sense of this second approach through the use of a parable:

> Two people are traveling together along a road. One
> of them believes that it leads to the Celestial City, the
> other that it leads nowhere, but since it is the only
> road there is, both must travel it. Neither of them has
> been this way before; therefore, neither is able to say
> what they will find around each corner. During their
> journey they meet with moments of refreshment and
> delight, and with moments of hardship and danger. All
> the time one of them thinks about the trip as a pil-
> grimage to the Celestial City. She interprets the pleas-
> ant parts as encouragements and the obstacles as trials
> of her purpose and lessons in endurance, prepared by
> the sovereign of that city and designed to make of her
> a worthy citizen of the place when at last she arrives.
> The other, however, believes none of this, and sees
> their journey as an unavoidable and aimless ramble.
> Since he has no choice in the matter, he enjoys the
> good and endures the bad. For him there is no
> Celestial City to be reached, and no all encompassing
> purpose ordaining their journeys; there is only the
> road itself and the luck of the road in good weather
> and in bad.[65]

Hick adds a rather short commentary to his tale:

> During the course of the journey, the issue between
> them is not an experimental one. That is to say, they
> do not entertain different expectations about the com-
> ing details of the road, but only about its ultimate des-
> tination. Yet, when they turn the last corner, it will be
> apparent that one of them has been right all the time
> and the other wrong. Thus, although the issue between
> them has not been experimental, it has nevertheless
> been a real issue. They have not merely felt different-

ly about the road, for one is feeling appropriately and the other inappropriately in relation to the actual state of affairs. The opposed interpretations of the situation have constituted genuinely rival assertions, whose assertion-status has the peculiar characteristic of being guaranteed retrospectively by a future crux.[66]

Thus, Hick sees an important connection between the moral quality theodicy mentioned earlier and its eschatological verification at the end of time, or, to use his metaphor, at the end of life's journey. It is at that time, Hick suggests, that it will be clear that the future harmony theodicy has been the proper interpretation of the way things are. At the end, all evils will be seen as actually resulting in good.

M.B. Ahern has suggested that Hick's theodical position can be summed up in six points:

(1) God's purpose in creating this world was to provide the logically necessary environment in which human persons could respond freely to His infinite love and freely accept a God centered rather than a self-centered life. Such a world is better than a world without evil, or a world with less evil but with morally determined beings.

(2) The freedom needed by human beings if they are to respond to God as free persons and not as automata logically supposes an element of unpredictability which makes it impossible for God to ensure that moral evil will never occur.

(3) Pain and suffering are part of the environment logically necessary for the moral growth of persons by trial and testing.

(4) The apparently excessive pain and suffering in the
world is due partly to its being the necessary condition of certain virtues and partly to the positive value
of mystery that challenges faith and trust.

(5) The joys of life after death will amply compensate
for the difficulties of this life and there will be no
human being who does not have them.

(6) The existence of animals which will suffer pain is
explained by their being a necessary part of an environment which sets men at a distance from God so
that no one is compelled to accept Him: their pain is
compensated for by animal good.[67]

Swinburne would most certainly agree that his position
includes (1) through (4) above. Since his position, the
moral quality theodicy, is subsumed in Hick's larger teleological perspective, we may effectively criticize them both
by attending to the shortcomings of Hick's approach.

First, from the standpoint of the sufferer Hick's position
leaves much to be desired. From a practical point of view,
evil cannot be regarded as instrumental to a greater good
without losing sight of the evil through a kind of objectification. If we regard all experiences of evil as related to a
higher good, it requires the victim to rise above or to transcend the evil, which is precisely what the victims of suffering often cannot do. This point becomes quite clear when
we bring the teleological theodicy to the bar of real experience. Something rings hollow when we approach the sur-
vivors of Auschwitz with the notion that their suffering has
brought about compassion, higher moral values, and rededi-
cation to the fight against genocide in other parts of the
world. To argue that the purpose of such atrocities is such

that certain goods can come out of them seems difficult, if not ridiculous. When this kind of approach is taken, it often seems to subordinate the individual experience of evil to the construction of an all-encompassing theological system that says nothing sincere to the victims of suffering. When the viewpoint of the individual sufferer is kept central, neither later goods nor a future harmony can be allowed to rob the suffering of its reality here and now. It is true that sometimes the sufferer, or someone totally sympathetic with him, may see that a particular evil has led or will lead to some good. This is particularly true in cases of self-sacrifice, where the victim willingly allows himself to be harmed in order to bring about a greater good. But a warrant for broadening these kinds of selected cases seems unclear.

On a philosophical level, there is another more serious problem with Hick's point of view. If his teleological approach is correct, why does there appear to be so much dysteleological evil, evil that cannot be seen to point to any obvious good? It is here that Hick resorts to such vague higher goods as "better moral character" or "higher awareness of the value of self-sacrifice." But I am not at all sure these "higher goods" do justice to the evils experienced. I am reminded of one Jewish theologian, reflecting on the Holocaust, who noted, "If one tries to hear a redeeming voice at Auschwitz, there is only silence."[68] This also seems to be the case with countless other evils: disastrous earthquakes, senseless accidents, serious birth defects. Even from a coldly dispassionate point of view, it is often very difficult to find even possible good ends for them.

If we could be guaranteed heavenly survival after death in reparation for the past evils we have experienced, the question could still be raised about whether eternal life would really make those evil experiences right. Doubts about the repairable character of survival after death have eloquently been voiced by Dostoyevski in the "rebellion" chapter of *The Brothers Karamazov*.

Here Alyosha and Ivan are discussing the problem of evil. Ivan, who always seems to take the viewpoint of the sufferer, describes the "unanswerably clear case" of suffering children and explains why he cannot accept that such suffering would in any way be repairable:

> I understand, of course, what an upheaval it will be, when everything in heaven and earth blends in one hymn of praise and everything that lives and has lived cries aloud: 'Thou art just, 0 Lord, for Thy ways are revealed.' When the mother embraces the fiend who threw her child to the dogs, and all three cry aloud with loud tears, 'Thou art just, 0 Lord.' Then, of course, the crown of knowledge will be reached and all will be made clear. But what pulls me up here is that I can't accept the harmony. And while I am here on earth, I make haste to make my own measures. You see, Alyosha, perhaps it may really happen that if I live to see the moment, or rise again to see it, I too, perhaps, may cry aloud with the rest, looking at the mother embracing the child's torturer, 'Thou art just, O Lord.' But I don't want to cry aloud now. While there is still time, I hasten to protect myself and so renounce the higher harmony all together. It's not worth the tears of that one tortured child who beat itself on the breast with its little fist and prayed in its stinking outhouse, with its unexpiated tears to 'dear, kind God.' It's not worth it, because those tears are unatoned for. They must be atoned for, or there can be no harmony.[69]

Alyosha then asks how these tears could be atoned for. Ivan responds:

> By their being avenged? But what do I care for aveng-
> ing them? What do I care for a hell for oppressors?
> What good can hell do since these children have
> already been tortured? And what comes of harmony, if
> there is a hell? I want to forgive. I want to embrace. I
> don't want more suffering. And if the suffering of
> children go to swell the sum of sufferings which were
> necessary to pay for truth, then I protest that the truth
> was not worth such a price. I don't want the mother to
> embrace the oppressor who threw her son to the dogs.
> She dare not forgive him. Let her forgive him for her-
> self, if she will, let her forgive the torturer for the
> immeasurable suffering of her mother's heart. But the
> suffering of her tortured child she has no right to for-
> give; she dare not forgive the torturer, even if the
> child were to forgive him. And if that is so, if they
> dare not forgive, what becomes of harmony? From
> love for humanity I don't want it. I would rather be
> left with an unavenged suffering and unsatisfied
> indignation, even if I were wrong. Besides, too high a
> price is paid for harmony; it's beyond our means to
> pay so much to enter it. And so I hasten to give back
> my entrance ticket, and if I am an honest man, I am
> bound to give it back as soon as possible. And that I
> am doing. It's not God that I don't accept? Alyosha,
> only I most respectfully return Him the ticket.[70]

I have quoted at length from this section of *The Brothers Karamazov* because it so forcefully represents the sympathetic point of view one must take in order to approach the reality of evil in a proper way. Rejecting a repaired and "happy world built on injustice and suffering,"

Ivan sees that if one reflects that evil is altered or repaired by certain circumstances, this thought at once loses sight of the real evil experienced by the sufferer and, in a way, demeans the integrity of the victim of suffering.

But beyond the question of the existential place of the sufferer in the theodicy of John Hick, there are also some logical and empirical confusions that must be cleared up regarding his view of survival.

In developing his view of eschatological verification, Hick appears to be committed to three distinct claims: First, that the self exists and continues to have experiences after death. The idea of verification makes little sense, Hick points out, if there are no selves left to do the verifying. Second, he suggests in the spirit of Biblical anthropology and much of modern analytic philosophy that it is unacceptable to conceive of people as disembodied spirits. Thus, he argues for a form of resurrection of the body rather than immortality of the soul.[71] Third, Hick suggests that these resurrected bodies will live and have experiences in a space totally different in kind from our present, physical space.

Some recent critics,[72] Anthony Flew spearheading the attack, have insisted that Hick's three claims are not false but rather they are meaningless. These philosophers suggest that the whole notion of the afterlife makes no sense because it is self-contradictory. There may, however, also be a confusion here among the critics. The real issue, if one reads Hick carefully, is not life after death, but rather experiences after death. It is true that there may be a contradiction about being biologically alive while at the same time being biologically dead, but there is nothing obviously contradictory about having experiences in a resurrected body. It is true that this would seem to require an act of omnipotence but that would appear to be no real obstacle for the

God of the Judeo-Christian tradition.

The key to Hick's view is that he is arguing that the notion of having experience in a resurrected body that exists in a disparate realm of space is an empirically meaningful claim.[73] This is, of course, a much stronger claim than suggesting that it is free of self-contradiction. Hick's main argument advanced in favor of his thesis is that the assertion "I am having experiences in a resurrected body in a disparate realm of space" could be verified by someone watching me. Now even if we concede that this is an empirically verifiable proposition, we must keep in mind at what time it becomes such. We might grant that it is an empirically meaningful proposition then; however, the problem seems to be whether it is empirically meaningful now. Indeed, Hick seems to come very close to admitting that this notion is meaningless now in the sense that we cannot now verify some state of affairs that would obtain then.[74] Such experiences cannot be shown to be false, Hick points out, but they can be shown to be true. In other words, if the proposition "I am having experiences in a resurrected body existing in a disparate space" is false, then I can never verify it by my experiences, but I could establish it with my experiences, and others could verify it the same way I do. But the difficulty still resides in the fact that the verification of these experiences could only be had then, while the problem we are addressing is whether they are meaningful now. As Hick has already suggested, since the verifying experiences could only be had then, presumably we can conclude that the whole matter is meaningless now. As Kai Nielson has suggested, "Hick in effect is trying to pull himself up by his own bootstraps."[75]

But perhaps there is a way out of this problem for Hick. The criticism we have outlined seems to rest on the verification principle of meaning. Although there have been various formulations of the principle since the publication of A.J. Ayer's *Language, Truth and Logic*,[76] the following, I think, is a fair rendering of the principle: an assertion is meaningful if and only if some sense observation would be directly or indirectly relevant to its confirmation or disconfirmation. If this really is the foundation for the argument against Hick, he may not be in serious difficulty after all.

One problem that has been discussed in regard to the verification principle is its restriction to sensory data. There may well be other types of experiences that are quite genuine and of real noetic significance but are not sensory experiences. Consider "remembering," for example. It is generally agreed among philosophers and psychologists alike that remembering is not, strictly speaking, a sense experience, though the object or objects remembered may have originally been apprehended by the senses. Does it make sense to talk about experiencing an object and then "experiencing the experiencing of an object"? Of course not, unless we want to say that we are restricted solely to our sense experiences.

The experience of having a headache is also not a sense experience, yet it makes good sense to talk about the experience of having a headache. Other problems may exist for the verification principle as well. The principle says nothing about who is to do the verifying nor when it is to be made. Indeed, one might ask what it is that verifies the verification principle. Certainly it is not sense experiences. If we use the verification principle to verify itself, it is a bit like asking a man if he always tells the truth and when he says yes believing him on the strength of his own testimony. If we use some other kind of verification principle, then we are still left with the sticky problem of verifying that principle.

Let us now return to what is at stake here to see what this has to do with Hick's argument. We have suggested that the difficulty with Hick's position is that the experiences that would verify the statement "I am having experiences in a resurrected body existing in a disparate realm of space" could only be had then, and are not available to us now, from which it would seem to follow that all talk about then is meaningless now. But consider the following example: Suppose after returning from a baseball game I were to say, "I saw the Baltimore Orioles play," and in the anticipation of another game in the future I were to add, "and I plan on seeing them again in the not too distant future." Now suppose these comments were made in the presence of a confirmed logical positivist. It seems to me that he would have to object to my statements on the grounds that all such talk about the future was meaningless, since the sense experiences that could confirm it were not available now. Indeed, the very same objection could be made to my reference to the game just past. Now suppose that any statements I made to this person, in an attempt to reply, were thought by him to be inadmissible unless they referred to my immediate sense experience. Indeed, he suggests that I am merely trying to pull myself up by my bootstraps.

But if we look at this positivist view very closely, it may have some unwanted side effects. Any statements about the positivist's own mind would be inadmissible since I am not given to myself in sense experiences. Any statements about his own past and future would also be meaningless, including that time in the past when he first happened upon Alfred Ayer's book. Also, statements about others' minds would be just as meaningless, which would put him in the rather bizarre position of trying to refute someone who may not even have a mind, since one does not come to know about another's mind, strictly speaking, through sense experience. If the positivist were then to argue for the meaningfulness of these concepts, we could accuse him of attempting to pull himself up by his own bootstraps.

If we were to grant that eschatological verification is an empirically meaningful concept, we must also say that Hick seems still to be going about his task in the wrong way. The critics insist on verification in this world, and Hick seems to fail to even meet them halfway in resorting to verification beyond the grave. In some ways Hick seems to be willing to do the verification dance but without paying the verification fiddler.

We must, of course, keep in mind that showing that a concept is meaningful is different from showing what kinds of experiences would confirm or disconfirm it. Hick says this about establishing the truth of eschatological verification:

> I shall not spend time in trying to draw a picture of a resurrected existence which would merely prolong the religious ambiguity of our present life. The important question for our purpose is not whether one can conceive of afterlife experiences which would verify theism (and in point of fact one can easily conceive of them), but whether one can conceive of afterlife experiences which would serve to verify them.[77]

Hick hopes to find some experimental situation in the next life that would conclusively verify the truth not only of his theodicy but also of Christian theism in general. But certainly he must tell us now what would show that his view is correct. This failure of Hick to specify when and how his brand of theodicy is to be verified has led to a problem discussed very clearly by J.E. Barnhart:

> Unfortunately, Hick's argument can be turned against him, for in the next life one could use Hick's argument to say, 'well things seem to support the view of God's loving providence, but the final word is not yet in. By and by we will see that what seems to us to be divine providence is really a mistaken impression rooted in our failure to grasp the entire picture, for in the eschaton that is still to come after heaven, we will actually verify that things are not at all like what they seem to be here in this temporary heaven.'[78]

Barnhart points out that if one suggests that this "survival after heaven" view seems a bit too fanciful for us to take seriously, the same charge could be leveled against Hick's initial view of heaven. Hick gives no specific point at which his eschatological view will be known to be the proper description of things. Barnhart argues that this vacillation might leave the residents of heaven in an epistemic quandary as to when the final word is in on eschatological verification.

In an earlier article,[79] Hick does suggest, however, that the Christian tradition offers two different accounts of verifying experiences after death: the Beatific Vision and/or the experience of Christ in his kingdom. But Hick doubts that these two accounts can be combined as readily as many traditional theologians assume, and he also raises serious doubts about whether the Beatific Vision is meaningful to us now, "for the exposition of it provides little more than the phrase itself for discussion."[80]

Hick seems to have a good deal more confidence in seeing Christ in his kingdom. He suggests that this might point unambiguously to the existence of a loving God. His notion of seeing Jesus in his kingdom appears to involve an experience of the fulfillment of God's purpose for ourselves in conjunction with the experience of communion with God as he revealed himself through Jesus.

It is important to note that this kind of experience, Hick suggests, would not prove his theodicy to be logically necessary and thereby conclusively established; rather, he wants to claim that this kind of experience would remove his theodicy from the realm of reasonable doubt.

But once again, this claim is beset with a host of difficulties. First, there is still the very real problem of observing Christ in his kingdom. It is very difficult to nail down exactly what he is talking about when he uses this expression. If it amounts to seeing Jesus in his resurrected body, presiding over all his subjects who were also in their resurrected bodies, how would this differ epistemically from Jesus' life on earth? Hick suggests that it would be different because the view of the onlookers would be radically different from the view they had on earth, for the truth of theism and the answer to the problem of evil were on earth still in the realm of reasonable doubt.[81]

This eschatological view would have to be sufficiently different in kind to make impossible the "faith response" that has been the hallmark of Christians for centuries. But if this were the case, there must also be an admission that we do not know now what kinds of observations could be made in heaven that would confirm Hick's particular brand of theodicy.[82]

There are a number of other points at which Hick's theodicy might also be criticized. One of the most obvious vulnerabilities is his insistence on answering one very large question, why do the righteous suffer, with an equally substantial question, do we survive death? We could very easily turn his argument around and say that the reason we can be certain of survival after death is that it will finally give us an answer to the problem of evil. In *Evil and the God of Love* hypotheses are built one on top of the other, with no real firm basis for speculation.

Hick's parable about the journey seems, in a real way, to be loading the dice. If we call what the two people are experiencing a "journey," then we quite rightly begin to ask questions about where they might be going, and we immediately sympathize with the individual who has some sense of what she is doing. But why should we use the analogy of the journey to begin with? Why not assume that they are out for a walk, with no destination in mind? In this version the one person sees all the events of the walk as enjoyable experiences to be savored for their own sake, while the other person continues to insist that there must be some overarching reason for all the experiences they are having on their stroll. In this example, it is clear that it is the latter person who has things all wrong and who suffers from an inability to garner various meanings from life depending on the situations that arise.[83]

Hick refers in his parable to difficult experiences as "obstacles" and "trials of purpose and lessons of endurance." And it would appear that if we are to take this image seriously, we must conclude that some people, because of extraordinary amounts of suffering, fail their trials. Indeed, this is precisely what is wrong with Swinburne's analysis as well. The adherents to the moral quality theodicy speak as though in each encounter with suffering there is a real possibility of "passing the test" and gaining in genuine moral insight.[84] In reality, this is clearly not always the case. And, more importantly, it is not always

the fault of the victims. H.D. Lewis points to this same difficulty with "soul factory" brands of theodicy akin to
Hick's:

> The trouble with this answer is that there is much suf-
> fering which it does not cover, suffering which
> degrades more than it ennobles, distress and debility
> which reduces men to a state akin to that of brutes and
> does little to deepen their character and sensitivity.
> The same applies to another answer that has much
> truth in it, namely that suffering and need bring out
> charity and sympathy. It would certainly be a poor
> world in which men never had the opportunity to bear
> one another's burdens, but again there is a surd which
> cannot be brought under this explanation; there is a
> wide range of ills which seem out of proportion to any
> benevolence they help display or elicit. There are situ-
> ations of sudden catastrophe and bereavement where it
> is perverse and provoking to proffer such consola-
> tion.[85]

When pressed on this point about excessive suffering,
Hick has the following to say:

> Our solution then to this baffling problem of exces-
> sive and undeserved punishment is a frank appeal to
> the positive value of mystery. Such suffering remains
> unjust and inexplicably haphazard. The mystery is a
> real mystery, inpenetrable to the rationalizing, human
> mind. It challenges the Christian faith with utterly
> baffling, alien, destructive meaninglessness.[86]

Yet theodicy and mystery would appear to be antitheti-
cal. The purpose of theodicy is, by and large, to show the
justice of God through appeals to reason. If the problem

collapses into mystery, we have clearly left the arena of reason.

Another major problem with Hick's point of view is that an ambiguity seems to exist in his position as to whether evil is real or not. Hick's theological justification for the disasters and the morally heinous acts of life is to aver that they are "genuine evils" but contained and overruled by God's ultimate purpose; he insists that they are utterly real and yet relative to a final good in which "nothing will have been finally and sheerly evil." This ambiguity is engendered by Hick's desire, I think, to escape the answer given by the religions of solution, which would make evil ultimate and beyond God's sovereignty, and monism, which would ultimately deny the reality of evil altogether. In the end, Hick seems to yield to the latter in order to save God's omnipotence. And to be certain that omnibenevolence will also be preserved, he adds universal salvation after death. "Evil is really evil, really malevolent, and deadly...and yet in the end it will be defeated and made to serve God's purpose."

In Camus' novel, *The Plague*, Father Paneloux's second sermon points to the same kind of ambiguity. You will remember that in the first of his homilies, the priest suggested that the plague could be understood as deserved punishment. You will also recall that a crucial event occurs between the first and second sermons that changes Father Paneloux's view of theodicy. The event, the death of an innocent child, forces the priest to abandon the retributive justice position.

In the second sermon, the priest introduces a new theodicy. The first sermon had attempted to demonstrate God's justice through the use of a kind of empirical method. The priest took stock of who had sinned and, consequently, who had died. Unfortunately, his equation, with the death of the small child, was shown to be too simplistic a view of the problem. The second sermon might be called a theodicy of last resort. It sounds very reminiscent of what Hick has said about the positive value of mystery. Father Paneloux says

> I understand that sort of thing is revolting because it passes our human understanding. But perhaps we should love what we cannot understand.[87]

Yet, it is of some interest that the priest does not, in the final analysis, resort to Hick's eschatological verification:

> In other manifestations of life God made things easy for us and, thus far, our religion had no merit. But in this respect he put us, so to speak, with our backs to the wall. Indeed, we all were up against the wall that plague had built around us, and under its lethal shadow we must work out our salvation. He, Father Paneloux, refused to have any recourse to simple devices enabling him to scale that wall. Thus he might easily have assured them that the child's suffering would be compensated for by an eternity of bliss awaiting him. But how could he give that assurance when, to tell the truth, he knew nothing about it? For who would dare to assert that eternal happiness can compensate for a single moment's human suffering.[88]

At least one other thorny problem with Hick's theodicy remains to be discussed. Hick maintains throughout *Evil and the God of Love* that moral choices required by God's purposes for creation are, at least in part, unpredictable. In these sections of the book, Hick appears to be suggesting that God cannot know what these human choices will be until after the decisions have been made. Now if this is true, it is difficult to see how God could have known in advance that his purposes for creation would be achieved in the end. M.B. Ahern points to this same problem:

> How could God be certain, before creating, that a free response to the good would be made in even one case or at least in enough cases to justify the world's evils. Uncertainty about the good outcome of the world makes it doubtful whether God was justified in creating. The risk seems too great. Furthermore, although he believes all men, no matter how evil in this world will share the blessedness of an afterlife, Hick gives no clear ground for certainty of this. If unforced moral response to God and to good is a supreme value, it is difficult to see how it could be certain, either before creation or after it, and that all men will actually make this response in this life or in the next. For his belief Hick claims not absolute certainty but practical certainty because of God's power to win people to himself. However, he does not explain how this power of God's is to be reconciled with unforced moral response in every instance.[89]

If Hick's view included foreknowledge of the events of the world, the theory would not suffer from these problems. His view of the positive character of suffering might also be better accepted. But he has chosen not to take this route. Richard Swinburne's position does not suffer from these particular problems, for Swinburne argues rather convincingly for God's omniscience, which includes foreknowledge. But Swinburne is not arguing for eschatological verification.

As I have attempted to show, Hick's proposed theodicy suffers from a number of difficulties. He all too often seems to employ the old theological trick, "if you can't refute it,

incorporate it into your argument." This is particularly true
of his arguments about the positive value of mystery and
"eschatological verification." Hick's theodicy in its present
form would account for a world twice, five times, even ten
times as evil as the present one. Indeed, because he suggests that senseless, irrational evil always has teleological
worth, he could account for an almost boundless amount of
evil, a kind of hell on earth. Were the world suddenly to
turn into a giant Auschwitz, where all suffered in unspeak-
able agony but which produced an occasional development
of moral character, Hick's theodicy would remain unshaken.
It would still be descriptive of the facts. Surely a theodicy
that accounts for a world with any degree of evil must be
seen as inadequate.

John Hospers seems troubled by this very point, as we
can see from the following passage of his *An Introduction
to Philosophical Analysis:*

> It is true that people have to suffer pain in order to
> recover health, our medical knowledge being what it
> is, and the laws of nature (particularly of biology in
> this case) being what they are. But this consideration
> which does justify a physician in inflicting pain on a
> patient in order that the patient may recover, applies
> only to limited beings who can achieve the end no
> other way. Once we suspect, however, that the physi-
> cian could achieve the goal without inflicting suffer-
> ing on his patients, and that he is inflicting anyway,
> we call him a cruel and sadistic monster. Now God,
> unlike the physician, is omnipotent; he could bring
> about a recovery without making a patient go through
> the excruciating pain. Why then does he not do this?
> If it is objected that this would require a miracle and
> that it would upset the orderliness of nature to contin-
> ually perform miracles, it can be replied that the laws

of nature could have been so set up that no miracle would be required in each case. After all, who is the author of the laws of nature? Why did God set up the causal order in such a way as to require his creatures to die in pain and agony? There is not the excuse in the case of God that there is in the case of the physician who can bring about his patient's recovery only by causing suffering, for God, being omnipotent as well as benevolent, could bring about the recovery without such means; indeed, he could have kept the patient from being sick in the first place. What would we think of a patient who first inflicted his child's leg and then decided to amputate it, although a cure was in his power and the infection was of his own giving to begin with? But this would be precisely the position of an omnipotent God, for being omnipotent, he does not need to use evil means to bring about a good end.[90]

A similar comment can be found in Josiah Royce's *The Problem of Job*. In that work, Royce, keeping in mind the perspective of the victims of suffering, makes a pertinent comment on the inadequacy of theodicies that rely on a soul factory interpretation of evil:

This talk of medicinal and disciplinary evil, perfectly fair when applied to our poor fate-bound human surgeons, judges, jailers, or teachers, becomes cruelly and even cynically trivial when applied to explain the ways of God.... I confess, as a layman, that whenever, at a funeral, in the company of mourners who are immediately facing Job's own personal problem, who ask that terrible and uttermost question of God himself...and require the direct answer — that whenever, I say, in such a company I have to listen to these half-

way answers, to these superficial splashes in the
wavelets at the water's edge of sorrow, while the black
unfathomed ocean of infinite evil spreads out before
our wide open eyes — well, at such times this trivial
speech about useful burns and salutary medicines
makes me, and I fancy others, simply wearily heart-
sick. Some words are due children at school, to pee-
vish patients in the sickroom who need a little tempo-
rary quieting. But quite other speech is due to men
and women when they are wakened to the higher reason of Job by fierce anguish of our mortal life's ultimate facts. They deserve either our simple silence, or
if we are ready to speak, the speech of people who
ourselves inquire as Job inquired.[91]

Royce's comments lead us quite naturally to the next
chapter, an analysis of the speeches of Yahweh and the
repentance of Job. There we will discuss the notion of "seeing God" as an "answer" to the problem of suffering. Before
doing this, however, let us make some final comments
about what has been accomplished in this chapter.

We began this chapter by offering a critical analysis of
most, if not all, of the major theodicies offered in the
Judeo-Christian tradition. In the course of this study, we
have delineated four major kinds of answers to the problem
of evil: punishment and warning theodicies; "unreality of
evil" theodicies; "evil is logically necessary" theodicies;
and teleological theodicies. In each of these four categories,
we explored a number of variations. In all of the examples
of the first three types, however, we have attempted to show
that there is at least one basic logical flaw that renders
those answers to the problem of evil invalid. In the fourth
type, the teleological theodicies, the inadequacy is not to be
found on logical grounds; rather, it lies in the fact that

these answers seem to pay so little heed to the victims of suffering. Although John Hick's answer to the problem of evil is logically possible, from the standpoint of the victim of suffering, it is not particularly appealing. We have also attempted to show that although there are no logical problems that sound the death knell for Hick's approach, there are still a number of logical difficulties that render his position on the problem of evil at times unclear and ambiguous.

In the following chapter we shall take a close look at the perspective offered by the *Book of Job* in the hope of laying the groundwork for a response to the problem of evil, offered in chapter five, that is logically consistent, true to the Christian form of life and at the same time sensitive to the needs and the point of view of the victim of suffering.

Notes

1. Gabriel Marcel, *The Philosophy of Existence* (London: Harvill Press, 1948) pp. 260-261.

2. M. Hay, "Europe and the Jews," *Religion From Tolstoy to Camus*, edited by Walter Kaufmann (New York: Harper Brothers, 1961) pp. 339ff. I am indebted for the reformulation of (b) to members of Prof. McBride's seminar in Old Testament Theodicy, Yale Divinity School, 1975.

3. John Hick, *Evil and the God of Love*, p. 10. Austin Farrer is even more bold in excluding the perspective

of the victim. See p. 11 of his *Love Almighty and Ills Unlimited* (Garden City: Doubleday, 1961) p. 11.

4. Leo Tolstoy, "The Death of Ivan Illych," in *The Cossacks, Happy Ever After, and the Death of Ivan Illych* (Harmondsworth: Penguin Books, 1982) pp. 127-128.

5. Ibid., p. 137.

6. Ibid., p. 152.

7. Judges 2:15; Deut. 11: 13-21; Deut. 28; Lev. 23; Num. 12: 1-5.

8. Is. 3:10f.

9. II Kings 21:5, 10-13.

10. Jer. 12:1.

11. F.M. Cross, "Will You Lie For God?" Convocation address delivered at the Memorial Church, Harvard University, September 24, 1958, p. 3.

12. Job 4:7-9.

13. Ibid., 5:11, 12, 15, 16.

14. Ibid., 21:5-9, 13, 28-30.

15. Ibid., 13:7-10.

16. Albert Camus, *The Plague*, translated by Stuart Gilbert (New York: Modern Library, 1948) p. 87.

17. Ibid.

18. Ibid., pp. 88-90.

19. Ibid., p. 192.

20. Ibid., pp. 198ff. It is to the priest's credit that at this point he abandons the punishment and warning theodicy altogether, considering he might have made a last ditch effort by falling back on Exodus 20: 5, "I the Lord your God am a jealous God, visiting the iniquity of the fathers upon the children unto the third and fourth generations of them that hate me."

21. Anthony Schillani, *Movies and Morals* (Notre Dame: Fides Press, 1968) p. 102.

22. Moses Maimonides offers a similar kind of rebuttal to the punishment and warning theodicy in his *Guide to the Perplexed* (London: Frielander, 1904) chapter 24.

23. Augustine, "On Free Will" II ix 53 in *Augustine's Early Writings* (London: SCM, 1958) p. 135.

24. Jean Jacques Rousseau, *Emile,* translated by M. Nugent (London: Everyman's Library, 1971) p. 12.

25. For a fuller view of Rousseau's conception of human nature, see his *Essays on the Origins of Inequality* (London: Everyman's Library, 1973).

26. One of the clearest uses of this position in literature is William Golding's *Lord of the Flies* (London: Faber and Faber, 1954).

27. Ralph Barton Perry, *The Thought and Character of William James* (New York: Macmillan, 1935) vol. I pp. 28-29.

28. Ninian Smart, "Omnipotence, Evil and Superman," *Philosophy* (April-July 1961) p. 192.

29. Ibid., pp. 190-191.

30. J.L. Mackie, "Evil and Omnipotence," p. 209.

31. Anthony Flew, "Are Ninian Smart's Temptations Irresistible?" *Philosophy* (January 1962) p. 58.

32. Anthony Flew, "Divine Omnipotence and Human Freedom," p. 149.

33. This point is also made by D.J. Hoitenga, "Logic and the Problem of Evil," *American Philosophical Quarterly* vol. IV, (1967) pp. 114-126. There he suggests that the traditional Christian doctrine of heaven holds that the blessed will be confirmed in goodness without loss of their freedom of choice. Thus, Hoitenga suggests, it is not clear why God could not have created rational creatures who always freely choose the good.

34. Alvin Plantinga, *God, Freedom and Evil* (New York: Harper and Row, 1974) and *The Nature of Necessity* (London: Oxford University Press, 1974) pp. 173-189.

35. Ibid., pp. 173ff.

36. Plantinga, *God, Freedom and Evil*, p. 53.

37. J.L. Mackie, *The Miracle of Theism*, p. 174.

38. C.S. Lewis, *The Problem of Pain* (New York: Macmillan, 1978) pp. 55f.

39. Moses Maimonides argues a version of this presumption argument in chapter 24 of T*he Guide to the Perplexed.*

40. David Hume, *Dialogues Concerning Natural Religion* (London: Thomas Nelson, 1947) p. 198.

41. For Jewish responses to the Holocaust, see Emile Fackenheim, *God's Presence in History* (New York:

University Press, 1960); and Richard Rubenstein, *After Auschwitz* (Indianapolis: Bobbs-Merrill, 1966).

42. As Harnack points out in his *History of Dogma* (London: Williams and Norgate, 1898) vol. V, p. 114, this analogy to a work of painting is well established in western theology, at least since the time of the neo-Platonists.

43. Alexander Pope, "Essay on Man" in *The Works of Alexander Pope* (London: Murray, 1889) vol. II. This argument is also often identified with G.H. Joyce's *Principles of Natural Theology* (London: Longmans Green, 1957), particularly chapter 17.

44. Fyodor Dostoyevski, "Rebellion," in Walter Kaufmann, *Religion From Tolstoy to Camus* (New York: Harper Brothers, 1961) pp. 142-143.

45. F.R. Tennant, *Philosophical Theology*, vol. II (Cambridge: Cambridge University Press, 1930) p. 181.

46. H.D. Lewis, *The Philosophy of Religion* (London: Cambridge University Press, 1965) pp. 308-309.

47. John Wisdom, "God and Evil," *Mind*, vol. 44 (1935) p. 2.

48. Ibid.

49. Augustine, *Enchiridion* (Edinburgh: T. and T. Clark, 1965) III, 11.

50. Errol Harris, *The Problem of Evil* (Milwaukee: Marquette University, 1977) pp. 31-32.

51. Germain Grisez, *Beyond the New Theism: A Philosophy of Religion* (South Bend: University of Notre Dame Press, 1976) p. 293. A similar position is also held by M.C. D'Arcy in his *The Pain of the World and the Providence of God* (London: Longmans Green, 1935).

52. *On Free Will*, I, iii, 6; *The City of God*, XI, 22.

53. F.R. Tennant, *Philosophical Theology*, vol. II., p. 181.

54. H.J. McCloskey, "Evil and Omnipotence," pp. 100ff in Nelson Pike's *God and Evil*.

55. W. I. Wallace, *The Existence of God* (Ithaca: Cornell University Press, 1965) pp. 142-143.

56. For two criticisms of Leibniz's theodicy, see M.B. Ahern, *The Problem of Evil*, pp. 53-63; and James Ross's *Introduction to the Philosophy of Religion* (Toronto: Collier-Macmillan, 1969) pp. 127-130.

57. Baruch Brody, *Beginning Philosophy* (Englewood Cliffs, N.J.: Prentice Hall, 1977) p. 116.

58. Plato, *The Republic*, translated by F.M. Cornford (London: Oxford University Press, 1970), particularly Book X.

59. David Hume, *Dialogues Concerning Natural Religion*, part X.

60. Baruch Brody, *Beginning Philosophy*, p.116.

61. Richard Swinburne, *The Existence of God*, p. 210.

62. Ibid.

63. John Hick, *The Philosophy of Religion* (Englewood Cliffs, N.J.: Prentice Hall, 1983) pp. 45-46.

64. John Hick, *Evil and the God of Love*, p. 291-292.

65. John Hick, *The Philosophy of Religion*, p. 101.

66. Ibid.

67. M.B. Ahern, *The Problem of Evil*, p. 63.

68. Unsigned article, "In Search of God at Auschwitz," *New York Times*, June 9, 1974, p. E-5.

69. Fyodor Dostoyevski, "Rebellion" in Kaufmann's *Religion From Tolstoy to Camus,* p. 143.

70. Ibid.

71. See Lou H. Silberman, "Death in the Hebrew Bible and Apocalyptic Literature," in *Perspectives on Death*, edited by L.O. Mills (Nashville: Abingdon Press, 1969), pp. 13-32.

72. See the two articles on death by Flew and MacKinnon in *New Essays in Philosophical Theology.*

73. John Hick, "Theology and Falsification," *Theology Today*, vol. XXXVII (April 1960) p. 20.

74. Ibid., pp. 14ff.

75. Kai Nielson, "God and Verification Again," *Canadian Journal of Theology*, vol. XI, (1965) p. 137.

76. A. J. Ayer, *Language, Truth, and Logic* (London: Victor Gollancz, 1956).

77. John Hick, "Theology and Verification," pp. 25-26.

78. J.E. Barnhart, *The Study of Religion and Its Meaning* (The Hague: Mouton, 1977) p. 63.

79. John Hick, *Faith and Knowledge* (Ithaca: Cornell University Press, 1957) pp. 150-163.

80. Ibid.

81. Ibid.

82. Edward Madden and Peter Hare, *Evil and the Concept of God* (Springfield: Charles Johnson, 1968) pp. 83-90, provide a line of criticism other than those I have taken here.

83. Compare Tolstoy's *Confession*, for example, with Albert Camus's *The Myth of Sisyphus*.

84. This position can be found in all William James's writings about the problem of evil.

85. H.D. Lewis, *The Philosophy of Religion*, p. 312.

86. John Hick, *Evil and the God of Love*, p. 371.

87. Albert Camus, *The Plague,* p. 201.

88. Ibid., pp. 201-202.

89. M.B. Ahern, *The Problem of Evil*, p. 64.

90. John Hospers, *An Introduction to Philosophical Analysis* (Englewood Cliffs, N.J.: Prentice Hall, 1963) pp. 464-465.

91. Josiah Royce, "The Problem of Job," in Kaufmann's *Religion From Tolstoy to Camus*, p. 244.

IV.
"Seeing God" as an "Answer" to the Problem of Suffering

'Did you say the stars were worlds, Tess?'
'Yes.'
'All like ours?'
'I don't know; but I think so, they sometimes seem to be like apples on our stubbard tree, most of them splendid and sound — a few blighted.'
'Which do we live on — a splendid one or a blighted one?'
'A blighted one.'

Thomas Hardy
Tess of the d'Urbervilles

"Solomon and Job have known best and spoken best of man's misery. The one the most fortunate, the other the most unfortunate of men; the one knowing by experience the emptiness of pleasure; the other the reality of sorrow."

Blaise Pascal
Pensees, no. 357

'I have been young, and now am not too old,
And I have seen the righteous forsaken,
His health, his honours and his quality taken.
This is not what we were formerly told.'

Edmund Blunden

The Book of Job is perhaps the greatest poetic work produced by the ancient Israelite community, both in terms of its poetic form and its intellectual perceptiveness and honesty. Thomas Carlyle has called it "the most wonderful poem of any age and language; our first, oldest statement of the never-ending problem — man's destiny and God's way with him here on earth...there is nothing written in the Bible or out of it of equal literary merit."[1] Professor Rowley has referred to the Book of Job as a "supreme literary masterpiece in the Old Testament, and one of the greatest creations of world literature."[2] Similar sentiments have been expressed by such Jewish philosophers and exegetes as Gersonides and Maimonides, as well as other prominent thinkers of the Middle Ages. In the modern period, the works of disparate artists, thinkers, and writers such as Martin Luther, Immanuel Kant, Robert Burton, William Blake, Alfred Tennyson, Carl Jung, Martin Buber, H.G. Wells, Robert Frost, and Archibald MacLeish give evidence of the profound influence the Book of Job continues to exercise over the hearts and minds of sensitive people. Yet, despite its almost universal appeal and the wide range of excellent commentaries available on the book,[3] the work still possesses a number of characteristics that remain enigmatic.[4]

The author may very well have lived in Judah shortly after the fall of Jerusalem in 586, though the time and authorship of the book are also matters of great debate.[5] The influence of the prophet Jeremiah in chapter three appears to be quite clear,[6] but the poet is most certainly working in the large genre of Wisdom literature.

Some scholars have thought the author to be a non-Israelite,[7] perhaps from Edom, but this view is not widely accepted. The principal reason for the development of this minority position is the lack of direct references in Job to the Covenant with Yahweh as well as the omission of any mention of the Temple at Jerusalem. These omissions might just as well be understood, however, by taking cognizance of the difficult spiritual situation out of which the poet may be speaking. What is Israel's honest hope now that the Temple has been destroyed? Is it possible for the Israelite people to continue to believe in Yahweh's steadfast love at a time like this?[8]

Still, the major questions of the book seem to be couched on the personal level rather than a grand metaphor for the nation as a whole. Indeed, the book can be seen as a continuation of questions raised by Jeremiah regarding the justice of the suffering of the righteous.[9] The poet clearly sets out to deal with such questions. The Book of Job is important for the purposes of this book for it raises issues, often in a quite philosophically sophisticated way, about how one should go about asking and perhaps answering the problem of evil. The author takes as his framework an ancient and no doubt popular narrative about a blameless and upright man named Job, whom Yahweh tested and afflicted to see whether his faith would endure the adversity. The archaic tale may date to as early as the ninth century,[10] and could also have circulated throughout the ancient Near East. The poet has incorporated the tale as the prologue (chapters 1 and 2) and the epilogue (42:7-17) of the present work, though it is likely that he has reworked this material for his own purposes.

A number of scholars have suggested that the epilogue is intrusive and that it destroys the poetic insights that immediately precede it in 42:1-6. But it may well be the case that the author, having laid out his poetic conclusion, was nevertheless willing to let the denouement of the older narrative stand. Had he not added the older conclusion, the community as a whole may have done so.[11] Another interpretation, as I shall show later, is that the importance of the epilogue lies not in what is given but in how much and in what manner.

It is sometimes argued that the prologue might have been eliminated as well. But the logic of the prologue is quite clear, and its transition to the main body of poetry is quite natural. The prologue is essential to the purposes of the poetry and therefore is an important reworking of the prose narrative. The Satan of the prologue is not the personification of evil to be found in later Judaism. Here he is the tester of man's faith; he is more like a devil's advocate than a devil. This adversary maintains that Job's piety is the direct result of his having been blessed by Yahweh — that God has continually rewarded Job for his good faith. If his prosperity were taken away, Satan argues, Job would curse God. The adversary is permitted to visit various calamities on Job, but through it all, the protagonist holds fast to his faith in the justice of Yahweh. Satan now maintains that if Job himself were smitten with evil, he would surely curse the deity.

> The Satan answered the Lord saying,
> Skin for skin!
> All a man has
> he will give for his life.
> But put forth your hand
> and touch his own flesh and bones
> and he will surely curse you to your face.
> Then the Lord said to Satan,
> He is in your power
> but preserve his life.[12]

Job soon contracts a loathesome disease. Earlier he had lost his children and all of his worldly possessions. Job's wife, in the face of these calamities, has had enough. She suggests an alternative to Job:

> "Are you still holding fast to your piety?
> Curse God and die."[13]

But Job is ready, at least for the present, to receive evil from the Lord as well as good. When they hear of Job's misfortunes, three friends come to comfort him, but first they sit stunned with him in silence for seven days and nights:

> Then Job's three friends heard all the trouble that had come upon him. And they came, each from his place — Eliphaz the Temanite, Bildad the Shuhite, and Zophar the Noamathite — having arranged together to come to condole with him and comfort him. Now when they caught sight of him from afar, they could not recognize him. So they raised their voices and wept and rent their robes and threw dust over their heads towards the heavens. They sat with him on the ground for seven days and for seven nights, no one saying a word, for they saw his agony was very great.[14]

We have learned much earlier from the prose narrative that Job "... was blameless and upright, fearing God and avoiding evil."[15] Clearly, it is Job's present condition, combined with this realization that he is innocent, that creates the problem of suffering for the poet. Eventually the friends become less sympathetic. They begin to maintain Job has sinned, no doubt unwittingly. Eliphaz, the oldest and wisest of the comforters, is the first to speak. He reminds Job how often the protagonist himself has consoled sufferers in the past by recalling a great religious truth:

> Think now, what innocent man was ever destroyed; and where were the upright cut off? Whenever I have seen those who plow iniquity and sow trouble — they reap it! By the breath of God they are destroyed, and by the blast of his wrath they are consumed.[16]

The other friends soon follow suit, and Job in turn protests his innocence. In anguish, he eventually suggests that Yahweh either come to his aid or take his life. He appeals for an umpire or a mediator to adjudicate his case:

> If only there were an arbitrator between us
> who could lay hands upon us both,
> who would remove God's rod from me
> so that my dread of Him would not terrify me.[17]

A second and third time the friends speak, advancing from gentle suggestion to specific accusation; indeed, by Eliphaz's third speech, Robert Gordis suggests that the first of the comforters has been stripped of his urbanity by Job's continued recalcitrance:

> Finding his theory of Divine Justice contradicted by the facts, Eliphaz proceeds to the time-honoured device of adjusting the facts to the theory. Accordingly, he invents a long catalogue of crimes committed by Job, of which we previously have heard nothing. Eliphaz is able to explain these alleged actions of Job on the ground God is so far away from him.[18]

In the words of Eliphaz:

> It is because of your piety that He reproves you and
> enters into judgement with you? In fact, your wicked-
> ness is immense, for there's no end in your iniquities.
> For you have taken pledges even from your kinsmen
> without reason, and stripped the naked of their cloth-
> ing. No water have you given to the weary, and from
> the hungry you have withheld bread.[19]

But through all of this Job vehemently asserts his right-
eousness. From the cruel and unyielding dogmatism of his
friends, he turns again and again to God, but he receives no
answer.

A fourth comforter, Elihu, enters the debate. For the
most part, he vainly enlarges on what the other friends have
already said, but he also adds a new possibility as to the
cause of suffering: that it sometimes comes even to upright
men as a discipline, as a warning to prevent them from slip-
ping into apostasy.

> Or a man may be chastened by pain upon his bed, by a
> perpetual strife in his bones, so that he loathes his
> bread, and his appetite abhors the daintiest food. His
> flesh wastes away so that it cannot be seen, and his
> bones protrude and cannot be looked upon. He himself
> draws near to the pit and his life approaches the emis-
> saries of Death. But if there be one spokesman for
> him, one advocate among a thousand to vouch for
> man's uprightness, God is gracious to him, and He
> commands, 'Free him from descending to the pit; I
> have found a ransom for him.'
>
> Then his flesh becomes fresh as in youth; he returns to
> the days of his vigor. He then prays to God, and finds

favor, and joyfully enters His presence. He recounts to
men His goodness and proclaims to men, saying, I
sinned and perverted the right, but it was not to my
advantage. He has redeemed me from going down to
the pit, so that I might see the light of life.[20]

But Job remains unmoved, even by the eloquence of
Elihu. Finally, from the majestic voice in the midst of a
whirlwind,[21] God replies to Job. He forcefully enumerates
the marvels of his creation:

> Then the Lord answered Job out of the whirlwind,
> saying, Who is this that darkens my plan by words
> without knowledge? Gird up your loins like a man; I
> will ask you, and you tell Me. Where were you when I
> laid the foundations of the earth?
>
> Tell Me, if you have any understanding. Who marked
> out its measure, if you know it, who stretched the
> plumb line upon it? Upon what were the earth's pillars
> sunk: who laid down its cornerstone, when the morn-
> ing stars sang together and all the sons of God shout-
> ed for joy? Who shut in the sea with doors when it
> broke forth from the womb whence it came, when I
> made the clouds its garments and dark clouds its
> swaddling clothes, prescribing My limit for the Sea,
> and setting for it bolts and doors, saying, 'Thus far
> shall you come, and no farther, and here shall your
> proud waves be stayed?'[22]

Robert Gordis points out there is much more than sheer
power to be found in God's speeches from the whirlwind.
He suggests there are at least two very important implied
points:

There are, in addition, two other significant ideas
implicit in the Lord's words. In accordance with
Semitic rhetorical usage they are not spelled out, but
are left to be inferred by the reader. The first is that
the universe was not created exclusively for man's
use, and therefore, neither it not its Creator can be
judged solely by man's standards and goals. The second is even more significant. The natural world,
though it is beyond man's ken, reveals to him its beauty and order. It is therefore reasonable for man to
believe that the universe also exhibits a moral order
with pattern and meaning, though it is beyond man's
power to fully comprehend it, Who then is Job, to
reprove God and dispute with Him?[23]

Indeed, Job responds to the marvel of God's creation by
confessing that his denial of God's justice was due to igno-
rance:

Then Job answered the Lord,
'I know that you can do all things
and that no purpose of Yours can be thwarted.'
You have said,
'Who is this that hides My plan without knowledge?'
Indeed, I have spoken without understanding,
of things too wonderful for me which I did not grasp.
You have said,
'Hear and I will speak;
I will ask you, and do you inform Me.
I had heard of You by hearsay,
but now my own eyes have seen You.
Therefore, I abase myself
and repent in dust and ashes.'[24]

The poet closes the book by adding a few verses to

serve as a bridge between the poetry and the conclusion of the traditional prose narrative,[25] which now becomes the epilogue. Earlier, Eliphas assured Job that if he repented, God would forgive him, and the protagonist would once again be able to intercede for sinners like himself. In a marvelously ironic passage, the Lord now castigates Eliphaz and the other comforters. God suggests that they can only be forgiven through the intercession of Job, who has spoken the truth about Him.

> After the Lord had spoken these words to Job, the Lord said to Eliphaz, the Temanite, 'My anger is kindled against you and against your two friends, for you have not spoken the truth about Me as has My servant Job. Now then, take seven bulls and seven rams, and go to My servant Job, and offer them as a burnt offering to yourselves. My servant Job must intercede for you, for only to him will I show favor and not expose you to disgrace for not speaking the truth about Me as did my servant Job.'[26]

In the very end, Job's wealth is restored twofold; he receives fourteen sons, three beautiful daughters and a happy life of one hundred and forty years.[27]

The final meaning and message of Job, like its composition and textual problems, has elicited a wide variety of responses over the centuries. The chief problem of interpretation arises from the fact that the speeches of Yahweh (chapters 38 to 42) majestically seem to ignore the issues as Job has posed them. The problem for Job is a straightfoward one: Why do the innocent suffer? But instead of giving a clear answer to that question, God confronts Job with a series of seemingly irrelevant questions destined to convince the protagonist of the paltriness of human knowledge and power. Indeed, some readers of the Book of Job have remarked that Yahweh responds from the whirlwind with a magnificent display of his power, when, in fact, his omnipotence has never seriously been in question. What has been suspect, however, at least from the perspective of Job, is God's goodness and justice, and the deity remains curiously silent about those attributes. We will return shortly to the problem of the Yahweh speeches, but let us first turn for a few moments to some other answers to the problem of Job's suffering that may be found elsewhere in the text.

There are at least three other answers to the problem of suffering suggested in the Book of Job: (a) that suffering is a divine test; (b) that suffering is retribution for past sins; and (c) that suffering is a discipline of warning to the just.

The first of these answers is suggested most strongly in the prologue. In the first scene of the book Satan is seen as a kind of prosecuting angel in the heavenly court, ironically insisting that Job has remained blameless and upright only because he has been well rewarded:

> Is it for nothing that Job has feared God? Have you not safely hedged him in, and his house, and all he owns, on every side? You have blessed the work of his hands and his possessions have increased in the land. But put forth Your hand and touch whatever he owns, and he will surely curse You to Your face![28]

If we accept this answer to Job's suffering, then the poetic body of the work is seen as the actual testing of Job's metal, first by removing all his worldly goods, and then by inflicting him with a dreaded disease.

But this perspective is clearly inadequate for at least three reasons. First, although Job receives all his worldly goods back in double proportion, the double restitution suggests not that Job has been tested, but rather that he has been unjustly deprived of his possessions, and therefore should be compensated doubly.[29] An interesting point to note is that this penalty is the same penalty as that exacted as compensation from thieves and negligent trustees, as Exodus 22:3, 6, and 8 clearly indicate.

A second good reason for dismissing the test argument as cogent is that Satan never appears in the epilogue and consequently God is never actually declared the winner of the wager. Nor could it be said that Yahweh in any way collects his bet. It is inconceivable that these elements would have been left out of the narrative if they were germane to the central meaning of the text.

A third point that contradicts this test interpretation of Job's suffering involves a realization of the way the world works outside the Book of Job. If we grant that the text is ostensibly about why the innocent suffer, and we answer this question by suggesting that the blameless are being tested and shall receive their just desserts eventually, then we must reckon with all those individuals throughout history who seem to have hung on stalwartly so that they might endure the test, and yet have not been rewarded. Keep in mind that nowhere in the text is it suggested that the reward might come in some life beyond the grave.[30]

Job's view of death is starkly naturalistic:

> For there is hope for a tree —
> it if be cut down, it can sprout again
> and its shoots will not fail.
> If its roots grow old in the earth
> and its stump dies in the ground,
> at the mere scent of water it will bud anew
> and put forth branches like a new plant.

> But man grows faint and dies;
> and breathes his last, and where is he?
> As water vanishes from a lake,
> and a river is parched and dries up,
> So man lies down and rises not again;
> till the heavens are no more he will not awake,
> nor will he be roused from his sleep.[31]

The poet refuses to dissolve the problem by taking refuge in a compensation beyond the grave. In this regard, he seems quite close to the sentiments of the author of Ecclesiastes:

> Naked from his mother's womb he came, as naked as he came he will depart again; nothing to take with him after all his efforts...The living know at least that they will die, the dead know nothing; no more reward for them, their memory has passed out of mind. Their loves, their hates, their jealousies these all have perished, nor will they ever again take part in whatever is done under the sun.[32]

It should be clear that "evil as just punishment" for sins is also a weak interpretation of Job's suffering, given the internal logic of the book. In fact, the work begins by telling us quite unambiguously that Job is "blameless and upright,"[33] and this bit of information is provided by the omniscient narrator of the tale. In 29:11-20 we gain an important insight about the logic of Job's former life style:

> Every ear that heard me called me blessed, and every eye that saw me encouraged me, because I delivered the poor man crying out, and the fatherless who had none to help them. The beggar's blessing came upon

> me, and I brought a song to the widow's heart. I put
> on righteousness and it clothed me; justice was my
> robe and my turban. Eyes to the blind was I and feet
> to the lame. A father to the poor was I, and I took up
> the cause of the stranger. I broke the fangs of the evil
> doer and snatched the prey from his teeth; and I
> thought, I shall die in my nest, and shall multiply my
> days as the phoenix, with my roots open to the water,
> and the dew all night on my branches, my glory fresh
> within me, and my bow ever new in my hand."[34]

Job had initially lived with the same retributive perspective as the unbending comforters. But in the grips of
his suffering, which is clearly ascribed to God, the problem
with that old syllogism becomes painfully clear. Since Job
is aware of his innocence, with the same consistency with
which his logical friends accuse him, he now must accuse
God. To give into the friends would be tantamount to denying reality. Although Elihu does suggest in chapter twenty-
two that Job has, in fact, sinned a great deal, Yahweh in
chapter forty-two sharply rebukes all of the comforters for
not speaking the truth, with the implication being that Job's
repeated protestations of innocence have been right all
along. If one were to employ the argument from silence, in
the absence of any incriminating evidence against Job,
God's reply in chapter forty-two may well indicate a divine
vindication of the protagonist as well as his argument.
Nothing within the logic of the text could be construed as
evidence for the truth of the comforters' position. And thus
retributive justice for past sins cannot be considered as a
tenable answer to Job's question.

The third position, that "suffering serves as a discipline
or warning to the just," is most clearly indicated by Elihu in
chapter thirty-three. There the fourth comforter argues that

God often uses evil to chastise even the just, so that they may not take their position for granted. Although Elihu's position may legitimately be seen as a compromise between the rigid friends, and their traditional view of punishment, and Job who from the depths of his own experience cries out that he is blameless, it is, nevertheless an inadequate point of view. Elihu's position is inadequate because it ignores the facts. At no point in the text could Job be accused of pride or intellectual hubris. Indeed, the artistry with which Job is kept from sounding arrogant and self-righteous as he answers his questioners is impressive.[35] Job is certainly angry, confused, and at times seemingly on the verge of giving up, but he is never proud. Elihu's comments do violence to the facts in much the same way as the suggestions of Job's impropriety. In the final analysis, the real problem with Elihu's position is that there is no good evidence for it. James Wood points out that Job himself comes to the same conclusion:

> The fact of his innocence prevented him from accepting any view of his suffering which sought to explain it as punishment for sin, or a corrective of misbehavior toward God. Because he was conscious of his moral integrity, it was psychologically impossible for him to find peace of mind in a course of behavior which assumed that he needed to repent for sins he did not commit.[36]

What is of interest about the three answers discussed here is that the poet dismisses them all, first on logical grounds, but also for existential reasons — they don't seem to take the sufferer seriously enough. It might accurately be said, I think, that the comforters fix on the second criterion of a viable theodicy, that it be true to the Judaic religious form of life, at the expense of ignoring the importance of the first and third.

Another point concerning the Book of Job that is often overlooked but is nevertheless central to an understanding of the text is that the author makes a clear distinction between natural and moral evils. In chapters one and two, the first and third calamities to befall Job and his family are man-made, while the second and fourth are natural catastrophes.[37] This clear distinction points not only to the philosophical sophistication of the poet, but it also contradicts the belief among some Biblical and Near Eastern scholars that the ancient Jews were a "proto-logical people," who tended to be associative rather than logically coherent and relevant.[38] In the Book of Job, the poet seems to be suggesting in a not-too-subtle way that any answer to the problem of suffering that might follow in the body of his poem must honestly grapple with the reality of both kinds of evils.

We have attempted to show that there are at least three answers to the problem of evil that the poet himself seems to have thrown open to serious doubt. We must now consider whether any other answer is to be found to the problem of Job's suffering. If a coherent answer could be found in the text, it would be of immense value to a constructive theodicy which would aspire at once to be cognizant of the Biblical tradition, logically sound, and sensitive to the integrity of the individual sufferer.

But first we must take a small diversion. As has been suggested earlier, it is sometimes argued that chapters thirty-eight to forty-two should not be considered as part of the original autograph. But as Driver and Gray have noted:

> The only ground for questioning this section as a whole lies in the nature of the contents which have appeared to some incapable of reconciliation with the standpoint of the author of the dialogue.[39]

It has not been uncommon for commentators to view the speeches of Yahweh as one spectacular irrelevance to the plot of the book. However, if the general line of thought in the remainder of this chapter is judged to be correct, such doubts about the originality of the speeches from out of the whirlwind will, it is hoped, be seen as considerably less forceful, if not completely unjustified.

Regarding the account of the theophany, Marvin Pope observes, "Either the book ends in a magnificent anticlimax, or we must see the highlight in the Divine speeches."[40] As has been suggested earlier, however, on first reading the Yahweh speeches seem a disappointment, a kind of Divine *non sequitur*. In the heart of the work, Job has demanded on several occasions to be given an explanation for what he held to be his undeserved suffering. But in chapter thirty-eight to forty-two no direct answer is given to Job's complaint. Rather, Job himself is put under questioning: "Who is this that darkens My plans by words without knowledge?"[41] In an overwhelming and stunning rhetorical blast, Yahweh depicts the divine creative power and glory in such a way that Job's rebellion ceases. The same Job who has so defiantly called Yahweh into account soon recants and repents in dust and ashes.

What has happened to Job to produce such a profound change of heart? We must now return to our original question: Is there an answer to the problem of suffering to be found in the Book of Job? In order to attempt to answer that query, our attention must focus on the Yahweh speeches.

In 42:5, Job "sees" God. Before the theopany, Job had only heard of Yahweh through the intellectual speculation and traditional dogma of his friends. Now, he "sees" Yahweh for himself. In this immediate experience with Yahweh, Job seems to find an answer, though it is clearly not the type of answer he had been expecting in the dialogue.[42] Job is overwhelmed by Yahweh's creative power and glory and consequently comes to see his own suffering in a new light. In Nahum Glatzer's selection [43] of modern commentaries (Judaic, Christian, and generally philosophical) on the Book of Job, an impressive number of writers understand Job's "seeing God" as the key to his apparent change of heart, though they go on to interpret his repentance in a number of vastly differing ways. Consider the following examples:

> (1) Job has appealed to God to appear and is prepared 'as a prince to enter his presence' (31:37), bearing a convincing statement of his case with him. God does not answer this challenge and presents himself in all his creative majesty. At once Job forgets his case and ceases to be urged by his problems. In the presence of God these things vanish away, and only God is left.[44]

> (2) What is God's answer? It is powerful, at once crushing and uplifting, and, as far as it goes, of eternal validity: it is God Himself. This means that God does not involve Himself with arguments for and against His dominion, but lets Himself be seen. His answer consists in manifesting His greatness in powerful speech and creative deeds. This, rather than the arguments of God's defenders, causes Job to grow silent and beg God's forgiveness.[45]

> (3) It is the vision of God that has released him from his problem. His suffering is as mysterious as ever, but, plain or mysterious, why should it vex him any longer? He has seen God, and has entered into rest.[46]

> (4) God offers Himself to the sufferer, who, in the

depth of his despair, keeps to God with his refractory complaint; He offers Himself to him as an answer.[47]

(5) It is often asked why he became convinced by, and what it is that he became convinced of; but the answer is surely that whereas there had been brought before him the wonders of creation, what he saw was the far greater wonder, the wonder of the Creator. He does not say: 'Mine eyes seeth behemoth and leviathan.' He says: 'Mine eyes seeth Thee.'[48]

(6) For if the rebellious hero here becomes a joyous confessor, and recognizes the divine omnipotence and voluntaristic purposefulness of God, this is not entirely due to the effect of the arguments of chapters 38f. on his reason, but is partly the result of his experience of the divine reality.[49]

(7) He has pictured Job as finding the solution to his problem, not in a reasoned explanation or a theology, but in a religious experience...His hero, Job, finds his satisfaction in a first hand experience of God.[50]

Other authors might be quoted here, but the point, I think, has already been made: Many commentators suggest that Job's "seeing God" was crucial in bringing about his repentance. But we must now probe a little more deeply into just how the theophany provoked this change of heart.

One avenue we might follow is to examine the kind of religious encounter the poet is attempting to depict in the Yahweh speeches. As R.A.F. MacKenzie has observed, we must consider the presence of a third dialogue in the book. In addition to the conversations between Job and his friends, and the dialogue between Job and God, there is also to be considered the dialogue of the author with his readers.[51] It is this third dialogue, MacKenzie claims, that provoked the composition and inclusion of the Yahweh speeches. Beyond merely affirming that an encounter between Job and Yahweh happened, the author attempts to depict the inner dynamics of Job's profound religious experience. The poet tries to convey

> Not merely that the theophany occurred but the effect it had upon Job. And that can best be done by means of God's self-expression in word. As the other characters have expressed and revealed themselves in speech, so must the divine arbiter. Hence, the need for the Yahweh speeches.[52]

But if Yahweh is to speak, what is He to say? MacKenzie speculates:

> He might simply tell the story of Satan's challenge and its acceptance; or might contribute yet another analysis of the function of suffering in human life. But...either of these would be quite unsuited to the function that the speech must fulfill. It must be some form of self-revelation, which will at least remotely symbolize the impact on the human soul of an immediate encounter with God.... It must at the same time convey the overwhelming Otherness of God and His transcendence with respect to the man who is before Him.[53]

For MacKenzie, the divine speeches of chapters thirty-eight to forty-two are a poetic expression of Job's "seeing God." It is a "sense impression of what the experienced presence of God is like."[54] In the Yahweh speeches, the poet attempts to interpret and display the significance of the theophany for Job, though "mystery cannot be made clear in human language and concepts."[55]

MacKenzie contends that the poet succeeded brilliantly in his portrayal of the divine-human encounter. For him, the two little syllables *Mi zeh* ("who is this...") at the very beginning of the speeches from the whirlwind represent the "Most shattering question that was ever posed,"[56] a question that sets the tone of the whole theophany section of the text and provides a basis for Job's radical change of heart. MacKenzie believes the message of the theophany is abundantly clear:

> God is God, and Job is a creature — the experience of that simple but fundamental fact is the primary effect of this encounter. The remorseless piling-up of the subsequent questions, each one reducing poor Job further into his state of debasement, indicates to us the penetration of this truth into his inmost being.[57]

Another commentator, the German Protestant theologian and historian of religions, Rudolph Otto, sees a religious encounter with God underlying the Yahweh speeches. In his *The Idea of the Holy*,[58] Otto describes how the "holy" or "numinous unnamed something" at the heart of religious experience "transcends the ethical, moral sphere and focuses on the awful, the mysterious, the tremendum, the majestic, the wholly other."[59] For Otto, chapters thirty-eight to forty-two of the Book of Job are a goldmine of expressions of the numinous:

> In the 38th chapter of Job we have the element of the mysterious displayed in rare purity and completeness, and this chapter may well rank among the most remarkable in the history of religion. Job has been reasoning with his friends against Elohim (God), and,

— as far as concerns them — he has been obviously in
the right. They are compelled to be dumb before him.
And then Elohim appears to conduct his own defense
in person. And he conducts it to such an effect that
Job avows himself to be overpowered — not merely
silenced by superior strength.[60]

Otto continues by suggesting that Job is presented with
a theodicy that goes beyond the rational ideas and solutions
of the dialogue's comforters; here Job encounters a resolution to the problem of suffering that relies on "the sheer
absolute wondrousness that transcends thought, on the
mysterium, presented in its pure, nonrational form."[61] The
accounts of the eagle, ostrich, wild ass, wild ox, behemoth
and leviathan, all of the glorious examples from nature

> express in masterly fashion the downright stupendous-
> ness, the wellnigh demonic and wholly incomprehen-
> sible character of the eternal, creative power; how
> incalculable and 'wholly other,' it mocks all conceiv-
> ing but yet stirs the mind to its depths, fascinates and
> overbrims the heart.[62]

Driver and Gray make a similar observation when they
comment:

> The first speech of Yahweh transcends all other
> descriptions of the wonders of creation or the great-
> ness of the Creator, which are to be found either in the
> Bible or elsewhere.[63]

To use the language of Otto, this absolutely mysterious
and frightening *numen* acts to fascinate Job in his encounter
with God; it acts to overpower him in such a way that he
repents and recants in dust and ashes.

As helpful as these accounts may be, they still leave us in the dark as to what particulars were involved in Job's "seeing God." What is it exactly that led him to reevaluate his stance of protest? Can the motivation for Job's repentance be explained further? If it cannot, this answer would seem barely to help any more than the old cliche "God's ways are not man's ways." Indeed, that sort of answer, at least at first blush, would not seem to take the individual sufferer very seriously. So we must ask: Is there anything that might be helpful in constructing a theodicy that aims at taking the victims of evil seriously? To simply say, "Job saw God, and that answered his question about undeserved suffering," will not do. It seems to beg the question. We must ask further: Why did seeing God benefit Job?

George Dennis O'Brien attempts to answer this as well as related questions in his article, "Prolegomena to a Dissolution to the Problem of Suffering." Here he argues, as we have in earlier chapters, that the problem of suffering only arises when we hold "at once to the notion of an all good, all powerful Creator of the world, and this world, as we experience it, full of travail. If we change the notion of God (or the world) in certain ways the dilemma simply vanishes."[64] O'Brien does not, however, mention the attribute of omniscience, which we have shown must also be included to generate the problem of evil as it is posed for the religions of paradox.

Quoting Anthony Flew with approval, O'Brien claims that the problem of evil cannot cast doubt on the notion of an omnipotent, and benevolent God "for anyone who adopts any variant of the position that infinite creative power is its own sufficient justification, or leaves no room for justification."[65] O'Brien observes that Thomas Hobbes successfully accomplishes a dissolution to the problem of suffering by holding that power is self-justifying. And though we may disagree in the end with Hobbes' position, we have much to learn from his unsentimental treatment of Job's repentance. Hobbes wrote:

> And Job, how earnestly does he expostulate with God, for the many afflictions that he suffered, notwithstanding his righteousness. The question in the case of Job is decided by God Himself, not from arguments derived from Job's sin, but His own power.[66]

O'Brien claims that here Hobbes "can still maintain that God is all powerful and good, but he conceives of the relationship between power and goodness in such a way that the supposed antinomy of God's power and goodness cannot arise;"[67] here there is a "transformation of the frame of reference in such a manner that questions of justification in the ordinary sense cannot be raised at all."[68] O'Brien labels this movement in Hobbes a "transfer from a formal to an existential frame of reference,"[69] a common shift which takes place when an overriding concern for an existential relation displaces the need for formal explanations. This shift operates, as follows, in Hobbes' view of Job's repentance:

> We begin with a 'formal' situation — a question of justification is asked, and it is expected that grounds or reasons for God's actions will be forthcoming. But what happens is that the voice from the whirlwind transforms it into an existential situation in which the relation between the questioner and the question becomes paramount. The 'formal' problem of justification is set aside because of the overriding situation between man and God. The shift is from question and

answer to questioner and questioned....What occurs in
this dialogue? Surely Job's question is not answered at
all; rather, God simply asserts that He is, after all,
God, and as the result of this 'answer' Job repents in
dust and ashes. If some sort of radical shift in the
framework is not involved, then the story is simply
pointless because Job never gets an answer. Yet he
repents.[70]

An exactly analogous frame of reference that shifts
from the formal to the existential occurs, O'Brien suggests,
in the case of a military situation where a soldier asks the
General why he should obey the latter's orders. Very often
in such a situation the soldier would accept as an answer a
shift in the frame of reference to the existential: "Because I,
the General, say so, that's why."[71] Here the existential relationship of the General to the soldier displaces any formal
concern about the justification of the command. Job, like
the soldier, is enlightened by "seeing God," in the sense
that he discovers he has been asking all the wrong questions. Once he discovers the overriding reality of the existential relation between God and himself, O'Brien believes,
the problem of suffering is transformed. As O'Brien suggests, "Once we realize that it is God who acts and man
who receives, there is no real question of justifying God's
acts or condemning Him for His injustice to Job."[72] The
blank assertion that "God is God" rules out any independent
standard of justification by which the deity might be questioned. "The answer to Job, then, is to remind him that he is
in the ruler-ruled relation which he cannot escape."[73]
Although I would agree with O'Brien on the point that
the context of Job's encounter with God changes from a formal one to an existential one, I would part company with
him on the reasons he suggests bring about the change. I am

not entirely convinced that O'Brien's position is sufficiently different from that of Hobbes. O'Brien mentions God's other attributes, but he still seems to base his view on Hobbes' claim that power gives the right to command. His choice of a military metaphor to describe the relation between God and Job is an indication of just how seriously he takes Hobbes' view of the self-justifying nature of power.

In order to see clearly the difference between my position and that of O'Brien's, as well as how they both differ from a third point of view, we must consider three possible interpretations of Job's repentance: (a) Job bows to Yahweh's power, but his submission is carried out "tongue-in-cheek;" (b) Job sincerely repents when he perceives Yahweh's power to be self-justifying; and (c) Job sincerely repents because of the realization of Yahweh's power but also for a number of other relevant reasons. Let us first consider possibility (a).

David Robertson's interpretation of Job's repentance is a good example of (a). In his article, "The Book of Job: A Literary Study," Robertson attempts to demonstrate that "irony pervades the entire book, and indeed, provides the key to a consistent and adequate reading of God's speeches from the storm."[74]

For Robertson, Job's repentance is more a "rolling with the punches" than a heartfelt change of position. He bases his position on Job's propensities in the dialogue of the speeches of Yahweh and Job's response to those speeches. Already in the ninth chapter, Robertson argues, Job foresees that God "would not come to listen patiently to Job's charges; he would come in a tornado, toss Job about, and scare him out of his wits."[75]

> If I summoned and he answered,
> I do not believe he would heed me.
> He would crush me with a tempest
> And multiply my wounds without cause.[76]

Robertson also suggests that Job predicts his own "tongue-in-cheek" confession. Again, as early as chapter nine, Job sees that it will be necessary to calm God's wrath with a phony repentance:

> No good can withstand his wrath,
> Rahab's troops cringe beneath him.
> The less could I refute him,
> Or match words with him.
> Though innocent I could not reply...
> I would have to beg for mercy.
> Though guiltless, my mouth would declare me guilty.[77]

By his insincere confession of guilt, Job wins the renewed favor of Yahweh but at the expense of deceiving God and making him the object of an ironic joke. Robertson sees the author or Job offering an antidote to perennial maladies such as man's fear of fate, destiny, and the unknown. He points out that the poet attempts to cure fear

> by means of its opposite, ridicule of the subject feared. We do not fear that which we feel beneath us in dignity; rather we scorn it.... While God may be more powerful than we are, He is beneath us on the scales that measure love, justice and wisdom. So we know of him what we know of all tyrants, that while they may torture us and finally kill us, they cannot destroy our personal integrity.[78]

While I am inclined to agree that Robertson has provided a consistent reading of the Book of Job, I remain unpersuaded that his is the most adequate interpretation of Job's change of heart. Robertson may find a good deal more irony in the book than is actually there. He admits that his essay is a "child of its age, the ironic age."[79] He invites us to consider his argument, unorthodox as it is, because "we need to take a variety of critical approaches to the Book of Job in order to better understand its truly remarkable scope and profundity."[80]

In the final analysis, however, I must agree with Edwin Good who, in responding to Robertson, suggests that he finally "tells us that both of its principal subjects are frauds — even righteous frauds,"[81] which, I might add, are usually the worst kind. I would hold that it is more faithful to the text to see Job's repentance as a sincere change of heart, but we are still left with two competing views as to why that repentance comes about.

We must now consider (b) Job sincerely repents because of the realization that Yahweh's power is self-justifying. We have already observed that this is the position suggested by Hobbes and in a more subtle fashion by O'Brien. It is also a view expressed by Gilbert Murray, who sees Job's God as a deity who has no real duties toward men; Job cannot complain of injustice because God owes Job nothing:

> If God's rule conflicts with human morality, that is because human morality is such a limited thing, not valid beyond particular regions of time and space. It is impertinence in man to expect God to be righteous.[82]

Murray understands Yahweh's answer out of the whirlwind as a "long insistence on the puny and ephemeral nature of Job."[83] The story culminates in the central argument: "Wilt thou disannul my judgement? Wilt thou condemn me, that thou mayest be righteous? Hast thou an arm like God, or canst thou thunder with a voice like him?"[84]

Yahweh's only answer to Job's complaint, Murray claims, is a reassertion of His divine power:

> God does not show, or even say, that he is righteous by human standards of righteousness; what he does assert is that he is, in Nietzsche's phrase, *Jenseits von Gut und Bose* (Beyond Good and Evil), and that the puny standards by which man judges right and wrong do not apply to the power that rules the universe.[85]

Murray concludes his essay by contrasting Job with the ancient Greek philosophers:

> If Plato or Aristotle had been present at this discussion I think they would have felt as explosive as Elihu the Buzite, but on different grounds. They would have pointed out that Jehovah was not answering the real question at all. No one had doubted his power, it was his justice they had questioned; and his only answer had been to reassert his power again and again in a storm of magnificent rhetoric, and demand how a worm like Job dares to ask any questions at all.[86]

Murray suggests that the "oriental" Job, unlike the Greeks, was "accustomed to the rule of a despot or patriarch, and cared most for obedience to the supreme power; such power was in Job's view completely self-justifying."[87] Although this may well be true for the time and place in which Job was written, we must ask whether this view of power is something that is still viable for twentieth century seekers of an answer to the problem of evil. If Murray's view is all that can be said about Job's repentance, it seems to help contemporary people very little, for our doctrine of God bears little resemblance to an "oriental despot."

A somewhat more profound view of (b) is given in Peter Geach's *God and the Soul.* In the chapter entitled, "The Moral Law and the Law of God," Geach raises the interesting question concerning whether it makes sense, given that there is an almighty God, to defy him. Geach clearly answers this question in the negative. He suggests that the world's "whole *raison d'etre* is to effect God's good pleasure."[88] Considering this, Geach argues, it is "insane" to set out to defy God:

> For Prometheus to defy Zeus made sense because Zeus had not made Prometheus and had only limited power over him. A defiance of an almighty God is insane; it is like trying to cheat a man to whom your whole business is mortgaged and who you know is well aware of your attempts to cheat him, or again, as the prophet said, it is as if a stick tried to beat or an axe to cut the very hand that was wielding it.[89]

Geach believes that because God is "the supreme power, wholly different from earthly powers," his might is self-justifying and worthy of worship:

> This reasoning will not convince everybody; people may still say that it makes sense, given that there is a God, to defy him, but this is only so because, as Pritchard said, you can no more make a man think than you can make a horse drink. A moral philosopher once said to me: 'I don't think that I am morally obliged to obey God unless God is good.' I asked him how he understood the proposition that 'God is good.' He replied, 'Well, I have no considered view of how it should be analyzed; but provisionally I'd say it meant

something like this: God is the sort of God whom I'd choose to be God if it were up to me to make the choice.' I fear that he has never understood why I found the answer funny.[90]

Geach seems content to leave his argument on more or less an intuitive level: when one fully realizes what the almighty power of God means, one simply cannot hold that defying God is a good option.

But we must raise a question in regard to Geach's view and the view of Hobbes as well. Exactly what is the guarantee that benevolence and justice are tied up with the self-justifying power of God? We have shown earlier that it is logically possible to be omnipotent but demonic. Are we to submit to God on the basis of his power alone? Geach's straw man moral philosopher is clumsily expressing an important point. On worshipping God for his power alone are we not, as J.S. Mill so forcefully put it, "bowing down to a gigantic image of something not fit for us to imitate?"

Interpretations (a) and (b) of Job's repentance may not be as far apart from one another as they initially appear. In a real way there is a decision made in both points of view that one horn of the Euthyphro dilemma must be saved at what seems like the expense of the other. Position (a) opts for the side that says ethical principles are independent of the will of God and that these values can and should be used in measuring even His conduct. In this regard, Robertson's position is very much like Dostoyevski's Ivan Karamazov. In interpretation (b), on the other hand, its proponents come very close to making the suggestion that God is worthy of worship no matter what. Thus, the believers of this second view settle for the pole of the Euthyphro dilemma that insists that goodness is good just because God says so. Geach's affinity with that horn of the dilemma can be seen in his rather curt reply to the moral philosopher. Murray's preference for that side of the problem can be ascertained in his remark that God is beyond good and evil. But the notion that we somehow need to choose one pole or the other of the Euthyphro dilemma, as we have shown in chapter two, rests on a mistake,

We could agree with Robertson that the ascertaining of what is good usually precedes any claims we may have about the will of God. Indeed, one of the main tests available to us concerning whether a revelation is genuine or spurious is a test of the moral goodness of what is willed. We would usually not be inclined to call something good, in a moral sense, unless it fulfilled our criteria for a moral good.

However, if one does not wish to make the morally good completely dependent upon the knowledge of God's will, neither is it advisable to make it superior to the will of the divine or even an independent entity.

We have already identified in chapter two a coherent avenue of escape from this conundrum. One way to reiterate what Mackie has suggested there is to say that the problem dissolves as a logical dilemma if we identify the will of God with the realm of values that constitutes the goodness of things. This divine will, Mackie argues, is also cognizant of what constitutes the most appropriate non-morally good life and reveals it to us through a set of prescriptions designed to have us follow that life. Thus there is a descriptive as well as a prescriptive resolution of the problem when he comments:

> The moral experience is one index of what we mean
> when we speak of God. Thus we do not have a prior
> conception of God, which must subsequently be
> brought in some sort of relation with our notion of the

realm of values so that either they depend upon him or he is conditioned by them. Rather, it is by starting with and developing a notion of values that we come to gain some idea of part of what is meant by the term 'God.'[91]

In addition to the major criticism discussed above which covers both interpretations (a) and (b) of Job's repentance, some further remarks might also be made regarding their individual inadequacies as a proper view of why Job repents.

One particular problem with Robertson is that he seems to want to have it both ways. On the one hand, he tells us that he is an "ironic child of his age," an age that, presumably, contains a modern conception of God, even if as "ironic" people we decide to reject it. Yet, in his essay he constructs an archaic, cardboard characterization of God, one much older even than the Book of Job itself. This divine figure of Robertson's lacks enough knowledge of others, not to mention self-knowledge, to be able to see through the calculated "repentance" of Job. Robertson measures an archaic conception of God by modern ethical standards and seems oddly surprised by the results.

Position (b) suffers from another important problem if it is to be regarded as a proper interpretation of Job's repentance: it is not true to the text. Murray suggests that suddenly in the speeches out of the whirlwind Job becomes aware of the awesome power of God. But it is clear that on numerous occasions before the Yahweh speeches Job is fully aware of God's power and his own powerlessness against it. Consider, for example, this passage from chapter twelve:

Behold, He destroys and it cannot be rebuilt,
He imprisons a man and he is not released.

He shuts up the waters and they dry up,
or He sends them forth and they overwhelm the earth.
With Him are strength and sound counsel;
The misled and the misleaders — are all His.
He drives the counselors mad,
and of judges he makes fools.
He opens the belt of kings
and removes the girdle from their loins.
He drives priests into madness
and temple votaries into confusion.[92]

It should be apparent that as early as chapter twelve Job is quite clear about the power of God. I would venture to say that if the Yahweh speeches were not intended to show Job something more than the display of Yahweh's power, there would be no real reason for the change of heart. Why should another display of Yahweh's strength break down Job's integrity at the end, when all hope for vindication of his life seems lost?[93]

Job's "seeing God" must involve something more than witnessing a display of sheer power. It must involve something new, something that helps to make proper sense of the theophany. In order to see what that something might be, we must return to the formulation (c) of Job's repentance: (c) Job sincerely repents because of the realization of Yahweh's awesome power but also for a number of other relevant reasons.

What we need to get clear about here are the other relevant reasons that might be sufficiently important to cause Job's change of perspective. As I have said before, I think that O'Brien is essentially right about a shift taking place where, because of the Yahweh speeches, the context of the God-Job encounter moves from a formal one to an existential one. I believe, however, that O'Brien is wrong on two points. First, it is not just power that changes Job's mind; it is omnipotence in consort with God's other attributes. Second, O'Brien's choice of a military metaphor to describe the new relation between God and Job obscures more than it enlightens. A more appropriate metaphor, I would suggest, for understanding the God-Job encounter is the relation between parent and child. Let us now return to the first point so that we may more fully develop an interpretation (c) of Job's repentance.

In chapter two of this book I suggested that it is important to understand each of the divine attributes: omnipotence, omniscience, omnibenevolence, and creator of the universe, within the context of each other. One cannot adequately be discussed without understanding its relationship to the others. The author of Job seems to make this same point. Consider again, for example, the opening lines of the speeches from the whirlwind:

> Where were you when I laid the earth's foundations?
> Tell me, if you know and understand.
> Who settled its dimensions? Surely you should know.
> Who stretched his measuring-line over it?
> On what do its supporting pillars rest?
> Who set its corner-stone in place,
> when the morning stars sang together
> and all the sons of God shouted aloud?
> Who watched over the birth of the sea,
> when it burst in flood from the womb
> when I wrapped it in a blanket of cloud
> and cradled it in a fog.
> When I established its bounds,
> fixing its doors and bars in place,
> and said, 'Thus far shall you come and no farther,
> and here shall your surging waves halt.'
> In all your life have you called up the dawn

or shown the morning its place?
Have you taught it to grasp the fringes of the earth
and shake the dog-star from its place;
to bring up the horizon in relief as clay under a seal,
until all things stand out like the folds of a cloak
when the light of the dog-star is dimmed
and the stars of the Navigator's Line go out one by
one?[94]

In these original queries God is not just displaying his power, He is challenging Job's comprehension of the original governing structure of the universe. In addition to displaying His creative genius, God is also making a specific comparison of His divine intelligence with that of Job's. In doing so He leads Job back to the primordial scene to experience the original mystery of the cosmos.

If Job were the first man endowed with wisdom, where was he when the rest of the heavenly council was celebrating the founding of the earth? Was he absent that day? Does he know how it was controlled by the creator? Can he summon the dawn to shed light on the mystery?

In the Lord's second speech, attention is given to divine justice. Earlier, in 9:19-24, Job accuses God of all but ignoring the evil done to Job; in 40:6-14 God addresses the problem directly. He does not accuse Job of lying about his innocence but rather of violating God's integrity. Job has mistakenly assumed that he had a proper perspective on the larger teleological context of God's justice. The Lord reminds Job that it is not necessary to condemn the divine in order to affirm one's own integrity.

One of the realizations Job makes, then, which may have much to do with his change of heart, is the discovery that the various attributes that go into the making of any meager description of God cannot properly be separated.

The other element in Job's repentance involves the point I have made about the inappropriateness of O'Brien's military metaphor. In Job's encounter with God in chapters thirty-eight to forty-two, he comes to "see" two things that the military metaphor does not capture. The first of these is that God is the creator and sustainer of Job in much the same way a good, intelligent and effective parent is the creator and sustainer of his or her child.

A child, of course, is ordinarily thought to have an obligation to obey his parents. Indeed, a child who makes no effort to please a benevolent, wise, and effective parent who has created and nurtured him is normally thought to be behaving reprehensively. The child's obligations to the parent are fulfilled by conforming to the wishes of the parent, provided those wishes are in the child's best interest.[95]

If all of this is correct, then we might rightly say that Job is under a similar moral obligation to obey God. In the midst of listening to the whirlwind speeches, he suddenly realizes this obligation. For unlike the parent-child relation where the older the child becomes, the less the parent is responsible, in the case of the God-Job relation the sustenance is permanent.

Another element that may go into the making of Job's change of heart is connected to the point made above. In addition to Job perceiving that God is the creator and sustainer of himself, He is also the creator and sustainer of the entire universe. He brought it into existence and continually keeps it in existence through His will, so that in a real way God could be said to be the legitimate owner of the universe. The owner of any property, of course, under normal circumstances has the right to tell those to whom he has loaned it what they are allowed to do with that property. Thus, God has a legitimate right to tell Job how he should conduct his life. Indeed, this view that God is the creator, sustainer, and therefore the owner of His creation is continually reiterated throughout the divine speeches of Job as well as the rest of scripture.

If we understand these two points about Job's obligation to God in light of Job's change of heart, it becomes clear that the context shifts from a formal to an existential relation, not merely because of the Lord's display of sheer power, but also because God has created and sustained Job as well as the world around him.

Still, one might raise an objection here that there are clearly lots of morally corrupt parents and pernicious landlords. Given the facts of the story of Job, could we not say that although Job had a *prima facie* duty to be obedient and long-suffering in respect to God, that obligation was abrogated by the moral degradation in which he was forced to live?

In order to meet this objection we must recall that God's power cannot be understood as being independent of His other attributes. Divine omnipotence can only be fully comprehended in consort with God's nature as the omniscient and benevolent creator of the universe. The suggestion that Job is under no moral obligation to obey and respect God because He is like an ethically corrupt parent does not work, for unlike even the best of earthly parents, by His very nature God cannot be morally corrupt.

Thus, Job's repentance is related, I believe, to his profound realization that this all-good all-powerful and all-knowing God has created and sustained him as well as the world around him, and it is this realization that changes the context of the God-Job encounter from a formal relation to an existential one.

Job is not left with particulars of a philosophical theodicy. In the end, what he does have is trust that God does have a teleological view by which evil will be overcome. Thus, in our final analysis of Job it can be said that he settles for a position that is logically coherent, true to his religion's form of life, and takes the individual sufferer most seriously.

With this realization of what Job has learned firmly in mind, I shall discuss in the final chapter the framework of a viable Christian theodicy that goes beyond the Book of Job.

Notes

1. Thomas Carlyle, *On Heroes* (London: The New University Library, 1957) p. 67. Much of the material for this chapter was taken from papers presented in Prof. McBride's seminar in Old Testament Theodicy, Yale Divinity School, 1975.

2. H.H. Rowley, *Job* (London: Thomas Nelson, 1970) p. 6.

3. S.R. Driver, *A Critical Exegetical Commentary on the Book of Job*, 2 vols. (New York: Chas. Scribner's Sons, 1921); Robert Gordis, *The Book of Job* (New York: Jewish Theological Seminary of America, 1978); Marvin Pope, *Job* (Anchor Bible Commentary Series) (Garden City, N.Y.: Doubleday, 1965).

4. For a sampling of the textual problems in Job consult the three sources mentioned above.

5. H.H. Rowley, *From Moses to Qumran* (London: Lutterworth Press, 1963) pp. 173ff.

6. Jeremiah 11:18 - 12:6.

7. Samuel Terrien, *Interpreter's Bible* vol. 3 (Nashville: Abingdon, 1954) pp. 884-888.

8. The analogical use of Job as a symbol of Israel is also suspect. One of the chief shortcomings of this view is that Job is innocent while Israel was not.

9. John Bowker, *The Problems of Suffering in the Religions of the World*, pp. 5-24.

10. Rowley, *Job*, pp. 21ff.

11. Ibid.

12. Job 2:4-6. All quotations except where otherwise specified from the Book of Job are taken from the translation of Robert Gordis.

13. Job 2:9-10.

14. Job 2:11-13.

15. Job 1:1-2.

16. Job 4:7-9.

17. Job 9:33-35.

18. Robert Gordis, *The Book of Job*, pp. 238-239.

19. Job 22:4-8.

20. Job 33:19-28.

21. Some scholars, R.A. Watson among them, have suggested that Elihu's words in chapter 37 have portended the whirlwind speech of Job 38:1ff.

22. Job 38:1-11.

23. Robert Gordis, *The Book of Job*, p. 435.

24. Job 42:1-6.

25. Job 42:7-17.

26. Job 42:7-8b.

27. Job 42:11-17.

28. Job 1:10-11.

29. Robert Gordis, *The Book of Job*, p. 498.

30. R. Martin-Archard, *From Death to Life: A Study of the Development of the Doctrines of Resurrection in the Old Testament* (Edinburgh: Oliver and Boyd, 1960).

31. Job 14:7-12.

32. Eccles. 5:14; 9:5ff (Revised Standard Version).

33. Job 1:1.

34. Job 29:11-20.

35. Job 6:24; 7:20; 9:1-3; and 19:4-6.

36. James Wood, *Job and the Human Situation* (London: Geoffrey Bles, 1966) pp. 108-109.

37. See Job 1:13-20.

38. For a good exposition of this position, see W.F. Albright, *From Stone Age to Christianity* (Baltimore: Johns Hopkins University Press, 1940).

39. S.R. Driver and G.B. Gray, *A Critical and Exegetical Commentary on the Book of Job,* vol. I, p. 65.

40. Marvin Pope, Job, p. 80.

41. Job 38:2 (Pope's translation).

42. Job 23:3.

43. Nahum Glatzer (ed.), *The Dimensions of Job* (New York: Schocken Books, 1969).

44. W.O.E. Oesterley and T.H. Robinson, "The Three Stages of the Book," in Glatzer's *The Dimensions of Job*, pp. 214-217.

45. Leonhard Ragaz, "God Himself is the Answer," in Glatzer, pp. 128-131.

46. Arthur Peake, "Job's Victory," in Glatzer, pp. 197-205.

47. Martin Buber, "A God Who Hides His Face," in Glatzer, pp. 56-65.

48. Leo Roth, "Job and Jonah," in Glatzer, pp. 71-74.

49. Emile Kraeling, "A Theodicy — and More," in Glatzer, pp. 205- 214.

50. G.A. Barton, "The Book of Job: Seeing God," *The Journal of Biblical Literature,* vol. 30. (1911).

51. R.A.F. MacKenzie, "The Purpose of the Yahweh Speeches in the Book of Job," *Biblica*, 40 (1959) p. 438.

52. Ibid., p. 440.

53. Ibid., p. 441.

54. Ibid., p. 443.

55. Ibid.

56. Ibid., p. 442.

57. Ibid.

58. Rudolph Otto, *The Idea of the Holy*, translated by John Harvey (London: Oxford University Press, 1950).

59. Ibid., pp. 5-7.

60. Rudolph Otto, "The Elements of the Mysterious," in Glatzer, pp. 225-226.

61. Ibid., pp. 226-227.

62. Ibid., p. 228.

63. S.R. Driver and G.B. Gray, *A Critical and Exegetical Commentary on the Book of Job*, p. 261.

64. George D. O'Brien, "Prolegomena to a Dissolution to the Problem of Suffering," *Harvard Theological Review* vol. 57 (1964) p. 304.

65. Ibid., p. 303.

66. Ibid.

67. Ibid., p. 304.

68. Ibid.

69. Ibid., p. 305.

70. Ibid., pp. 305ff.

71. Ibid., p. 306.

72. Ibid., p. 308.

73. Ibid., p. 310.

74. David Robertson,"The Book of Job: A Literary Study,"
    Soundings, vol. 56 (1973) p. 446.

75. Ibid., p. 462.

76. Ibid., p. 466.

77. Ibid., p. 468 (Robertson's translation).

78. Ibid., p. 446.

79. Ibid., p. 447.

80. Ibid.

81. E.M. Good, "Job and the Literary Task: A Response,"
    Soundings, vol. 56 (1973) p. 479.

82. Gilbert Murray, "Beyond Good and Evil," in Glatzer,
    p. 196.

83. Ibid.

84. Ibid.

85. Ibid.

86. Ibid.

87. Ibid.

88. Peter Geach, *God and the Soul* (London: Routledge
    and Kegan Paul, 1969).

89. Ibid., p. 127.

90. Ibid.

91. W. G. MacLagan, *The Theological Frontiers of Ethics* (London: Allen and Unwin, 1961) p. 90.

92. Job 12:14-19.

93. For further criticisms of Geach's position, see D.Z. Phillips, *Death and Immortality* (London: Macmillan, 1970), particularly chapter 2.

94. Job 38:4-15. (Norman Habel's translation).

95. For a similar point of view, see Richard Swinburne, *The Coherence of Theism*, pp. 183ff., and Baruch Brody, "Morality and Religion Reconsidered," *Readings in the Philosophy of Religion* (Englewood Cliffs, N.J.: Prentice Hall, 1974).

V.
Prolegomena to a
Christian Theodicy

If there were no obscurity, man would not feel his cor-
ruption, and if there were no light, man would not
hope for a remedy. Thus, it is not only just, but useful
to us that God is hidden in part and discovered in part,
for to man it is as dangerous to know God without
knowing his own misery as it is to know his misery
without knowing God.

Blaise Pascal

Despair over the earthly or over something earthly is
really a despair about the eternal and over oneself,
insofar as it is a despair, for this is the formula for all
despair. But the despairer...did not observe what was
happening behind him, so to speak; he thinks he is in
despair over something earthly and constantly talks
about what he is in despair over, and yet he is in
despair about the eternal.

Soren Kierkegaard

Man, the scientists say, is an animal that thinks. They
are wrong. Man is an animal that loves. It is in man's
love that life is beautiful; in man's love that the
world's justice is resolved. To hold together in one

> thought those terrible opposites of good and evil
> which struggle in the world is to be capable of life,
> and only love will hold them so. Our labor always,
> like Job's labor, is to learn through suffering to
> love...to love even that which let us suffer.
>
> Program notes to Archibald MacLeish's *J.B.*,
> Yale Drama School (1958)

In chapter three we attempted to make a distinction between theodicies prohibited by reason and those allowed by reason. We have discovered that in the first group we find the punishment and warning theodicies: retributive justice and the free will defense; the unreality of evil theodicies: the amount of evil is insufficient to create a problem, evil is an illusion, and evil is privation of good; and the evil is logically necessary theodicies: certain versions of the free will defense and the contrast perspective. Because of one or more logical flaws, all of these responses fail as logically consistent answers to the problem of evil.

Those theodicies that are allowed by reason include both the classical Hindu and Hinayana Buddhist versions of monism, the dualistic responses to the problem of evil offered by Plato, Zoroastrianism, process thought, and limited God theories such as that offered by J.S. Mill and the various possibilities suggested by David Hume in the *Dialogues Concerning Natural Religion.*[1] We have also seen that despite some logical problems, John Hick's version of the teleological theodicies can be numbered among those responses to the problem of evil that are allowed by reason. All of the members of this second group are logically consistent and therefore possible candidates for the job of answering the question: "Why does evil exist?"

As we have mentioned earlier, however, logical consistency is not the only criterion by which theodicies might be measured. In addition to the first criterion, it has also been suggested that any viable theodicy must be true, at least in a broad way, to the form of life out of which it arises or out of which an answer is sought. And thirdly, we have suggested that any workable response to the problem of evil must take the individual sufferer seriously.

If we examine carefully those theodicies that have already passed our first test of logical consistency, we find that the monistic faiths, classical Hinduism and Hinayana Buddhism, fail on both the second and third criteria. The purpose of this entire discussion has been to discover whether there is some answer or group of answers within the Christian form of life that might respond adequately to the problem of evil. Both of these monistic responses deny some of the basic ontological presuppositions on which the Christian faith is based. Indeed, it would be logically impossible to call oneself a member of the Christian tradition while still adhering to either of these positions. Because the basic metaphysical presuppositions on which the monistic faiths are built are so radically different from those of Christianity, they cannot be considered as viable responses in the Christian tradition. In a curious way, because of the same metaphysical presuppositions, classical Hinduism and Hinayana Buddhism also seem to fail the third criterion. Since both traditions would have us believe that at bottom level individual personalities, as well as evil itself, do not really exist, there seems to be a fundamental denial of the importance of the individual sufferer.

The dualistic responses would seem to do well in meeting the third criterion. The writings of J.S. Mill and Hartshorne, as well as the ethical dialogues of Plato, give ample evidence of a genuine concern for the plight of the individual sufferer. None of these dualistic approaches, however, seem as effective in meeting the second criterion. All of the limited God theorists, Plato, Zoroastrianism, and the process thought of Charles Hartshorne deny at least one of the traditional attributes of God discussed in chapter two. For Plato, Zoroastrianism, and J.S. Mill, God is not omnipotent. The same can be said for the process thought of Hartshorne if we construe omnipotence as the ability to do anything that is logically possible. Additionally, it could be argued that God does not create the world *ex nihilo* in any of these dualistic points of view. It might be said that each of these responses denies at least one aspect that seems to be fundamental to the classical Christian conception of God.

Upon closer examination, even the theodicy of John Hick seems to fail the second criterion. On one level we might simply say that his position is not an adequate Christian response because he holds a view of omniscience that is radically different from the classical position that God knows all true propositions. This point, perhaps, could be argued. Nevertheless, on a more fundamental level, it may also be said that Hick fails to give sufficient weight to the person of Christ in his theodicy. Quite simply, the crucifixion and atonement seem to serve no central role in his answer to the problem of evil. The same criticisms might seem also to apply to the Book of Job. But since Job was written several hundred years before the advent of Christianity, it might more sensibly be said that the Book of Job meets our criteria for viable Judaic response to the problem of evil but it is, as I shall soon show, still incomplete as a Christian theodicy.

Still, we may have managed to tether ourselves in a kind of doublebind. On the one hand, it would seem to be the case that the only theodicies that meet our first criterion of logical consistency are those that appear doomed by the second or third tests. On the other hand, if Mackie is correct, any theodicy that adheres to the belief in the traditional attributes of God, as well as the reality of evil, seems to be prohibited by reason.

But let us return at this point to the work of J.L. Mackie in the hope of showing that he may have overstated his case when he suggests, in effect, that all Christians' answers to the problem of evil, which adhere to the classical conception of God, are prohibited by reason. If Mackie is correct, then there can be no logically consistent theodicy in the Christian tradition.

In chapter two we presented J.L. Mackie's case for viewing the problem of evil as a logical problem, that is, as a "problem of clarifying and reconciling a number of beliefs." According to Mackie, the Judeo-Christian theologian must (but cannot consistently) hold to the following theistic set of beliefs:

> i. God is omnipotent.
> ii. God is omniscient.
> iii. God is omnibenevolent.
> iv. There is evil in the world.

Mackie states the problem quite clearly in his recent book, *The Miracle of Theism*:

> According to traditional theism, there is a God who is both omnipotent (and omniscient) and wholly good, and yet there is evil in the world. How can this be? It is true that there is no explicit contradiction between the statement that there is an omnipotent and wholly good God and that there is evil. But if we add the at

least initially plausible premises that good is opposed
to evil in such a way that a being who is wholly good
eliminates evil as far as he can, and there are no limits
to what an omnipotent being could do, then we do
have a contradiction. A wholly good omnipotent being
would either eliminate evil completely, if there really
are evils, or, there cannot be such a being.

The problem of evil in the sense I am using the phrase
is essentially a logical problem: it sets the theist the
clear task of clarifying and if possible reconciling the
several beliefs which he holds. It is not a scientific
problem that might be solved by a decision or action.
And the problem in this sense signally does not arise
for those who view the world differently from traditional theism.[2]

Alasdair MacIntyre explains the two possible ways of
resolving the logical problem of evil as Mackie has posed
it:

With an argument that seems to involve us in a contradiction, two courses are open to us. We can scrutinize
the meaning of the terms employed in the argument
more carefully, and ask whether we have not perhaps
made a mistake in supposing a contradiction to arise.
Or we can accept the fact that a contradiction does
arise and avoid it by abandoning one of those statements, the joint affirmation of which leads to the contradiction.[3]

Traditional Christian theism is, of course, committed to
the truth of propositions i through iv. Consequently,
MacIntyre's second suggestion is out of the question. If the
groundwork for an answer to the problem of evil is to be

laid, it is the truth of MacIntyre's first course that must be established.

If we keep Mackie's phrasing of the dilemma before us, we will recall his admission that "the contradiction does not arise immediately" among the terms "evil," "omnipotent," "omnibenevolent" and "omniscient." Rather, some "quasi-logical rules" or "additional principles" are needed to demonstrate the contradiction. Earlier, in chapter two, we added a fifth premise (v, God created the world *ex nihilo*) to see whether that would produce the logical inconsistency. We saw that it did not. Consequently, we added Mackie's additional principles as premises vi and vii.

> vi. Good is opposed to evil in such a way that a good thing always eliminates evil as far as it can.

> vii. There are no limits (other than logical ones) to what an omnipotent and omniscient being can do.

From these two "at least initially plausible" premises, Mackie derives something like the following:

> viii. An omnibenevolent, omnipotent and omniscient being would eliminate evil completely.

> ix. 'An omnibenevolent, omnipotent, and omniscient being exists' and 'evil exists' are logically incompatible.

If Mackie's conclusion (ix) follows from his premises (i through viii), then it would also follow that any answer to the problem of evil that accepted the traditional attributes of God would be logically inconsistent and therefore prohibited by reason. In charging that such a contradiction exists Mackie has attempted to show that all of the initial premises (i through iv) cannot be true at the same time, under any circumstances. He has added premises vi through viii to support his charge of inconsistency.

It must be admitted that if premises vi and vii are true, then viii and ix follow quite nicely and, indeed, we would be faced with a logical contradiction. Certainly vii is true, at least by virtue of Mackie's definition of omnipotence. For the moment then, let us grant him the truth of vii. But why should we assume that vi is true?

If vi is true, what kind of truth is it? Certainly it is not a necessary truth, for no inherent contradiction would arise from its denial. If it is not a necessary truth, it must be a contingent truth. But if it is a contingent truth, then it is possible that it is not true at all. If it were the case that vi is not true at all, then the truth of viii and ix would collapse, for their supposed truth rests on the prior truth of each of the premises i through vii .

The question essentially becomes one of what sort of evidence we can give for and against the truth of vi. Mackie must argue that the evidence is overwhelmingly in favor of the truth of vi. But the critic of Mackie's formulation might attempt to show that certain counter evidence might be brought forth that would contradict the notion that "good is opposed to evil in such a way that a good thing always eliminates evil as far as it can."

Suppose, for example, there was some greater good to be achieved in a particular situation by the endurance of a certain amount of pain. Indeed, suppose it were the case that this greater good could only be accomplished through the endurance of this very real pain. We would then have a case where good was not opposed to evil in such a way that a good thing always eliminates evil.[4] This situation is certainly possible logically.[5] Mackie has not shown why this could not be the actual descriptive account of the attitudes and actions of God. Indeed, it may well be the sort of view that Job finally settles on. What we are suggesting here is "at least initially plausible" and would give us a new look at premise vi.

> vi. (b). Good is not necessarily opposed to evil in such a way that a good thing always eliminates evil as far as it can.

If we add our new premise vi(b) to the truth of Mackie's vii, we get something like the following:

> vii. There are no limits, other than logical ones, to what an omnipotent being can do.

> viii (b). An omnibenevolent, omnipotent, and omniscient being would not necessarily eliminate evil completely.

> ix (b). 'An omnibenevolent, omnipotent, and omniscient being exists' and 'evil exists' are not logically incompatible.

One way to show what we have done in the above argument is to recall our remarks regarding the distinction between "genuine evil," "apparent evil," and "*prima facie* evil." As we have suggested earlier, it may be the case that all *prima facie* evil is actually genuine evil. It is also logically possible that some *prima facie* evil is genuine and some is merely apparent. Both of these conclusions would follow from Mackie's argument. But there is also still a third logically possible state of affairs in which all *prima facie* evil is actually only apparent. The key point to understand here is that all three of these situations are logically possible states of affairs and therefore allowed by reason. It could be the case that Mackie is correct, but there is nothing logically necessary about his formulation of premise vi nor about his conclusion in ix.

Another way to phrase the same point is to look at Christianity as a religion of *prima facie* paradox. The *prima facie* paradox may indeed be actual, as Mackie has suggested, but it is also logically possible that it is merely apparent. John Wisdom makes a helpful remark that comes close to the heart of this issue:

> One might have expected that in the sphere of religion everyone would have learned by now to move carefully and neither at once to accept nor hastily reject what sounds bewildering. But no, even here we find a tendency to reject strange statements with impatience, to turn from them as absurd or unprovable or to write them down as metaphor — deceptive, or at best, merely picturesque. Only a few months ago someone came to me troubled about the old but bewildering statement that Christ was both God and man. He asked those who taught him theology how this could be true. Their answers had not satisfied him. I was not able to tell him what the doctrine means. But I did remind him that though some statements which seem contradictory are self-contradictory, others are not, that indeed some of the most preposterous statements ever made have turned out to convey the most important discoveries.[6]

It is important to understand two features of Wisdom's comment. First, the *prima facie* religious paradoxes or contradictions may indeed turn out to be genuine self-contradictions, though there is also the possibility that they will later be seen as merely apparent. And second, it is only those that turn out to be merely apparent that may be illuminating or "tremendous discoveries."

Some commentators on the work of Professor Wisdom seem to miss this second point and in the process make him out to be something akin to a believer in Tertullian's dictum: I believe because it is absurd. T.F. Torrance, for example, makes the following observation about Wisdom's view as applied to Christian theology:

> The task of a living and constructive theology is to discover and work out the interior logic of our knowledge of God, but in the nature of the case it will not be able to avoid constant tension between the material logic thrusts upon it from the side of the redeeming operations of God in Christ, and the logico-verbal atoms of our thought and speech that are already schematized to this world, for the Truth of God as it is in Christ breaks through all our linguistic and logical forms.[7]

But if we examine again the words of Wisdom that occasioned this remark, we can see that in Wisdom's view the fruitful paradoxes are those that turn out not to be self-contradictory. Torrance seems to be saying just the opposite and, in so doing, relegates language about God to the same class as language about round squares and married bachelors.

Wisdom's point is quite relevant for our discussion of Mackie's argument, for it at least points to the possibility that Mackie has overstated his case. In a similar vein, Nelson Pike has attempted to show that the believer need not be cowed by an appeal to Mackie's construction of the supposed logical contradiction. Pike challenges those of the Mackie-Flew persuasion to prove the falsity of a claim like: "A good God could have a morally sufficient reason for allowing evil to exist." Pike suggests that just as a child may not be old enough to understand why his mother causes him so much pain in curing him of a certain sickness, and yet the mother has morally sufficient reasons for doing so, so a limited human being may not understand what a perfect God's sufficient reasons could be for allowing evil.[8] Indeed, this is precisely the position the author of Job seems to be suggesting.

M.B. Ahern arrives at a similar conclusion about the argument proposed by Mackie, as well as incompatibility arguments in general that attempt to argue that any answer in the Judeo-Christian tradition that adheres to the traditional attributes of God must be prohibited by reason:

> There are two general conclusions from this study: (1) Apart from positive proofs of God's existence, it cannot be shown that the world's evil is logically compatible with the existence of a wholly good, omnipotent and omniscient being, or that the conditions for incompatibility are in fact met. (2) It cannot be shown that the world's evil is logically incompatible with God's existence, or that the conditions for compatibility are not in fact met.[9]

Ahern continues by arguing that although it cannot be shown that there is a logical connection between evil and the nonexistence of God, it may be possible to show that there is a synthetically necessary connection between them:

> We saw that such a connection cannot be made by means of the principles used by Epicurus, Augustine,

Hume and others. Perhaps it can be established by other principles, e.g. a good being always prevents suffering to innocent children. It might be argued that such principles are synthetically *a priori* and necessarily true. Strictly speaking, this view does not come within the scope of the present study. It involves questions about the notion of synthetically *a priori* principles which could only be discussed in a separate study. But since the chapter on the general problem has no fewer than eight principles about goodness which could be proposed as synthetically *a priori* and all were held to be false it seems reasonable to believe that satisfactory principles will probably not be found. The question here is noted as a possible non-theist position which the study has not discussed. The study has dealt with problems about logical compatibility raised for them by evil and claimed that none of them can be shown to be decisive.[10]

This indefinite conclusion has real significance for our study. Far from containing airtight solutions to the problem of evil, Christian revelation may very well leave the problem shrouded in mystery, as we have seen in chapters thirty-eight to forty-two of Job. If this indefinite conclusion is the best honest Christians can do, it lays open the possibility that the evils of this world may be merely apparent. Any teleological theodicy that suggests that in the end the *prima facie* paradox of evil may be shown to be merely apparent would therefore appear to be a candidate for the class of the responses to the problem of evil that are allowed by reason. If one or more of these theodicies at the same time appears to be true, at least in a broad way, to the Christian form of life, then it would appear that we have one or more Christian theodicies that are both logically sound and religiously acceptable. If it could be demonstrated that one or more of these theodicies was also quite sensitive to the needs and perspective of the individual sufferer, then the task of this book would be complete. In the remainder of this chapter I shall attempt to sketch the bare framework of a response to the problem of evil that may well meet these three conditions.

One way to begin our discussion of a viable Christian response to the problem of evil is to recall two of the principle flaws in the theodicy developed by John Hick in his *Evil and the God of Love*. The first of these was that Hick's view of omniscience does not allow for God's knowing future contingent human actions. In chapter two we have demonstrated that by understanding the distinction between necessity *de dicto* and necessity *de re* it can be shown that God's knowledge of future free human choices is not logically contradictory. By taking this view of omniscience we may make an important step in developing a teleological theodicy that is true to the conception of God as conceived in classical Christian theism.

We have suggested that the other deficiency in Hick's point of view occurs at a more fundamental level — he seems to deny any central role to Christ in the formulation of his answer to the problem of evil.

Some might suggest the reason Hick spends so little time discussing the role Christ should play in any distinctively Christian response to the problem of evil is that it is clear from the outset that any doctrine of the incarnation rests on a number of murky and logically contradictory claims. Consequently, any theodicy that uses as its centerpiece the dual nature of Jesus fails to meet our first criterion for a viable theodicy—logical consistency.[11] These critics might argue further that Hick has wisely avoided any central references to the person of Christ in his theodicy precisely so his position might be numbered among those that are allowed by reason.

There is at least ample circumstantial evidence to be found in *The Myth of God Incarnate*[12] for the view that Hick has carefully left out any reference to Jesus in *Evil and the God of Love* because he thinks any traditional view of the incarnation is self-contradictory. Indeed, in the former work Hick argues the orthodox doctrine of Jesus' nature has no clear content and therefore no non-metaphorical interpretation. Hick suggests that to say that the historical Jesus was also God is to utter a contradiction so devoid of meaning as to say that a circle is also a square.[13]

If Hick is correct, any answer to the problem of evil that relies heavily on the person of Christ would contain some central elements that are not only *prima facie* paradoxical but are genuinely paradoxical and therefore logically incoherent.

I think, however, Hick's perspective is profoundly mistaken for at least two important reasons. First, in a real way Hick throws out the proverbial baby with the bath water. By removing the person of Christ from his theodicy, he ceases to hold a distinctively Christian point of view. Indeed, he has abandoned the Christian form of life altogether. Second, I think it can be successfully argued that the doctrine of the incarnation is not a logically inconsistent or incoherent doctrine. In fact, it may well be the one doctrine that gives a special kind of coherence to the problem of evil as it is expressed in the Christian form of life. In order to make this claim, however, we must first show that the doctrine of the incarnation is a belief that is not prohibited by reason.

In order to develop a satisfactory response to Hick's doubts about the classical conception of the incarnation, we must engage in two different but related tasks: we must get clear as best we can on what it means in philosophical terms to say that something is an x, where x is a member of a certain class. Additionally, we must also discern, at least in a broad way, the clearest interpretation of what it means to say that "Jesus was fully human and fully divine." The first task can be completed, I think, in a fairly straightforward manner. Something is an x if and only if that thing possesses all the essential properties of x. By an essential property of x we mean one that must be present in order to call that thing an x. [14]

If we keep this analysis of the identity of members of a class in the backs of our minds for a moment we may proceed in an attempt to answer the question regarding the proper interpretation of "Jesus was fully human and fully divine." Let us begin then with a philosophical interpretation of this phrase:

> (a) Jesus possessed all the characteristics of men, while at the same time having all the characteristics of God.[15]

Formulation (a) will not do as a proper interpretation of "Jesus was fully human and fully divine," for there is clearly a difference between kinds of attributes, be they predicated of man or God. Some men are tall and some are short. Some humans are bald, while others have full heads of hair. It is clear that Jesus could not possess all the characteristics of men, for that would require him to be simultaneously tall and short, bald and hairy, and so on.

To solve this problem we might suggest another formulation of what it means to say that Jesus was fully human and fully divine:

> (b) Jesus had all the essential attributes of God while at the same time possessing all the indispensable properties of a man.

We have seen that an essential property of x is one that must be present in order to call that thing an x. Now the question arises: Can a being who possesses the essential attributes of God simultaneously possess the essential attributes of human beings? Another way to phrase this question is to ask whether a being who is omniscient, omnipotent, omnibenevolent, and creator of the universe can at the same time be limited in knowledge, power, and so on.

At first blush it would appear the answer to this question is no. The Jesus of the New Testament, for example, seems at times to be lacking in knowledge.[16] As MacIntyre has pointed out, when faced with a *prima facie* paradox, two routes are open to us. We can either say that Jesus Christ in some sense had both sets of properties, and thereby reduce discussions of the nature of Jesus to arguments about matters akin to round squares, or we can take what is sometimes referred to as a kenotic approach to the incarnation and thereby argue that the paradox is merely apparent. In this second point of view it is readily admitted that Jesus did not have properties like omniscience, omnipotence, or any other divine attributes inconsistent with being a human being. But at the same time he continued to possess those divine attributes that were consistent with his humanity, and was also capable of regaining in his ascension those essential properties given up. This perspective brings us to a third formulation of the notion that Jesus is fully human and fully divine:

> (c) Jesus was in possession of certain essential divine attributes, as well as certain human attributes, and there was no logical contradiction between them.

At first this seems like an initially plausible interpretation, but it also suffers from a major flaw. Formulation (c) would be satisfied even if Jesus only possessed, say, the attribute of omniscience but at the same time was deficient in all other divine properties. If this were a proper description of the nature of Jesus, he would seem to be inferior, for example, to the God of J.S. Mill. We must once again, therefore, amend the definition of fully human and fully divine to look like this:

> (d) Jesus was in possession of certain divine attributes as well as certain human attributes, and there was no logical contradiction between them. The divine properties were sufficient to make him God, while the human properties were sufficient to make him man.

But perhaps this new formulation leaves us with a major difficulty. How could Jesus be truly God if he lacked some essential attribute(s) of the divine. Earlier, we have seen, for example, that the Jesus depicted in the New Testament appears not to have been omniscient. In order to answer this difficulty we must make distinctions between what Stephen Davis calls "Jesus simpliciter" and "Jesus as truly God."[17] It would be false to say that Jesus had all the divine attributes or was God simpliciter. But the traditional conception of the incarnation does not necessarily imply this.[18] What it does insist, however, is that Jesus Christ was truly human and truly God. Another way to put this is to say that during the earthly life of Jesus, he was God as best he could be revealed in human form.

There are certain things he could not have done unless he were God (forgive sins, for example). And there were also clearly things he could not have done without a "truly human" nature (die on the cross, worry in the Garden of Gethsemane). But at the same time it is clear that only one person forgave sins and died on the cross.

This brings us to our major response to Hick's suggestion about the incoherence of any traditional doctrine of the incarnation. In the same way that a skilled cricket batsman could choose to play a match from his weaker side of the wicket, so too an omnipotent being could choose to temporarily limit his power so he might truly become human. The same can be said, it seems to me, about omniscience. An omniscient being could choose not to know the truth of certain propositions or a whole range of propositions for that matter.

But another objection might once again be raised at this point. One might grant that an omnipotent being could choose not to exercise his power, but how is it that an omniscient being could abandon the knowledge of certain propositions without ceasing to be omniscient? Can a being who is potentially omniscient choose not to know something? At first, this seems like a very peculiar idea, but I see no logical problems with an omniscient being giving up some of his knowledge. In order to understand this as a logical possibility, consider the following example. Suppose person A were to ask person B what the 148th digit of *pi* happens to be. B, who is quite a good mathematician, nevertheless finds the question trivial and unimportant. Consequently, he responds to A by saying, "I know what to do in order to discern the answer, but at this point I do not know it, nor do I wish to."

We might say about person B that in a curious kind of way he could both be said to know what the 148th digit of *pi* is and at the same time to not know it. The sense in which he does not know it is clear, for if he were told to answer yes or no to the question, his response would clearly be no. Yet, at the same time his answer does not do justice to the fact that B *could* know the answer any time he liked.

In a roughly analogous way, the same could be said about Jesus: He was omniscient in the sense that he could have exercised his knowledge of all true propositions at any time, but freely chose to live as a human being without that knowledge. At the same time, there is also a sense in which Jesus could still be said to be omniscient, since in freely choosing to limit his knowledge he still had the potential for omniscience. The first sense of omniscience is sufficient for Jesus to have retained his human nature, whole the second sense was sufficient to make him divine.[19]

Still, the notion of kenotic incarnation is not without its critics. Don Cupitt, Maurice Wiles, and John Hicks, among others, are all highly critical of this approach. Cupitt seems to argue on the basis of three points. First, "kenosis is not a theory designed to account for the facts, but rather about how one can go on believing in the incarnation in a time when the old arguments have broken down."[20] Second, kenosis leads to anthropomorphisms. And third, kenosis leads to an incoherent "triple consciousness in the incarnate Lord."[21]

I find the first of Cupitt's criticisms puzzling for at least three reasons. First, even if Cupitt were correct about the motivation of Christian apologists, and I think he is not,[22] the origin of their argument would say nothing about the truth or falsity of it, unless Cupitt can show that the genetic fallacy is no longer a fallacy.

A second reason I find Cupitt's first objection a bit odd is that the way the objection is raised displays a kind of ambiguity in regard to what counts as a "fact." Certainly, we must count Jesus as a man born in Palestine during the first century as a fact, but are we also to count Jesus' performance of miracles as facts or might we not be better off to see miracles in Wisdom's terms as a certain connecting technique of the facts? A third peculiarity of Cupitt's first criticism is that he seems to be selective in reading the New Testament text. Any ambiguous passages that might be counted in favor of kenosis are ignored. Consider this example from Philippians 2: 5-8

> His state was divine,
> yet he did not cling
> to his equality with God
> but emptied himself
> to assume the condition of a slave,
> and became as men are,
> he was humbler yet,
> even to accepting death,
> death on a cross.[23]

Certainly this passage should not be used as a definitive proof text for kenosis. Nevertheless, it can be used as credible evidence in its support, but Cupitt seems curiously to ignore this and other New Testament passages.

Cupitt's other two objections to kenotic interpretations of the incarnation have been dealt with rather effectively by Brian Hebblethwaite in "The Logical Coherence of the Doctrine of the Incarnation."[24] About Cupitt's charge that kenotic theories lead to anthropomorphisms Hebblethwaite says the following:

> These [Cupitt's] objections fail because they them-
> selves depend wholly on what we can imagine anthro-
> pomorphically. I notice that anthromorphisms come
> from critics who themselves, at least in considering
> their opponents' views, think only anthromorphically.[25]

Concerning the criticism that kenosis leads to an incoherent triple consciousness for the son of God,
Hebblethwaite comments:

> It is a travesty to suggest that for kenotic Christology,
> divinity is predicated of Jesus' humanity. This is cer-
> tainly to confuse the natures. We predicate divinity of
> Jesus, because we believe his humanity to be the vehi-
> cle and expression of the eternal son. There is no con-
> version of the Godhead into flesh. To think this is to
> operate with some crude picture of two kinds of stuff.
>
> Nor is there any reason to postulate three conscious-
> nesses where God incarnate is concerned. Indeed, it is
> hard to take such playing around with theological con-
> cepts seriously. All we need is Jesus' own sense of fil-
> ial dependence on the one hand, and God's awareness
> of his [God's] own acts through incarnation on the
> other.[26]

Maurice Wiles' criticisms of kenosis are directed primarily at Hebblethwaite's version of the theory. Although
Wiles proposes several different lines of attack, one of the
most interesting of his objections to Hebblethwaite's view
can be found in the following passage:

> But Hebblethwaite's argument can be turned on its
> head, and I am genuinely uncertain which way up it
> functions better. For if it is logically conceivable (as

Hebblethwaite's view of the incarnation insists that it
is) for God to be actually identified with a human person without in any way taking away from the full and
genuine humanity of that human person, it follows
that God does not, in fact, draw near to us as individual men and women or share our suffering as directly
as he apparently could.[27]

Wiles seems to be suggesting that if Hebblethwaite's
view of the incarnation is true (and not merely allowed by
reason), it would have the unwanted consequence of putting
Jesus in a position of not sharing in our suffering as directly as he might have.

Although Wiles' point is correct, I am not sure why this
should count as a criticism against Hebblethwaite's view in
particular on the concept of kenotic incarnation in general.
One might agree with Wiles at the same time pointing out
Jesus had temporarily given up his divine ability to sympathize with us all by taking on his own human suffering as
an individual man. It could be said that Jesus had voluntari-
ly given up divine sympathy in favor of a very real human
empathy, not an unwanted consequence by any means.

John Hick's criticisms of kenosis are many and varied.
Most of them can be summed up, however, in his claim that
if kenosis

is to be put forward as an answer to our problems,
it needs to be expounded and discussed at first hand.
If there is a viable understanding of incarnation here,
let someone lay it on the table.[28]

Although Hick's call for discussion is commendable, we
must keep in mind that he already seems to have made up

his mind about any but the most mythological accounts of
the incarnation:

> I have suggested that the incarnation motif should in
> fact be understood as a basic metaphor. If this is right,
> then the centuries long attempt of Christian orthodoxy
> to turn the metaphor into metaphysics was a cul-de-
> sac....[29]

Later, he concludes

> ...the idea of divine incarnation is a basic metaphor,
> functioning as a religious myth, and that it is a cate-
> gory mistake to try to specify it as a hypothesis of
> theological science.[30]

Despite an initial Kierkegaardian remark that I must
confess to being unable to understand what the expression
"theological science" might mean, two general remarks
might be made concerning Hick's view of the viability of
any orthodox interpretation of the incarnation. The first of
these is that he appears to have decided in some kind of *a
priori* way against the possibility of any nonmythological
view of the incarnation, be it kenosis or otherwise. And
second, anyone who suggests a nonmythological account of
the incarnation in Hick's view is making an error by trying
to specify the position as a hypothesis of "theological
science." I think that Hick is, quite simply, mistaken on
both of these points.[31]

I have already suggested in a very general way an interpretation of the expression "Jesus is fully human and fully
divine" that I believe is not logically incoherent, nor is it
metaphorical. More specifically, I have also suggested that
this particular kenotic view of the incarnation is one that is

allowed by reason. I will have more to say about this view of kenosis in the following section. Additionally, I will argue in the last part of this chapter that religious assertions like "Jesus is fully human and fully divine" are more than just expressive or evocative utterances, though, as we shall see, they do not function with the same logical status as scientific hypotheses. For the moment, however, let us return to our original task in this chapter: the amending of John Hick's teleological theodicy. What we have done in the last several pages is to attempt to show that there is nothing logically contradictory about the phrase "Jesus was fully human and fully divine." We may now use this traditional Christological doctrine, with its newer kenotic twist, as the centerpiece for constructing a distinctively Christian response to the problem of evil that at the same time takes the pain of the individual sufferer seriously.

In summarizing the second section of this final chapter we might once again call to mind Wisdom's observation that sometimes *prima facie* paradoxes turn out to be merely apparent, and it is those apparent paradoxes that may be theologically illuminating or "tremendous discoveries." We have suggested Job's "discovery" may have been the possibility of a larger teleological framework in which to view his suffering. In the classical doctrine of the incarnation as well, we may have one of these "tremendous discoveries." This situation is by no means a necessary conclusion but, certainly one that is allowed by reason. Let us now, in the third part of this chapter, return to the person of Christ, with an emphasis on his kenotic incarnation, as the foundation of our proposed theodicy.

In an article entitled "The Problem of Suffering: A Dialogue," which appeared in the *Expository Times*, Cyril Rodd makes a remark about the special attitude of the reflective Christian toward the problem of evil: "As a Christian I cannot consider the problem without turning to Jesus."[32]

In his *Church Dogmatics* IV/1, Karl Barth observes:

> What God is and what it means to be divine is some-thing we have to learn where God has revealed Himself and His nature, the essence of the divine. And if He has revealed Himself in Jesus Christ as the God who does this, it is not for us to be wiser than He and to say that it is in contradiction with the divine essence. We have to be ready to be taught by Him that we have been too small and perverted in our thinking about Him within the framework of a false idea.[33]

The same spirit is expressed in this passage from *The Christian Life:*

> As we search for a knowledge of God in the world that is unequivocally achieved both objectively on God's side and subjectively on man's, as we look for a point where his name might be clearly and distinctly hallowed on both sides in and for the world, we can think only of the one Jesus Christ. In him the knowl-edge of God in the world does not lack either the definitiveness of the objective element, as in the case of the attestation by the Church and Christians, or that of the subjective element, as in the case of the hidden glory of God in his creation. In him the circle closes which elsewhere is disturbingly open on one side or the other.[34]

Although God would have been capable of revealing himself through a dead dog if he wished, the message that the Christian form of life is obligated to proclaim is that

God has revealed himself in the person of Christ Jesus. In a real way, in Christ the adherents to Christianity "see God." Consequently, we must attend very carefully to what God has done in Christ in order to answer the question: *Qualis sit Deus?* (What kind of God is this?)

Barth's point of departure is the particular revelation of God in Christ. He sees as "untenably corrupt and pagan" any conferring of general conceptions (such as "absolute in contrast to all that is relative, exalted in contrast to all that is lowly") to God.

Rather, we must learn "to correct our notions of the being of God, to reconstitute them in the light of the fact that he has done this."[35] If we assume Barth's general Christological point of departure, we can see, in returning to Mackie's premise vii (There are no limits, other than logical ones, to what an omnipotent being can do) that this is an inadequate definition of omnipotence for the believing Christian. For Barth, God reveals himself, through Christ, to be a victim of suffering. By following this line of reasoning, Barth broadens our conception of evil to include a distinctively theological element. This added dimension revolutionizes the existential relation between God and humankind, thereby recasting the question of theodicy.

Barth suggests that we must re-evaluate the meaning of "omnipotence" in light of the story of Christ, where God has allegedly chosen to reveal himself. If this approach is not used when discussing Christian responses to suffering, then we run the risk of denying one of the major tenets of the Christian form of life. Barth seems to understand this point quite clearly when he makes the following remark in *The Doctrine of the Word of God*:

> Theology follows the language of the Church, as far

as in its questions as to the correctness of the
Church's procedures therein, it measures it, not by a
standard foreign to it, but by her very own source and
object.[36]

No theologian has reflected more extensively on the
relation between the person of Jesus Christ and the concept
of God's omnipotence than the twentieth century kenoticist,
P.T. Forsyth. In his book, *The Person and Place of Jesus
Christ*, Forsyth makes a strong appeal for a kenotic conception of the incarnation as well as what he calls a "moraliza-
tion of dogma" in light of the revelation of God in Christ.
Seeing Jesus Christ as "holy love" (which is God's essence),
Forsyth describes how the divine attribute of omnipotence
comes to be moralized:

> ...God is not God physically but morally, not by power
> but by love... That is the Christian revelation. The
> nature of the Godhead is holy Love. There lies the
> region, the nature and the norm of his omnipotence. It
> is no arbitrary or casual omnipotence, which puts out
> power just for the sake of doing it or showing it. It
> can do, not everything conceivable to freakish fancy,
> but everything that is prescribed by Holy Love. To a
> physical omnipotence it is indifferent. Such being its
> nature its object with humanity is a kingdom of holy
> love.[37]

This divine love is revealed to us through the person of
Jesus Christ, whose love

> is not a love which might itself be finite, only with a
> miraculous physical omnipresence; but it is an
> almighty love in the sense that it is capable of limiting
> itself, and, while an end, becoming also a means, to an

extent adequate to all love's infinite ends. This renouncing, self-retracting act of the son's will, this reduction of Himself from the supreme end to the supreme means for the soul, is no negation of His nature; it is the opposite, it is the last assertion of his nature as love. It is no negaton of His freedom; it's rather the freest energy of His whole will. He never willed something so mightily as freely as the subjective, the renunciation of self-will to the holy requirement of God. It is the concentrated omnipotence of love, and not of mere power, that underlies His earthly existence.[38]

In much the same way that we argued in part two of this chapter, Forsyth suggests that the divine qualities of omniscience and omnipotence were present in Christ, but "He consented not to know, and was mighty not to do." The action of the divine attributes in Christ "was at once reduced, concentrated, intensified within the conditions of the saving work."[39]

Forsyth continues:

The divine qualities were kept, but only in the mode that salvation made necessary. Jesus did not know everything actually, empirically, but only what was needed for the work. But as that is the central final work in human nature, the knowledge required for it contains the promise and potency of all knowledge. And, as to the exercise of power, he did what God alone could do in forgiving human sin, a salvation which is a nucleus and germ of all worthy power besides. His vocation was not to apply or exhibit omnipotence, but to effect the will of infinite love, and master all that set itself against that. All that

divine vocation was only possible to one who had a
divine position. The world's redeemer must be the son
of God.[40]

In his essay, "The Manhood of Jesus in the New
Testament," C.F.D. Moule stands with those who express an
even more radical conception of kenosis. Indeed, he goes
well beyond the kenotic point of view of Forsythe, who, he
says

> explain[s] the human limitations suffered by the
> divine Son of God in terms of the deliberate act of
> self-emptying, as though the pre-existent Son of God
> voluntarily emptied himself of divine prerogatives for
> a time, in order to share to the full the human lot, and
> resumed his full capacities only after the death on the
> cross.[41]

Citing the passage in Philippians that I quoted earlier,
Moule suggests that Paul points to a "divine paradox which
stands every human scale of values on its head." He
observes:

> I agree with those who interpret *harpagmos* not, con-
> cretely, as 'something worth snatching,' but, abstract-
> ly, as 'the act of snatching' (i.e., virtually 'acquisitive-
> ness'), and who render the phrase in which it occurs in
> some such way as: 'Jesus did not reckon that equality
> with God meant snatching: on the contrary, he emp-
> tied himself....' This would mean that, whereas ordi-
> nary human valuation reckons that God-likeness
> means having your own way, getting what you want,
> Jesus saw God-likeness essentially as giving and
> spending oneself out.[42]

For Moule, it was because Jesus was in the form of God that he "recognized equality with God as a matter not of getting but of giving." In this context "*kenosis* actually is *plenosis*," which means the human limitations of Jesus are seen as a positive expression of his divinity rather than as a curtailment of it.

Kenosis is understood by Moule not just as a negative emptying out but also as a positive fulfilling. He thinks this may teach us something terribly profound about the divine attribute of omnipotence. Moule notes, "It is easily forgotten that the omnipotence of a personal God is exhibited (to quote the collect) 'most chiefly in showing mercy and pity.'"[43]

Following Forsythe and Moule, Geddes MacGregor, in his book *He Who Lets Us Be*, argues for a new vision of God as essentially self-emptying and thus self-fulfilling. MacGregor sees the idea of kenotic power as the most profound and useful insight in the history of Christian thought. He emphasizes that the omnipotence of God is not properly to be conceived as the ability of an unrestrained or unfettered deity to do anything and everything. For MacGregor, such a definition of the theistic attributes makes God "seem like an oriental despot twenty feet tall."[44] Rather, he says, divine omnipotence should be understood as it is revealed in Christ, as the creative power of self-sacrificing and self-emptying love.

MacGregor criticizes philosophers of religion such as Mackie and Flew, whose positions indicate an

> uncritical acceptance of the traditional way of formulating the character of divine omnipotence as though it were the infinite exercise of a super-sultanic power, and of a radical failure to take seriously enough the theological proposition that God is love.[45]

In his *Philosophical Issues in Religious Thought,*
MacGregor makes the same point:

> The modern philosophers who try their hand at restat-
> ing the old objections with which the problem of evil
> confronts theism, use as their model what theologians
> aver about the nature of God and his relation to
> nature. They do it so properly, of course, since the
> problems with which they purport to deal arise only in
> a theological context. They do not usually take into
> account, however, the whole theological context. It
> would be pointless apart from the context, preferring
> to confine themselves rather to certain doctrinal
> propositions that may be accounted the most easily
> manageable for logical treatment. In the case of the
> forms of argument put forth by Flew and Mackie, the
> neglect of the rest of the theological picture to which
> the propositions belong is so conspicuous as to make
> theologians wonder how they could rest content with a
> model that is distorted and diminished, a caricature
> that ludicrously traduces the theological situation in
> which the problem arises.[46]

Wittgenstein had much to say on this matter of framing
pictures that might be of relevance here. He suggests the
disagreement between a philosopher (such as Mackie or
Flew) and a theologian (such as Forsyth or MacGregor) on
religious issues is not a matter of discovering empirical
facts. The disagreement is much more fundamental. What it
comes down to is the use of different kinds of pictures —
or in some cases, where the believer uses a certain picture
and the unbeliever does not.[47] MacGregor is suggesting
Flew and Mackie are willing to accept only a small part of
the Christian picture.

John Wisdom is another philosopher who holds the position that disagreements concerning religious matters usually do not involve empirical facts but rather the picturing of the facts. Wisdom quotes a passage from J.P. Marquand's novel, *H. M. Pulham, Esquire*, to illustrate how it is possible to have all the items of a pattern and to still miss the pattern. A man confides to a friend that "Kay and I are pretty happy; we've always been happy." But when the skeptical friend challenges this remark, the first man offers an explanation that although he and Kay have had their skirmishes during the marriage, the sum total of the facts of their lives "adds up" to happiness. Wisdom is quick to point out that it is not at all a question of addition, as if one could sit down and tally up a balance sheet. Rather, he suggests, it is a matter of interpreting the marriage or seeing the marriage in a certain way.

Wisdom offers a second example that will make this point about picturing the world a bit clearer. Two friends are engaged in a discussion about a particular character in a story they both have read. One says, "Really, she hated him," but the second protests, "She didn't, she loved him." Both friends have read the entire book. They begin to trade information back and forth in case the other has missed a critical point in the story. But alas, they have both read it very carefully. At this point, Wisdom asks a question about what their dispute really involves. The disagreement cannot be about the facts of the story, since they are in full accord as to the actual episodes depicted in the book. The dispute, Wisdom argues, is about their different interpretations or "picture preferences" regarding the facts.[48]

A third example offered by Wisdom has become the source of much theological discussion over the last forty years. Two people return to their "long neglected garden."

Seeing a number of flowers still growing, one concludes that a gardener has tended the plot in their absence. Concentrating on the numerous weeds also growing in the garden, the other concludes that the gardener does not exist. After a lengthy investigation, they fail to detect the presence of the gardener. Still, the first person holds fast to his view that the gardener exists, only now his conclusion is that the gardener is invisible.

At this point in the story, Wisdom makes a very perceptive remark. He suggests, as I think Wittgenstein would have been inclined to do,[49] that the two are no longer in disagreement about the facts. Each agrees as to which organic items in the garden can properly be referred to as flowers and which should be called weeds. There is no disagreement about the facts of the case. Their difference of opinion concerning the presence of the invisible gardener is due, not to a dispute over the facts, but rather to their different picture preferences. Let us label the picture preferences of the first person the "garden story." This labelling will be quite instructive when looking at what Anthony Flew has to say in the retelling of Wisdom's tale.

In Flew's version of the story the two people are turned into "explorers who come upon a jungle clearing."[50] Nevertheless, Flew still has the first explorer view the clearing, discover the flowers, and proclaim that "some gardener must tend this plot." And, once again, after a series of experiments fails to confirm the assertions of the first, he moves to speak of an invisible gardener. At this point Flew asks an important question: "What remains of the original assertion?" [51]

But perhaps an even more fundamental question can be raised. Flew's version is perhaps better referred to as the "jungle story." After looking at both versions of the tale, one might ask: How is it that two philosophers start out to tell a story about the same mix of flowers and weeds and one sees the picture of a garden while the other prefers to see it as a jungle clearing? The answer to this question can be quite illuminating concerning the ways in which different people may view the problem of evil. Some, like Anthony Flew, begin by picturing the world as a series of natural events fraught with blind pain, disease, misfortune, etc. Forsyth and MacGregor, however, begin by picturing the world containing these evils as coming into existence by the creative power of God. All three men would agree, I think, as to what events and situations in the world count as *prima facie* evils. Their disagreement arises when they begin to discuss the ultimate meaning of that *prima facie* evil. Flew, of course, would suggest that the *prima facie* evil in reality is actual evil, while Forsyth and MacGregor would insist that it is merely apparent. Clearly, their dispute is not about the "facts" of the world; it has to do with the interpretation of the world as a whole, a picturing of the world that goes beyond or lies behind the facts.

It is important to understand in these examples of Wisdom that he is not advocating religious belief. What he is suggesting is that given ambiguous "facts," different picture preferences are possible. Wittgenstein's use of the duck-rabbit example is designed for the same purpose. Because the facts may be read in more than one way, we may come to the picture illustrated below[52] with the notion of "seeing" a duck. Indeed, if we come with that notion, then a duck will appear before our eyes. Conversely, we will find a rabbit if we are ready to see a rabbit. With a genuinely ambiguous picture like the duck-rabbit, we simply "see it as" one or the other. In order to change to the other perspective, Donald Hudson argues,[53] a certain kind of conversion must take place, though the "facts" of the picture do not change. What can be said about the duck-rabbit can also be said about the garden-jungle clearing, and, it seems to me, by extension to picturing the world as a whole. We may either come to picture the world as created by an omnipotent, omniscient, and omnibenevolent God, or, in the case of Flew and Mackie, as a closed physical system that had no beginning and perhaps will have no end.

Although Wisdom is not advocating religious belief, what he does recommend is that

> We must not forthwith assume that there is no right and wrong about it [picture preferences], no rationality or irrationality, no appropriateness or inappropriateness, no procedure which tends to settle it, nor even that this procedure is in no sense a discovery of new facts.[54]

Indeed, the kind of "connecting technique" suggested by Wisdom has been used in discussion of works of art for some time. There are, for example, many different interpretations of Shakespeare's *Hamlet*. Some argue that the young Hamlet is hopelessly mad throughout most of the play; others claim that he has crafted his craziness in order to catch his father's murderers. No new lines may be added to the play to decide the dispute. It can only be arbitrated by making reference to what is already there. The best interpretations of the play, Wisdom would most surely suggest, are those that do the best job of connecting the known facts. It would be absurd and unreasonable, for example, to argue that *Hamlet* should be played as a comedy or a farce. For much the same reasons, it would be ludicrous to propose that the duck-rabbit picture was in fact a profile depiction of Ronald Reagan's head. Preferred connections, in

Wisdom's view, are those that best accommodate the available evidence.[55]

One way to appreciate this point about the logical consistency of picture preferences, or "preferred connections," is to say that it is simply another way of referring to our first criterion of a viable Christian theodicy. Does a particular "picture" present a logically consistent view? Do all of its parts fit in an organic whole? How does it answer challenges to internal consistency?[56]

If we return to our discussion of the concept of God's omnipotence within the context of the Christian picturing of things, the importance of this digression should be clear. Anthony Flew, in his "Theology and Falsification," insists on his particular picturing of the concept of omnipotence, indeed, of his picturing of the world as a whole. In the process, he ignores the possibility suggested by Wisdom in the beginning of this chapter that certain concepts used in the religions of paradox may be only apparently contradictory. We might also criticize Flew on the front suggested by MacGregor. He seems to be unable to see the larger Christian form of life in which the classical attributes of God find their home. Flew fixes on those elements of the theological problem of evil that are most amenable to logical analysis, but at the same time he neglects some of the logical possibilities — possibilities that are fundamental to any Christian answer to the problem of evil.

So far in this final chapter we have attempted to accomplish a number of tasks. First, we have tried to show that none of the theodicies we have analyzed thus far has been able to pass at the bar of our three criteria for a viable Christian response to the problem of evil. Along the way, we also proposed that Mackie has overstated his case when he argues in effect that all answers to the problem of evil that adhere to the traditional Christian conception of God are prohibited by reason. After making these remarks about Mackie, we then went on to show that John Hick's teleological theodicy might become a viable Christian response to the problem of evil if we were to adjust his conception of omniscience as well as make a central place for the person of Christ in his teleological answer.

Next, we attempted to show that Hick's reticence in discussing the role Christ might play in Christian theodicy is probably couched in his belief that any nonmythological account of the incarnation is logically contradictory. By entertaining various nonmetaphorical formulations of what it means to say that Jesus is "fully human and fully divine," and finally settling on one that we have shown is allowed by reason, we have attempted to demonstrate that Hick is incorrect about the possibility of a coherent doctrine of the incarnation.

As we have seen, the view shown to be one that is allowed by reason is associated with a family of approaches to the doctrine of the incarnation that are often called "kenotic." After entertaining various criticisms of kenosis offered by Hick, Wiles, and Cupitt, we further explicated the notion of kenosis with insights provided by Barth, Forsyth, Moule, and MacGregor.

A comment of MacGregor's led us to a discussion of the notion of "picturing" facts. With the help of Wittgenstein and Wisdom we have suggested that the difference between philosophers such as Flew and Mackie and theologians like Forsyth and MacGregor is not in terms of "facts" but, in Wisdom's words, different "connecting techniques."

In the section that is to follow, we must continue our task of constructing a viable Christian theodicy. This will be done by first making some remarks regarding our third criterion, the requirement that any viable Christian theodicy must take the individual sufferer seriously. We will be concerned with showing how the story of Christ might serve to confirm the importance of understanding the practical reality of suffering. Additionally, we will also more fully explicate the particulars of the teleological Christian theodicy we are proposing.

Finally, in the last section, we will attempt to grapple with a host of questions related to why we should believe this theodicy in particular or the message of the Christian faith in general. What justification can be given for holding religious assertions? The answer to this question is clearly related to a number of vexing issues about foundational principles, the logical status of religious propositions, and the rationality of religious beliefs.

We have made some very general remarks about a Christocentric answer to the problem of evil that is both logically consistent and true, in a broad way, to the Christian form of life. For the next several pages, we must now make some remarks concerning just how the story of Christ might confirm what has been said in previous chapters about the importance of understanding the practical reality of suffering. Once again, in order to do this, we must return to the person of Jesus Christ, in whom God Himself became a victim of suffering.

It would be difficult to think of anyone who has reflected more profoundly on the problem of evil in the context of the New Testament than D.M. MacKinnon. In his *Borderlands of Theology,* he openly criticizes the "convention of Christian practice" that allows the Gospel narratives about Jesus to be read as if they were oriented toward a happy ending,

> as if the resurrection faith which gave them birth was
> powerful enough to obliterate memory of the sombre
> events which they describe.[57]

MacKinnon acknowledges that the Gospels are expressions of the Easter faith, but he also lingers on the practical reality of suffering that is so evident in the Gospel accounts of the life and death of Jesus. On the Gethsemane narratives, for example, MacKinnon says the following:

> If I am honest, I think I must say that I should cease
> to believe altogether unless I believed that Jesus had
> indeed prayed that the hour might indeed pass from
> him, had indeed been left alone to face the reality of
> absolute failure. It is fashionable nowadays to speak
> of Christ as victor, as if the agony and the disillusion,
> the sheer monstrous reality of physical and spiritual
> suffering which he bore were a kind of charade. The
> idiom of a superficial cosmic optimism, often express-
> ing itself ritually in patterns of liturgical symbolism,
> is currently fashionable, as if a world that knows, as
> ours does, extremities of terror as well as hope, could
> be consoled by a remote metaphysical chatter. But the
> Gospels, including that of John which does not chron-
> icle the episode of Gethsemane, recall our imagina-
> tions to a figure prostrate on the earth, afraid and des-
> olate, bidding men and women see in him the ground
> of all creation.[58]

Even in the fourth Gospel, MacKinnon reports, Jesus is properly seen as a victim of suffering. Before the author of John "reminds his readers that the Word through whom all things take their origin became flesh he insists that the word so came among his own and he was rejected." MacKinnon states

> Yet behind the language of the prologue something more can be discerned, something whose appeal is universal, even if the appeal is grounded in the author's appraisal of the One concerning whom he writes. In these verses the reader finds himself raised to a level that is beyond optimism and pessimism, as one usually understands those two contrasted attitudes. The author is sure that the ground of the world is itself good; he is sure of this because he identifies the ground with what men have heard and seen in Jesus; yet Jesus was rejected, and his glory was most fully revealed when he was lifted up from the earth upon a Roman gallows.[59]

MacKinnon sees in the incarnation that God in Christ takes on a "contingency so sheer and unequivocal that inevitably at all levels we shrink from it, preferring necessary absolutes whether abstract values, or institutions, or even spiritual experiences."[60] But the realization that there is no escape from contingency with Christ is especially evident in the "supremely revealing and supremely authoritative moment in human history" when the Son of God, the ultimate victim of suffering, cries upon the cross: "My God, my God, why have you forsaken me?" In this cry of dereliction

> [i]t was made plain that the Son of God's acceptance of the ultimate triviality and failure of human existence, whose depths at the moment he finally plumbed, the whole language of perplexity, uncertainty, bewilderment, hopelessness and pain, even of God-forsakenness, was laid hold of and given a sense by the very God himself and converted into the way of his reconciling the world unto himself."[61]

We will talk more about this reconciliation in a moment; what is important now, however, is to attend to a subtle point made by Professor MacKinnon. If Jesus was the son of God, and if *sub specie aeterni* and *sub specie crucis* are in some sense the same perspective, then the rejection and crucifixion of Jesus can only be "evil itself."

MacKinnon agrees with Barth in seeing the figure of Judas Iscariot "as where the problem of evil is raised with archetypal and definitive seriousness," for there is God's actual engagement with the issue. For MacKinnon, the problem of evil, in its ultimate sense, must not be seen "apart from, but in terms of, the betrayal and rejection of Christ."[62]

What is one to say about this "evil itself" in which God in Christ becomes the victim? Certainly this evil was no mere illusion, deprivation of good, nor deserved punishment for sin. The agony and passion of Christ was not deleted by a later interpretation, right or wrong, that his suffering and death was an occasion, indeed *the* occasion for good. In the Gospel accounts, as MacKinnon so skillfully points out, the evil and the good of Christ's fate are simply juxtaposed:

> There is no solution offered...of the riddle of Iscariot through whose agency the son of man goes his appointed way. It were good for him that he had not been born. The problem is stated; it is left unresolved, and we are presented with the likeness of the one who bore its ultimate burden, and bore it to the end, refusing the trick of bloodless victory to which the scoffers, who invited him to descend from the cross, were surely inviting him.[63]

Finally, we see in the account of Christ's death that even the Father's sympathy with the son as he cried out those last words from the cross could not alter the dreadful reality of Christ's suffering. In an analogous kind of way, perhaps the same can be said about our suffering as well. What can also be said, without contradiction, about our suffering, is that through the suffering of Christ we have more than a sympathetic response to our plight, we have in him a real, human empathetic attitude toward our suffering. In the crucifixion of Christ the plight of the individual sufferer is understood most poignantly.

But it must also be emphasized that in Christ's suffering we see not only the practical reality of evil in all its graphic horror, we may also perceive a widening of its reference. Earlier we saw that Hick defines evil as that "which we dislike, shun and avoid." But if the story of God suffering in Christ is accepted as true, a new dimension or context to the practical reality of evil must be understood: ultimate evil must be that which opposes God and his will. That which is an affront to God is that which is finally evil. If we comprehend this point on an existential level, we are led directly to the concept of sin, a distinctively theological concept that defines people as out of relationship with God. Sin cuts people off from the revolutionizing existential relationship between God and humankind accomplished in Christ Jesus.

Earlier, in our remarks about Job in chapter four, we discussed the existential relationship that is produced by an awareness of the ontological gulf between God and humankind that radically alters the context of doing theodicy. Here we shall examine how, given the notion that God and people are reconciled in Christ, the task of justifying God cannot be seen apart from the work of Christ. We shall use some insights gained from P.T. Forsyth's *The Justification of God* to help us accomplish that task.[64]

No theologian, past or present, has taken the perspective of the victim of suffering as seriously as Forsyth. He writes during the height of The Great War as a person who has "witnessed the lid coming off hell." But while he affirms evil's "bloody and tortured stream," he clings fast to an interpretation of the saving work of Christ and discovers that only at the cross can an adequate theodicy be constructed. In *The Justification of God* Forsyth develops a theodicy that he hopes will not only be helpful to the Church at large but also to suffering soldiers in the trenches.

Forsyth sees the war as "making at least one contribution to human salvation — it is sin's apocalypse."[65] The war came as such a shock because people had forgotten the heinous acts of which people are capable. John Hick, in discussing Forsyth's theodicy, suggests that he "brought teleological theodicy back to reality, both divine and human."[66] In Forsyth's view, the evolutionary perspective that tended to view mankind as continually developing and advancing in knowledge, goodness, and spirituality, has led to a gross underestimation of humankind's capacity to do evil. A kind of evolutionary optimism, Forsyth believed, has also led to an inadequate conception of God. Forsyth suggests that in the period immediately preceding the war the divine was seen as "a tender God, in no sense judge...an attractive God, more kindly than holy, more lovely than good."[67] He argues that the evil of that particular war had begun to correct these misconceptions and force a new context for theodicy:

> What is it that would justify God to you? You have grown up in an age that has not yet got over the delight of having discovered in evolution the key to

creation. You saw the long expanding series broadening to the perfect day. You saw it foreshortened in the long perspective, peak rising on peak, each successfully catching the ascending sun. The dark valley, antres vast, and deserts horrible, you did not see. They were crumpled in the tract of time, and folded away from sight. The roaring rivers and thunders, the convulsions and voices, the awful conflicts latent in nature's ascent and man's — you could pass these over in the sweep of your glance...but now you have been flung into one of those awful valleys. You taste what it has cost, thousands of times over, to pass from range to range of those illuminated heights. You are in bloody, monstrous and deadly dark....Every aesthetic view is blotted out by human wickedness and suffering. The air is as red as the rains of hell. The rocks you stood on fall on you....[68]

In the sixty years since Forsyth's death, we have seen German death camps, Stalin's purges, the bombings of Hiroshima and Nagasaki, tragic wars in Korea and Vietnam, and other heinous acts of people done to people too numerous to mention. His suggestion about the need for a new context for understanding the problem of evil is today clearly just as appropriate:

We are bidden to recognize that God's demand on man takes the lead of man's demand on God. And both are overruled by God's demand on God — God's meeting his own demands. And we learn unwillingly that only God's justification of man gives the secret of man's justification of God....In a word, there is but one theodicy, and it is evangelical.[69]

In contrast to the discredited evolutionary optimism,

Forsyth sees Christianity finding its hopes not in the order of this world:

> The world's convulsions, therefore, need not destroy it. Rather, it rose from the sharpest cries, the greatest war, the deadliest death, and the deepest grave the world ever knew — in Christ's cross.[70]

In this context a "religious and theological theodicy is our only refuge....The only vindicator of God is God. And his own theodicy is the cross of his son Jesus Christ."[71]

Forsyth further elaborates the dynamics of his theodicy:

> The world does not ask the question as it is put by the Church. The Church, starting from the Holy One, asks how man shall be just with that God, and she owes her existence to the answer in Christ's cross and Gospel .... but the world, with its egoist start, asks how God shall be just with man. The one brings man to God's bar, the other brings God to man's. Christ deals with both. The first question he answers with God's free justification of man, the second question he makes us recast. He does not bring God to man's bar but to God's own, since there is none greater. He brings God's providence to the bar of God's own promise — His own Gospel. He attunes it to God's own conscience, His own nature; he embodies the self-justification of God.[72]

Forsyth insists that the only possible kind of theodicy in the Christian tradition is "an adequate atonement."[73] For him the justification of God is not a philosophical nor even a systematic answer. It is a religious one, and above all, a practical one. God thought it best not to put the thought about the problem of evil on a new line but rather to place "the thinker in a new life."[74]

> The final theodicy is in no discovered system, no revealed plan, but in effective redemption. It is not in the grasp of ideas, nor in the adjustment of events, but in the destruction of guilt and taking away the sin of the world....It is not really an answer to a riddle but a victory in a battle....We do not see the answer; we trust the Answerer, and measure by Him. We do not gain the victory; we are united with the Victor.[75]

Forsyth argues very forcefully that the Christian experience places the believer in a new perspective, a new picture of the world, if you will, wherein one's suffering comes to be seen as less than ultimate given God's own suffering in Christ. The context of theodicy is radically shifted as the center is altered from the justification of God to the existential relation between God and humankind, radically altered through Christ's victory over sin and evil.

It is of interest that Forsyth goes on to develop a teleological theodicy, which, we have attempted to show earlier in this chapter, is one of the few members of the class of responses to the problem of evil that are allowed by reason. Forsyth suggests that "all things will work together for the good." But his teleological response is not based on a shallow optimism about world history. It must be grounded in the saving work of Jesus Christ. Apart from Christ, evil cannot be seen as an occasion for good and thus Forsyth's position differs from Hick's in a radical way. Hick believes that any discussion of the incarnation of Christ must be undertaken with the realization in mind that all such references are metaphorical, while Forsyth literally makes the dual natures of Jesus as the centerpiece for the construction of his response to the problem of evil. The importance of Christ as the focal point in Christian theodicy is also clearly expressed by D.M. MacKinnon. Indeed, MacKinnon suggests that the notion of a teleological answer to the problem of evil, at least within the Christian form of life, cannot be understood any other way: "Such concepts as reconciliation, and the overcoming of evil by good, are to be interpreted in terms of the *opus operatum* of the ministry of Jesus, and not vice-versa."[76]

Oliver Quick is another writer who insists that teleological theodicy is impotent outside the context of the cross. He says

> All attempts to deal with the problem of evil, which are not grounded upon the power of self-sacrifice of love, may by its passing away be instrumental to fulfilling the goodness of an eternal world which is already in some partial sense expressed and embodied within it.[77]

Forsyth sees the divine destiny of the world "not simply revealed in Christ, but secured in him." In the final analysis, he argues for a salvation where all souls might "come to the fullness and quality of the universal and eternal Christ." [78] For Forsyth the redemptive possibilities go beyond death until all are brought in: "the worst and most intractable lost — since freedom may not be forced."[79] As Forsyth comments, "there is eternity to do it in."[80]

Still, it is quite possible that the victim of suffering might wish to raise some objections concerning Forsyth's point of view. The sufferer might ask why God did not create people without free will, or perhaps, as Mackie has suggested, as agents who always freely choose the good. If God possesses the attributes of omnipotence, omniscience, and omnibenevolence, why should there be evil at all? Forsyth begins to respond by pointing out:

> It is easy to set up an expectation and call on God to comply. It is so easy to frame some high *a priori* way, and pitch our demand accordingly, as to what God would do. It is not so easy to ask what God has done, penetrate it, and accept His own account of His way of doing it.[81]

Again Forsyth observes, "We create difficulties for ourselves, I say, by our wrong start, by expectations formed at other sources than God's own account of His profound and supreme way."[82]

The victim of suffering might still be tempted, like Dostoyevski's Ivan Karamazov, to "stumble at the cost" of the future order. But Forsyth was not unaware of this kind of criticism. Indeed, he raises the sufferer's complaint in a series of interrogatories: "Why such a dreadful and ineffable suffering along the whole course, suffering both of those taken and those left? Why does it cost so much at every stage...?"[83]

To answer these questions, Forsyth once again brings us back to the cross of Christ. He contrasts the suffering of man with the deeper pain provoked by God's conquest of evil in Christ. Forsyth seems to be replying on behalf of the divine, but he insists that ultimately it is also the perspective of the sufferer that merits his attention:

> Do you stumble at the cost? It has cost me more than you — Me who sees and feels it all more than you who feel it but as atoms might. 'Groanings and moanings, none of it I lose.' Yea, it has cost me more than if the price paid were all mankind. For it cost me my

only and beloved son to justify my name of righteous-
ness, and to realize the destiny of my creatures in holy
love. And all mankind is not so great and dear to me
as he. Nor is its suffering the enormity in a moral
world that his cross is. I am no spectator in the course
of things, and no spectator on the result. I spared my
own son. We carried the load that crushes you. It
bowed him to the ground. On the third day he rose
with a new creation in his hand, and a regenerate
world, and all things working together for good to
love and holy purpose in love. And what he did I
did.[84]

But the skeptic might still ask about the specifics by
which all of this will be accomplished. Forsyth has doubts
that we can know what the exact contours of God's plan for
salvation might be:

This you know not now....Be still and know that I am
God whose mercy is as his majesty, and his omnipotence is chiefly in forgiving and redeeming, and settling all souls in worship of the temple of a new heav-
en and earth full of holiness. In that day the anguish
will be forgotten for joy that a new humanity is born
into the world.[85]

It is important to notice that Forsyth insists that the suffering of this world will be "forgotten for joy," not
repaired. "Heaven does not laugh loud but it laughs last —
when all the world will laugh in its light."[86] Forsyth is also
careful not to couch his point of view in the language of
verification, eschatological or otherwise. He is content to
make a suggestion — because of the sacrifice of Jesus
Christ

The evil world will not win at last. It failed to win at the only time it ever could. It is a vanquished world where men play their devilries. Christ has overcome it. It can make tribulation, but desolation it can never make.[87]

All of the criticisms of Forsyth's kenotic theodicy we have mentioned in the last few pages had been voiced from the standpoint of the religious skeptic. But there had also arisen among his theological contemporaries a number of objections to his point of view that also deserve some discussion.

Some of the clearest and what many suggest are the most significant criticisms of Forsyth come from William Temple in his *Christus Veritas*.[88] In that work, Temple, who for many years was the Bishop of Manchester, seems to stress at least two major objections to Forsyth's kenotic position. The first of these can be seen in the following quotation:

The difficulties are intolerable. What was happening to the rest of the universe during the period of our Lord's earthly life? To say that the infant Jesus was from his cradle exercising providential government over it all is certainly monstrous; but to deny this and to say that the Creative Word was so self-emptied as to have no being except in the infant Jesus, is to assert that for a certain period the world was let loose from the control of the Creative Word, and 'apart from him' very nearly everything happened that happened at all during those thirty odd years, both on this planet, and throughout the immensities of space.[89]

The second of his criticisms follows the passage cited above. Temple suggests that the idea of kenosis makes the period of Jesus' earthly life look like an episode in the life of the Word. But since the Word is eternal there can be no episodes in his life.[90] Because of these two major shortcomings, Temple suggests an alternative view of the incarnation: "All these difficulties are avoided if we suppose that God the Son did most truly live the life recorded in the Gospel, but added to this the other work of God. There are indications that this is the Johannine view."[91]

Earlier in this chapter we have suggested that God is in time, but a time that stretches eternally in both directions. Thus it makes perfectly good sense to speak of "episodes in the life of the world." Additionally, in the first of these criticisms Temple seems to ignore the possibility that the "providential government" of the universe during the time of Jesus was being carried on quite adequately by the Father and the Spirit. In order to hold this view, of course, we would have to be able to show that the concept of the Trinity is such that three distinct persons in one God is not a logically contradictory notion. Although I will not argue that position here, I will mention that W.L. Power, in his article "Symbolic Logic and the Doctrine of the Trinity," has, I think, demonstrated satisfactorily that the *prima facie* paradox of the Trinity may be only apparent.[92]

Temple's second objection would also only seem to hold for a position that sees God as "timeless" or "outside of time." Since I have argued earlier that the proper interpretation of God's eternity is "infinite duration in time" this criticism does not hold for my view. Forsyth's view of God's relation to time is not clearly spelled out, and consequently Temple may be entirely correct in his second criticism of Forsyth. But we need not hold Forsyth's view of God's relation to time and thus can escape Temple's second objection.

It must also be added at this point that the alternative view of the incarnation suggested by Temple may present us with its own set of difficulties. Quick has pointed out, for example, that the "addition" of human experiences to the life of the divine Word itself may imply the addition of its own peculiar set of limitations.[93] Indeed, it might also be argued that Temple's view does succumb to one of Cupitt's criticisms — that it involves a doctrine of two consciousnesses. Ironically, this problem could be solved if the kenotic principle were applied.

One final kind of negative comment about the kenotic theodicy of Forsyth might be voiced from those of the Mackie and Flew persuasion or indeed even from the believing theist. These critics might concede, after some argument, that the position we have been describing here is a logically possible state of affairs. But they might still ask why we should believe it.

The answer to this important question is bound up, I think, with a host of other questions about the logical status of foundational principles, the rationality of religious beliefs, and more particularly about the justification of religious assertions like those expressed by Forsyth about the problem of evil. In the remaining portion of this chapter we will attempt to answer these questions through the use of some insights once again provided by Ludwig Wittgenstein in his *On Certainty*, as well as some observations suggested by John Wisdom.

Since the time of Augustine, and probably much earlier, there has existed a certain ubiquitous view about the logical status of religious propositions. It has been popular among believers and nonbelievers alike to view religious assertions as empirical hypotheses. Since the time of Hume and Kant and their arguments against the philosophical proofs,

most philosophers have taught that it is wise to confine religious assertions to matters of belief, since we are not now
in a position to know whether they are true. In this widely
held view, religious assertions like those made by Forsyth
regarding the problem of evil look like "hypotheses" —
uncertain statements whose truth or falsity might be known
in principle, if not in practice, by the gathering together of
some set of relevant facts. As this view goes, until the facts
are in, we cannot ascertain the truth of any given religious
proposition, and so it must remain a hypothesis.

In this view, the only real difference between religious
propositions and other kinds of beliefs is that it seems so
difficult to gather together the right set of facts so that our
religious hypotheses might be upgraded to the level of
truth. Treating religious propositions as hypotheses gives us
the image of someone who waits by his mailbox for a report
from the committee studying the Shroud of Turin, so that
his religious hypotheses might finally be confirmed.
Certainly, John Hick has committed himself to the
"hypotheses view," albeit a sophisticated version, by suggesting his criterion of eschatological verification.

There are, nevertheless, two major problems with the
notion of religious propositions as hypotheses. First, many
faithful practitioners of Christianity show little tentative-
ness in their adherence to religious teachings, despite how
difficult it might be to justify these assertions on empirical
grounds. And second, the role religious assertions play in
the thought and lives of believers, as well as the believers'
facility for connecting the facts, may be more germane to
questions about their credibility than any other kind of criterion that could be applied.

What I shall argue here, with the help of some insights
from Wittgenstein, is that the major propositions on which

Forsyth's theodicy are built need not be construed as hypotheses at all. Indeed, it is probably much closer to their use to refer to them as "'truths' to live by" or "foundational principles." These kinds of "truths" tend to prove themselves in their use, not by being tested by some empirical method. If this could be established, then it would seem that the regulative function of religious assertions might be their most distinctive logical feature, though I will not suggest that religious assertions have no objective referents. However, it may well be that the power of a certain body of beliefs to change a person's life may have more to do with the resolution of doubt than the proportioning of belief to the available evidence.

The real trouble arises for a view like Forsyth's when we realize that in order to conform to a particular body of religious assertions we must first have a prior belief that the body of religious assertions is true. In a real way, the practical use these beliefs acquire as "'truths' to live by" does not solve the problem of their truth status; it only confounds it. This sometimes makes the tendency to view religious assertions as hypotheses very captivating. Most people, including a good many philosophers and theologians, are attracted to the notion that religious assertions must first "prove" themselves as truth claims before they may properly be labelled as "truths to live by." Thy must have a logical status like every other truth claim, or so these people argue. And it is precisely at this point that we shall introduce Wittgenstein.

In his book, *On Certainty*,[94] Wittgenstein suggests that some beliefs lie so deeply ingrained in our thinking that it would make little sense to doubt them. They neither need nor allow the kind of justification we ordinarily require of hypotheses that are offered as truth claims. Wittgenstein suggests that reasonable people, nevertheless, take these kinds of beliefs, which he calls "certainties," for granted. They have this status not because they have been empirically verified but because with these assertions believing and behaving come together. The reasonableness of certainties is not a function of evidence; rather, it is because thinking and acting in the world entail conforming to these certainties.[95]

Before discussing what relevance Wittgenstein's *On Certainty* may have for religious assertions like those of Forsyth, we must make a distinction between different kinds of certainties — a distinction that Wittgenstein himself does not seem to make. We might label the first kind of certainty "paradigmatic" and the second "foundational." Examples of paradigmatic certainties are "I have two hands," or "My name is Stephen Vicchio." These propositions have the status of certainties by virtue of the role they play in a particular game or set of language games to which we seem to adhere. This role can be understood as having two separate but related elements. First, Wittgenstein believed, if a paradigmatic certainty were to turn out to be false, it would have such repercussions throughout the language game or set of language games that the survival of that language game or set of language games would be put in question.[96] And second, if the context in which that paradigmatic certainty is placed were to change, it could, with very little trouble to the language game as a whole, cease to be a certainty.

Thus, if in ordinary circumstances G.E. Moore stands before an audience of philosophers and declares, while looking at his wiggling fingers, that he has two hands, it would most assuredly count as what we have called a paradigmatic certainty. The falsity of the proposition "G.E.

Moore has two hands," given the context mentioned above, would prove to be problematical for a whole network of propositions related to it such that the whole language game in which it was placed might be called into question.

But consider what happens if we change the context to the morning following a terrible automobile accident in which G.E. Moore has been involved. Now when visiting Professor Moore in his hospital room, we might very well look down at his bandaged limbs and say, "I wonder if G.E. Moore has two hands." Clearly the change of context also changes the proposition "G.E. Moore has two hands" from a paradigmatic certainty to an empirical proposition whose truth is now in doubt.

The other kind of certainty, what I have labelled "foundational" certainty, can be characterized by propositions like "there are physical objects," and "the earth has existed in the past." This type differs from the paradigmatic certainties in that the first type are indubitable statements within the language game, whereas the second type specify the formal conditions of the language game being played. Foundational certainties, then, are distinct from paradigmatic certainties because the latter are context dependent and therefore contingently true, while the former are held to be the case regardless of any context within that particular language game in which they may be placed.

One could perhaps argue that the denial of one or more of the paradigmatic certainties would not throw the language game "entirely off the rails," as Wittgenstein puts it. Language games and forms of life may be more flexible than Wittgenstein's account in *On Certainty* seems to suppose. But the denial of any of the foundational certainties must bring the language game to a halt. Since foundational certainties express the formal presuppositions of the lan-

guage game, if any of them are denied, the underpinnings of
the language game itself come apart.

In the case of paradigmatic certainties, a change in context or the development of new empirical evidence might
count against their believability, and thus their status as
certainties. This can never occur, however, in regard to
foundational certainties, for first, they can never be construed as empirical hypotheses, no matter what the change
of context might be, and second, they are the foundations
on which any judgment within the language game is based.[97]

With all this said, we must add that Wittgenstein was
probably not thinking about religious propositions when he
made his remarks about certainties. The kinds of beliefs he
had in mind were things about which all the the dyed-in-
the-wool skeptics would agree. Yet, his observations about
certainties may contribute more to the understanding of the
problem of criteria for truth in religion than any of his
other works, including his lectures on aesthetics and religious belief.[98] The general problem of the rationality of religious belief, as well as the larger problem about foundational principles, and the more specific answer to the question concerning why we should hold Forsyth's religious
assertions as "'truths' to live by" become clearer when we
apply a certain interpretation to *On Certainty*.

We must begin the explication of this interpretation by
admitting that religious assertions are neither paradigmatic
nor foundational certainties, at least not the kind to which
Wittgenstein refers. But religious assertions may, nevertheless, share a great deal with certainties. One of the chief
similarities is that they both may reasonably be held without being justified on prior empirical grounds. This interpretation of *On Certainty* opens up the possibility that reasonable faith may have little or nothing to do with the

defense of empirical hypotheses, for most important religious assertions, like Wittgenstein's foundational certainties, are not hypotheses to be tested.

A second way that specific religious assertions may be analogous to foundational certainties is that in both we find the connection between believing and behaving to be so inextricably bound together that one's understanding of the way the world works depends on the prior acceptance of these beliefs.[99] In both religious foundation principles and foundational certainties learning a certain form of life that is based on these principles or certainties is always logically and temporally prior to any claims of doubt.

Throughout much of *On Certainty*, Wittgenstein's purpose is to discuss philosophical skepticism.[100] In brief, he thought any thoroughgoing version of skepticism was really a type of philosophical confusion. Instead of answering the skeptics' arguments, he treated their doubts as spurious and unfounded because they raised questions about foundational certainties or fundamental beliefs without which human beings could not function. He never claims in *On Certainty*, however, to be able to give a logical or empirical refutation of skepticism nor that he could furnish proofs for all his fundamental beliefs. [101]

Wittgenstein believed that the purely philosophical doubts, like those raised in Descartes' *Meditations*, for example, are idle doubts, doubts that cannot and should not be taken seriously. Of course, on first blush religious doubts appear to be appreciably different because they do not appear to be idle.[102] Nevertheless, there is a third way in which many religious propositions are akin to Wittgensteinian foundational certainties. The religious believer is confronted by the doubts of the atheist or agnostic in the same way the ordinary believer in certainties is confronted with the doubts of the philosophical skeptic. Indeed, from a purely rational and empirical standpoint, the ordinary believer finds himself at a loss to provide logically compelling arguments against the philosophical skeptic. Similarly, the religious believer in a position such as Forsyth's may be hard pressed, in a post-Kantian age, to respond in a convincing way to the assaults of the nonbeliever. In both situations, the believer must readily admit that the skeptical position is a logically possible one.

It is clear that Wittgenstein held that evidential grounds are not perpetually needed to justify all reasonable beliefs. The possibility of doubt, it must be admitted, will never go away as long as empirical grounds are needed to justify foundational certainties.

Wittgenstein hints that the proper way to respond to the philosophical skeptic is to show that doubts are sometimes completely out of place. In order to do that the believer in ordinary certainties must show that the demand for empirical proof cannot apply to all claims of fact, and that the room for reasonable doubt diminishes the closer we get to those certainties that are the foundations of our judgments.[103]

Wittgenstein set out to show in *On Certainty* that all assertions about truth are not hypotheses. He accomplishes this task by making a distinction between certainty and knowledge.[104] Unlike knowledge, paradigmatic and foundational certainties are questionable in principle, though it would seem exceedingly odd to question them in practice. We *can* question certainties, but this is only because we can formulate the truth of their opposites without forming a logical contradiction. The mere fact that we can formulate the denial of certainties without contradiction, however, does not provide reasons for doubting them.

We can say, with Bishop Berkeley, "I wonder if the physical world exists," but this is only because we can formulate the negation of the certainty "the physical world exists" without a logical contradiction. But the mere fact that we can formulate the denial of this foundational certainty does not provide us with reasons for doubting it.

Wittgenstein's conclusion in *On Certainty* is that different truth claims sometimes have different logical statuses. Since the truth of foundational certainties is required as a condition for the possibility of judging other truth claims, the certainties occupy a kind of axiomatic status.

The analogy we have been implicitly building should now be made more explicit. In the Christian form of life specific religious propositions serve as the "foundational principles" on which that particular form of life is built. That Jesus is fully human and fully divine, that the atonement was necessary for our salvation, that Jesus was a vehicle for that atonement, are all religious assertions that within the Christian form of life have a status of "foundational principles." Without these prior beliefs, the Christian faith would make no sense. But we must be careful to notice that none of the religious assertions mentioned are empirical propositions, for their truths do not rest on some set of empirical facts to be discovered in the world. The Christian form of life provides the context in which these certainties are to be viewed.

The importance all this has for our discussion of the problem of evil should now be clear. We have suggested that our teleological theodicy is somehow bound up with the incarnation and atonement of Jesus Christ. These are certainly not empirical propositions. But they are foundational principles on which the Christian faith is based.

Since we have shown earlier that Forsyth's kenotic theodicy is one that is allowed by reason, and since it is within the Christian form of life that these assertions about the problem of evil are to be understood, the notion that all will be well because of the saving act of Jesus Christ takes on the status of a kind of foundational principle, one on which many other assertions about the Christian form of life are based. Moreover, these foundational principles go into the making of a form of life whose picturing of the world is one that is allowed by reason.

Of course, it is true that our position is not exempt from doubt, but the assertions on which it is based nevertheless take on the status of foundational principles when viewed as part of the Christian form of life. In that set of language games, compelling evidence should no more be expected than it should for foundational certainties.[105] Like foundational certainties, foundational religious beliefs play a governing role in the thinking of the adherents to that particular form of life. Thinking and acting become intermingled. The difficult task of justifying religious beliefs on empirical grounds often seems destined to failure, which puts the believer in the position of looking as though he or she has been defeated, when, in fact, the "defeat" may be a function of the difference in logical statuses between empirical propositions and foundational religious principles.

To some it may begin to look like we have been arguing for a kind of relativism by taking this line of Witgenstein's. Roger Trigg, in his work *Reason and Commitment,* for example, takes Wittgenstein and several of his followers to task for holding what he thinks is a relativistic view of truth:

One popular form of relativism apparently manages to avoid the slide into total objectivism by making reasoning as well as truth relative to groups or societies. Proponents of this view are usually very reluctant to be called relativists. Nevertheless, once it is stressed that the different cultures have different concepts, and that their members see the world differently, it is no very great step to saying that there is no right way of seeing the world and that it is pure arrogance to assume one's own society's understanding of things is the correct one. It thus becomes impossible to judge other cultures at all, since to do so we would have to rely on our own society's understanding of things being the correct one. We have to rely on our own conception of what really is the case, and this is to beg the question of what is really right. What we are left with are separate ways of thinking about the world, or a particular part of it. There can be no neutral way of describing the world, against which every conceptual scheme can be measured. It is obvious that we can only describe the world by means of some conceptual scheme, and so it is not logically possible to step outside of every conceptual system....The result is that we are unable to pass judgments on other systems without using our own. This is fine if it enables us to think of reality as it is, while other systems give us a false picture. Since, however, the adherents to each system are liable to think that theirs sets the standard of truth, an obvious compromise is to say that there is no such thing as truth when conceptual systems are being compared. Each system sets its own standards of truth, but they are not the kinds of things which themselves can be true or false. Such a position seems to be a paradigm case of relativism.[106]

Trigg continues by citing Peter Winch as one of the major perpetrators of this Wittgensteinian relativism:

> Winch fails to separate 'reality' from language, so that language actually seems to determine what is real. Even an objectivist, of course, would admit that there is a link between a language and what is regarded as real. A language expresses a community's beliefs about reality. The objectivist, however, would still wish to insist that reality exists apart from people's beliefs, and that their beliefs could be mistaken. An essential function of the language, he would maintain, is to concern itself with what actually is the case. Its business is to communicate truth. Winch will have none of this. He says: 'Reality is not what gives language sense. What is real and what is unreal shows itself in the sense that language has. Further, both the distinction between the real and the unreal and the concept of agreement with reality themselves belong to our language.' It follows that different languages cannot be thought of as different attempts to describe the same reality. 'Reality' is made relative to a language and if different languages portray 'the world' differently, then there must be different worlds. If one accepts this conclusion, one is remorselessly driven to unpalatable consequences. The result of granting that 'the world' or 'reality' cannot be conceived as independent of all conceptual schemes is that there is no reason to suppose that what the peoples of very different communities see as the world is similar in any way.[107]

It must be kept in mind in analyzing what Trigg has said that he begins by agreeing that it is impossible to argue outside of all conceptual frameworks in order to decide between or among them. There is no ideal observer status, at least not for human beings. Trigg is also in agreement that there is a close link between language and what is thought of as reality.

But it must also be said that Trigg does not seem to fully understand Winch's position. Nowhere in his article about Evans-Pritchard's work on the Azandes does Winch suggest either implicitly or explicitly that language describes reality. Rather, the speakers of a natural language express their beliefs about reality in that language. It is the beliefs, not the language, that can be true or false.

For Winch, and for Wittgenstein as well, different cultures have different concepts, and there is no neutral way of comparing them. But nowhere do either Winch or Wittgenstein suggest that the people of these different cultures also have different worlds. Trigg seems to confuse these two points. In Wisdom's terms, we might suggest that different cultures have different connecting techniques for making sense of the same world. Still, Trigg offers a rather detailed argument in support of the view that "different concepts mean different worlds":

> If the members of different societies live in different worlds and do not merely have varying and conflicting beliefs about the same reality, there will not necessarily be any point of contact between the concepts of one society and those of another. If different societies are dealing with the same world, it is possible in principle to examine how differently they describe the same thing. All that is necessary is to see what members of the respective societies say when confronted with a specific situation; if the assumption concerning the objectivity of what they describe is removed, there can be no justification for comparing what they say

because they may be talking about very different
things.[108]

In this passage Trigg uses the words "reality" and
"world" as though they are interchangeable. Both are used
in a very comprehensive way. He does not refer to different
aspects of the world or the different sorts of things and situations that go into the making of the world. Trigg's comment contains the naive assumption that all aspects of reality or parts of the world are made of the same stuff. But he
fails to see that there are criteria for distinguishing between
different senses of what is "real." For example, one may
walk by a department store window and say that the man-
nequin is not a real person. We can also point to an
acquaintance and say, because of a lack of self-knowledge
on the part of that person, that he or she is not a real person. Here we clearly have two different criteria for real and
unreal because they are two different aspects of the world
or different kinds of situations that go into the making of
the "world. "

Wittgenstein does use the term *weltbild* (usually translated as "world picture"), but he is not using it in the simplistic way that Trigg uses "reality"or "world." For
Wittgenstein, this world picture is one that comes together
through the conflation of a huge complex of different but
overlapping belief systems. They overlap in the same sense
that a belief system about what a person feels is different
from but related to the belief system about how a person
looks, for example. In these two systems of belief we use
two different sets of concepts and these concepts are not
subject to the same rules. Still, with all of that said, it is
clear that Wittgenstein believed that talking about different
concepts is not tantamount to "different worlds."

Trigg seems intent on concentrating on those examples in which it is supposed that different concepts are used to talk about the same thing, where "the same thing" does not mean different aspects of the same thing but the same aspect. It is in these cases where he speaks about the assumption of objectivity in relation to what is described. If this assumption is removed, Trigg argues, there can be no way of comparing what the two groups have to say. Although it could be pointed out that Trigg seems to have a rather peculiar notion of what counts as a thing, in that he seems not to realize that what counts as a thing is always decided in some quite specific context, in a way it could also be said that Trigg is correct. If the concepts of two cultures are radically different, there may not be enough shared notions for communication between them to be easy.

But the real violence Trigg seems to do to the Wittgensteinian position is that the former implies that in the latter's position there is no way of showing that any beliefs are false. Certainly, Wittgenstein does not make this claim. Indeed, any belief that has the logical status of an empirical hypothesis can, at least in principle, be shown to be false. Someone who thinks that the world is flat, to use one of Trigg's favorite examples, can be shown to be incorrect very easily. There are all sorts of empirical pieces of evidence for suggesting that this position is in error.

But we must recall that the logical status of Forsyth's religious assertions about the problem of evil are closer in form to Wittgensteinian foundational certainties than they are to empirical hypotheses. Therefore, it is inappropriate to use empirical criteria to determine the truth or falsity of these claims. Indeed, it is impossible to ascertain their truth in this way, for, as Wisdom has suggested, the supposed truth of these propositions goes beyond the "facts" of the world.

D.Z. Phillips attempts to make this same point when he suggests that a religious question like "What kind of reality is divine reality?" is not like the hypothetical question "Is this physical object real?" Rather, the religious question is more like the foundational certainty, "What kind of reality is the reality of physical objects?"

> I suggest that more can be gained if one compares the question, 'What kind of reality is divine reality?' not with the question, 'Is the physical object real or not?' but with the different question, 'What kind of reality is the reality of physical objects?' To ask whether physical objects are real is not like asking whether this appearance is real or not where often one can find out, but how can I find out whether the physical world is real or not. The latter question is not about the possibility of carrying out an investigation. It is a question of whether it is possible to speak of truth and falsity in the physical world; a question prior to that of determining the truth or falsity of any particular matter of fact.

> Similarly, the question about the reality of the divine is a question about the possibility of sense and nonsense, truth and falsity in religion. When God's existence is constructed as a matter of fact, it is taken for granted that the concept of God is at home within the conceptual framework of the reality of the physical world. It is as if we said 'We know where the assertions of God's existence belongs, we understand what kind of assertion it is; all we need to do now is determine its truth or falsity.' But to ask a question about the reality of God is to ask a question about a kind of

reality, not about the reality of this or that, in much the same way as asking about the reality of physical objects is not to ask about the reality of this or that physical object.[109]

At this point in our discussion we must attempt to avoid a possible misunderstanding that the use of this Phillips' quotation might engender. My position is closer to John Wisdom's use of Wittgenstein than it is to the position of Phillips. Wisdom wrote nothing about *On Certainty*.[110] Nevertheless, I think he would agree with Phillips' claim that a religious question like "What kind of reality is divine reality?" is more like the question "What kind of reality is the reality of physical objects?" rather than "Is this particular thing real?" Wisdom would be in agreement with Phillips on this point, I think, because he would also say that religious propositions are not empirical propositions, not experimental hypotheses to be proved. For Wisdom, in the case of experimental hypotheses, further evidence should always be relevant and may make a difference to what can reasonably be believed. In the case of religious assertions, however, there is no further evidence to be collected. It is a matter rather of how most reasonably to construe or connect the evidence. Wisdom points out that religious apologists have nothing to tell us when it comes to what the facts are except what is already known.

At the same time, Wisdom would probably profoundly disagree with Phillips on a number of very important points. He would not admit, for example, that religious propositions have their own "sense," though he would say that often religious language is metaphorical or sometimes initially paradoxical. All religious propositions, Wisdom would suggest, from any form of life, must pass the initial test of logical consistency and intelligibility. It is true that one form of life's religious propositions may be difficult to understand by those in another form of life, but this is no warrant for believing in round squares.

In reading *Death and Immortality*,[111] one wonders whether Phillips' case for religious language does not turn out to be a subtle denial of what it is usually thought to be about. In a real way Phillips seems to have given up any attempt to defend theism except in terms of social function and meaning. Wisdom, unlike Phillips, would argue that although religious assertions are not empirical hypotheses, they may, nevertheless, refer to realities that exist independently of the language games in which these entities are mentioned. Phillips would deny that the concept "God" refers to something that is there independent of whether people believe in him or not. He also holds a similar position about the soul:

> To say of someone "He'd sell his soul for money" is a perfectly natural remark. It in no way entails any philosophical theory about the duality of human nature. The remark is a moral observation about a person, one that expresses the degraded state that person is in. A man's soul, in this context, refers to his integrity, to the complex of practices and beliefs which acting with integrity would cover for that person. Might not talk about the immortality of the soul play a similar role?[112]

Later in the same work, Phillips answers his rhetorical question:

> ...questions about the immortality of the soul are seen to be not questions concerning the extent of a man's life, and in particular concerning whether that life can

extend beyond the grave, but questions concerning the
kind of life a man is living.[113]

Certainly, Phillips' suggested use of the term "soul" is a
proper one given the context he has supplied, but that is not
the only context in which the word soul is used. Indeed,
when the devout believer says, "I believe in the life of the
world to come," he is most frequently voicing a belief that
he *will* survive death.

In contrast to Phillips Wisdom would hold that although
religious propositions are not empirical hypotheses, they
may, nevertheless, have cognitive significance. His position, in a real way, closes the gap between the cognitive and
noncognitive functions of religious language. Wisdom proposes that religious language may contribute to cognitive
inquiry while at the same time not being subject to the rules
of verification. In some ways, his position is not unlike
some of the insights of Immanuel Kant.

Kant grants that religious language, even within the
domain of pure theoretical reason, has certain heuristic
functions that are similar, I believe, to the function of
Wisdom's connecting technique. Imagining God as a cosmic
designer can give shape and direction to the framing of our
observations. Kant admitted that God concepts can never be
cognitively justified, but he did believe, nevertheless, that
the terms '"God" and "immortality" actually refer to something.[114]

Nevertheless, even with these caveats, Phillips still has
something important here to tell us. Because the question
"What kind of reality is divine reality?" is much more like
the foundational certainty "physical objects exist" than it is
like the hypothesis "unicorns exist," justification for holding that there is a divine reality should not be required in

the same way it is for empirical hypotheses. The reality of physical objects is one of Wittgenstein's certainties. It is a foundational principle on which other assertions about the world are based. In an analogous way, positing the existence of God is a foundational principle, a principle on which many of our other religious assertions are based. One should not be required to justify this religious assertion on empirical grounds because it functions with a different logical status than do hypothetical assertions about which we usually have or ask for proof.

The importance this point has for our study should be apparent. When Forsyth makes religious assertions about the problem of evil, he is making a set of claims that are based largely on a number of foundational principles on which the Christian form of life is based. He has taken as his starting point certain nonempirical propositions about the saving work of Jesus Christ and his central role in Christian theodicy.

Having assumed this Christological perspective, I have attempted in this chapter to show that P.T. Forsyth's answer to the problem of evil is one that is allowed by reason and that is firmly rooted within the Christian form of life. It is true that critics might still respond by suggesting that I have reneged on my original promise to keep the victim of suffering central in my response to the problem of evil. Some might suggest that by resorting to Forsyth's teleological perspective I have ceased to give justice to the pain of the sufferer.

It may be the case that outside the context of an existential relation with God it would only be rational and correct to claim that the experience of suffering is so real that it cannot be seen as an occasion for good, and that no amount of divine suffering can change the original terror of evil.

But within the existential relation, the picturing of the world is quite different. Here the crushing reality of evil is not disputed; indeed, it is confirmed. But at the same time, the attributes of God come to be realized within the context of "seeing God." This process occurs in different ways, both in Job's encounter with Yahweh and with the Christian's encounter with Christ. When Job "sees God," as we have shown in chapter four, the problem of evil radically changes in focus. He suddenly understands the foundational principles on which his faith is based.

A similar alteration of the context for theodicy occurs in the case of the Christian's personal relation to God in Christ. For the Christian, it is in Jesus that one "sees God." In the context of this existential relation, the sufferer comes to see the son of God's victory over death as not diminishing the horror of evil but rather confirming it in a most graphic way.

That God had to die on the cross becomes for the Christian *the* problem of evil, and this realization totally recasts the way in which the victim approaches theodicy. God's transformation of judgment into mercy in the cross of Christ allows the Christian sufferer to see evil as an occasion for good, but only on the basis of the work of Christ. God conquered evil in Christ, but this does not diminish its reality here and now. Rather, it gives the sufferer who is in Christ the power to transform his experience of evil into an occasion of good and to see in a future order the possibility of a respite from evil, not a repairing of it.[115]

It might still be asked why God chooses to do things this way. Why must we "accept the ticket"? The answer, very plainly, is that the experience of "seeing God" leads the victim not in the direction of a theoretical theodicy that answers all our questions about natural and moral evil, but rather it sets the sufferer in a new life and provides the basis for a practical response to the problem of evil. As Forsyth puts it, the Christian theodicy he is advocating is "not really an answer to a riddle but a victory in a battle."[116]

This situation is where the Christian response to evil goes well beyond the Book of Job. Job could only go his way with the realization of the ontological gulf between himself and God and the trust in a teleological answer; the Christian receives the Good News that God has reconciled the two in Christ. In Christ, the sufferer finds a firm position from which to take a stand against evil. Participating in the suffering of Christ, the victim can partake in the victory of the ultimate victim over the powers of sin, evil, and suffering. Rather than being paralyzed by the experience of evil, the victim, in Christ, is able to share in the practical struggle against it. As Oliver Quick puts it, "Our Lord's victorious self-sacrifice was not achieved in order to make our own unnecessary, but to make it possible."[117] Indeed, if the Christian believes that God "empties himself" in Christ, he has the comforting assurance, as C.S. Lewis has expressed it, that in "self-giving, if anywhere, we touch a rhythm not only of all creation but of all being."[118]

Austin Farrer gives a good description of how the victim of suffering who continues to abide in the Christian existential relation with God may respond to the problem of evil with the acceptance of his practical calling in the world:

> An overmastering sense of human ills can be taken as the world's invitation to deny her Maker, or it may be taken as God's invitation to succor His world. Which is it to be? Those who take the practical alternative become more closely acquainted with misery than the onlookers; but they feel the grain of existence, and the

movement of the purposes of God. They do not argue, they love; and what is loved is always known as good. The more we love the more we feel the evils besetting or corrupting the objects of love. But the more we feel the force of the besetting harms, the more certain we feel of the value residing in what they attack; and in resisting them we are identified with the action of God, whose mercy is over our flesh.[119]

In the final analysis, more than any carefully reasoned theodicy, we must come to the realization that it is the figure of Christ, the God become man, who enables us to endure and indeed to transcend suffering. At the heart of the Christian message we must find a God who identifies himself so thoroughly with his creatures that he becomes one of them.

It is true that the particulars of Forsyth's theodicy are not entirely clear. But we must trust that at bottom level the *prima facie* Christian paradox of evil is merely apparent. In the final analysis, we must trust as does one of the Magi in a Dorothy Sayers play:

I do not mind being ignorant and unhappy —
All I ask is the assurance that I am not alone,
Some courage, some comfort against the burden of fear and pain.

If He is beside me, bearing the weight of His own creation,
If I may hear His voice among the voices of the vanquished,
If I may feel His hand touch mine in the darkness,
If I may look upon the hidden face of God
and read in the eyes of God
that He is acquainted with grief.[120]

Notes

1. David Hume, *Dialogues Concerning Natural Religion*,
    parts X and XI. Cf. also part V, where Hume suggests
    "this world, for all (we know) is very faulty and
    imperfect, compared to superior standard; and was
    only the first rude essay of some infant deity, who
    afterwards abandoned it...." Much of the material
    dealing with kenosis in this chapter was taken from
    papers presented in Prof. McBride's seminar in Old
    Testament Theodicy, Yale Divinity School, 1975.

2. J.L. Mackie, *The Miracle of Theism*, pp. 150-151.

3. Alasdair MacIntyre, *Difficulties in Christian Belief*
    (London: SCM Press, 1959) p. 17.

4. For a more detailed version of this objection, see
    James Ross's *Introduction to the Philosophy of
    Religion* (New York: Macmillan, 1969) pp. 120-123.

5. Another way to put this objection is to say that Mackie
    insists what is needed to falsify the claim that an all-
    powerful, all-loving, all-knowing God exists is one
    example of absolute, utterly useless evil that cannot be
    overcome. But it is not clear that we can give such an
    example. One might suggest that Mackie would have to
    disprove the existence of God in order to prove that
    any instance of evil is absolute; hence, Mackie's

appeal is circular, presupposing what it intends to prove.

6. John Wisdom, "Paradox and Discovery," in *Paradox and Discovery* (Oxford: Oxford University Press, 1965) p. 124. Later, we shall argue that the incarnation is, in fact, an excellent example of a religious paradox that is merely apparent.

7. T.F. Torrance, *Theological Science* (London: Oxford University, 1924) p. 279.

8. Nelson Pike, *God and Evil*, p. 102. Pike also points out in "Hume and Evil," *Philosophical Review* (1963), reprinted in *God and Evil*, that Hume overlooks the possibility that God permits evil for a good and justifying purpose.

9. M.B. Ahern, *The Problem of Evil* (New York: Schocken Books, 1971) p. 78.

10. Ibid., pp. 78-79.

11. Cf. Maurice Wiles' "Christianity Without Incarnation"; Michael Goulder's "Jesus, the Man of Universal Destiny"; Leslie Houlden's "The Creed of Experience"; and Don Cupitt's "The Christ of Christendom," all in *The Myth of God Incarnate* (London: SCM Press, 1977).

12. Ibid., pp. ix-xi and 167-185.

13. Ibid., p. 178f.

14. I do not mean to minimize the complicated debate on the problem of identity. Often this problem has been answered by fairly abstruse metaphyscial concepts such as "eternal forms," "substances," and "essences."

I do not wish to become embroiled in these debates
and suggest this simple analysis.

15. Many if not all of the insights for my approach to the
philosophical problem of the incarnation have come
from chapter eight of Stephen T. Davis' *The Logic and
Nature of God* (London: Macmillan, 1983).

16. Mark 5:30; 13:32.

17. Stephen Davis, *The Logic and Nature of God*, p. 128.

18. By the traditional conception, I mean the formulation
of the doctrine brought forth at the Council of
Chalcedon in 451 A.D.

19. A similar argument can be given, I think, for the other
major attributes.

20. *Incarnation and Myth*, p. 43

21. Ibid., p. 45.

22. Cupitt is, I think, mistaken when he implies that the
"invention" of the notion of kenosis has come along
recently as a stop-gap measure for giving some meager
credibility to a crumbling doctrine of the incarnation.
As early as Irenaeus' *Against Heresies* (iii, II, 3) there
is a suggestion of the possibility that Jesus' divine
attributes may have been "quiescent" or "sleeping"
during the temptation, cruxificion, and death of Jesus.
Cyril of Alexander, in *Quod Unus Sit Christus* (viii, I,
319), formulates a similar possibility when he offers
that the Logos "willed to permit human experience to
prevail over him." Similar though admittedly cryptic
remarks may also be found in Gregory of Nyssa's
Oratio Catechetica Magna (XXIV). On the continent,
various thinkers in the nineteenth century Lutheran

tradition, such as Thomasius in *Christi Person und Werk* (1853), Godet in his *Gospel of St. John,* and Dorner in *The Doctrine of the Person of Christ* (1861), had suggested by mid-century that Jesus may have depotentiated himself by abandoning his divine attributes for a while. In England, the nineteenth century congregational divine, A.M. Fairbain, in his *Christ in Modern Theology* (pp. 470-478), developed a distinction between the "physical" and "ethical" attributes of God, providing the way for subsequent kenotic theorists such as Charles Gore, Frank Weston, H.R. MacKintosh, and P.T. Forsyth. Perhaps A.M. Ramsay in *From Gore to Temple* sums up best the emergence of the kenosis doctrine of the incarnation when he says

> that doctrine has sprung from the consideration
> of the historical data of our Lord's life considered
> side by side with the belief in His deity. On
> the one hand the Gospels depict Jesus Christ as
> living a genuinely human life: He advances in
> knowledge. He learns. He asks questions as
> needing to know the answer. He shows ignorance
> (cf. Mark 13:32). On the other hand, the church
> worships Him as divine, and reads in the Gospels
> of His perfect revelation of the Father. How were
> Christian teachers to express the two aspects of the
> Incarnation, without allowing the one to override
> the other? It was one thing to assert the dogma of a
> perfect Godhead and perfect Manhood coexisting
> in the one Person. What was more difficult was to
> teach about the incarnate life without making the
> humanity seem unreal or the deity seem to be
> ousted by the human limitations. Inevitably, the
> problem may be more keenly felt in the modern
> church with its concern for history than it had been
> in the ancient church with the concentration upon

the framework of dogmatic definition. (London:
Longmans Green, 1959), pp. 31-32.

23. The Jerusalem Bible (London: Darton, Longman and
Todd, 1968).

24. In *Incarnation and Myth*, pp. 60-62.

25. Ibid., p. 61.

26. Ibid., p. 60.

27. Ibid., pp. 7-8.

28. Ibid., p. 50.

29. Ibid., pp. 48-49.

30. Ibid., p. 49.

31. It is of some interest that when Hick does specifically
criticize kenotic accounts of the incarnation he
concentrates on older versions such as that of Frank
Weston in *The One Christ* (London: Longmans Green, 1907)
and H.R. MacKintosh's *The Doctrine of the Person of
Christ* (Edinburgh: T. and T. Clarke, 1912).

32. Cyril Rodd, "The Problem of Suffering: A Dialogue,"
Expository Times, (August, 1972) p. 342.

33. Karl Barth, *Church Dogmatics* IV/1 (Edinburgh: T. and
T. Clarke, 1956) p. 60.

34. Karl Barth, *The Christian Life* (Edinburgh: T. and T.
Clarke, 1981) p. 123.

35. Karl Barth, *Church Dogmatics* IV/1 p.186.

36. Karl Barth, *The Doctrine of the Word of God*
(Edinburgh: T. and T. Clark, 1936) p.2.

37. P.T. Forsyth, *The Person and the Place of Jesus Christ* (London: Hodder and Stoughton, 1909) p. 313.

38. Ibid., pp. 313-314.

39. Ibid. A.D. Lindsay makes a similar remark in his posthumously published *Selected Addresses* (London: Hodder and Stoughton, 1957). On pp. 67ff he makes ample use of Kierkegaard: "If we rightly consider omnipotence, then clearly it must have the quality of so taking itself back in this very manifestation of all its powerfulness that the results of this act of the omnipotence can be independent. It is only a miserable and worldly picture of the dialectic of power to say that it becomes greater as it can compel and make things dependent. Socrates knew better: the art of using power is to make free."

40 Forsyth, *The Person and the Place of Jesus Christ*, p. 319

41. C.F.D. Moule, "The Manhood of Jesus in the New Testament," *Christ, Faith, and History*, edited by S.W. Sykes and J.P. Clayton (Cambridge: Cambridge University Press, 1972) p. 96.

42. Ibid., p. 97.

43. Ibid., p. 98.

44. Geddes MacGregor, *He Who Lets Us Be* (New York: Seabury Press, 1975) p. 72. MacGregor also provides a valuable critical survey of the concept of omnipotence.

45. Ibid.

46. MacGregor, *Philosophical Issues in Religious Thought*, pp. 167-168.

47. Ludwig Wittgenstein, *Lectures on Aesthetics, Psychology, and Religious Belief* (Oxford: Basil Blackwell, 1966), particularly his discussion of the last judgment.

48. John Wisdom, "Gods," *Proceedings of the Aristotelean Society,* vol. XLV (1944-1945) pp. 188ff. Also see Wisdom's *Philosophy and Psychoanalysis* (Oxford: Basil Blackwell, 1953) pp. 149-159.

49. Cf. Donald Hudson's *A Philosophical Approach to Religion* (London: Macmillan, 1974), particularly chapter 6.

50. Anthony Flew, "Divine Omnipotence and Human Freedom," pp. 149f.

51. Ibid.

52. Cf. *The Philosophical Investigation* part II, section xi.

53. Donald Hudson, *A Philosophical Approach to Religion*, pp. 148-150.

54. John Wisdom, "Gods," p. 197.

55. This is one of the major points that sets Wisdom's view off as different from R.M. Hare's "bliks." Cf. the latter's contribution to "Theology and Falsification" in Flew and MacIntyre's *New Essays in Philosophical Theology.*

56. These criteria do not push one in the direction of coherence theories of truth I shall try to show in the final section of this chapter.

57. D.M. MacKinnon, *Borderlands of Theology* (Philadelphia: J.B. Lippincott, 1968) p. 101.

58. Ibid., p. 92.

59. Ibid., p. 90.

60. Ibid., p. 81.

61. Ibid.

62. Ibid., p. 67.

63. Ibid., pp. 92-93.

64. P.T. Forsyth, *The Justification of God* (London: Latimer House, 1948).

65. Ibid., p. 19.

66. Hick, *Evil and the God of Love*, p. 249.

67. Forsyth, *Justification of God*, p. 35.

68. Ibid., p. 159.

69. Ibid., p. vi.

70. Ibid., p. 57.

71. Ibid., p. vi.

72. Ibid., p. 130.

73. Ibid., p. 167.

74. Ibid., p. 139.

75. Ibid., p. 53.

76. D.M. MacKinnon, *Borderlands of Theology*, p. 70.

77. Oliver Quick, *The Christian Sacraments* (London: Nisbet and Co., 1927) p. 82.

78. P. T. Forsyth, *The Justification of God,* p. 1 66 .

79. Ibid .

80. Ibid.

81. Ibid., p. 163-164.

82. Ibid., p. 168.

83. Ibid.

84. Ibid., p. 169.

85. Ibid., p. 215.

86. Ibid., p. 232.

87. Ibid., p. 169.

88. William Temple, *Christus Veritas* (London: Longmans Green, 1924). Other criticisms of kenotic doctrines can be found in D.M. Baille, *God Was in Christ* (London: Faber and Faber, 1948) pp. 94-98; E.L. Mascall, *Theology and the Gospel of Christ* (London: SPCK, 1978); and in various places in C.R. Fairweather and F.W. Beare, *A Commentary on the Epistle to the Philippians* (London: A. & C. Black, 1959), particularly their comments on 2: 5-8.

89. Ibid., pp. 142-143.

90. Ibid., p. 143.

91. Ibid.

92. W.L. Power, "Symbolic Logic and the Doctrine of the Trinity," *The Iliff Review* vol. XXXII no. 1 (Winter 1975).

93. Oliver Quick, *Doctrines of the Creed*, pp. 136-139.

94. Ludwig Wittgenstein, *On Certainty* (Oxford: Basil Blackwell, 1977). *On Certainty* is indexed by Marjorie Clay in *Philosophical Investigations* vol. 2 (1979) pp. 66-84.

95. Ibid., 246, 341-344.

96. This distinction, in slightly different form, has been raised by Professor C. Wright of the St. Andrew's University Department of Logic and Metaphysics, in his spring 1984 seminar on *On Certainty*. It can also be found in T. Morawetz's *Wittgenstein and Knowledge: The Importance of "On Certainty"* (Amherst: University of Massachuetts Press, 1978) pp. 12-13.

97. This distinction between paradigmatic and foundational certainties can perhaps best be seen in a somewhat cryptic remark in section 99 of *On Certainty*: "And the bank of the river consists partly of hard rock, subject to no alteration, or only to an imperceptible one, partly of sand, which now in one place now in another gets washed away or deposited."

98. Ludwig Wittgenstein, *Lectures and Conversations on Aesthetics, Psychology and Religious Belief* (Oxford: Basil Blackwell, 1966).

99. This interpretation of *On Certainty* has many affinities with that found in John Whittaker's *Matters of Faith and Matters of Principle* (San Antonio: Trinity University Press, 1981) though Whittaker's view seems much closer to the noncognitive position of our former teacher Paul Holmer than does my own.

100. Ludwig Wittgenstein, *On Certainty*, 37ff.

101. Ibid., 240f.

102. But when the religious person has doubts he does
     not disagree about the facts of the world; rather, he
     doubts the metaphysical principles on which the
     Christian view of the world is built. The disagreement
     is about picturing the world as a whole, not about the
     individual parts of the world.

103. Ibid., 128-131.

104. Ibid., 308f.

105. Norman Malcolm relates an incident in *Ludwig
     Wittgenstein: A Memoir* (London: Oxford University
     Press, 1958) that may illustrate that Wittgenstein
     could have believed the analogy between certainties
     and foundational religious principles. "When I once
     quoted him a remark of Kierkegaard's to this effect:
     'How can it be that Christ does not exist, since I know
     he has saved me?' Wittgenstein exclaimed: 'You see,
     it isn't a question of proving anything!'"

106. Roger Trigg, *Reason and Commitment*
     (London:Cambridge University Press, 1973) p. 6.

107. Ibid., p. 15.

108. Ibid., p. 14ff.

109. D.Z. Phillips, "Philosophy, Theology and the
     Reality of God", *Philosophical Quarterly* vol. 13
     (1963).

110. It is clear that Phillips' example comes directly from
     section 20 of *On Certainty*: "'Doubting the existence
     of the material world' does not mean for example

doubting the existence of a planet which later observation proved to exist."

111. D.Z. Phillips, *Death and Immortality* (London: Macmillan, 1970).

112. Ibid., p. 43.

113. Ibid., p. 49.

114. Immanuel Kant, *The Critique of Pure Reason: Kant Selections*, edited by T.M. Greene (New York: Charles Scribner's Sons, 1929) pp. 242ff. and 260-262.

115. The well-known eschatological statement of Mother Julian captures this quiet optimism: "But all shall be well, and all shall be well, and all manner of things shall be well." (Quoted in Hick's *Evil and the God of Love*, p. 264.)

116. P.T. Forsyth, *The Justification of God*, p. 211.

117. Oliver Quick, *Doctrines of the Creed*, p. 212.

118. C.S. Lewis, *The Problem of Pain* (London: Collins, 1940) p. 40.

119. Austin Farrer, *Love Almighty and Ills Unlimited* (New York: Doubleday, 1961) pp. 164.ff.

120. As quoted in John Kenner's *Suffering and Death: Two Theological Breaking Points* (New York: Macmillan, 1968) p. 315

Bibliography

Abbot, Edwin, *Flatlands: A Romance of Many Dimensions* (New York: Dover Publications, 1952)

Ahern, M.B., *The Problem of Evil* (New York: Schocken Books, 1971)

Albright, W.F., *From Stone Age to Christianity* (Baltimore: Johns Hopkins University Press, 1940)

Anselm, "The Proslogion," in *St. Anselm* Sidney Norton Dean (trans.) (Lasalle: Open Court Press, 1962)

Aquinas, Thomas, *Summa Contra Gentiles* Anton Pegis (trans.) (New York: Doubleday, 1955)

Aquinas, Thomas, *Summa Theologica. Great Books of the Western World* (London: Encyclopedia Britannica, 1952) Vols. 19, 20

Aquinas, Thomas, *Summa Theologica* (Latin text) (New York: McGraw Hill, 1963)

Aquinas, Thomas, *The Basic Writing of St. Thomas Aquinas* A.C. Pegis (ed.) (New York: 1945)

Aristotle, *The Prior and Posterior Analytics* W.D. Ross (ed.) (Oxford: Oxford University Press, 1949)

Augustine, *Enchiridion* (Edinburgh: T. and T. Clark, 1965)

Augustine, "On Free Will:" *Augustine's Early Writings* (London: SCM, 1958)

Augustine, *The City of God. Basic Writings of St. Augustine* Marcus Dods (trans.) (New York: Random House, 1948)

Augustine, *The City of God* W.J. Oates (trans.) (New York: Random House, 1948)

Augustine, *The Confessions and Enchiridion* A.C. Autler (trans.) (Philadelphia: Westminster Press, 1955)

Augustine, *The Confessions: Great Books of the Western World* (London: Encyclopedia Britannica, 1952) Vol. 18

Ayer, A.J., *Language, Truth and Logic* (London: Victor Gollancz, 1956)

Baier, Kurt, *The Moral Point of View* (Ithaca: Cornell University Press, 1958)

Barnhart, J.E., *The Study of Religion and Its Meaning* (The Hague: Mouton, 1977)

Barrett, Charles, *Understanding the Christian Faith* (Englewood Cliffs, N J.: Prentice Hall, 1980)

Barth, Karl, *The Christian Life* (Edinburgh: T. and T. Clark, 1981)

Barth, Karl, *Church Dogmatics* Vol. IV/1 (Edinburgh: T. and T. Clark, 1956)

Barth, Karl, *The Doctrine of the Word of God* (Edinburgh: T. and T. Clark, 1936)

Barton, G.A., "The Book of Job: Seeing God," *The Journal of Biblical Literature* Vol. 30, 1911

Becker, Ernest, *Escape From Evil* (New York: Free Press, 1975)

Berdyaev, Nicholas, *The Destiny of Man* (Glasgow: University Press, 1954)

Berger, Peter, *The Sacred Canopy* (New York: Anchor Books, 1969)

Bertocci, Peter, *Introduction to the Philosophy of Religion* (New York: Prentice Hall, 1951)

Blanshard, Brand, *Reason and Belief* (New Haven: Yale University Press, 1975)

Bochenski, I.M., "On Analogy," *The Thomist* Vol. II, no. 4 (1948)

Boethius, *The Consolation of Philosophy* Richard Green (trans.) (New York: Random House, 1962)

Bowker, John, "Intercession in the Qumran and Jewish Tradition," *Journal of Semitic Studies* Vol. 11 (1966)

Bowker, John, *The Problems of Suffering in the Religions of the World* (London: Cambridge University Press, 1970)

Brightman, E.S., *A Philosophy of Religion* (Englewood Cliffs, N.J.: Prentice Hall, 1940)

Brightman, E.S., *An Introduction to Philosophy* (New York: Henry Holt, 1925)

Brody, Baruch, *Beginning Philosophy* (Englewood Cliffs, N.J.: Prentice Hall, 1977)

Brown, Delwin and James, Ralph, *Process Philosophy and Christian Thought* (New York, 1971)

Buber, Martin, "A God Who Hides His Face," in *The Dimensions of Job* Nahum N. Glatzer (ed.) (New York: Schocken Books, 1969)

Burrows, Millar, "The Voice From the Whirlwind," *Journal of Biblical Literature* Vols. 47-48 (1928-1929)

Buttenwiesser, Moses, *The Book of Job* (New York: Macmillan, 1922)

Cabell, James Branch, *Jurgen* (London, 1919)

Calvin, John, *The Institutes of the Christian Religion Book I* John Allen (trans.) (Cheapside: T. Tegg and Son, 1838)

Campbell, C.A., *Selfhood and Godhead* (New York: Macmillan, 1957)

Camus, Albert, *The Myth of Sisyphus* (London: Hamish and Hamilton, 1955)

Camus, Albert, *The Plague*, Stuart Gilbert (trans.) (New York: Modern Library, 1948)

Carlyle, Thomas, *On Heroes* (London: The New University Library, 1957)

Castaneda, H.N., "Omniscience and Indexical Reference," *Journal of Philosophy*, Vol. 64 (1967)

Chesterton, G.K., *The Man Who Was Thursday* (London: Arrowsmith, 1944)

Cobb, John, *A Christian Natural Theology* (Philadelphia: Westminster Press, 1965)

Cross, Frank, "Will you Lie for God?" Convocation address delivered at the Memorial Church, Harvard University, Sept. 24, 1958

Cullmann, Oscar, *Christ and Time* (Philadelphia: Westminster Press, 1950)

Cupitt, Don, "Mr. Hebblethwaite on the Incarnation," in *Incarnation and Myth* Michael Goulder (ed.) (London: SCM, 1979)

Cupitt, Don, "The Christ of Christendom," in *The Myth of God Incarnate*, John Hick (ed.) (London: SCM, 1978)

D'Arcy, M.C., *The Pain of the World and the Providence of God* (London: Longmans Green, 1935

Damiani, Saint Peter, "De Divina Omnipotentia" in J. Migne's *Patrologia Latina* (Paris: no date) Vol. 145

Darrow, Clarence, *Attorney For The Damned* (New York: Macmillan, 1957)

Davies, A., *The Crisis of Conscience after Auschwitz* (London: 1969)

Davies, Brian, *Introduction to the Philosophy of Religion* (London: Oxford University Press, 1982)

Davis, S.T., *The Logic and Nature of God* (London: Macmillan, 1983)

Descartes, René, *Descartes' Letters* C. Adam and P. Tannery (eds.) (Paris, 1964)

Dhorme, E., *A Commentary on the Book of Job* Harold Knight (trans.) (London: Nelson, 1967)

Dodd, C.H., *Interpretation of the New Testament* (Grand Rapids: Eerdmans, 1977)

Dodd, C.H., *More New Testament Studies* (Manchester: Manchester University Press, 1968)

Dodd, C.H., *The Founder of Christianity* (London: Collins, 1971)

Doob, L.W., *Panorama of Evil* (London: Greenwood Press, 1978)

Dorner, J.A., *The Doctrine of the Person of Christ* (Edinburgh: T. and T. Clark, 1865)

Dostoyevski, F.M., *The Brothers Karamozov* Constance Garnatt (trans.) (New York: Modern Library, 1950)

Driver, S.R. and Gray, G.B., *A Critical and Exegetical Commentary on the Book of Job* (New York: Charles Scribner's Sons, 1921)

Durrant, Michael, *The Logical Status of "God"* (London: Macmillan, 1973)

Edwards, Jonathan, "Freedom of the Will," in *The Works of Jonathan Edwards,* P. Miller (ed.) (New Haven: Yale University Press, 1957)

Ehrenfels, Christian, *Cosmology* (New York: Comet Press, 1948)

Einstein, Albert, *Out of My Later Years* (New York: Grove Press, 1950)

Evans-Pritchard, E.E., *Witchcraft, Oracles and Magic Among the Azandes* (Oxford: Clarendon Press, 3rd ed., 1976)

Ewing, A.C., *The Definition of Good* (New York: Macmillan, 1947)

Fackenheim, Emile, *God's Presence in History* (New York: University Press, 1960)

Fackenheim, Emile, *Quest for Past and Future* (Bloomington: Indiana University Press, 1968)

Fairbairn, A.M., *Christ in Modern Theology* (London: Hodder and Stoughton, 1893)

Farberow, N.L., *Suicide in Different Cultures* (Baltimore: University Park Press, 1975)

Farrer, Austin, *Love Almighty and Ills Unlimited* (Garden City, N.Y.: Doubleday, 1961)

Ferre, Frederick, *Basic Modern Philosophy of Religion* (London: George Allen and Unwin, 1967)

Ferre, Frederick, *Language, Logic and God* (New York: Harper and Row, 1961)

Fleishner, Eva (ed.), *Auschwitz* (New York: KTAV, 1977)

Flew, Anthony, "Are Ninian Smart's Temptations Irresistible?" *Philosophy*, Vol. 37 (1962)

Flew, Anthony, "Death," in *New Essays in Philosophical Theology* (London: SCM, 1955)

Flew, Anthony, "Divine Omnipotence and Human Freedom," *New Essays in Philosophical Theology* (London: SCM Press, 1955)

Forsyth, P.T., *The Person and the Place of Jesus Christ* (London: Hodder and Stoughton, 1909)

Forsyth, P.T., *The Justification of God* (London: Lattimer House, 1948)

Frankfurt, H.G., "The Logic of Omnipotence," *Philosophical Review* Vol. 73 (1964)

Frazer, James, *Beliefs in Immortality and Worship of the Dead* Gifford Lectures, St. Andrews, 1913

Frazer, James, *The Golden Bough* Books II and X (London: Longmans, 1914)

Frey-Rohn, Lilane, "Evil From the Psychological Point of View," *Curatorium of the C.G. Jung Institute: Evil* (Evanston: Northwestern University Press, 1967)

Garrison, Jim, *The Darkness of God: Theology After Hiroshima* (London: SCM, 1982)

Geach, P.T., *God and the Soul* (London: Routledge and Kegan Paul, 1969)

Geach, P.T., *Providence and Evil* (Cambridge: Cambridge University Press, 1977)

Geertz, Clifford, *The Interpretation of Culture* (New York: Basic Books, 1973)

Gert, Bernard, *The Moral Rules* (New York: Harper and Row, 1970)

Glatzer, Nahum (ed.), *The Dimensions of Job* (New York: Schocken Books, 1969)

Godet, J., *The Gospel of St. John* (Edinburgh: T. and T. Clark, 1892)

Golding, William, *Lord of the Flies* (London: Faber and Faber, 1954)

Good, Edwin, "Job and the Literary Task: A Response," *Soundings* Vol. 56 (1973)

Gordis, Robert, *The Book of Job: Commentary, New Translation and Special Studies* (New York: Jewish Theological Seminary of America, 1978)

Gore, Charles, *Belief in Christ* (London: John Murray, 1902)

Goulder, Michael, "Jesus, the Man of Universal Destiny," in J. Hick's *The Myth of God Incarnate*

Griffen, D.R., *God, Power and Evil* (Philadelphia: Westminster Press, 1976)

Grisez, Germain, *Beyond the New Theism: A Philosophy of Religion* (South Bend, Ind.: Notre Dame University Press, 1976)

Hare, R.M., "Theology and Falsification," in Flew and MacIntyre's *New Essays in Philosophical Theology*

Harnack, Adolph, *History of Dogma* Vol. 5 (London: Williams and Norgate, 1898)

Harrelson, Walter, *Interpreting the Old Testament* (New York: Holt, Rinehart, Winston, 1964)

Harris, Errol, *The Problem of Evil* (Milwaukee: Marquette University Press, 1977)

Hartshorne, Charles, *The Divine Relativity* (New Haven: Yale University Press, 1948)

Hartshorne, Charles, "On Some Criticisms of Whitehead's Philosophy," *Philosophical Review* Vol. 44 (1935)

Hartshorne, Charles, *A Natural Theology for Our Time* (Lasalle: Open Court Press, 1973)

Hastings, James, *The Encyclopedia of Religion and Ethics* (London: Marshall, Morgan and Scott, 1981)

Hay, M., "Europe and the Jews," *Religion from Tolstoy to Camus* Walter Kaufmann (ed.) (New York: Harper Brothers, 1961)

Hebblethwaite, Brian, *The Adequacy of Christian Ethics* (London: Marshall, Morgan and Scott, 1981)

Hebblethwaite, Brian, *Evil Suffering and Religion* (London: Sheldon Press, 1979)

Hegel, G.W., *The Philosophy of History* (Cambridge: Cambridge University Press, 1975)

Helm, Paul, "God and Spacelessness" *Philosophy* Vol. 55 (1980)

Hick, John, *Evil and the God of Love* (London: Macmillan, 1977)

Hick, John, *Faith and Knowledge* (Ithaca: Cornell University Press, 1957)

Hick, John, "The Problem of Evil," *The Encyclopedia of Philosophy* Vol. III (New York: Macmillan, 1967)

Hick, John, "Theology and Falsification," *Theology Today* Vol. 37 (1960)

Hick, John, *The Philosophy of Religion* (Englewood Cliffs, N.J.: Prentice Hall, 1983)

Hobbes, Thomas, *The Leviathan* Michael Oakeshott (ed.) (Oxford: Basil Blackwell, 1957)

Hoitenga, D.J., "Logic and the Problem of Evil," *American Philosophical Quarterly* Vol. 4 (1967)

Hook, Sidney, "Toward the Understanding of Karl Marx," in *Determinism and Freedom in the Age of Modern Science* (New York: New York University Press, 1958)

Horowitz, David, "The Passion of the Jews," *Ramparts* Vol. 13 (1972)

Hospers, John, *An Introduction to Philosophical Analysis* (Englewood Cliffs, N.J.: Prentice Hall, 1963)

Hudson, Donald, *A Philosophical Approach to Religion* (London: Macmillan, 1974)

Hume, David, *Dialogues Concerning Natural Religion* (New York: Hafner Publishing Co., 1959)

Hume, David, *Dialogues Concerning Natural Religion* N.K. Smith (ed) (London: Thomas Nelson 1947)

Indinopulos, A., "Art and the Inhuman: A Reflection on the Holocaust," *The Christian Century* Vol. 41 (1974)

Jacks, L.P., *Religious Foundations* (New York: Macmillan, 1923)

James, William, *Pragmatism* (London: Longmans Green, 1907)

Jastrow, Morris, *The Book of Job* (Philadelphia: J.B. Lippincott, 1920)

Jerusalem Bible (London: Darton, Longman and Todd, 1968)

Journet, Charles, *The Meaning of Evil* (London: Geoffrey Chapman, 1963)

Joyce, G.H., *Principles of Natural Theology* (London: Longmans Green, 1957)

Jung, Carl, *Answer to Job* R.C. Hull (trans.) (Princeton: Princeton University Press, 1973)

Kane, G.S., "The Concepts of Divine Goodness and the Problem of Evil," *Religious Studies* Vol. 2 (1975)

Kant, Immanuel, "The Critique of Pure Reason" in *Kant Selections* T.M. Greene (ed.) (New York: Chas. Scribner's Sons, 1929)

Kenner, John, *Suffering and Death: Two Theological Breaking Points* (New York: Macmillan, 1968)

Kenny, Anthony, *Aquinas: A Collection of Critical Essays* (London: Macmillan, 1969)

Kenny, Anthony, *The God of the Philosophers* (Oxford: Oxford University Press, 1977)

Kierkegaard, Soren, *Concluding Unscientific Postscript* David Swenson (trans.) (Princeton: Princeton University Press, 1941)

Klubertanz, George, *St. Thomas Aquinas on Analogy* (Chicago: University of Chicago Press, 1960)

Kretzmann, Norman, "Omniscience and Immutability," *Journal of Philosophy* Vol. 63 (1966)

Kushner, Harold, *When Bad Things Happen to Good People* (London: Pan Books, 1982)

Leibniz, G.W., *Theodicy* E.M. Huggard (trans.) (London: Routledge Kegan Paul, 1952)

Lester, Gene and David, *Suicide: The Gamble with Death* (Englewood Cliffs, N.J.: Prentice Hall, 1971)

Lewis, C.S., *The Problem of Pain* (New York: Macmillan, 1978)

Lewis, Edwin, *The Creation and the Adversary* (New York: Abingdon and Cokesbury, 1948)

Lewis, H.D., *The Philosophy of Religion* (London: Cambridge University Press, 1965)

Lindsay, A.D., *Selected Essays* (London: Hodder and Stoughton, 1927)

Linton, Ralph, "Universal Ethical Principles," in *Moral Principles of Action* Ruth Nanda Anshen (ed.) (New York: Harpers, 1952)

Loemker, L.E., "Theodicy," In the *Dictionary of the History of Ideas* Vol. IV (New York: Chas. Scribner's Sons, 1973)

Lucas, J.R., *A Treatise on Time and Space* (London: Methuen, 1973)

Luther, Martin, *Luther Oder Erasmus* (Basil: Friedrich Rheinhart, 1972)

Luttkens, Hampus, *The Analogy Between God and the World* (Uppsala: University of Uppsala, 1953)

MacGregor, Geddes, *He Who Lets Us Be* (New York: Seabury Press, 1975)

MacGregor, Geddes, *Philosophical Issues in Religious Thought* (Boston: Houghton Mifflin, 1973)

MacIntyre, Alasdair, *Difficulties in Christian Belief* (London: SCM Press, 1959)

MacKenzie, R.A.F., "The Purpose of the Yahweh Speeches in the Book of Job," *Biblica* Vol. 40 (1959)

Mackie, J.L., *Ethics: Inventing Right and Wrong* (London: Penguin Books, 1977)

Mackie, J.L., "Evil and Omnipotence," *Mind* (April, 1955) reprinted in *God and Evil*, Nelson Pike (ed.) (Englewood Cliffs, N.J.: Prentice Hall, 1964)

Mackie, J.L., *The Miracle of Theism* (London: Oxford University Press, 1982)

MacKinnon, D.M., "Death," in *New Essays in Philosophical Theology* Anthony Flew (ed.) (London: SCM Press, 1955)

MacKinnon, Donald, *Borderlands of Theology* (Philadelphia: J.B. Lippincott, 1968)

MacKinnon, Donald, *The Problem of Metaphysics* (London: Cambridge University Press, 1974)

MacKintosh, H.R., *The Doctrine of the Person of Christ* (Edinburgh: T. and T. Clark, 1912)

MacKintosh, H.R., *The Miracle of Theism* (London: Oxford University Press, 1982)

MacLagan, W.G., *The Theological Frontiers of Ethics* (London: Allen and Unwin, 1961)

MacLeish, Archibald, *J.B.* (London: Secker and Warburg, 1959)

Madden, Edward and Hare, Peter, *Evil and the Concept of God* (Springfield: Charles Johnson, 1968)

Maimonides, Moses, *Guide to the Perplexed* (London: H. Friedlander, 1904)

Malcolm, Norman, *Ludwig Wittgenstein: A Memoir* (London: Oxford University Press, 1958)

Marcel, Gabriel, *The Philosophy of Existence* (London: Harvill Press, 1948)

Martin-Archard, R., *From Death to Life: A Study of the Development of the Doctrines of Resurrection in the Old Testament* (Edinburgh: Oliver and Boyd, 1960)

Mascall, E.L., *Existence and Analogy* (London: Longmans Green, 1949)

Mavrodes, George, "Some Puzzles Concerning Omnipotence," *The Philosophical Review* Vol. 72 (1963)

McCloskey, H.J., "God and Evil," *The Philosophical Quarterly* Vol. 10 (1960), reprinted in Nelson Pike's *God and Evil*

McTaggert, John, *Some Dogmas of Religion* (London: Edward Arnold, 1906)

Meynell, H., "The Euthyphro Dilemma" *Aristotelean Society Supplementary* Vol. 46 (1972)

Mill, J.S., "Mr. Mansel on the Limits of Religious Thought," *God and Evil* Nelson Pike (ed.) (Englewood Cliffs, N.J.: Prentice Hall, 1964)

Mill, J.S., *An Examination of Sir William Hamilton's Philosophy* (London: Longmans Green, Reader and Dyer, 1973)

Mill, J.S., *Three Essays on Religion* (London: Longmans Green, 1885)

Morawetz, Thomas, *Wittgenstein and Knowledge* (Amherst: University of Mass. Press, 1978)

Moule, C.F.D., "The Manhood of Jesus in the New Testament," in *Christ, Faith and History* S.W. Sykes and J.P. Clayton (eds.) (Cambridge: Cambridge University Press, 1972)

Muller, Max, *Lectures on the Origin and Growth of Religion* (London: Longmans, 1878)

Murray, Gilbert, "Beyond Good and Evil," in Glatzer's *The Dimensions of Job*

Nielson, Kai, "An Examination of the Alleged Theological Basis of Morality," *Iliff Review* Vol. 23 (1964)

Nielson, Kai, "God and Verification Again," *Canadian Journal of Theology* Vol. 11 (1965)

Niven, W.D., "Good and Evil," in *Hastings Encyclopedia of*

Religion and Ethics Vol. 6 (New York: Scribners, 1922)

O'Brien, George, "Prolegomena to a Dissolution to the Problem of Suffering," *Harvard Theological Review* Vol. 57 (1964)

O'Dea, Thomas, *Introduction to the Sociology of Religion* (Englewood Cliffs, N.J.: Prentice Hall, 1966)

Oesterley, W.O.E. and Robinson, T.H., "The Three Stages of the Book," in Glatzer's *The Dimensions of Job*

Otto, Rudolph, "The Element of the Mysterious" in Glatzer's *The Dimensions of Job*

Otto, Rudolph, *The Idea of the Holy* John Harvey (trans.) (London: Oxford University Press, 1950)

Owens, H.P., *The Christian Knowledge of God* (London: University of London, The Athlone Press, 1969)

Peake, Arthur, "Job's Victory," in Glatzer's *The Dimensions of Job*

Perry, Ralph Barton, *The Thought and Character of William James* (New York: Macmillan, 1935)

Petit, F., *The Problem of Evil* (New York: Hawthorn Books, 1958)

Pfeiffer, R.H., *Introduction to the Old Testament* (New York: Harper and Row, 1948)

Phillips, D.Z., "Philosophy, Theology and the Reality of God," *Philosophical Quarterly* Vol. 13 (1963)

Phillips, D.Z., *Death and Immortality* (London: Macmillan, 1970)

Pike, Nelson, "Divine Omniscience and Voluntary Action" *The Philosophical Review* Vol. 74 (1965)

Pike, Nelson, *God and Timelessness* (New York: Macmillan, 1970)

Pike, Nelson, "Hume and Evil," in *God and Evil* (Englewood Cliffs: Prentice Hall, 1964)

Plantinga, Alvin, "Rationality and Religious Belief," *Nous* Vol. 15 (1981)

Plantinga, Alvin, *God, Freedom and Evil* (New York: Harper and Row, 1974)

Plantinga, Alvin, *God and Other Minds* (Ithaca: Cornell University Press, 1967)

Plantinga, Alvin, *The Nature of Necessity* (Oxford: Oxford University Press, 1974)

Plato, *The Republic*, F. M. Cornford (trans.) (London: Oxford University Press, 1970)

Plato, *The Timaeus and Critias*, A.E. Taylor (trans.) (London: Methuen and Co., 1929)

Pope, Alexander, "Essay on Man," *The Works of Alexander Pope* Notes by Whitwell Elwin (London: Murray, 1889)

Pope, Marvin, *The Anchor Bible: Job* (Garden City, N.Y.: Doubleday, 1965)

Power, W.L., "Symbolic Logic and the Doctrine of the Trinity," *The Iliff Review* Vol. XXXII, No. 1 (Winter 1975)

Prior, A.N., "The Formalities of Omniscience," *Time and Tense* (Oxford: Clarendon Press, 1968)

Pucetti, Roland, "John Hick," *Religious Studies* Vol. 2 (1967)

Quick, Oliver, *Doctrines of the Creed* (London: Nisbet and Co. 1938)

Quick, Oliver, *The Christian Sacraments* (London: Nisbet and Co., 1927)

Ragaz, Leonhard, "God Himself is the Answer," in Glatzer's *The Dimensions of Job*

Ramsay, A.M., *From Gore to Temple* (London: Longmans Green, 1960)

Rawlinson, G., *Job* (London: Funk and Wagnalls, 1906)

Richman, Robert, "Plantinga, God, and Other Minds," *Australian Journal of Philosophy* Vol. 50 (1972)

Robertson, David, "The Book of Job: A Literary Study," in *Soundings* Vol. 56 (1973)

Robinson, Wheeler, "Hebrew Psychology," *The People and the Book* Arthur Peake (ed.) (London: Oxford University Press, 1925)

Rodd, Cyril, "The Problem of Suffering: A Dialogue," *Expository Times* (Aug., 1972)

Ross, F.H., *Personalism and the Problem of Evil* (New Haven: Yale University Press, 1940)

Ross, James, "Analogy and the Resolution of Some Cognitivity Problems," *The Journal of Philosophy* Vol. 67 (1970)

Ross, James, *Introduction to the Philosophy of Religion* (Toronto: Collier-Macmillan, 1969)

Roth, John, *A Consuming Fire: Encounter with Elie Wiesel and The Holocaust* (Atlanta: John Knox Press, 1979)

Roth, Leo, "Job and Jonah," in Glatzer's *The Dimensions of Job*

Rousseau, J.J., *Emile* M. Nugent (trans.) (London: Everyman's Library, 1971)

Rousseau, J.J., *Essays on the Origin of Inequality* (London: Everyman's Library, 1973)

Rowe, William, "Plantinga on Possible Worlds," *Journal of Philosophy* Vol. 70 (1973)

Rowley, H.H., *From Moses to Qumran* (London: Lutterworth Press, 1963)

Rowley, H.H., *Job* (London: Thomas Nelson, 1970)

Royce, Josiah, "The Problem of Job," *Religion From Tolstoy to Camus* W. Kaufmann (ed.) (New York: World Publishing Co. 1956)

Rubenstein, Richard, *After Auschwitz: Beginning a New Era* (Indianapolis: Bobbs-Merrill, 1966)

Rylaardsdam, J. Coert, *Revelation in Jewish Wisdom Literature* (Chicago: University of Chicago Press, 1946)

Sanders, Paul, *Twentieth Century Interpretations of the Book of Job* (Englewood Cliffs, N.J.: Prentice Hall, 1968)

Savage, C.W., "The Paradox of the Stone," *Philosophical Review* Vol. 76 (1967)

Schillani, Anthony, *Movies and Morals* (Notre Dame: Fides Press, 1968)

Schleiermacher, Friedrich, *The Christian Faith* H.R. MacKintosh and J.S. (eds.) (Edinburgh: T. and T. Clark, 1957)

Silberman, L.H., "Death in the Hebrew Bible and Apocalyptic Literature," in *Perspectives on Death* L.O. Mills (ed.) (Nashville: Abingdon Press, 1969)

Skinner, B.F., *Beyond Freedom and Dignity* (New York: Alfred A. Knopf Co., 1971)

Smart, Ninian, "Omnipotence, Evil and Superman," *Philosophy* (1961), reprinted in Nelson Pike's *God and Evil*

Solzhenitsyn, Aleksander, *The Gulag Archipelago* (New York: Harper and Row, 1974)

Spinoza, Benedict, *Ethics* W. Hale White (trans.) (London: Oxford University Press, 1930)

Sri Purchit Swami and Yeats, W.B., trans., "Katha Upanishad" in *The Principal Upanishads* (London: Faber and Faber, 1937)

Steuer, A.D., "Once More on the Free Will Defense," *Religious Studies* (Sept. 1974)

Swinburne, Richard, "The Problem of Evil," *Reason and Religion* Stuart Brown (ed.) (Ithaca: Cornell University Press, 1977)

Swinburne, Richard, *The Existence of God* (Oxford: Clarendon Press, 1979)

Swinburne, Richard, *The Coherence of Theism* (Oxford: Oxford University Press, 1977)

Taylor, Richard, *Good and Evil* (New York: Macmillan, 1970)

Temple, William, *Christus Veritas* (London: Longmans Green, 1924)

Tennant, F.R., *Philosophical Theology* Vol. II (Cambridge: Cambridge University Press, 1930)

Terrien, S.L., "Exegetical Commentary on Job," *The Interpreter's Bible* Vol. 3 (Nashville: Abingdon Press, 1954)

Terrien, S.L., *Job: Poet of Existence* (Indianapolis: Bobbs-Merrill, 1958)

Tolstoy, Leo, *The Confessions* (London: Bradda, 1960)

Tolstoy, Leo, "The Death of Ivan Illych," *The Cossacks, Happy Ever After and the Death of Ivan Illych* (Harmondsworth: Penguin Books, 1982)

Torrance, T.F., *Theological Science* (London: Oxford University Press, 1924)

Trethowan, Illtyd, "Dr. Hick and the Problem of Evil," *Journal of Theological Studies* Vol. 18 (1967)

Trigg, Roger, *Reason and Commitment* (London: Cambridge University Press, 1973)

Tylor, E.B., *Primitive Cultures* (London: Longmans, 1891)

Unsigned, "In Search of God at Auschwitz," *New York Times* June 9, 1974

Vicchio, S.J., "Against Raising Hopes of Raising the Dead," *Essence*, Vol. 3 (1979)

Von Fritz, Kurt, "Relative and Absolute Values," in *Moral Principles of Action* Ruth Nanda Anshen (ed.) (New York: Harpers, 1952)

Wainwright, W.J., "Christian Theism and the Free Will Defense," *International Journal of Philosophy of Religion* Vol. 6 (1975)

Wallace, W.I., *The Existence of God* (Ithaca: Cornell University Press, 1965)

Wallant, E.L., *The Pawnbroker* (New York: McFadden-Bartell, 1965)

Ward, James, "Naturalism and Agnosticism," Gifford Lectures, Aberdeen, 1896-98 (London: A. and C. Block, 1915)

Watson, R.A., *The Book of Job* (London: Hodder and Stoughton, 1942)

Webb, Dom Bruno, *Why Does God Permit Evil?* (London: Burns, Oates and Washbourne, 1961)

Weston, Frank, *The One Christ* (London: Longmans Green, 1907)

Whittaker, John, *Matters of Faith and Matters of Principle* (San Antonio: Trinity University Press, 1981)

Wiesel, Elie, *Night* (New York: Hill and Wang, 1960)

Wiesel, Elie, *One Generation After* (New York: Avon Books, 1972)

Wiesel, Elie, *The Oath* (New York: Random House, 1973)

Wiesel, Elie, *The Trial of God* (New York: Random House, 1976)

Wiles, Maurice, "Christianity Without Incarnation," in J. Hick's *The Myth of God Incarnate*

Williams, J.A., *Islam* (New York: Basic Books, 1961)

Williams, R.J., "Theodicy in the Ancient Near East," *Theodicy in the Old Testament* J.L. Crenshaw (ed.) (London: SPCK, 1983)

Winch, Peter, "Understanding a Primitive Society," *American Philosophical Quarterly*, Vol. 1 (1964)

Wisdom, John, "God and Evil," *Mind* Vol. 44 (1935)

Wisdom, John, "Gods," *Proceedings of the Aristotelean Society* Vol. XLV (1944-1945)

Wisdom, John, "Paradox and Discovery," in *Paradox and Discovery* (London: Oxford University Press, 1965)

Wisdom, John, *Philosophy and Psychoanalysis* (Oxford: Basil Blackwell, 1953)

Wittgenstein, Ludwig, *Lectures and Conversations on Aesthetics, Psychology and Religious Belief* (Oxford: Basil Blackwell, 1966)

Wittgenstein, Ludwig, *On Certainty* (Oxford: Basil Blackwell, 1977)

Wittgenstein, Ludwig, *The Philosophical Investigations* (Oxford: Basil Blackwell, 1953)

Wittgenstein, Ludwig, *Remarks on Frazer's The Golden Bough*, ed. Rush Rhees (London: Cambridge University Press, 1979.)

Wolff, Kurt, "For a Sociology of Evil," *Journal of Social Sciences Issues* Vol. 25, no. 1 (1969)

Wolterstorff, Nicholas, "God Everlasting," *God and the Good: Essays in Honor of Henry Stob* Clifton Orlebeke and Lewis Smedes (eds.) (Grand Rapids: Eerdmans, 1975)

Wood, James, *Job and the Human Situation* (London: Geoffrey Bles, 1966)

Zaehner, R.C., *The Teachings of the Magi: A Compendium of Zoroastrian Beliefs* (London: 1956)

Index